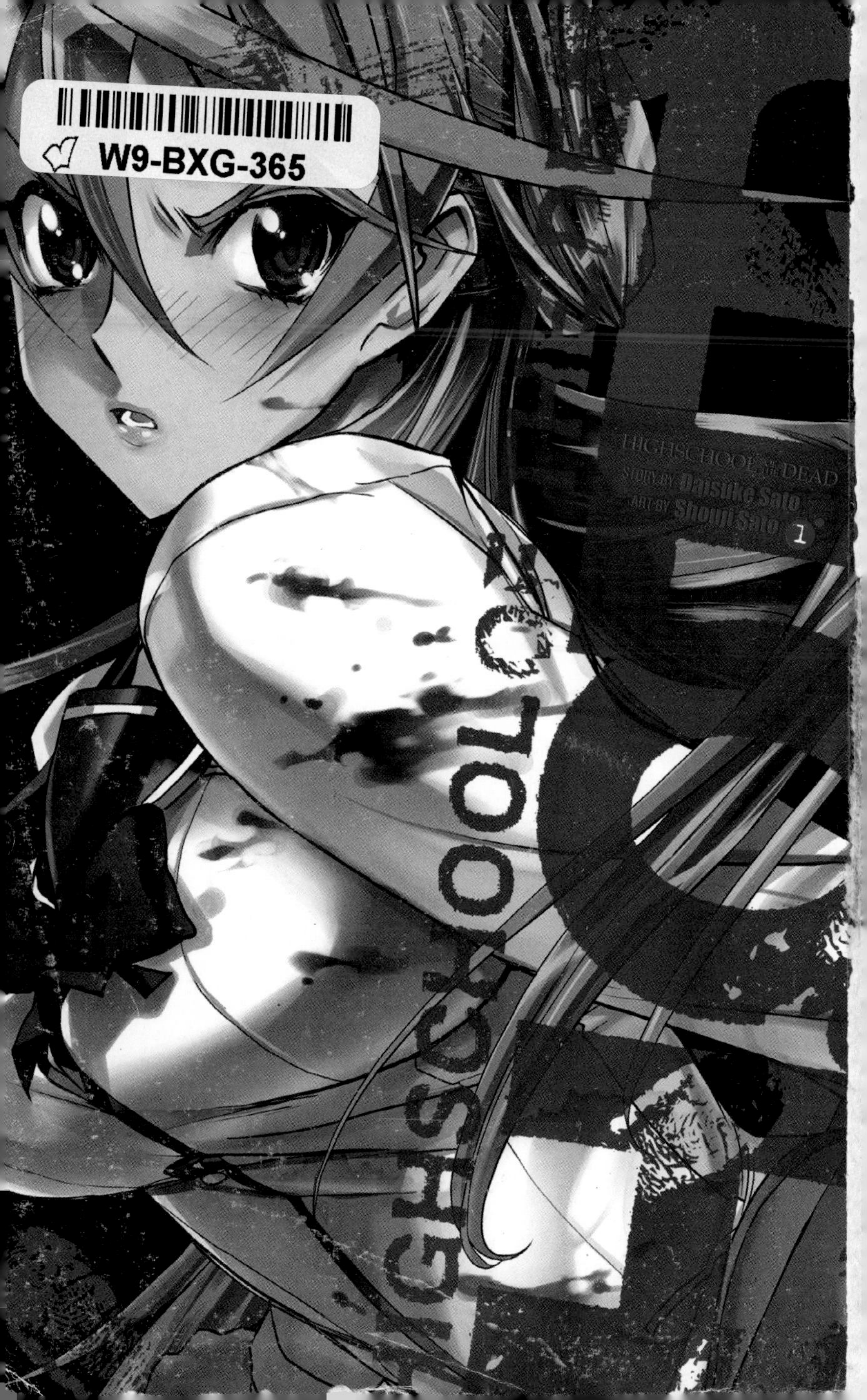
HIGHSCHOOL OF THE DEAD
STORY BY Daisuke Sato
ART BY Shouji Sato
1
HIGHSCHOOL

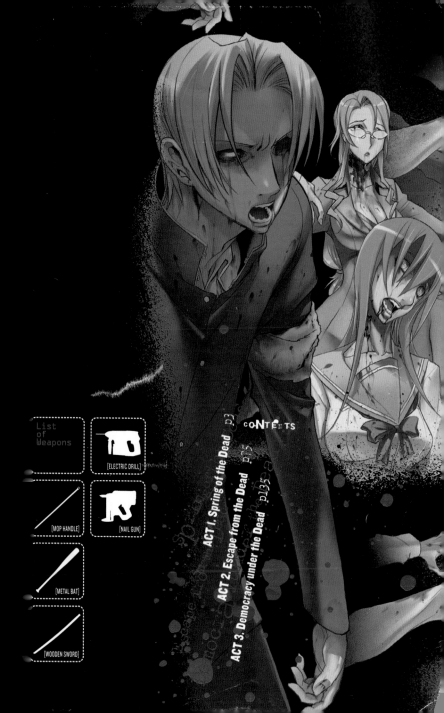

List
of
Weapons

[ELECTRIC DRILL]

[MOP HANDLE]

[NAIL GUN]

[METAL BAT]

[WOODEN SWORD]

CONTENTS

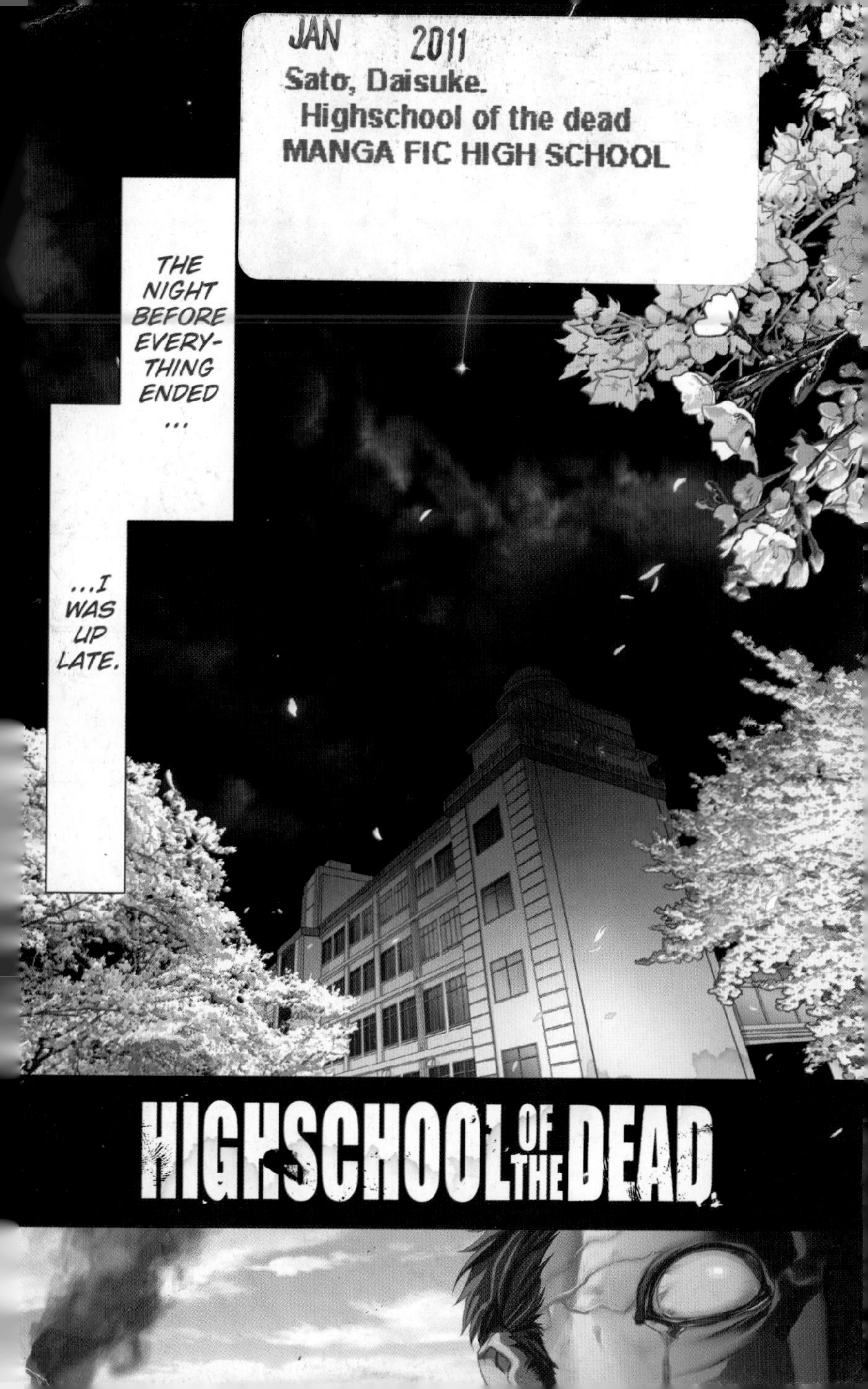
THE NIGHT BEFORE EVERYTHING ENDED ...
...I WAS UP LATE.
HIGHSCHOOL OF THE DEAD

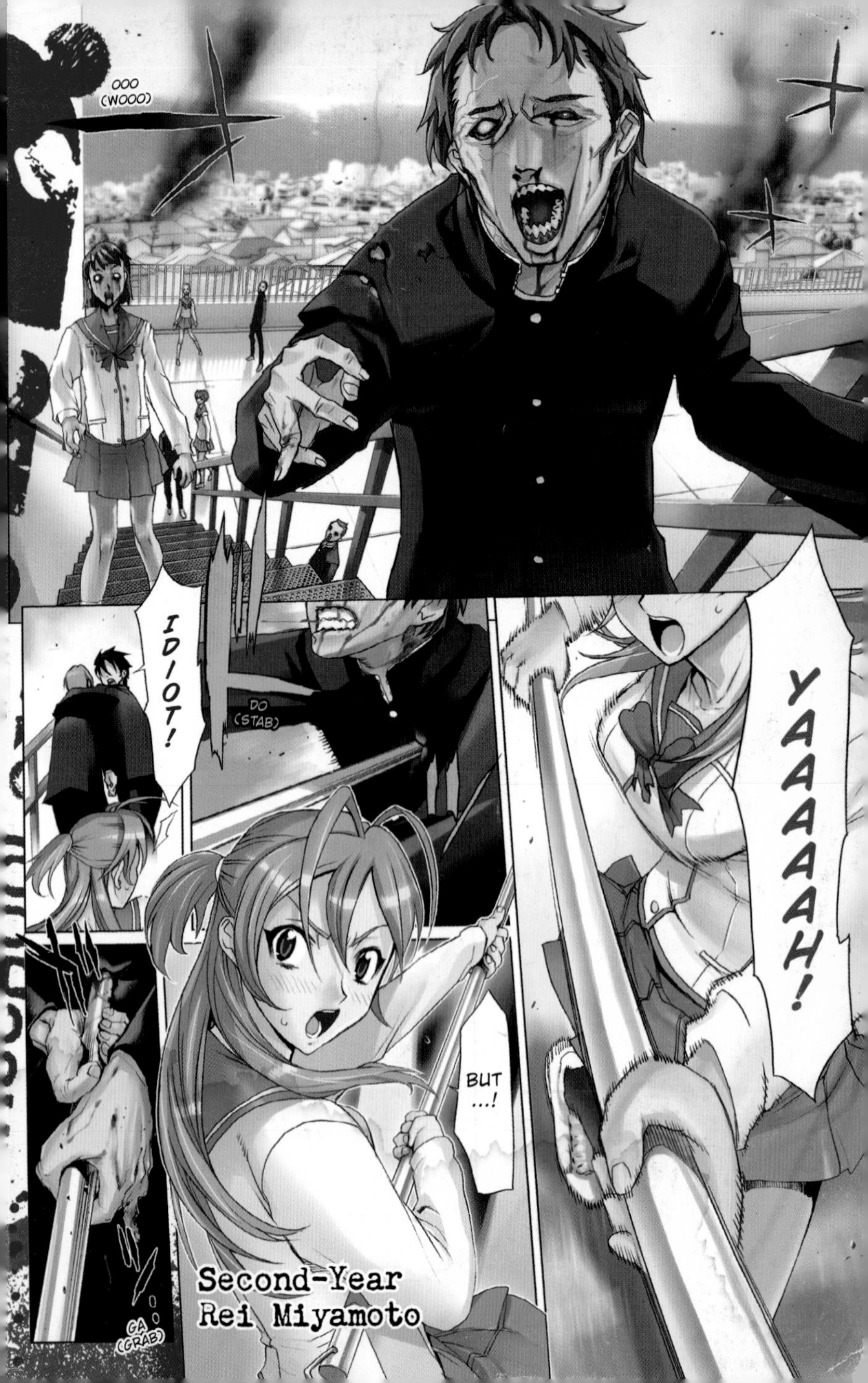
OOO
(WOOO)
YAAAAAH!
DO
(STAB)
IDIOT!
BUT
...!
Second-Year
Rei Miyamoto
GA
(GRAB)

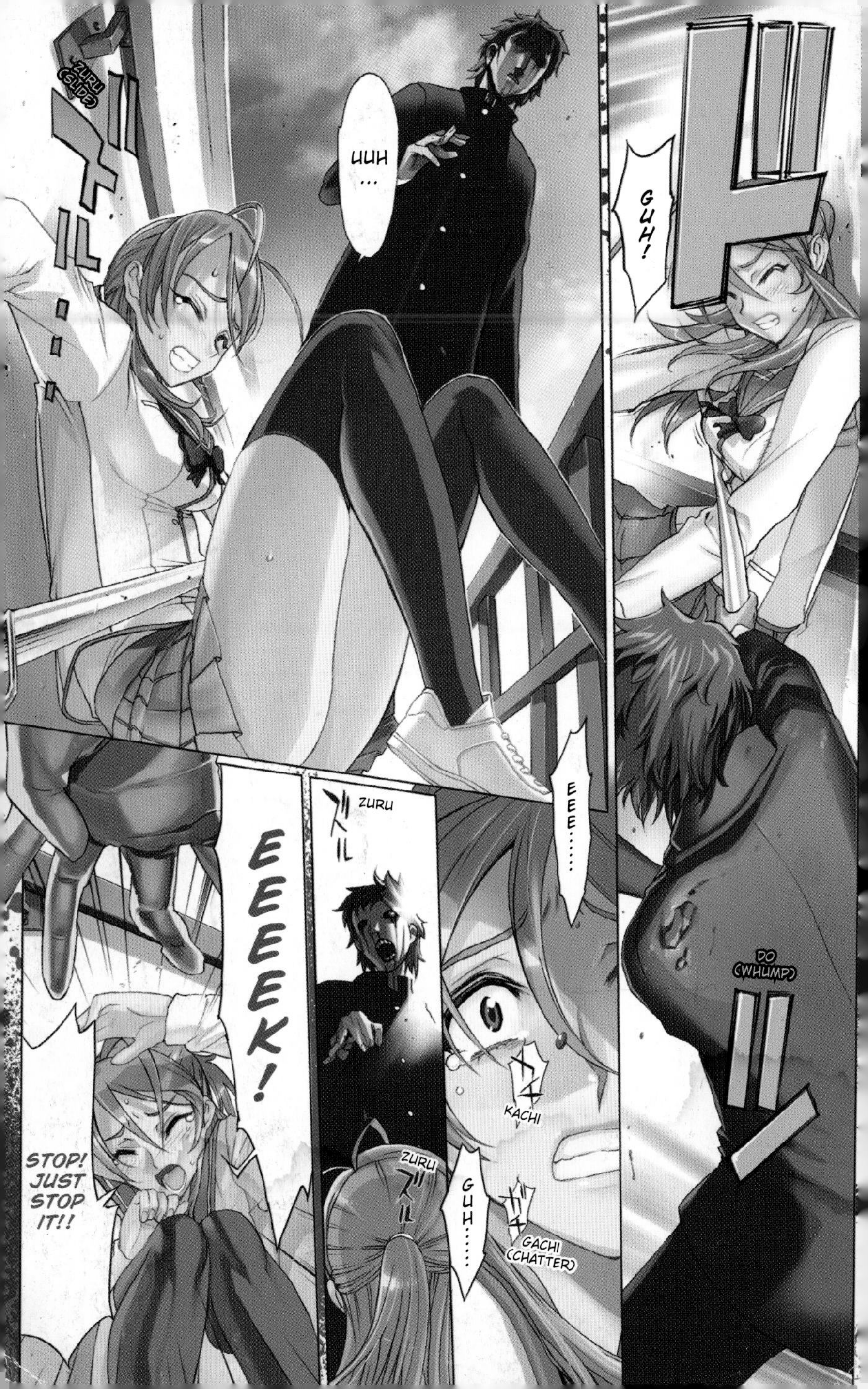
GUH!
DO (WHUMP)
UUH...
ZURU (GLIDE)
EEE......
ZURU
EEEEEK!
KACHI
GUH......
GACHI (CHATTER)
ZURU
STOP! JUST STOP IT!!

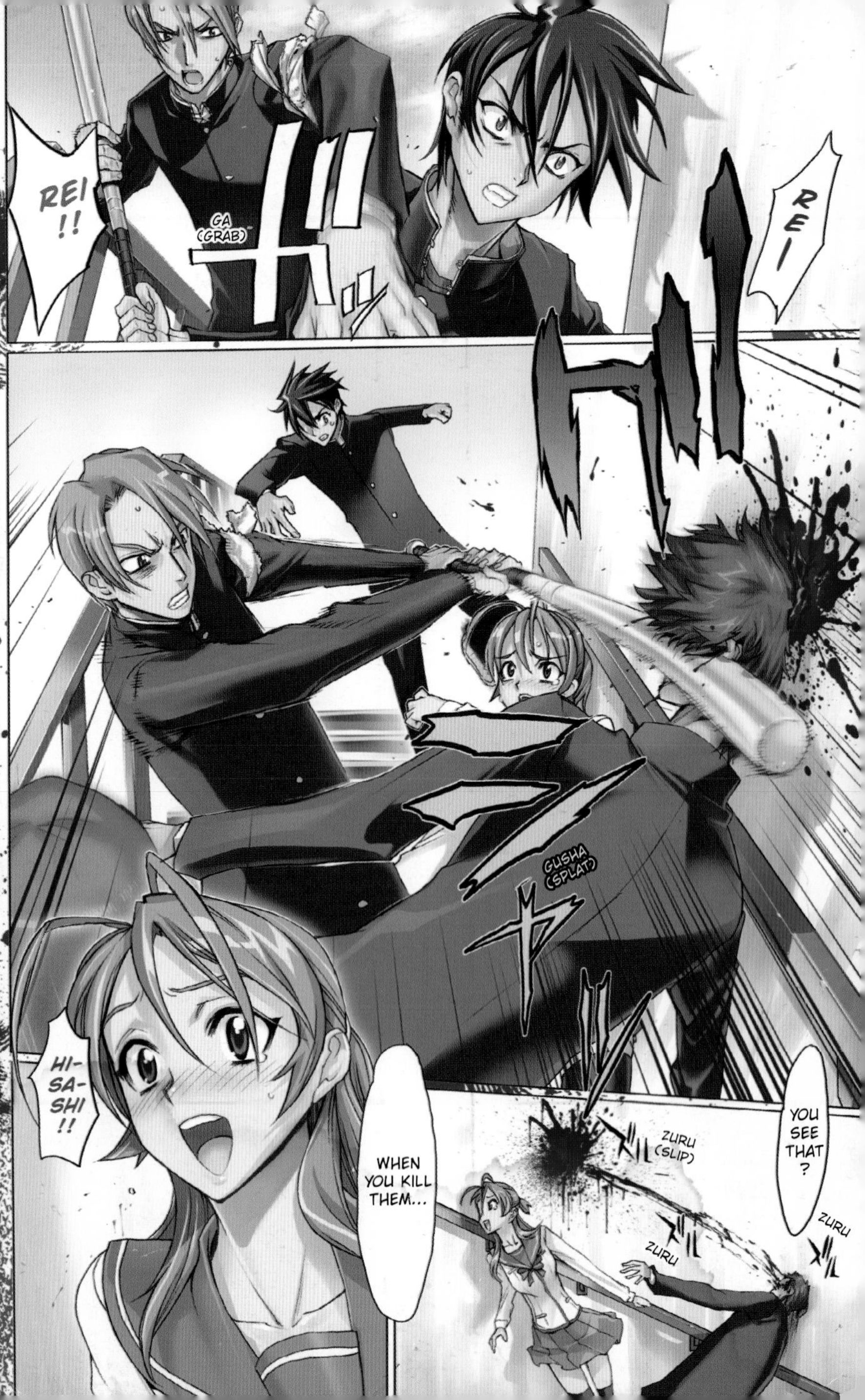

REI
GA (GRAB)
REI !!
GUSHA (SPLAT)
YOU SEE THAT ?
ZURU (SLIP)
ZURU
ZURU
WHEN YOU KILL THEM...
HI-SA-SHI !!

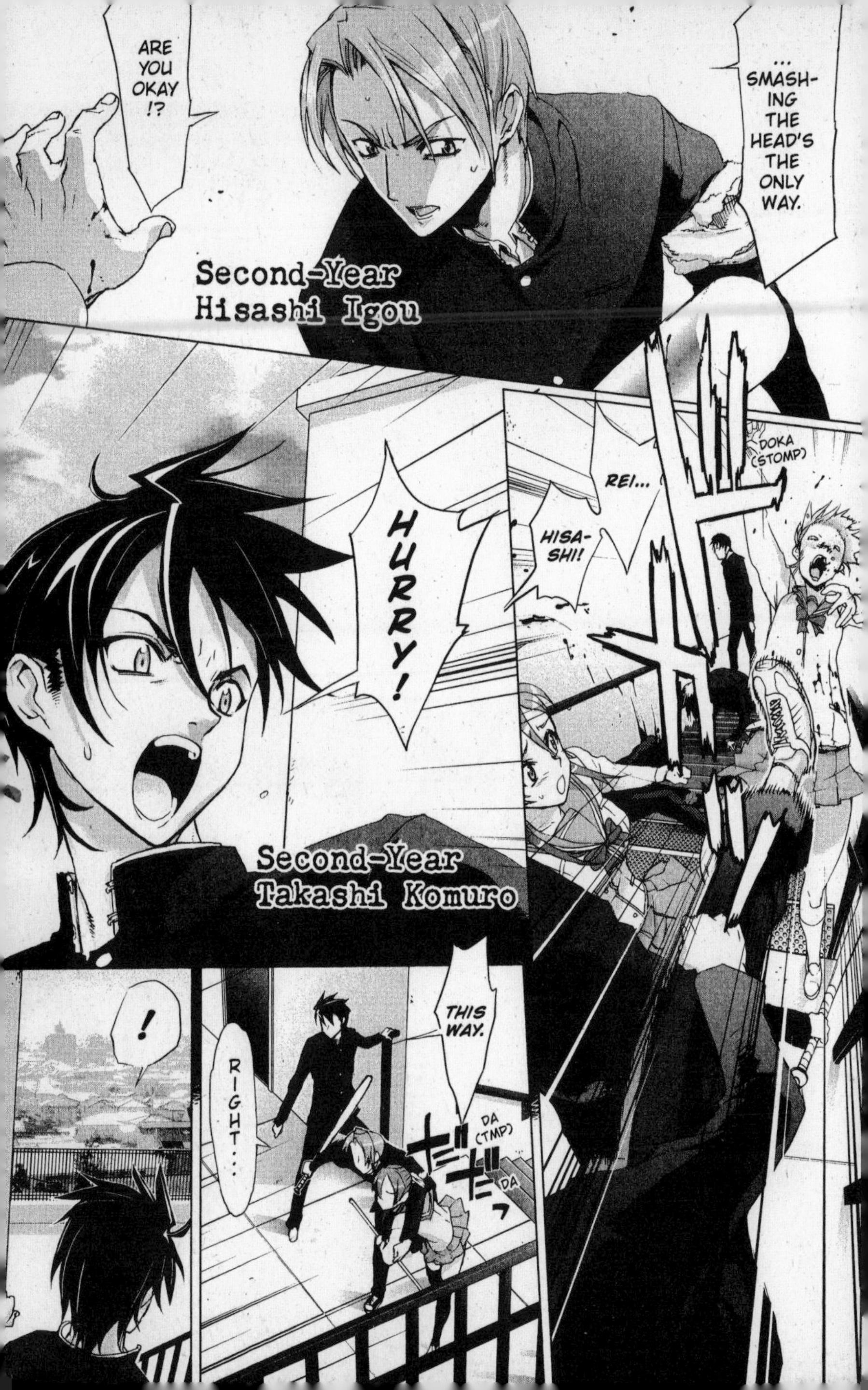
... SMASHING THE HEAD'S THE ONLY WAY.
ARE YOU OKAY !?
Second-Year Hisashi Igou
DOKA (STOMP)
REI...
HISASHI!
HURRY!
Second-Year Takashi Komuro
THIS WAY.
DA (TMP)
DA
RIGHT...
!

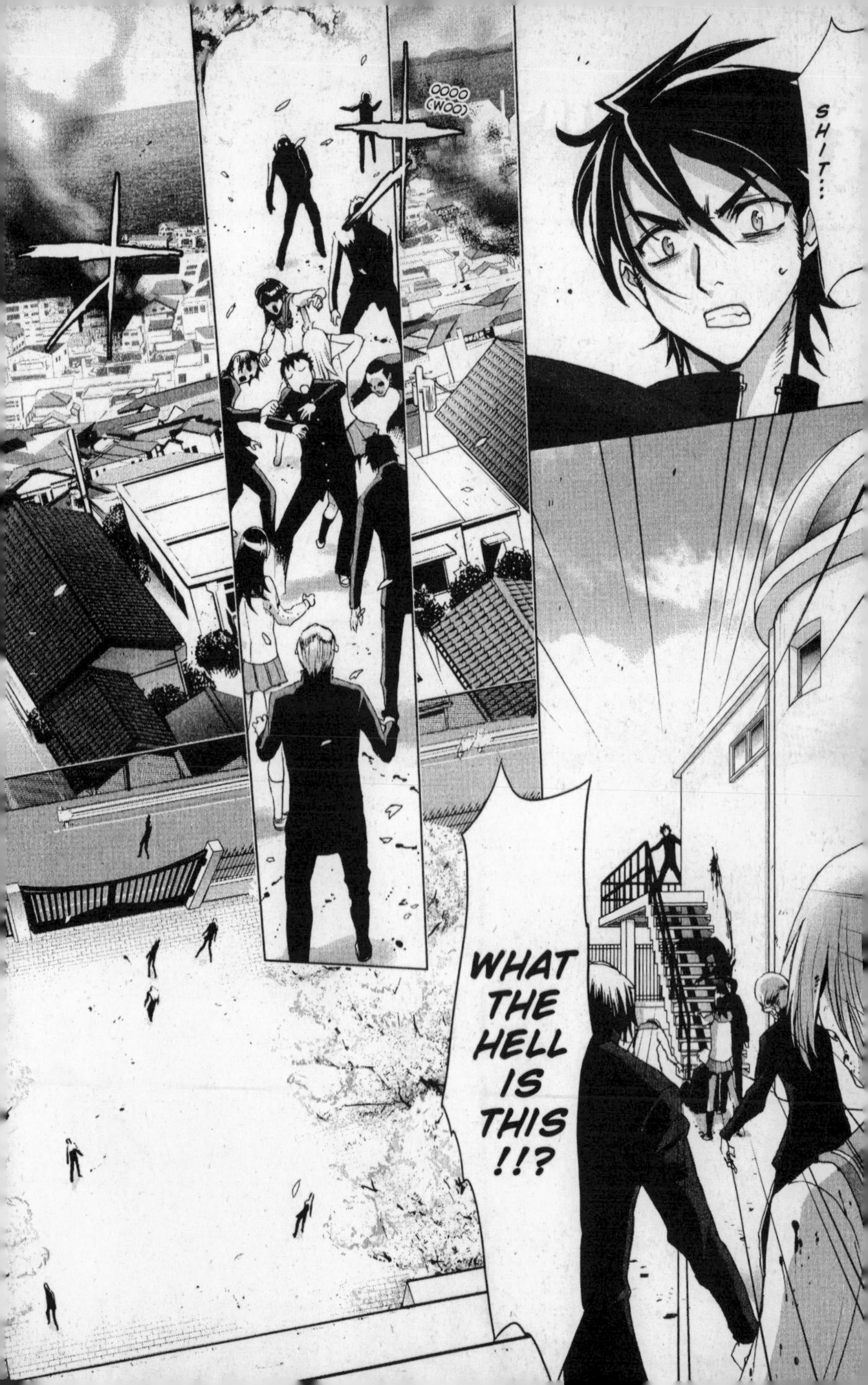
SHIT...
WHAT THE HELL IS THIS!!?
OOOO (WOO)

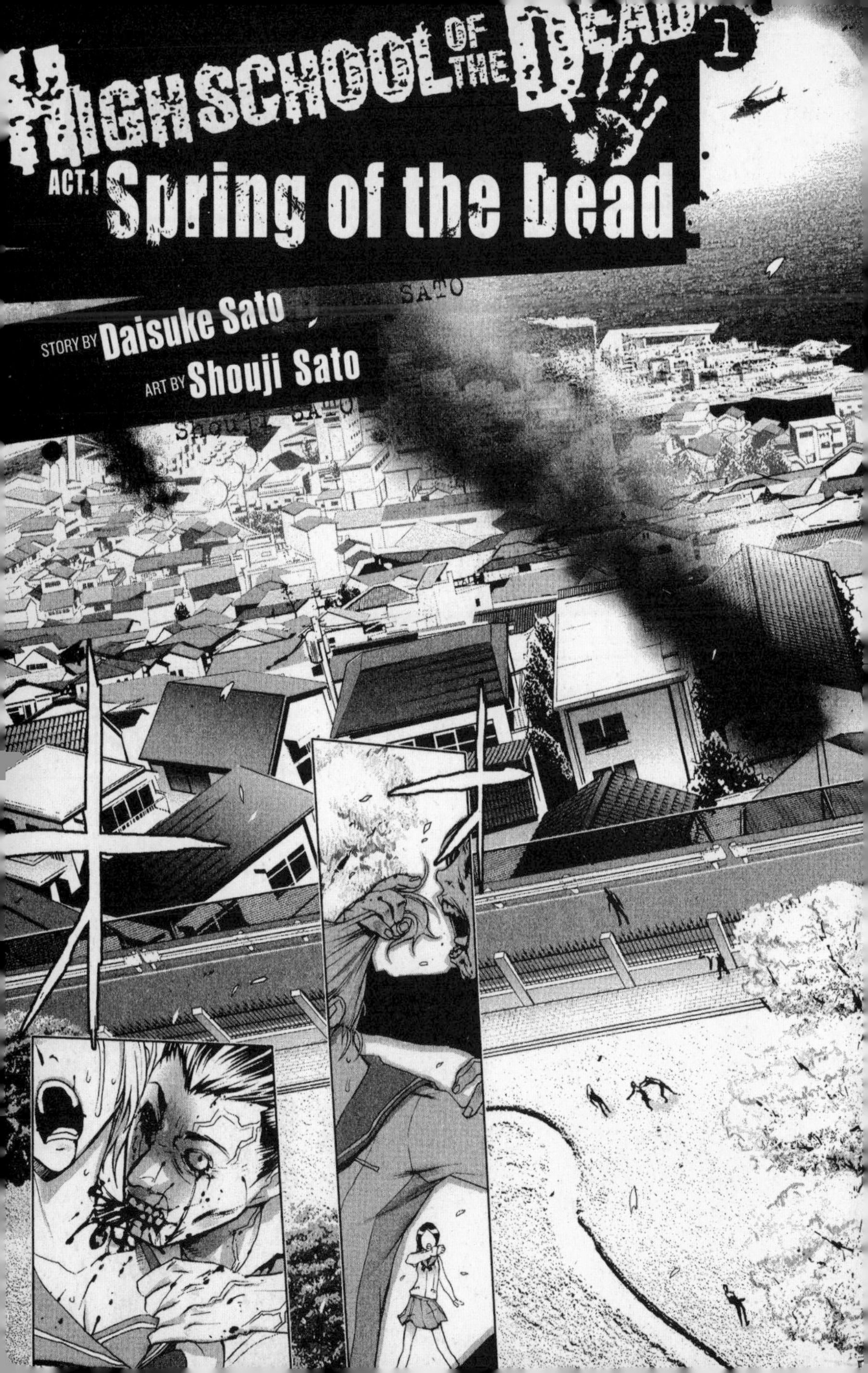
HIGHSCHOOL OF THE DEAD 1
ACT.1 Spring of the Dead
STORY BY Daisuke Sato
ART BY Shouji Sato

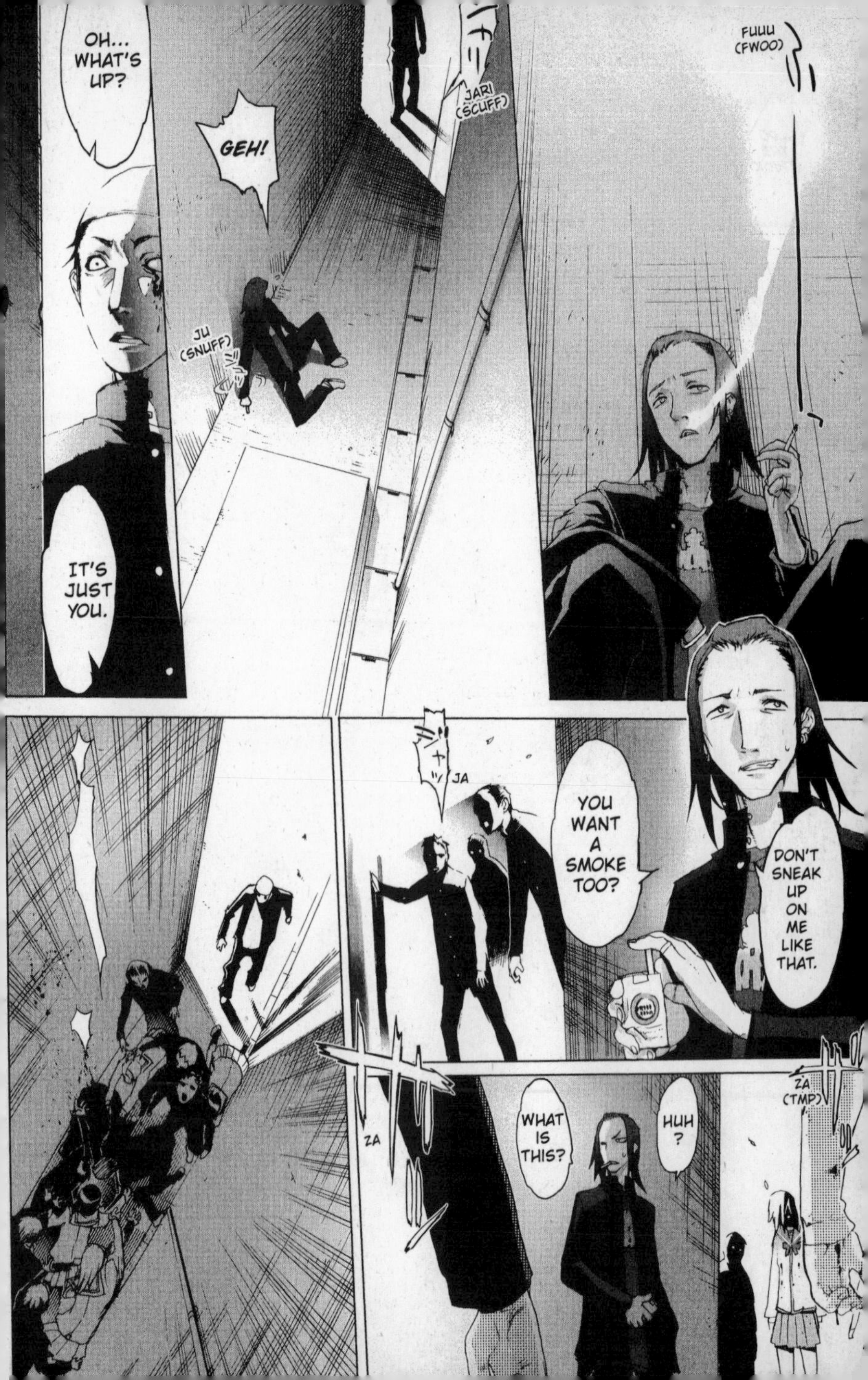
FUUU (FWOO)
JARI (SCUFF)
GEH!
JU (SNUFF)
OH... WHAT'S UP?
IT'S JUST YOU.
DON'T SNEAK UP ON ME LIKE THAT.
JA
YOU WANT A SMOKE TOO?
ZA (TMP)
HUH?
WHAT IS THIS?
ZA

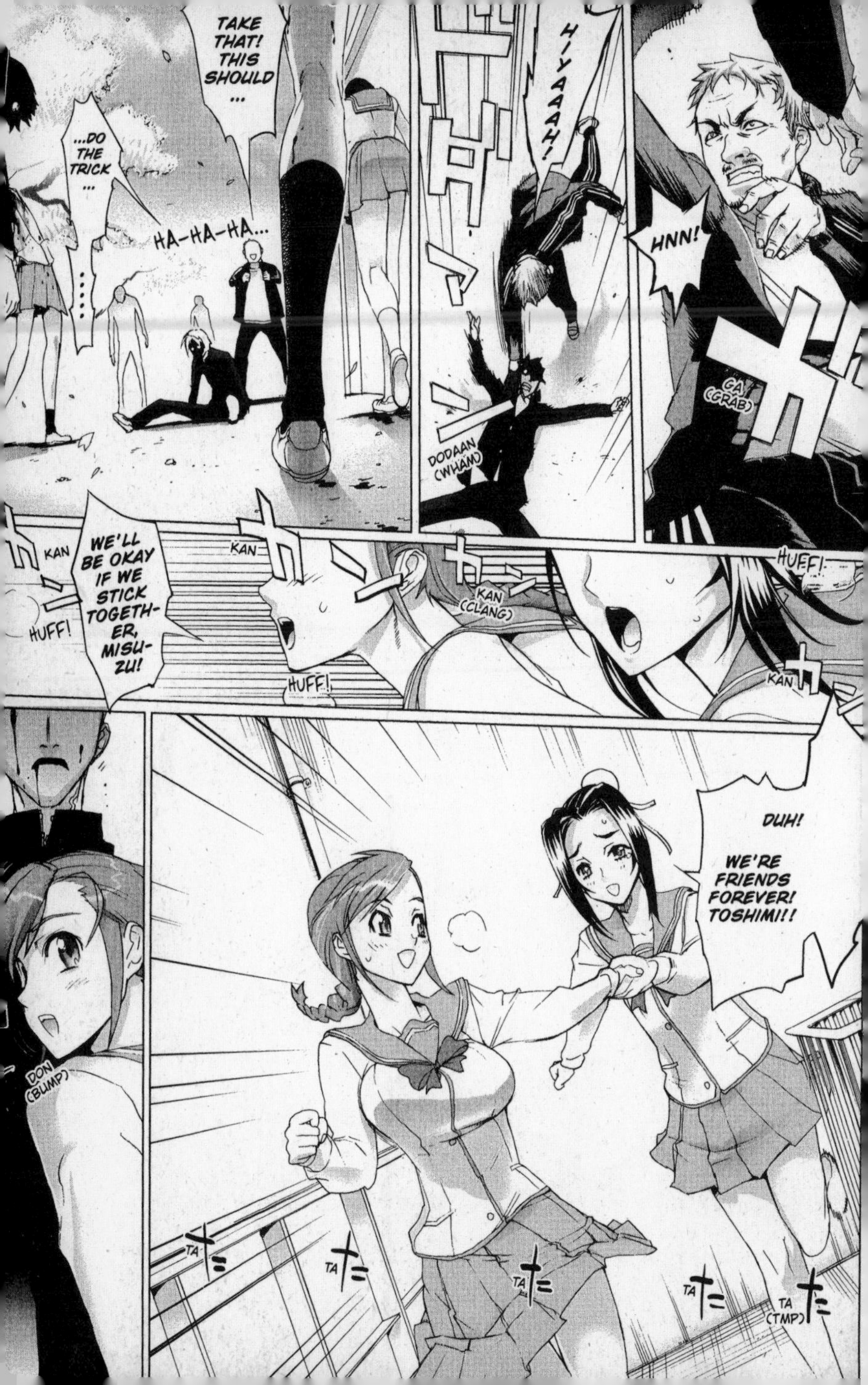
HNN!
GA (GRAB)
HIYAAAAH!
DODAAN (WHAM)
TAKE THAT! THIS SHOULD ...
...DO THE TRICK ...
HA-HA-HA...
......
HUFF!
KAN
KAN (CLANG)
KAN
HUFF!
KAN
WE'LL BE OKAY IF WE STICK TOGETHER, MISUZU!
KAN
HUFF!
DUH!
WE'RE FRIENDS FOREVER! TOSHIMI!!
TA (TMP)
TA
TA
TA
TA
DON (BUMP)

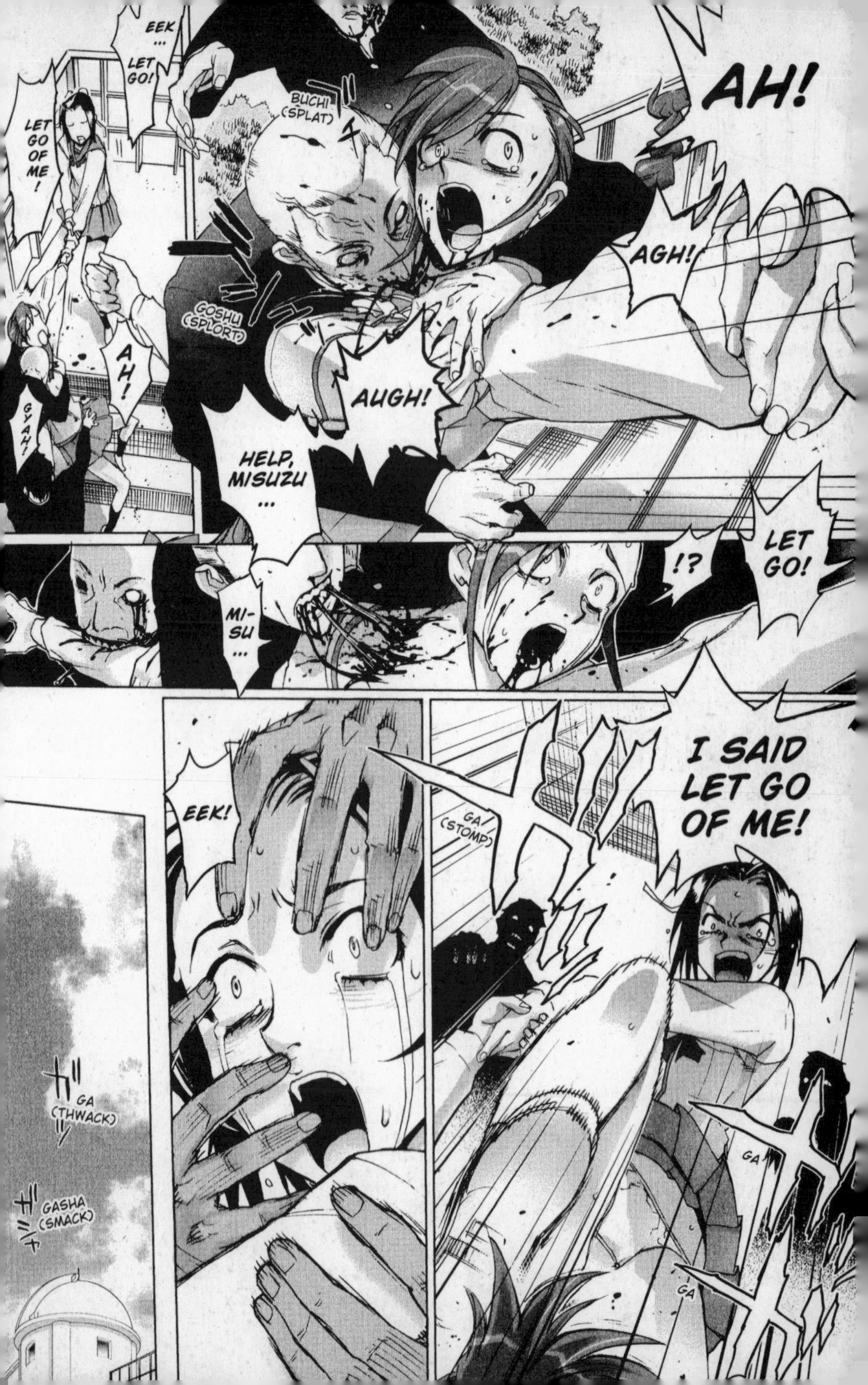
AH!
AGH!
BUCHI (SPLAT)
EEK ... LET GO!
LET GO OF ME!
GOSHU (SPLORT)
AUGH!
AH!
HELP, MISUZU ...
GYAH!
LET GO!
!?
MI-SU ...
I SAID LET GO OF ME!
GA (STOMP)
GA
GA
EEK!
GA (THWACK)
GASHA (SMACK)

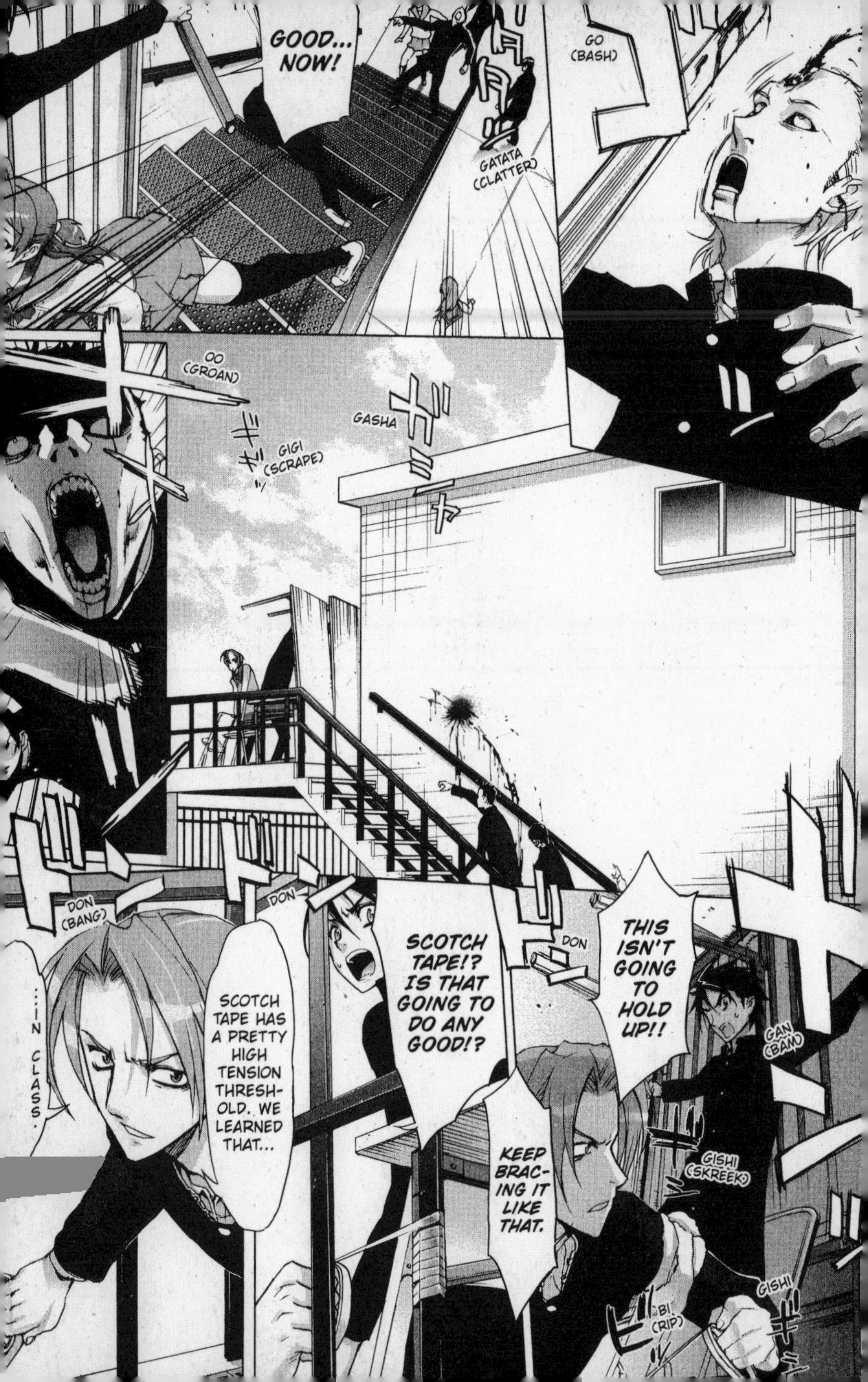
GO (BASH)
GATATA (CLATTER)
GOOD... NOW!
GASHA
OO (GROAN)
GIGI (SCRAPE)
THIS ISN'T GOING TO HOLD UP!!
GAN (BAM)
DON
GISHI (SKREEK)
KEEP BRACING IT LIKE THAT.
GISHI
BI (RIP)
SCOTCH TAPE!? IS THAT GOING TO DO ANY GOOD!?
DON
DON (BANG)
SCOTCH TAPE HAS A PRETTY HIGH TENSION THRESH-OLD. WE LEARNED THAT...
...IN CLASS.

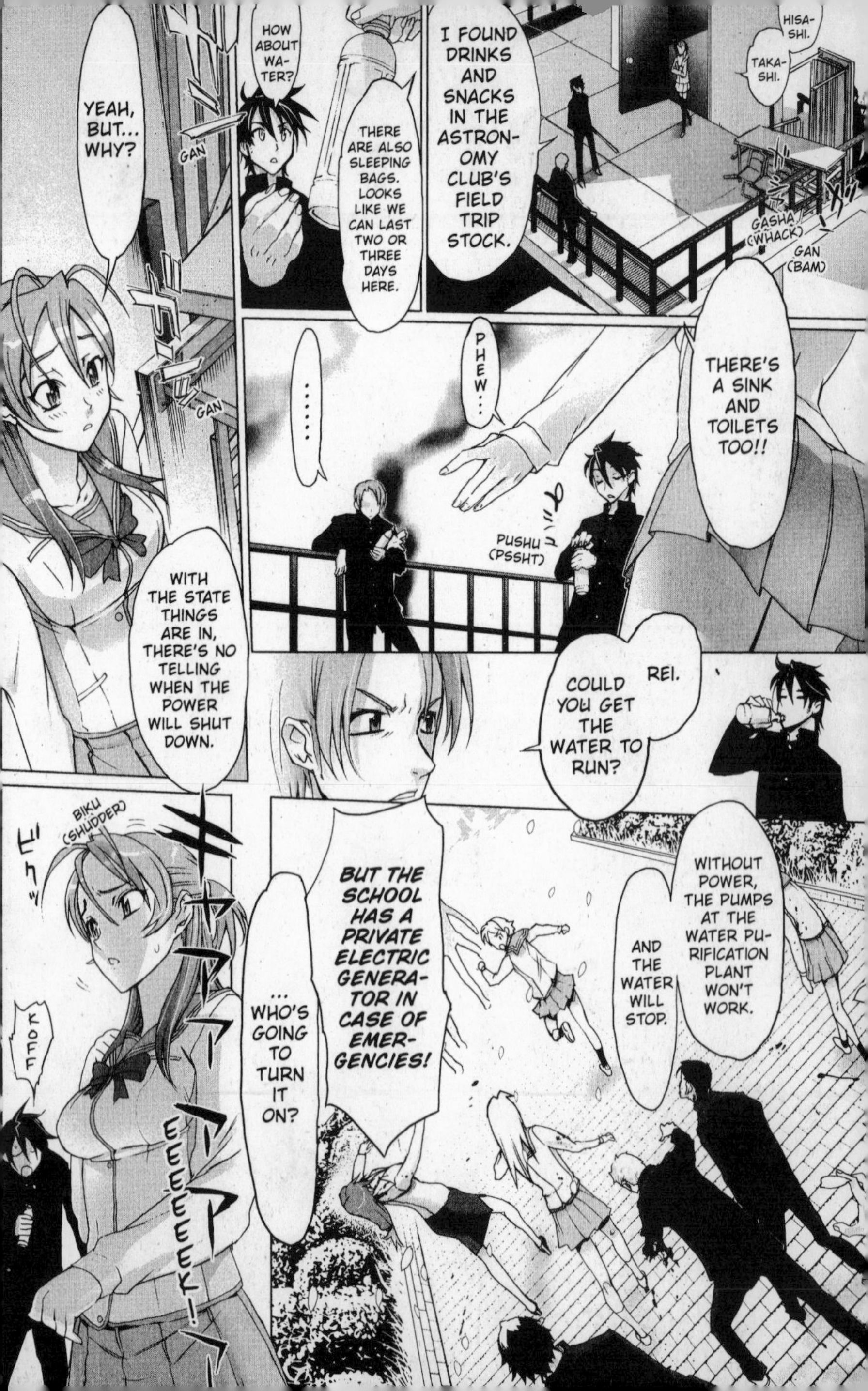
HISA-SHI.
TAKA-SHI.
GASHA (WHACK)
GAN (BAM)
I FOUND DRINKS AND SNACKS IN THE ASTRONOMY CLUB'S FIELD TRIP STOCK.
HOW ABOUT WATER?
THERE ARE ALSO SLEEPING BAGS. LOOKS LIKE WE CAN LAST TWO OR THREE DAYS HERE.
THERE'S A SINK AND TOILETS TOO!!
PHEW...
......
PUSHU (PSSHT)
REI.
COULD YOU GET THE WATER TO RUN?
YEAH, BUT... WHY?
GAN
GAN
WITH THE STATE THINGS ARE IN, THERE'S NO TELLING WHEN THE POWER WILL SHUT DOWN.
WITHOUT POWER, THE PUMPS AT THE WATER PURIFICATION PLANT WON'T WORK.
AND THE WATER WILL STOP.
BUT THE SCHOOL HAS A PRIVATE ELECTRIC GENERATOR IN CASE OF EMERGENCIES!
... WHO'S GOING TO TURN IT ON?
BIKU (SHUDDER)
KOFF
EEEEEEEK!

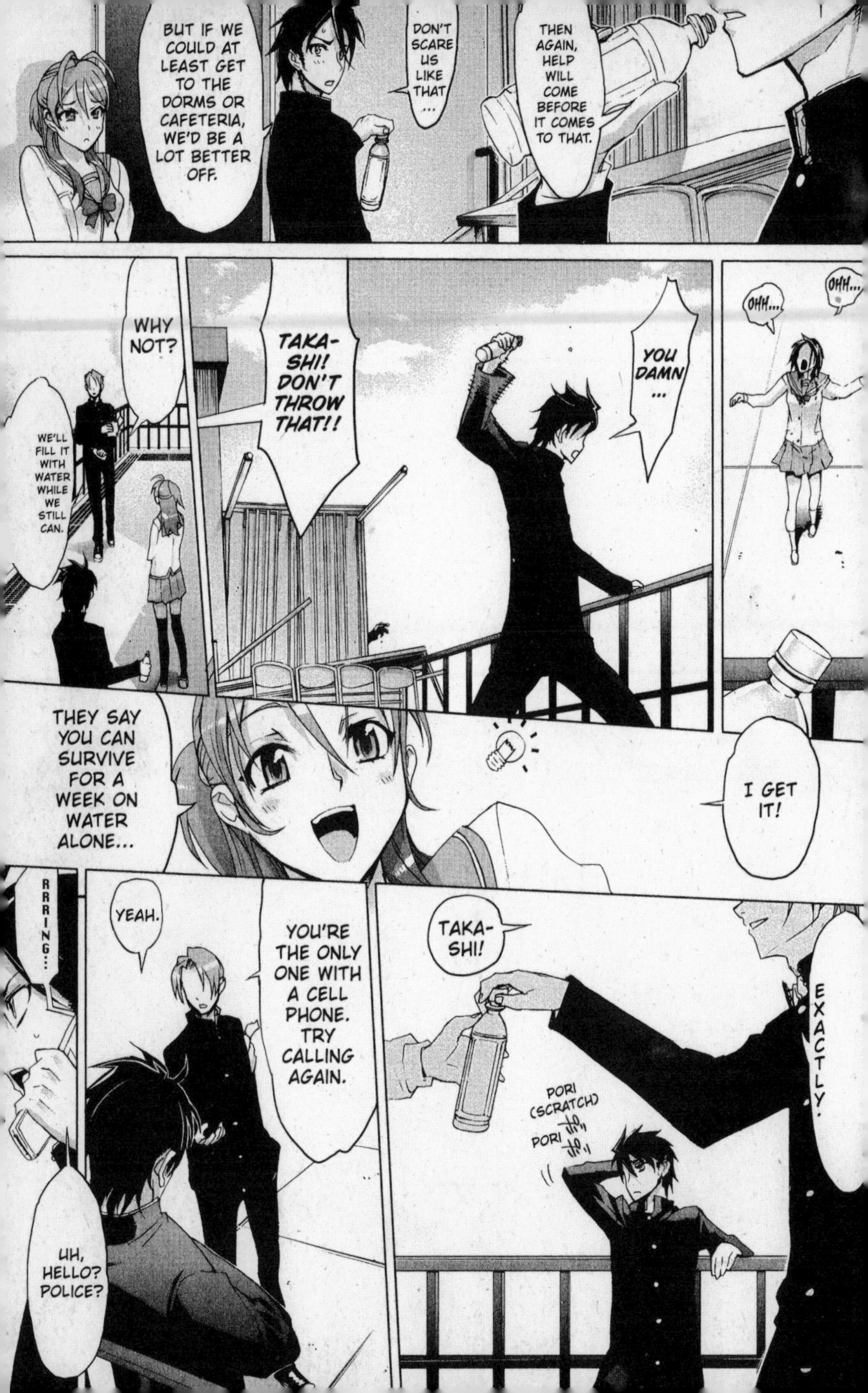
THEN AGAIN, HELP WILL COME BEFORE IT COMES TO THAT.
DON'T SCARE US LIKE THAT...
BUT IF WE COULD AT LEAST GET TO THE DORMS OR CAFETERIA, WE'D BE A LOT BETTER OFF.
OHH...
OHH...
YOU DAMN...
TAKA-SHI! DON'T THROW THAT!!
WHY NOT?
WE'LL FILL IT WITH WATER WHILE WE STILL CAN.
I GET IT!
THEY SAY YOU CAN SURVIVE FOR A WEEK ON WATER ALONE...
EXACTLY.
TAKA-SHI!
PORI (SCRATCH)
PORI
YOU'RE THE ONLY ONE WITH A CELL PHONE. TRY CALLING AGAIN.
YEAH.
RRRING...
UH, HELLO? POLICE?

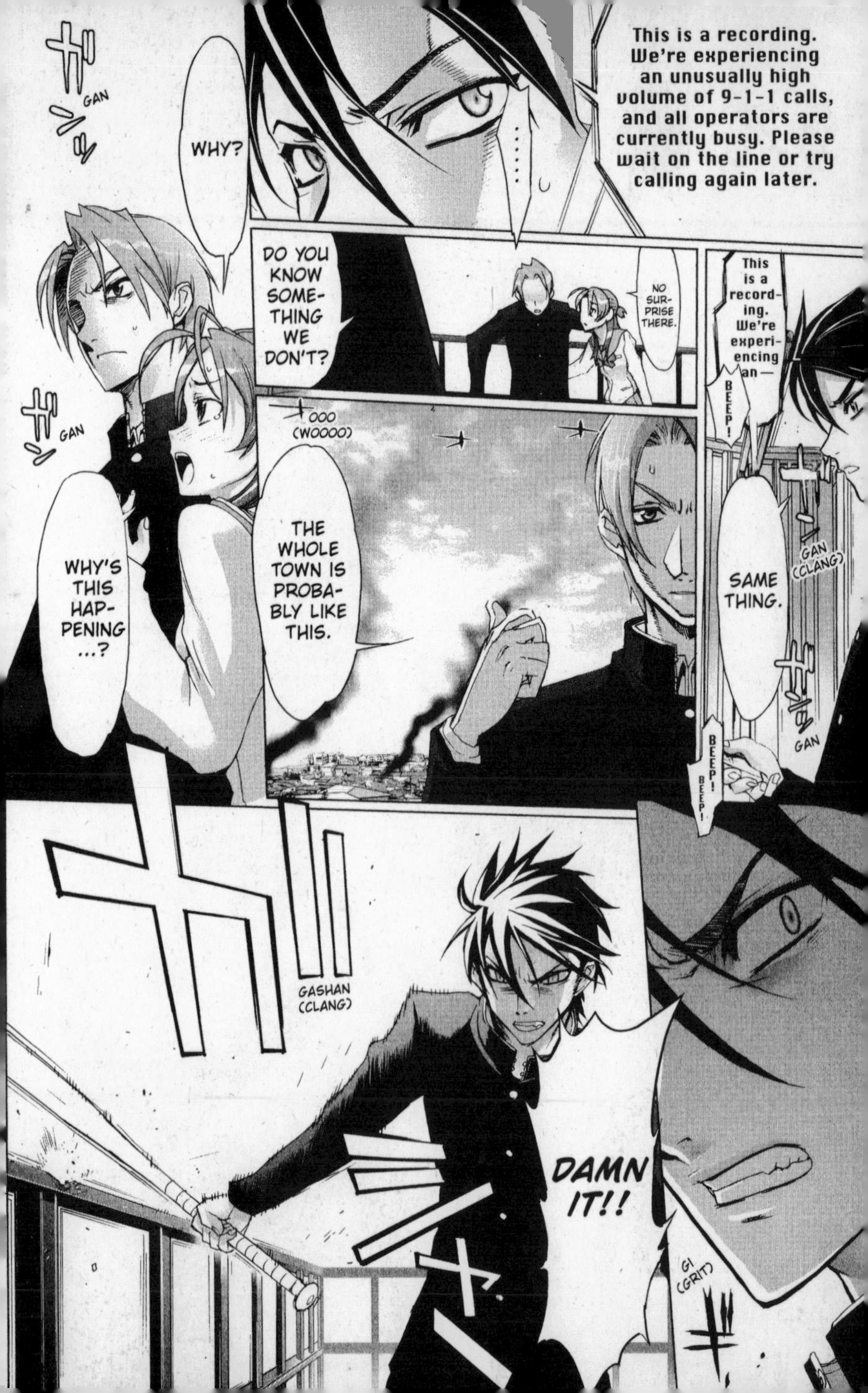
This is a recording. We're experiencing an unusually high volume of 9-1-1 calls, and all operators are currently busy. Please wait on the line or try calling again later.
WHY?
GAN
This is a recording. We're experiencing an—
BEEP!
SAME THING.
GAN (CLANG)
GAN
BEEP! BEEP! BEEP!
NO SURPRISE THERE.
DO YOU KNOW SOMETHING WE DON'T?
OOO (WOOOO)
THE WHOLE TOWN IS PROBABLY LIKE THIS.
GAN
WHY'S THIS HAPPENING ...?
GI (GRIT)
DAMN IT!!
GASHAN (CLANG)

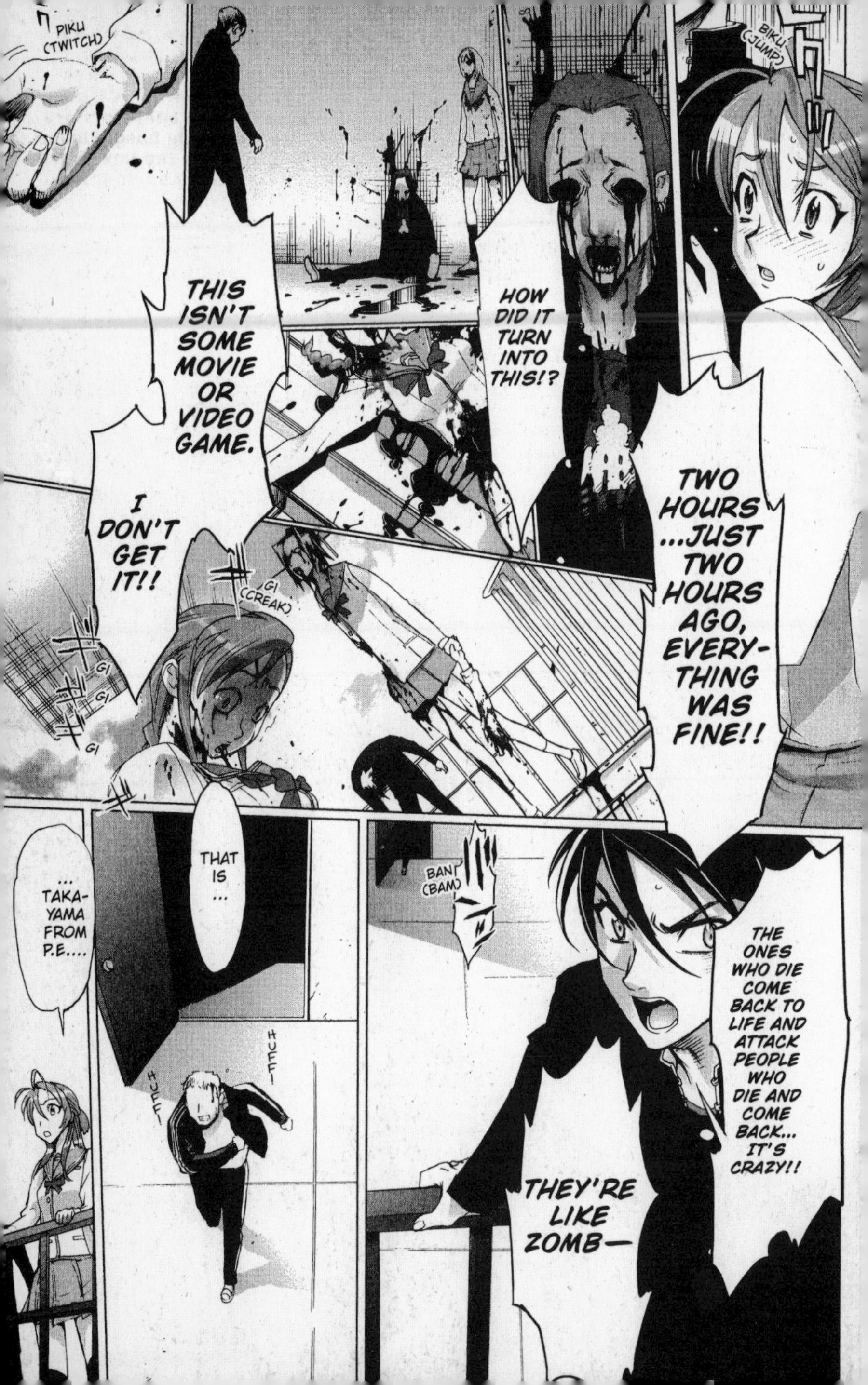
BIKU (JUMP)
HOW DID IT TURN INTO THIS!?
THIS ISN'T SOME MOVIE OR VIDEO GAME.
PIKU (TWITCH)
TWO HOURS ...JUST TWO HOURS AGO, EVERY-THING WAS FINE!!
I DON'T GET IT!!
GI (CREAK)
GI
GI
GI
BAN (BAM)
THE ONES WHO DIE COME BACK TO LIFE AND ATTACK PEOPLE WHO DIE AND COME BACK... IT'S CRAZY!!
THEY'RE LIKE ZOMB—
THAT IS ...
... TAKA-YAMA FROM P.E....
HUFF!
HUFF!

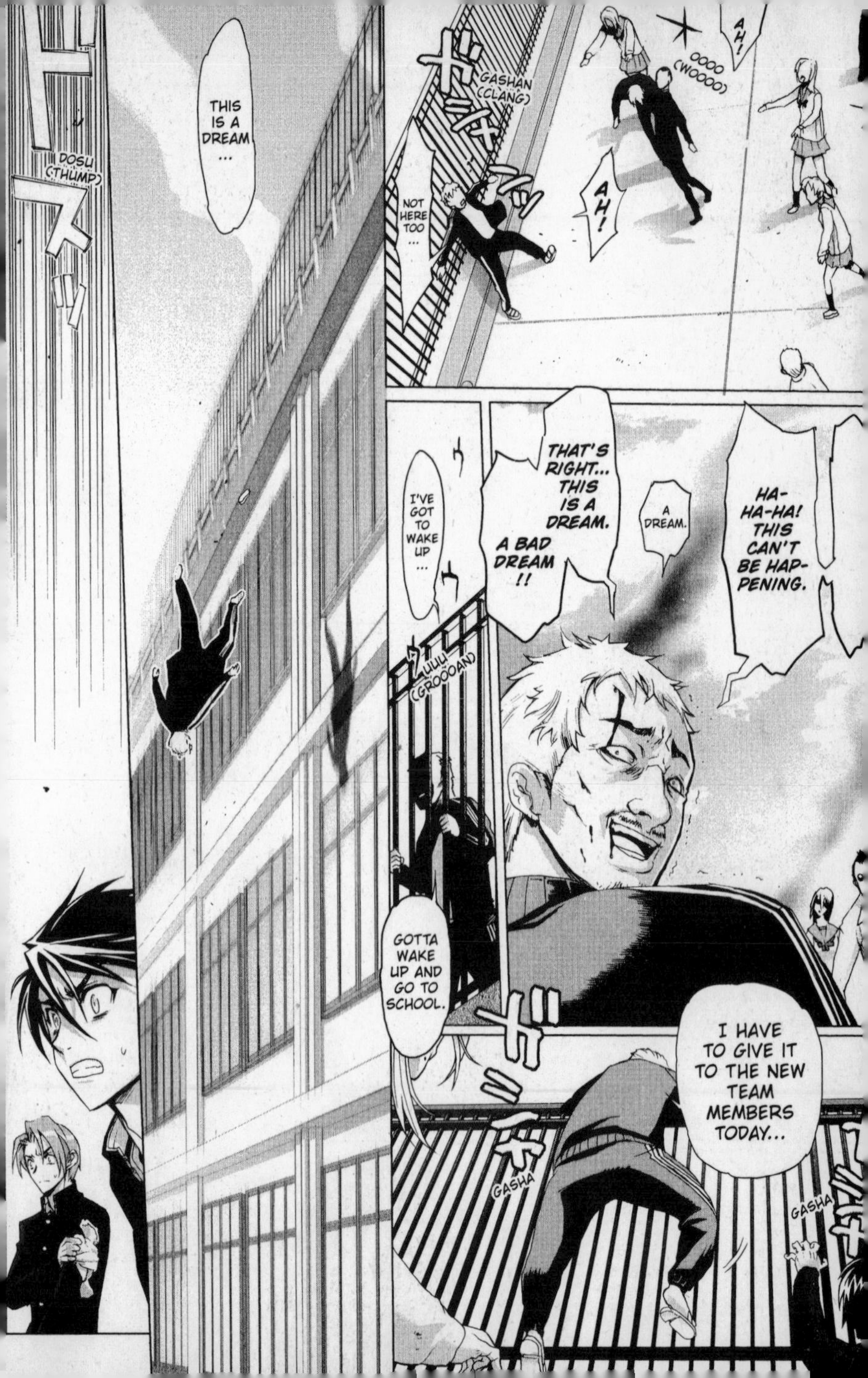
AH!
OOOO (WOOOO)
AH!
GASHAN (CLANG)
NOT HERE TOO...
HA-HA-HA! THIS CAN'T BE HAPPENING.
A DREAM.
THAT'S RIGHT... THIS IS A DREAM.
A BAD DREAM!!
I'VE GOT TO WAKE UP...
UUU (GROOOAN)
I HAVE TO GIVE IT TO THE NEW TEAM MEMBERS TODAY...
GASHA
GASHA
GOTTA WAKE UP AND GO TO SCHOOL.
THIS IS A DREAM...
DOSU (THUMP)

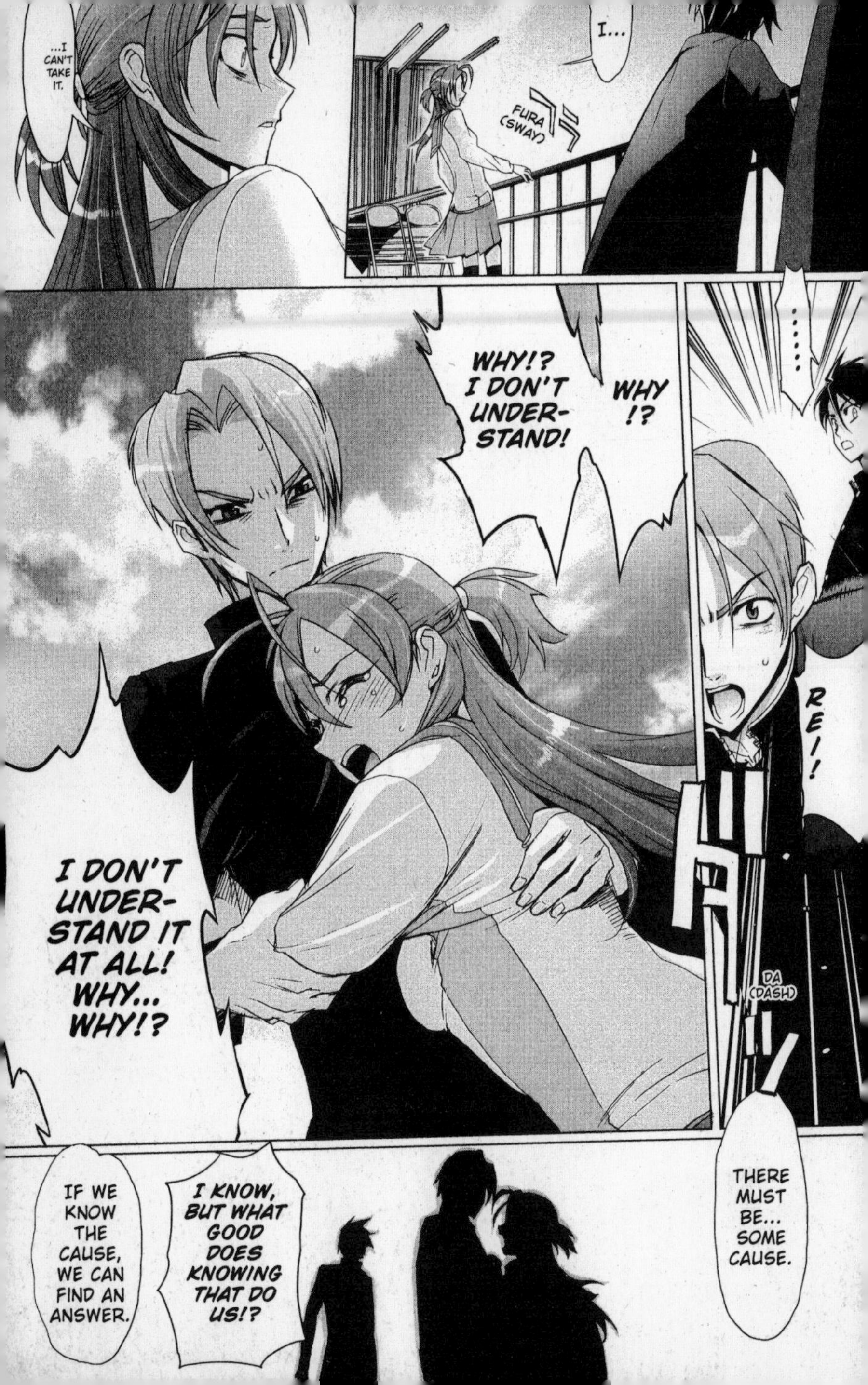
I...
FURA (SWAY)
...I CAN'T TAKE IT.
......
REI!
DA (DASH)
WHY !?
WHY!? I DON'T UNDERSTAND!
I DON'T UNDERSTAND IT AT ALL! WHY... WHY!?
THERE MUST BE... SOME CAUSE.
I KNOW, BUT WHAT GOOD DOES KNOWING THAT DO US!?
IF WE KNOW THE CAUSE, WE CAN FIND AN ANSWER.

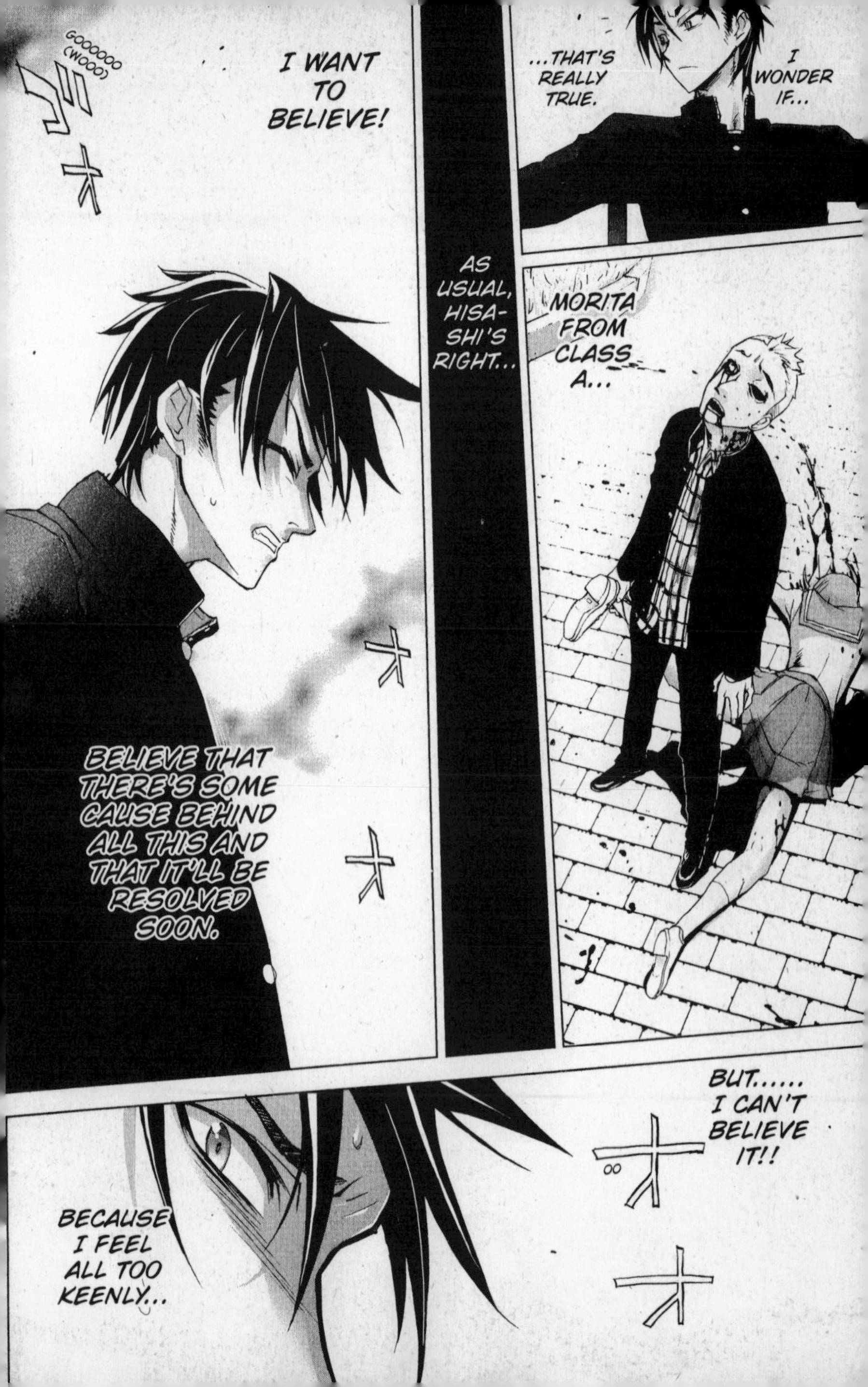
I WONDER IF...
...THAT'S REALLY TRUE.
MORITA FROM CLASS A...
AS USUAL, HISA-SHI'S RIGHT...
GOOOOOO (WOOO)
I WANT TO BELIEVE!
BELIEVE THAT THERE'S SOME CAUSE BEHIND ALL THIS AND THAT IT'LL BE RESOLVED SOON.
BUT...... I CAN'T BELIEVE IT!!
BECAUSE I FEEL ALL TOO KEENLY...

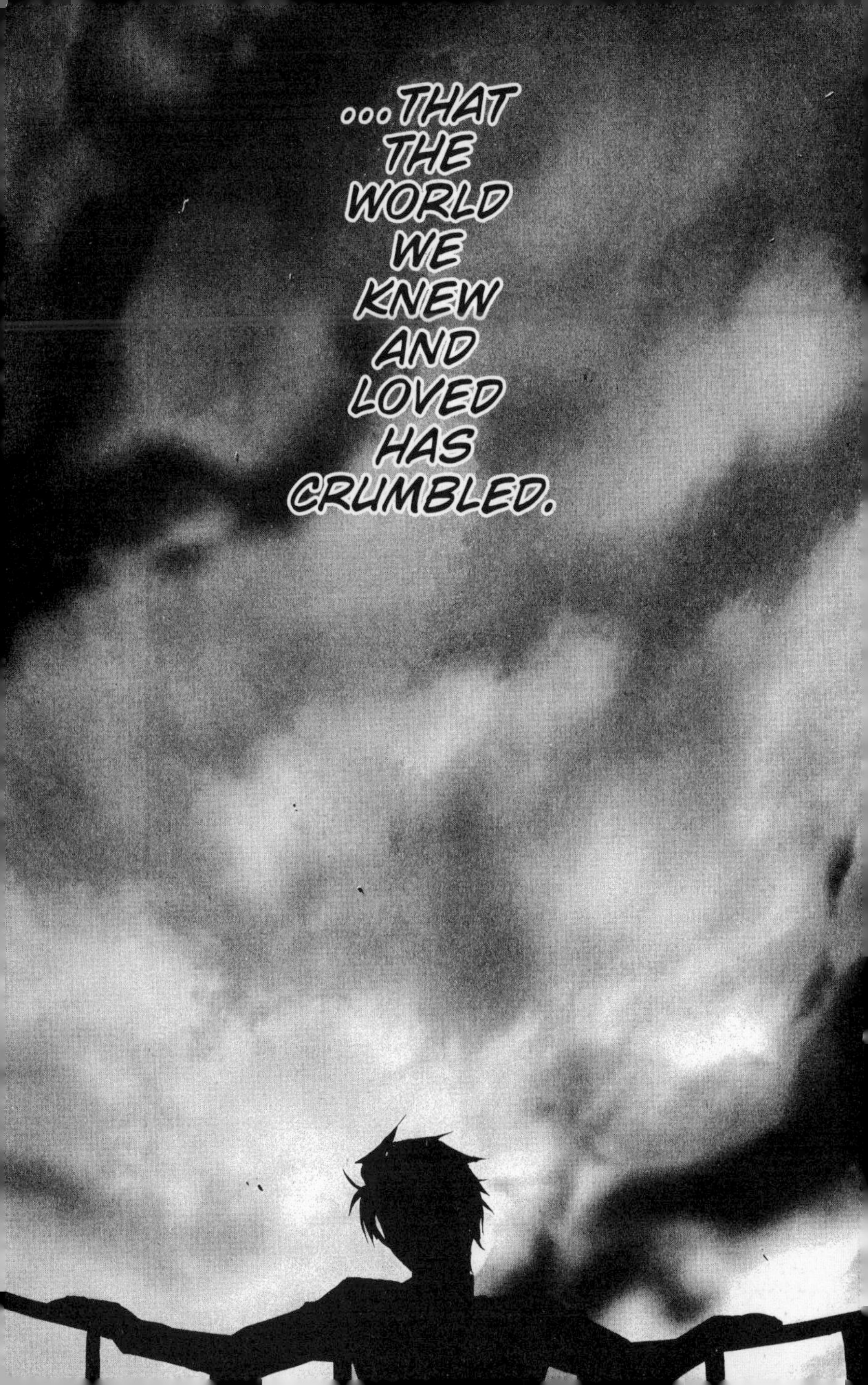
...THAT THE WORLD WE KNEW AND LOVED HAS CRUMBLED.

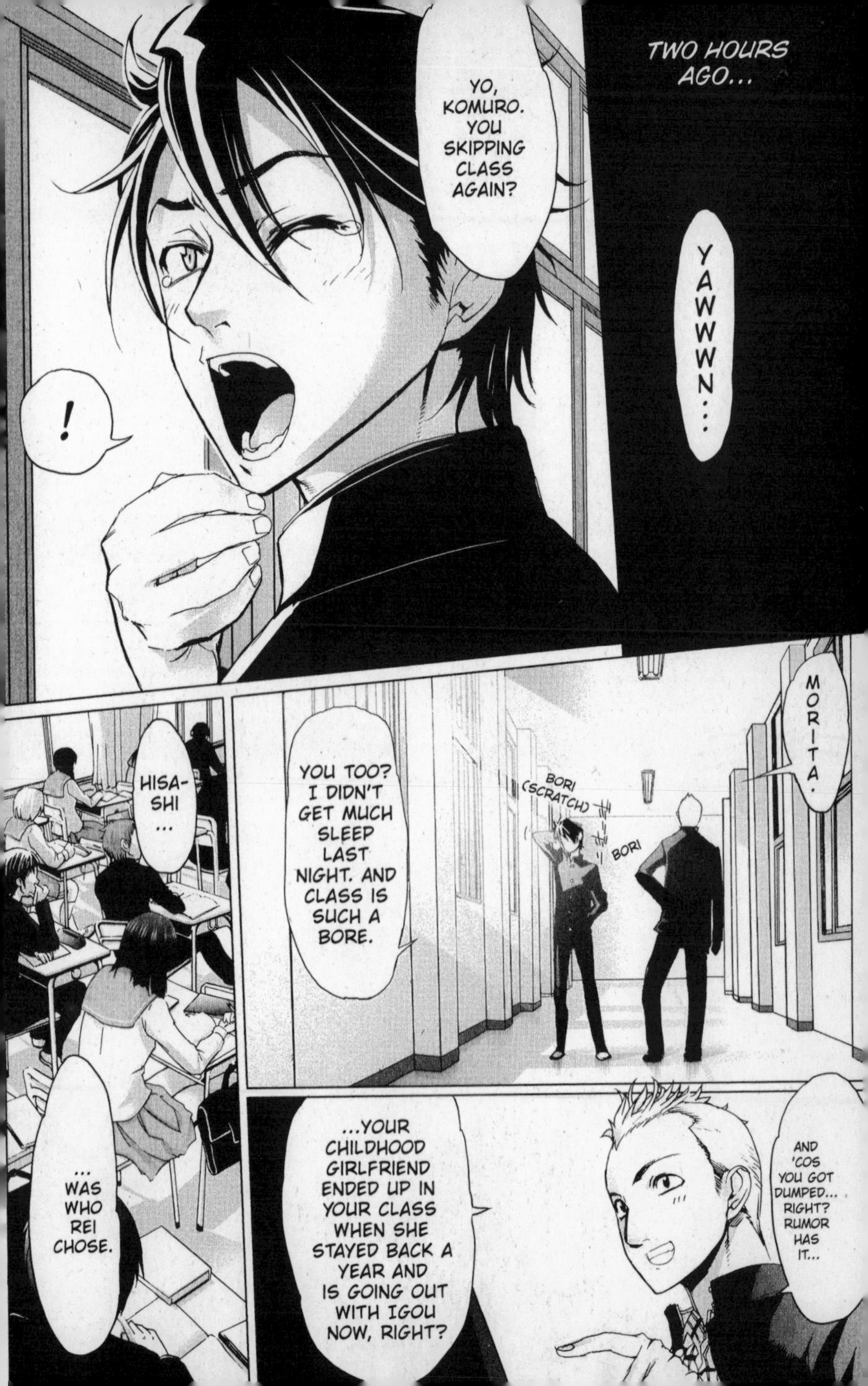
TWO HOURS AGO...
YAWWWN...
YO, KOMURO. YOU SKIPPING CLASS AGAIN?
!
MORITA.
BORI (SCRATCH)
BORI
YOU TOO? I DIDN'T GET MUCH SLEEP LAST NIGHT. AND CLASS IS SUCH A BORE.
AND 'COS YOU GOT DUMPED... RIGHT? RUMOR HAS IT...
...YOUR CHILDHOOD GIRLFRIEND ENDED UP IN YOUR CLASS WHEN SHE STAYED BACK A YEAR AND IS GOING OUT WITH IGOU NOW, RIGHT?
HISA-SHI...
...WAS WHO REI CHOSE.

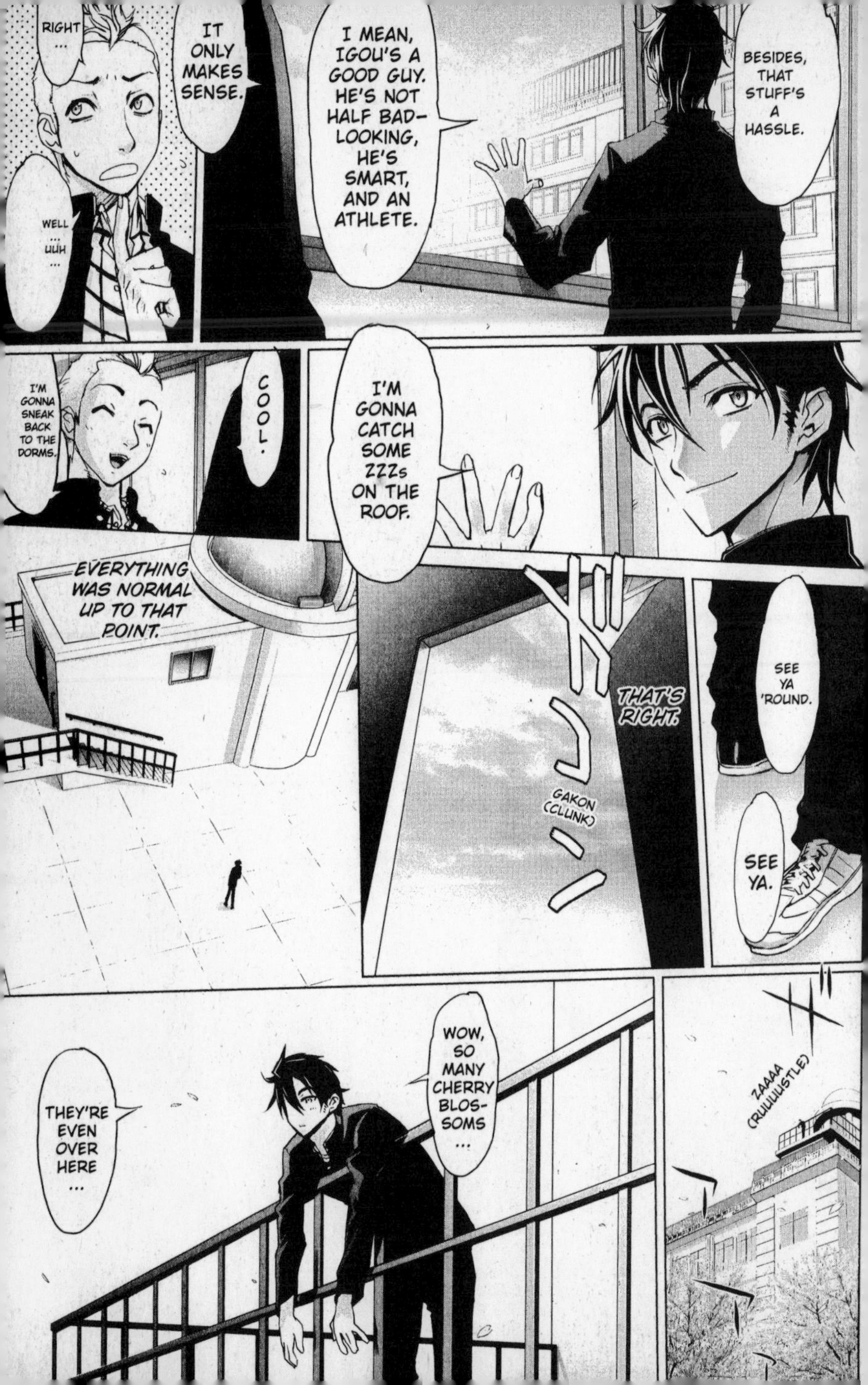
BESIDES, THAT STUFF'S A HASSLE.
I MEAN, IGOU'S A GOOD GUY. HE'S NOT HALF BAD-LOOKING, HE'S SMART, AND AN ATHLETE.
IT ONLY MAKES SENSE.
RIGHT...
WELL... UUH...
I'M GONNA CATCH SOME ZZZs ON THE ROOF.
COOL.
I'M GONNA SNEAK BACK TO THE DORMS.
SEE YA 'ROUND.
SEE YA.
THAT'S RIGHT.
GAKON (CLUNK)
EVERYTHING WAS NORMAL UP TO THAT POINT.
ZAAAA (RUUUUSTLE)
WOW, SO MANY CHERRY BLOSSOMS...
THEY'RE EVEN OVER HERE...

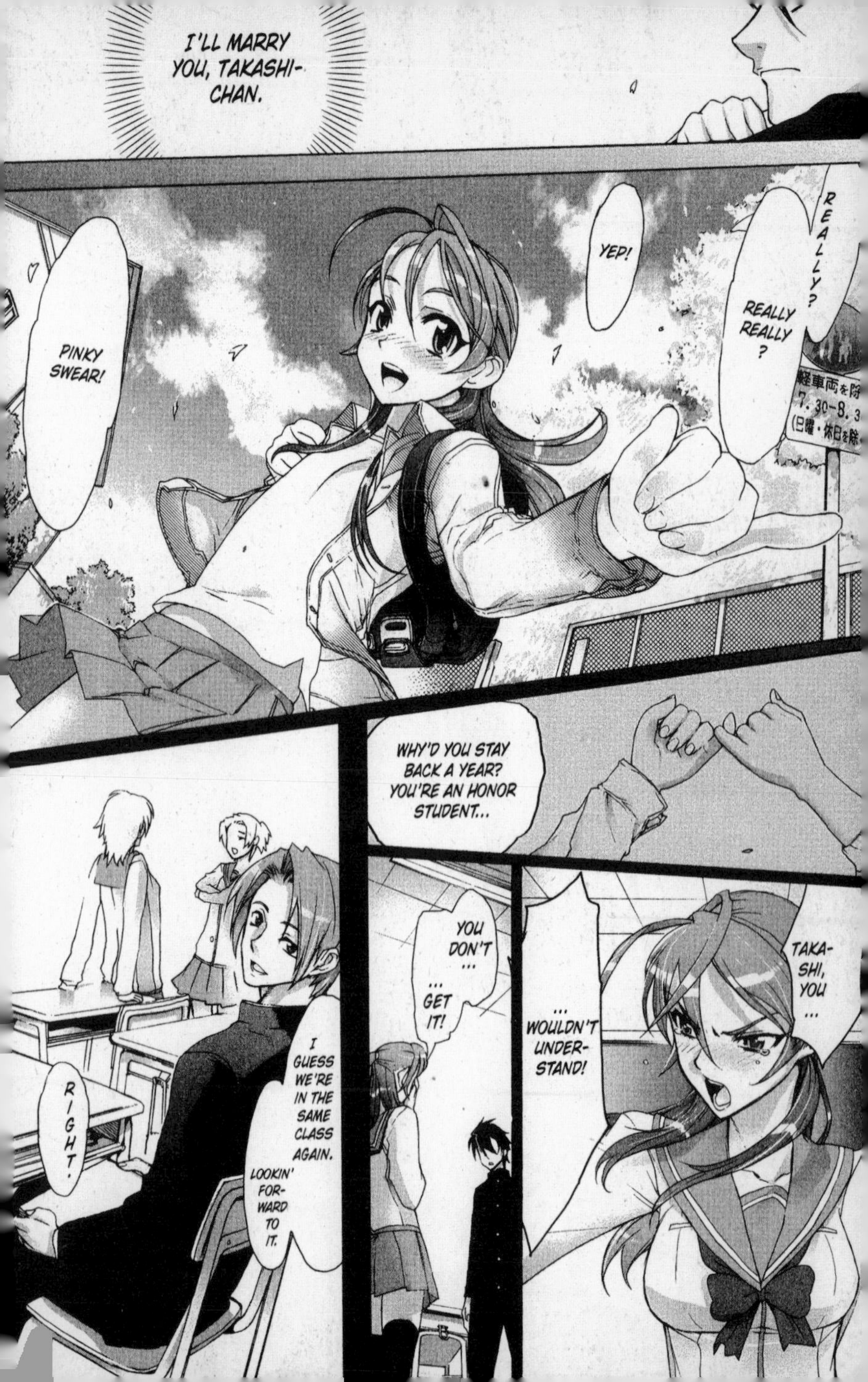
I'LL MARRY YOU, TAKASHI-CHAN.
REALLY? REALLY REALLY?
YEP!
PINKY SWEAR!
WHY'D YOU STAY BACK A YEAR? YOU'RE AN HONOR STUDENT...
TAKASHI, YOU ...
... WOULDN'T UNDERSTAND!
YOU DON'T ...
... GET IT!
I GUESS WE'RE IN THE SAME CLASS AGAIN.
LOOKIN' FORWARD TO IT.
RIGHT.

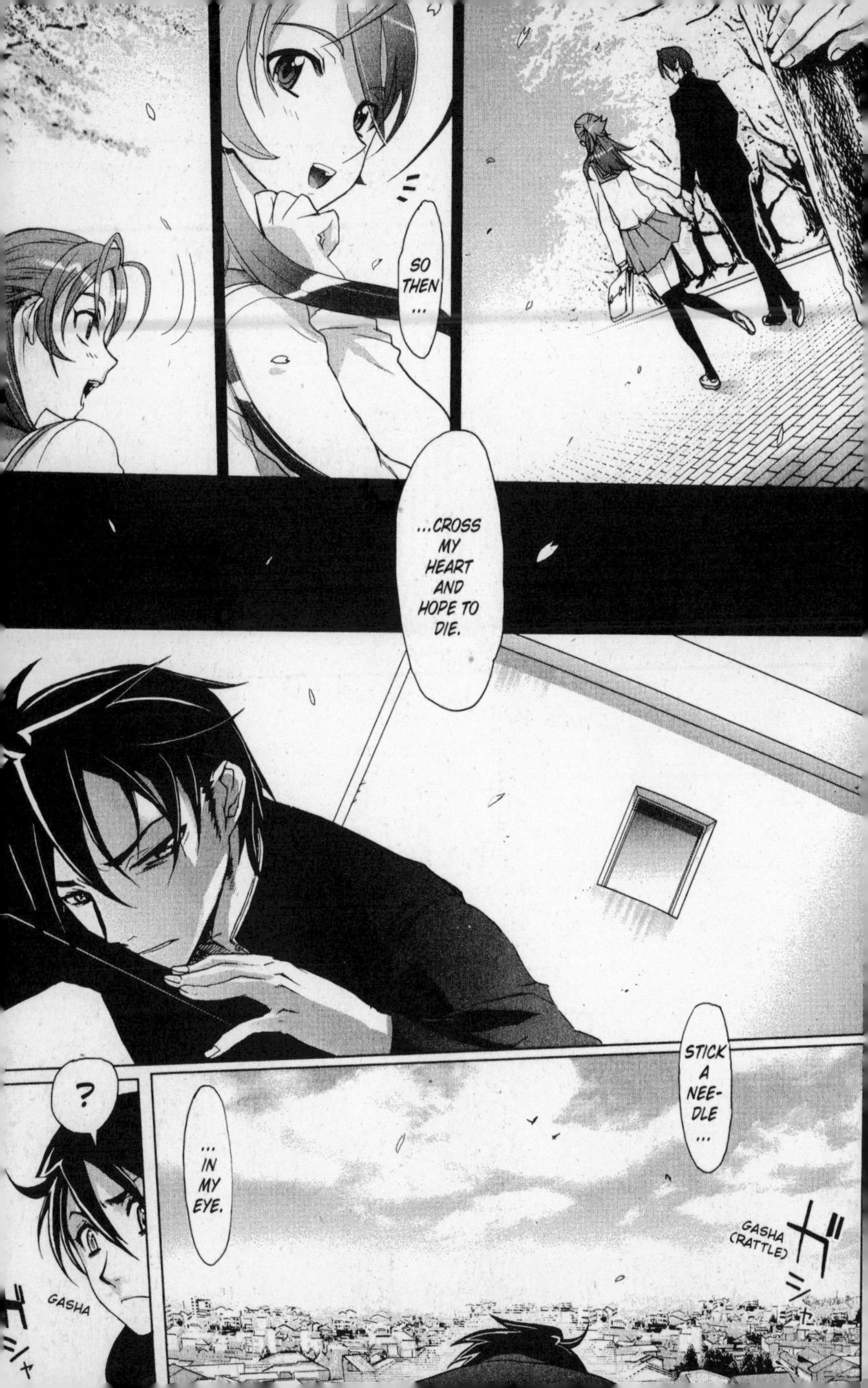

SO THEN ...
...CROSS MY HEART AND HOPE TO DIE.
STICK A NEE-DLE ...
... IN MY EYE.
GASHA (RATTLE)
?
GASHA

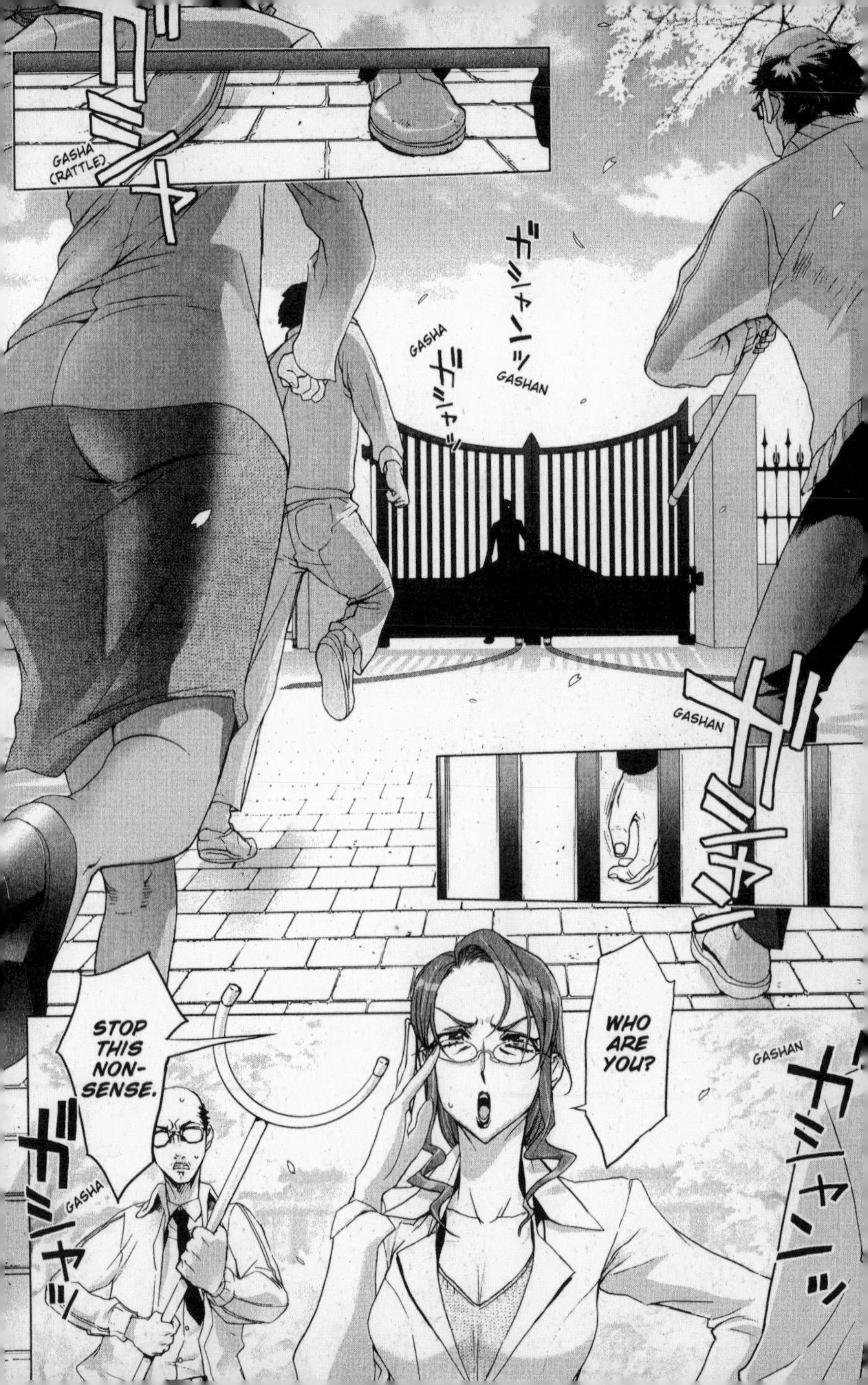
GASHAN
GASHA
GASHA (RATTLE)
GASHAN
GASHAN
WHO ARE YOU?
STOP THIS NON-SENSE.
GASHA

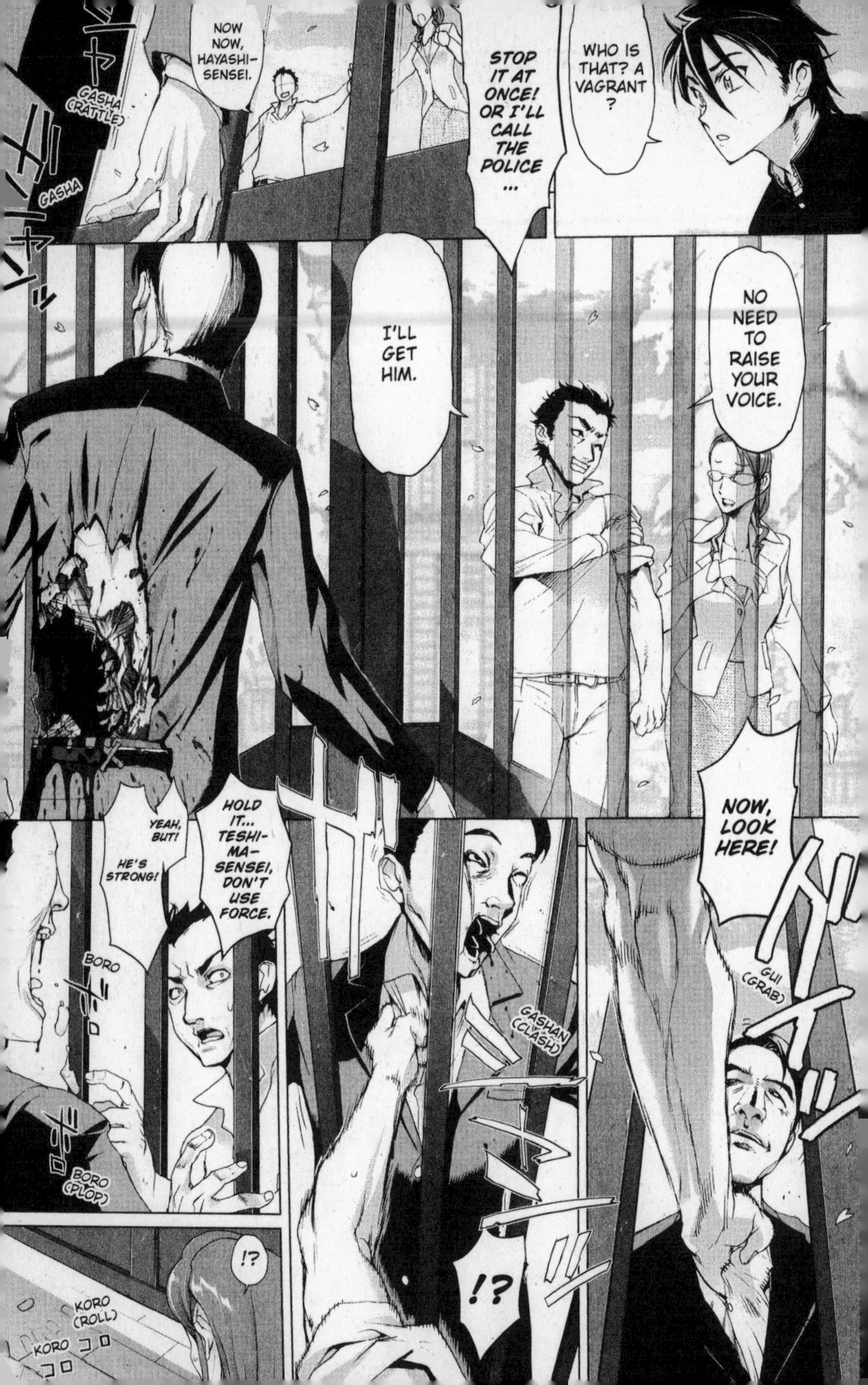
WHO IS THAT? A VAGRANT ?
STOP IT AT ONCE! OR I'LL CALL THE POLICE ...
NOW NOW, HAYASHI-SENSEI.
GASHA (RATTLE)
GASHA
NO NEED TO RAISE YOUR VOICE.
I'LL GET HIM.
NOW, LOOK HERE!
GUI (GRAB)
GASHAN (CLASH)
!?
HOLD IT... TESHIMA-SENSEI, DON'T USE FORCE.
YEAH, BUT!
HE'S STRONG!
BORO
BORO (PLOP)
!?
KORO (ROLL)
KORO

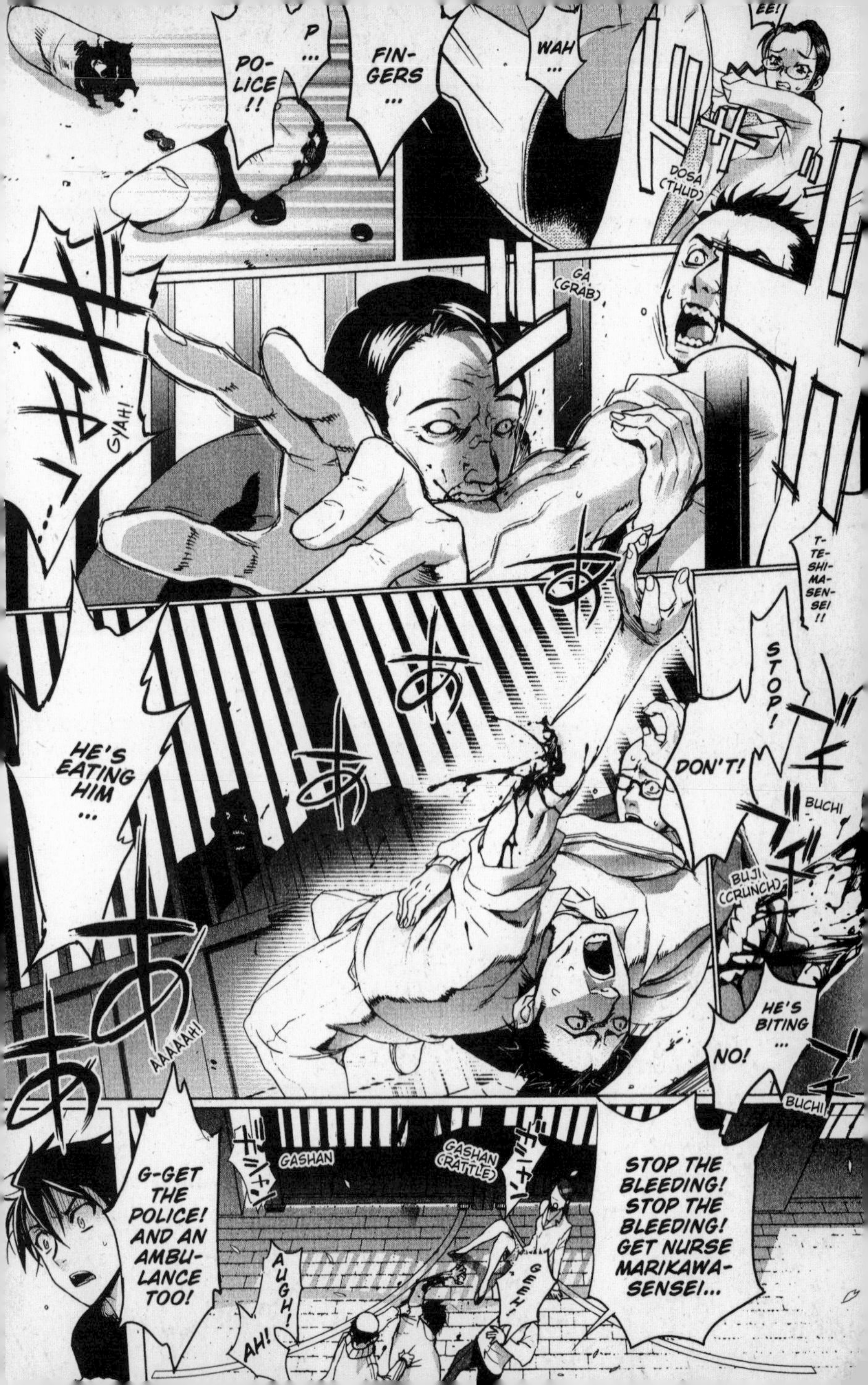
EE!
DOSA (THUD)
WAH ...
FIN-GERS ...
P ... PO-LICE!!
GA (GRAB)
GYAH!
T-TESHIMA-SENSEI!!
STOP!
DON'T!
BUCHI
BUJI (CRUNCH)
HE'S BITING ...
NO!
BUCHI
HE'S EATING HIM ...
AAAAAH!
STOP THE BLEEDING! STOP THE BLEEDING! GET NURSE MARIKAWA-SENSEI...
GASHAN (RATTLE)
GEEH!
GASHAN
AUGH!
AH!
G-GET THE POLICE! AND AN AMBULANCE TOO!

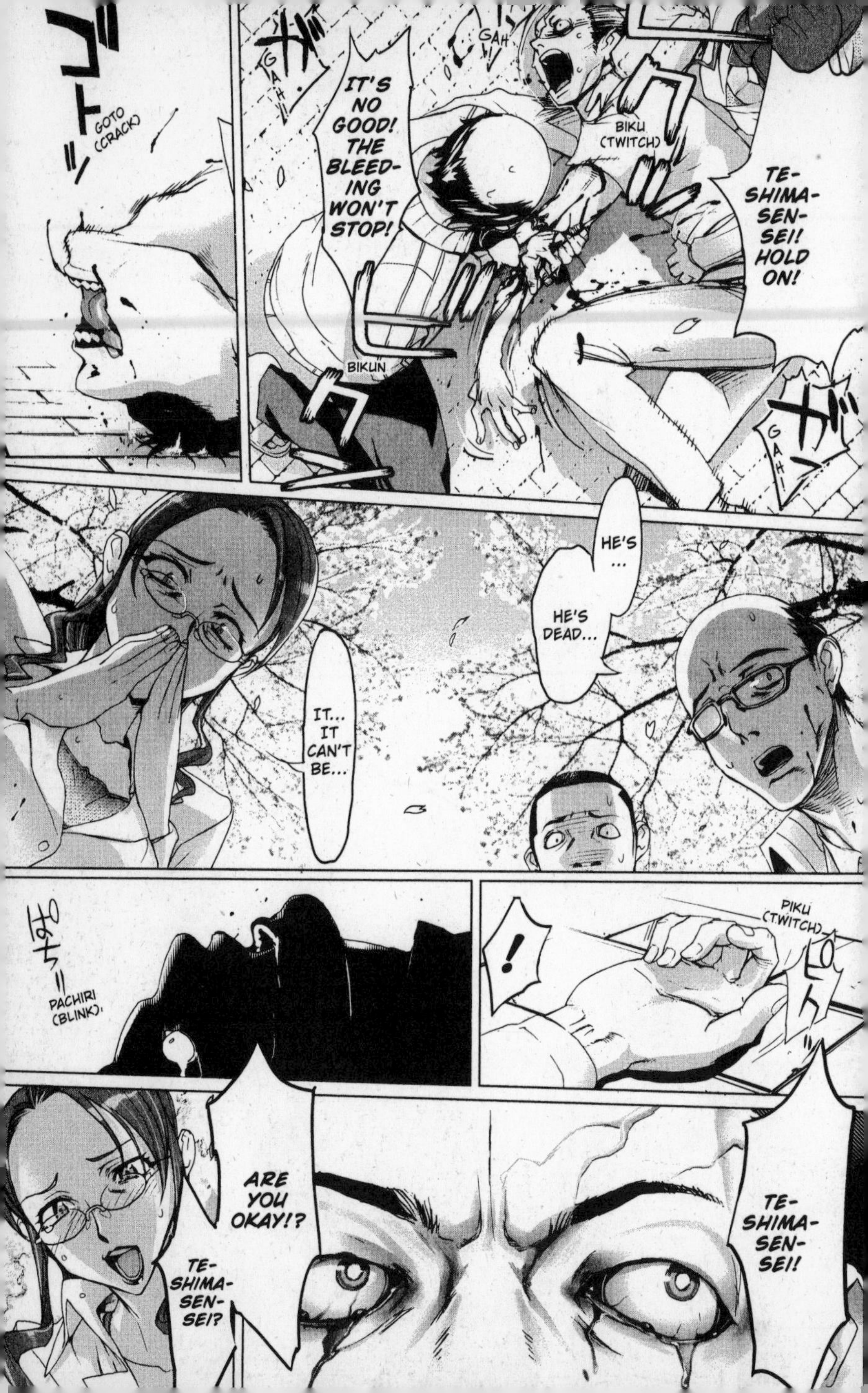

TE-SHIMA-SENSEI! HOLD ON!
GAH!
BIKU (TWITCH)
GAH!!
IT'S NO GOOD! THE BLEEDING WON'T STOP!
GAH!!
BIKUN
GOTO (CRACK)
HE'S...
HE'S DEAD...
IT... IT CAN'T BE...
PIKU (TWITCH)
!
PACHIRI (BLINK)
TE-SHIMA-SEN-SEI!
ARE YOU OKAY!?
TE-SHIMA-SEN-SEI?

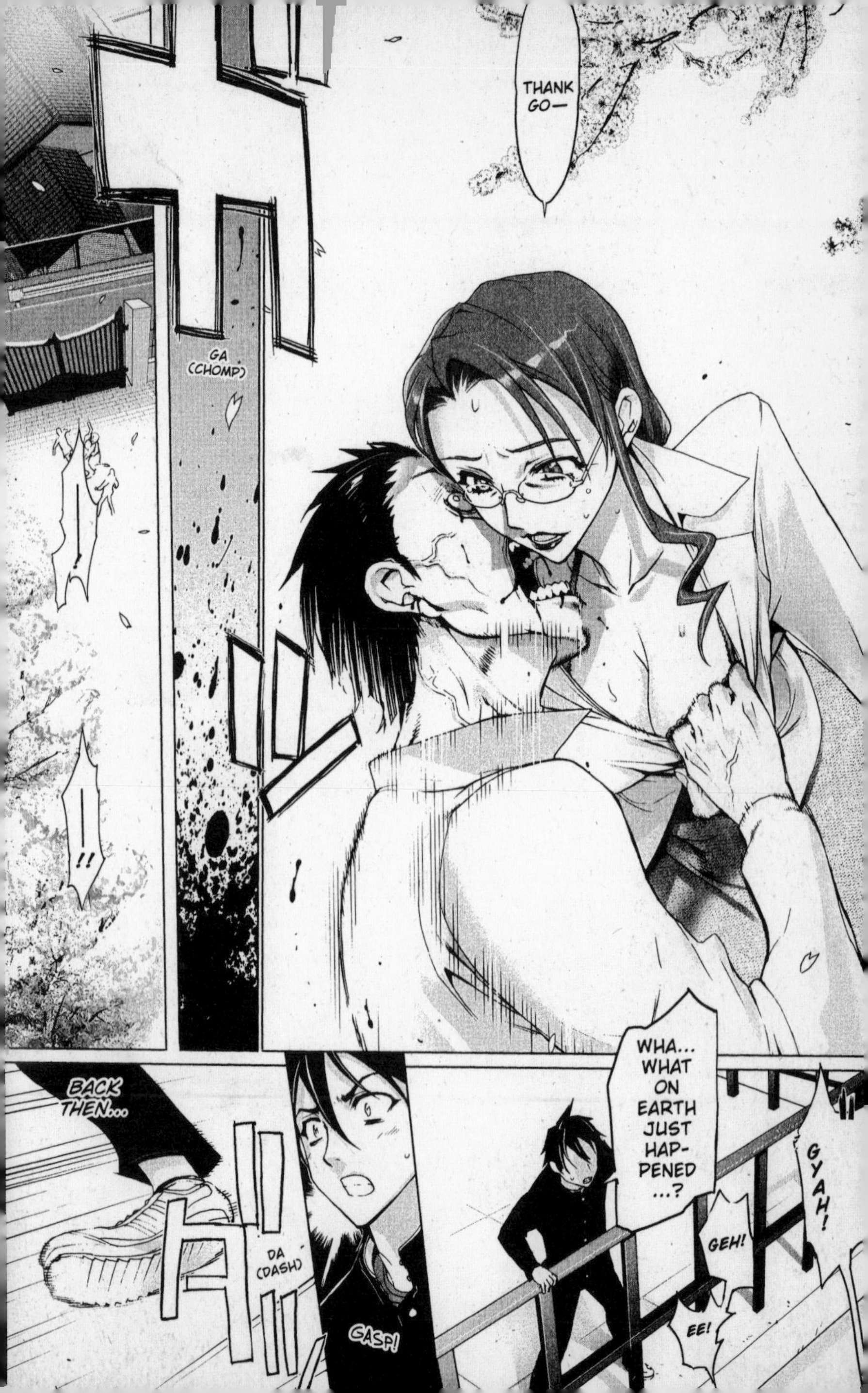
THANK GO—
GA (CHOMP)
!
!!
WHA... WHAT ON EARTH JUST HAP-PENED...?
GYAH!
GEH!
EE!
GASP!
BACK THEN...
DA (DASH)

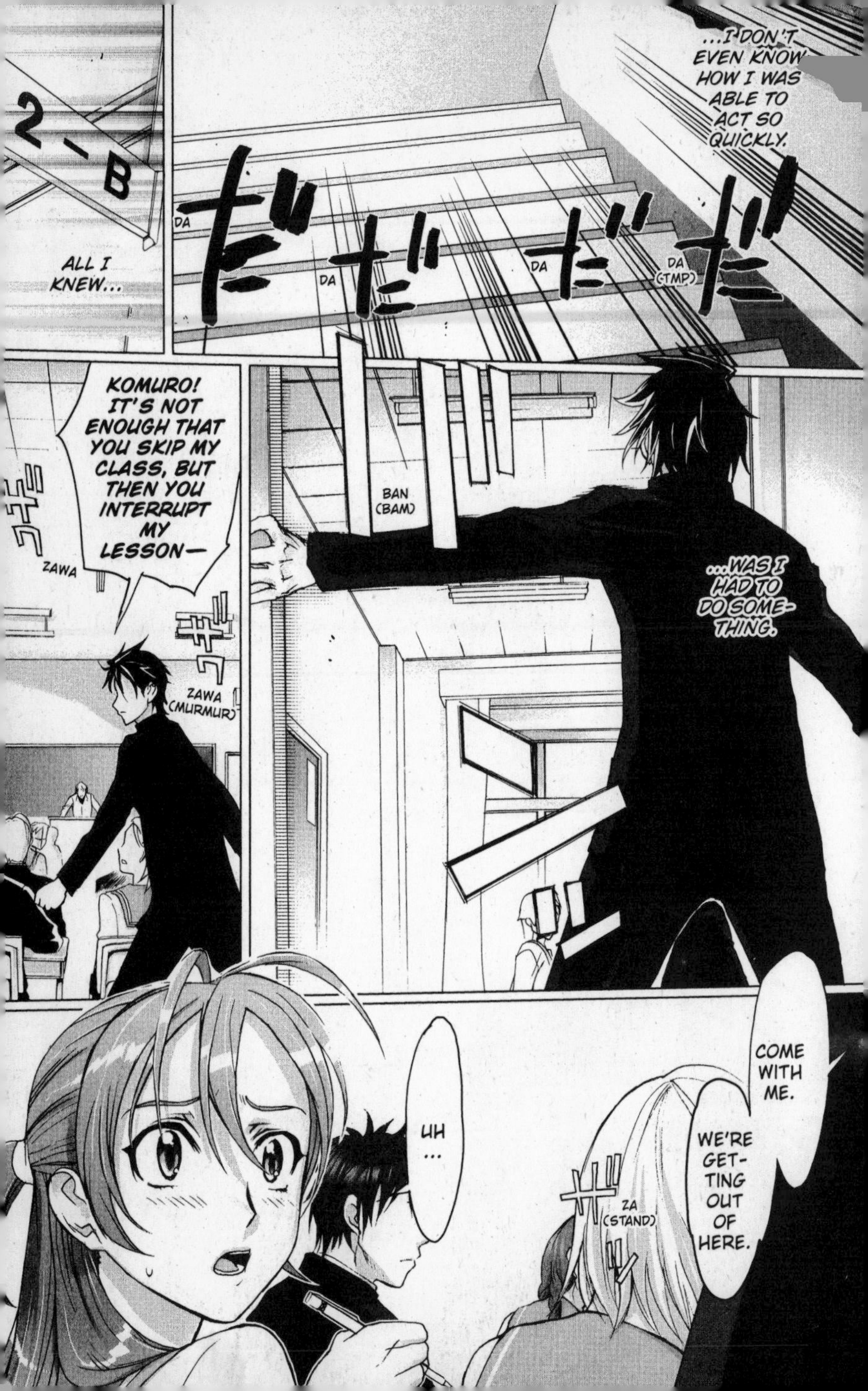
...I DON'T EVEN KNOW HOW I WAS ABLE TO ACT SO QUICKLY.
DA (TMP)
DA
DA
DA
2-B
ALL I KNEW...
BAN (BAM)
...WAS I HAD TO DO SOME-THING.
KOMURO! IT'S NOT ENOUGH THAT YOU SKIP MY CLASS, BUT THEN YOU INTERRUPT MY LESSON—
ZAWA (MURMUR)
ZAWA
COME WITH ME.
WE'RE GET-TING OUT OF HERE.
ZA (STAND)
UH ...

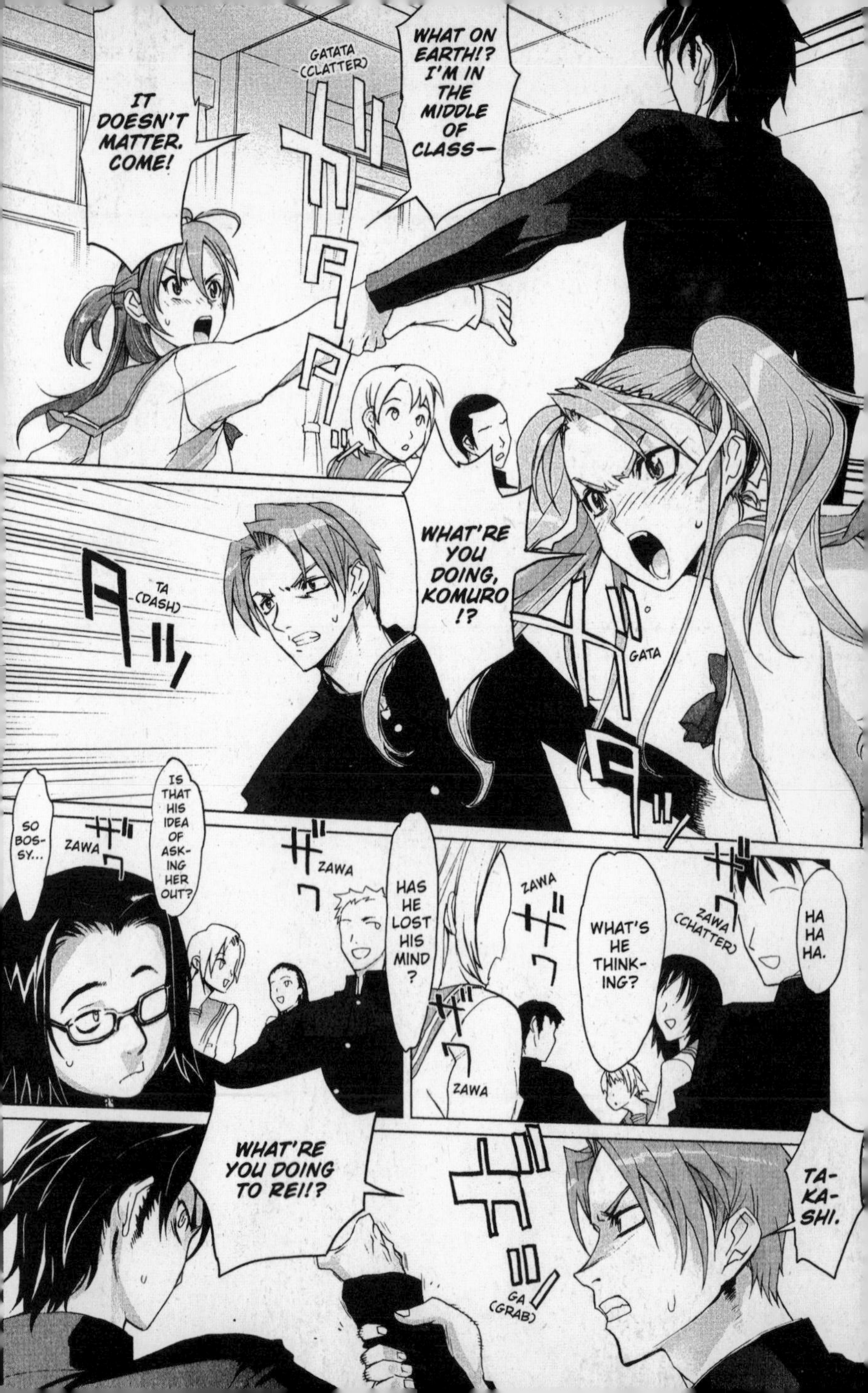

WHAT ON EARTH!? I'M IN THE MIDDLE OF CLASS—
GATATA (CLATTER)
IT DOESN'T MATTER. COME!
WHAT'RE YOU DOING, KOMURO!?
GATA
TA (DASH)
HA HA HA HA.
ZAWA (CHATTER)
WHAT'S HE THINKING?
ZAWA
HAS HE LOST HIS MIND?
ZAWA
ZAWA
IS THAT HIS IDEA OF ASK-ING HER OUT?
ZAWA
SO BOS-SY...
TA-KA-SHI.
GA (GRAB)
WHAT'RE YOU DOING TO REI!?

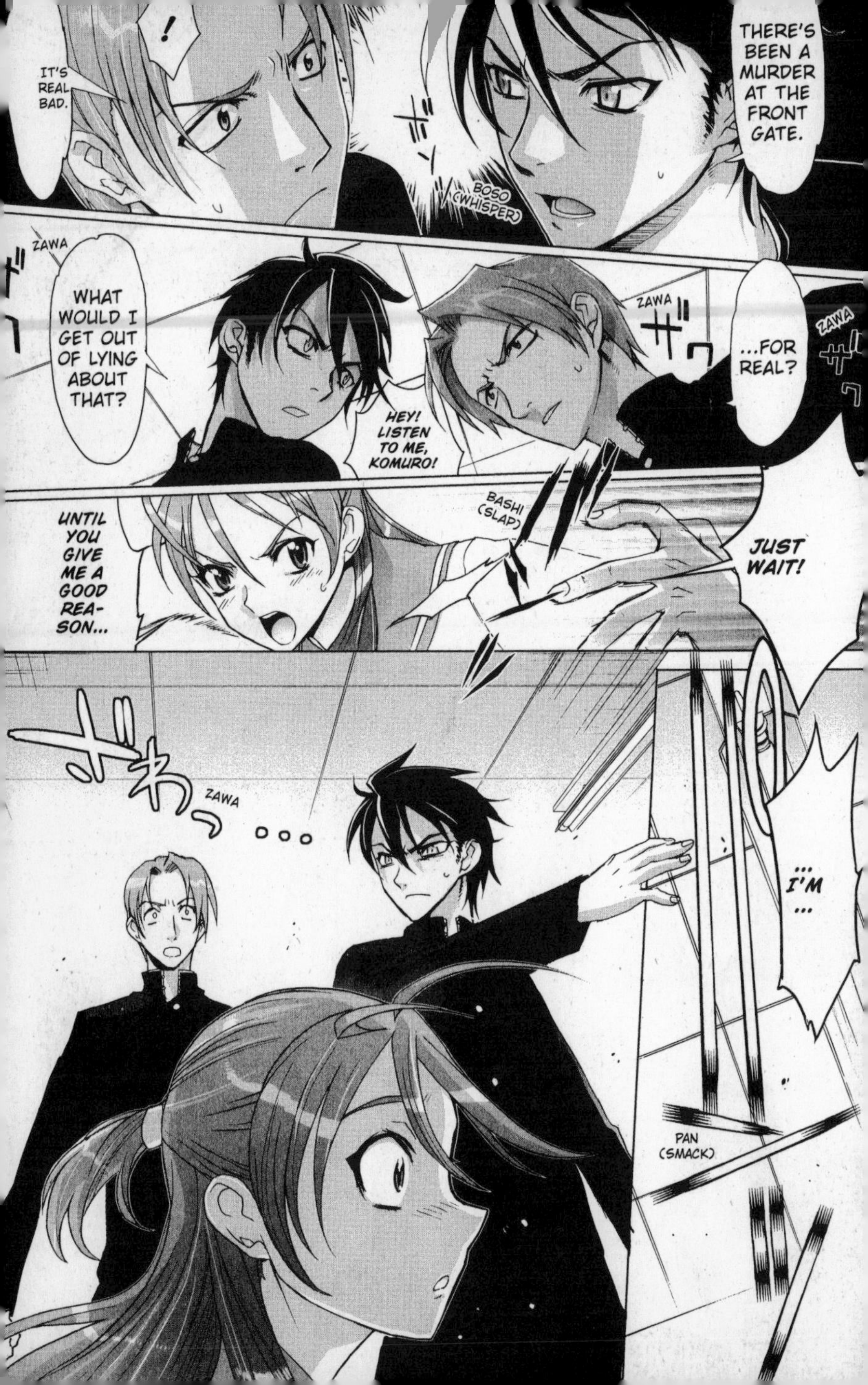
THERE'S BEEN A MURDER AT THE FRONT GATE.
BOSO (WHISPER)
!
IT'S REAL BAD.
ZAWA
...FOR REAL?
ZAWA
HEY! LISTEN TO ME, KOMURO!
WHAT WOULD I GET OUT OF LYING ABOUT THAT?
ZAWA
JUST WAIT!
BASHI (SLAP)
UNTIL YOU GIVE ME A GOOD REA-SON...
...I'M...
PAN (SMACK)
ZAWA
...

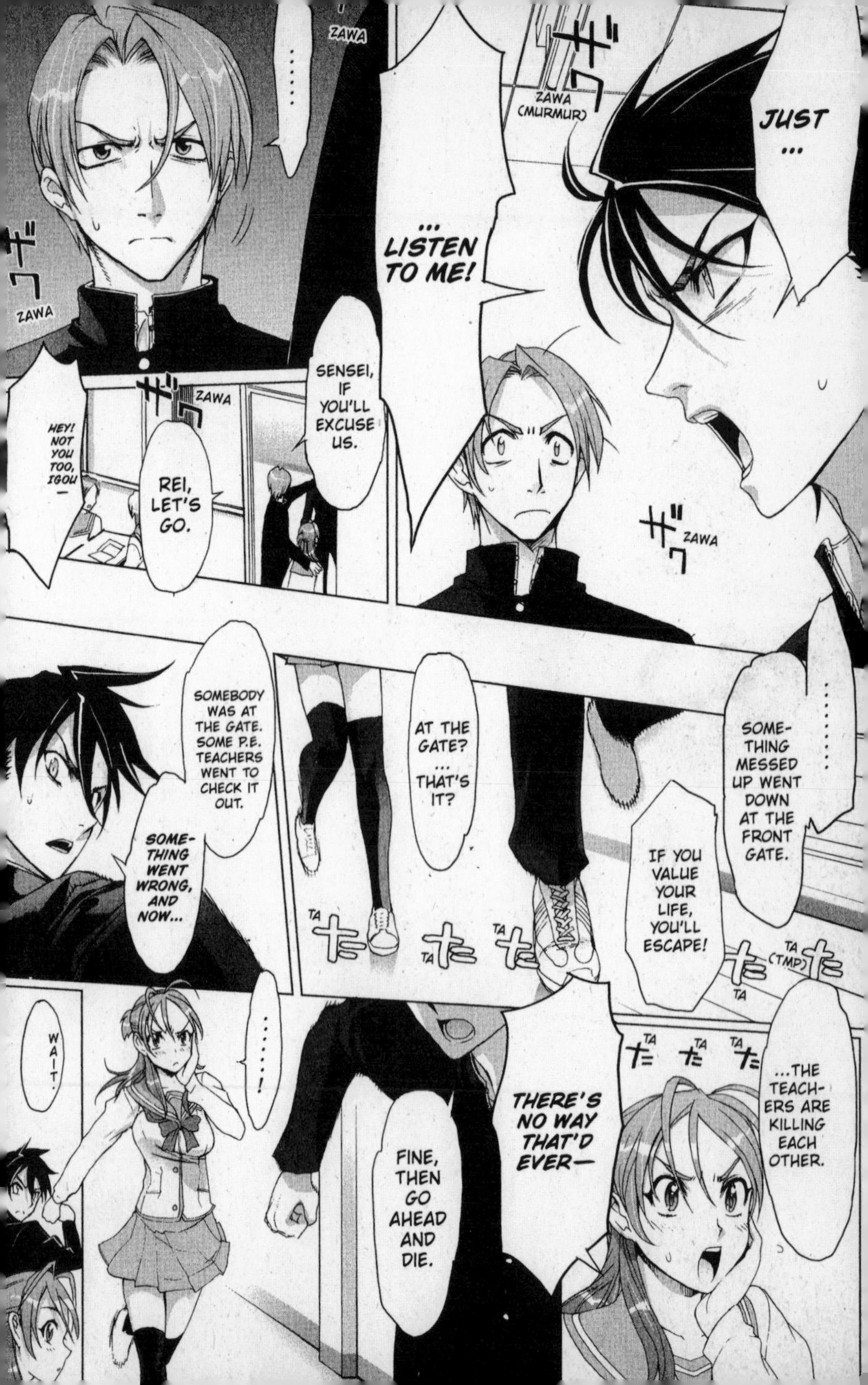
ZAWA (MURMUR)
JUST ...
... LISTEN TO ME!
ZAWA
ZAWA
.....
ZAWA
ZAWA
SENSEI, IF YOU'LL EXCUSE US.
REI, LET'S GO.
HEY! NOT YOU TOO, IGOU—
SOME-THING MESSED UP WENT DOWN AT THE FRONT GATE.
......
IF YOU VALUE YOUR LIFE, YOU'LL ESCAPE!
TA (TMP) TA TA
AT THE GATE? ... THAT'S IT?
TA TA TA
SOMEBODY WAS AT THE GATE. SOME P.E. TEACHERS WENT TO CHECK IT OUT.
SOME-THING WENT WRONG, AND NOW...
...THE TEACH-ERS ARE KILLING EACH OTHER.
TA TA TA
THERE'S NO WAY THAT'D EVER—
FINE, THEN GO AHEAD AND DIE.
......!
WAIT.

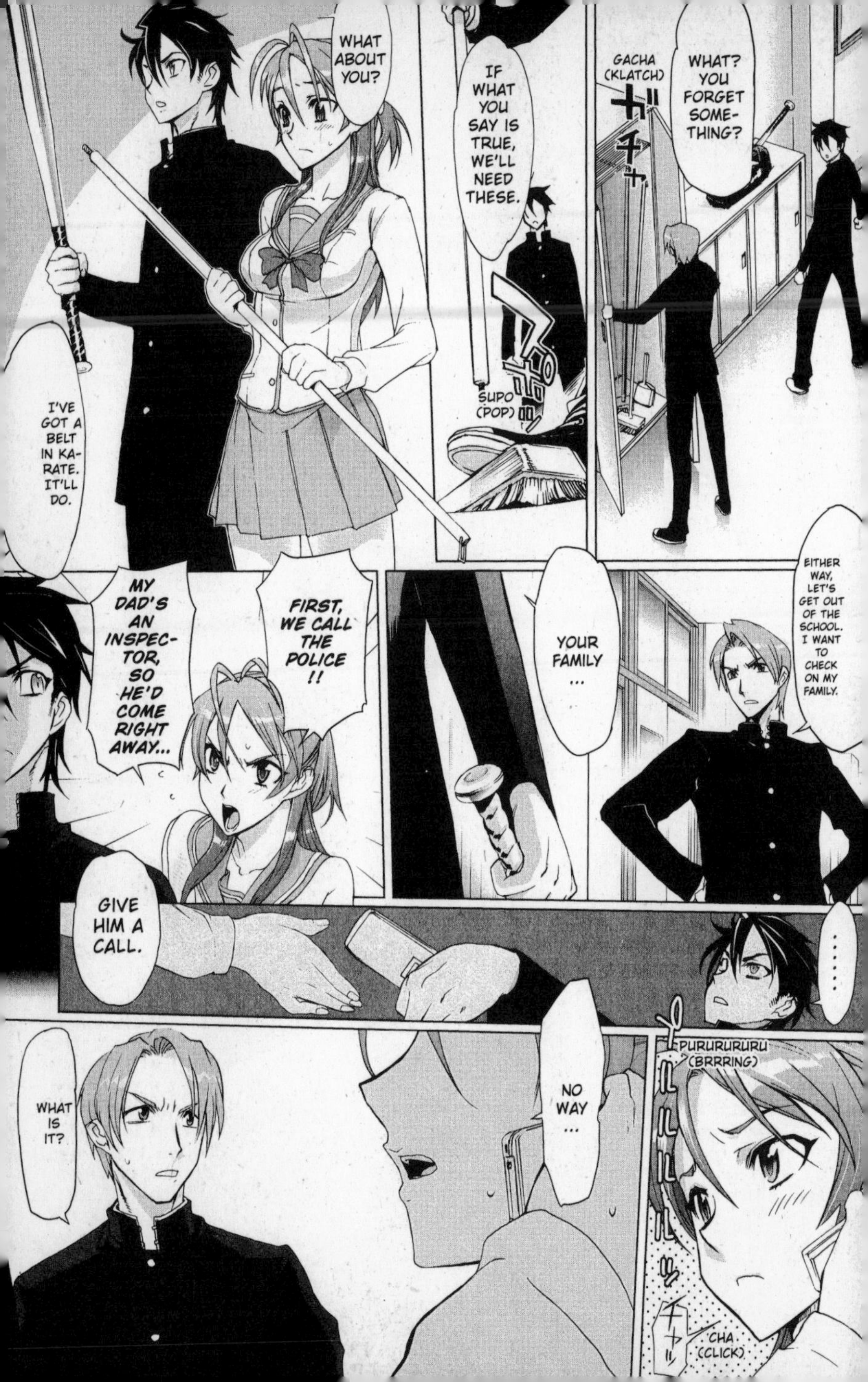
GACHA (KLATCH)
WHAT? YOU FORGET SOME-THING?
IF WHAT YOU SAY IS TRUE, WE'LL NEED THESE.
SUPO (POP)
WHAT ABOUT YOU?
I'VE GOT A BELT IN KA-RATE. IT'LL DO.
EITHER WAY, LET'S GET OUT OF THE SCHOOL. I WANT TO CHECK ON MY FAMILY.
YOUR FAMILY ...
FIRST, WE CALL THE POLICE !!
MY DAD'S AN INSPEC-TOR, SO HE'D COME RIGHT AWAY...
......
GIVE HIM A CALL.
PURURURURU (BRRRING)
CHA (CLICK)
NO WAY ...
WHAT IS IT?

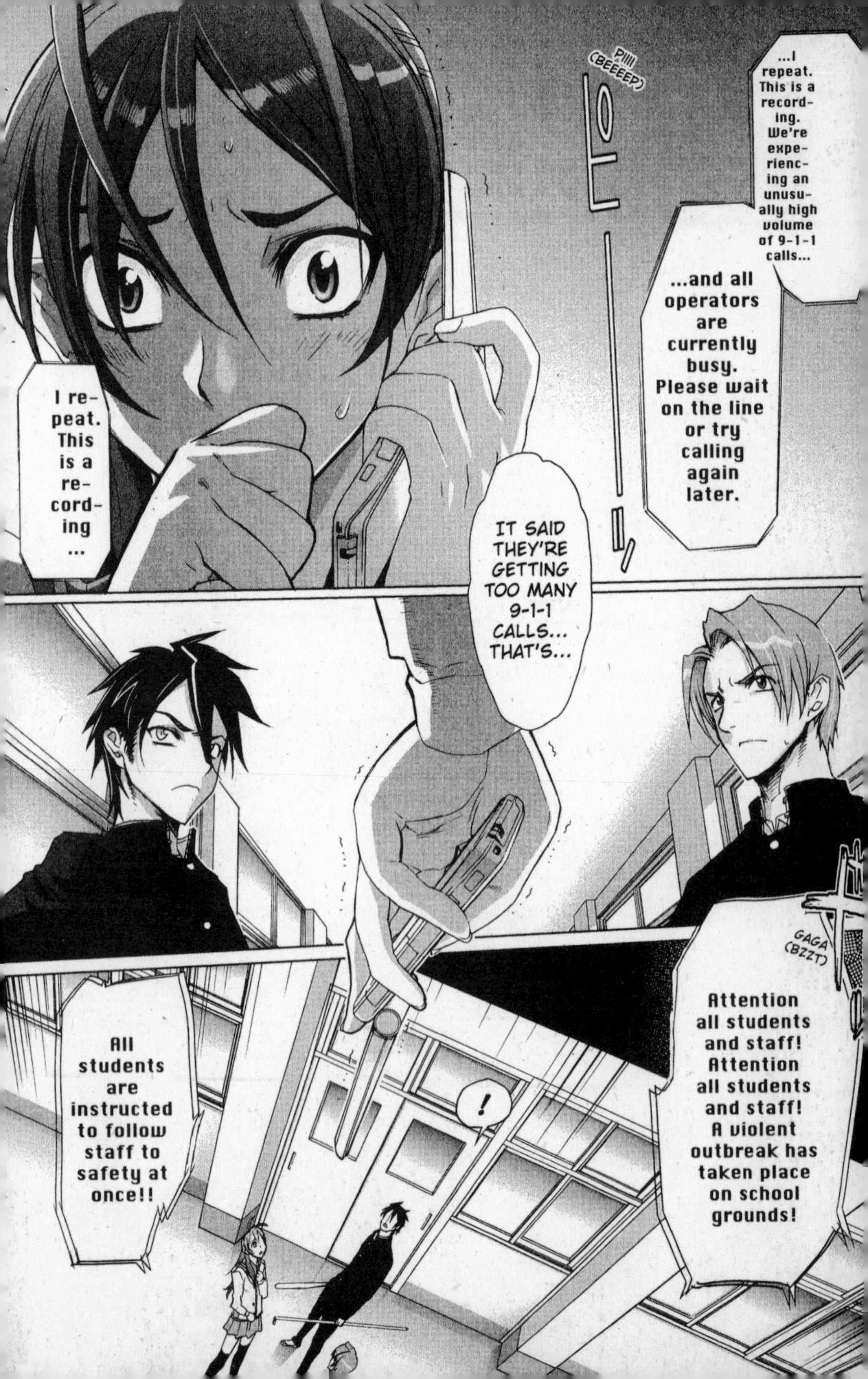
...I repeat. This is a recording. We're experiencing an unusually high volume of 9-1-1 calls...
PIIII (BEEEEP)
...and all operators are currently busy. Please wait on the line or try calling again later.
I repeat. This is a recording...
IT SAID THEY'RE GETTING TOO MANY 9-1-1 CALLS... THAT'S...
GAGA (BZZT)
Attention all students and staff! Attention all students and staff! A violent outbreak has taken place on school grounds!
!
All students are instructed to follow staff to safety at once!!

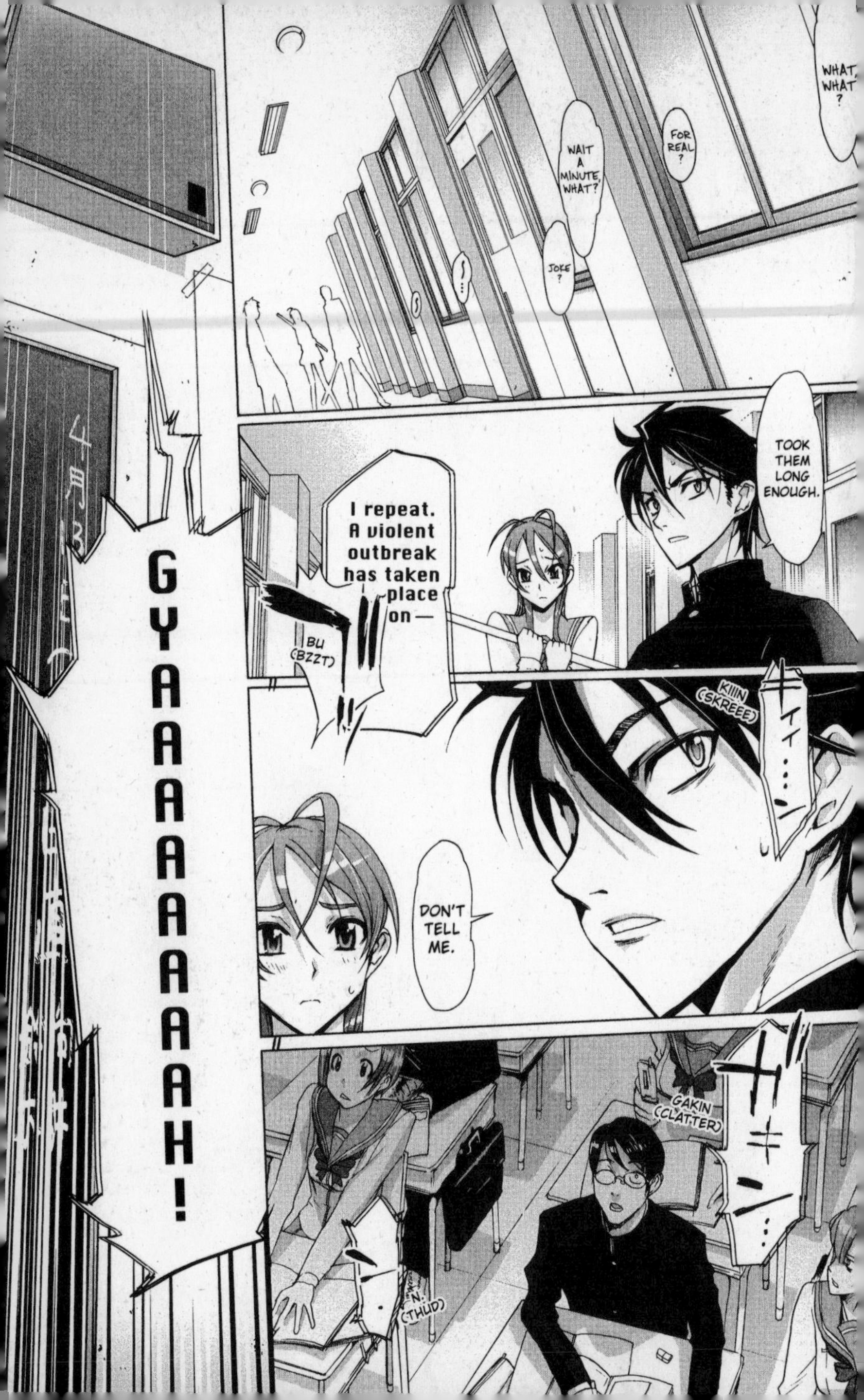
WHAT, WHAT?
FOR REAL?
WAIT A MINUTE, WHAT?
JOKE?
TOOK THEM LONG ENOUGH.
I repeat. A violent outbreak has taken place on—
BU (BZZT)
KIIIN (SKREEE)
DON'T TELL ME.
GYAAAAAAAAH!
GAKIN (CLATTER)
N. (THUD)

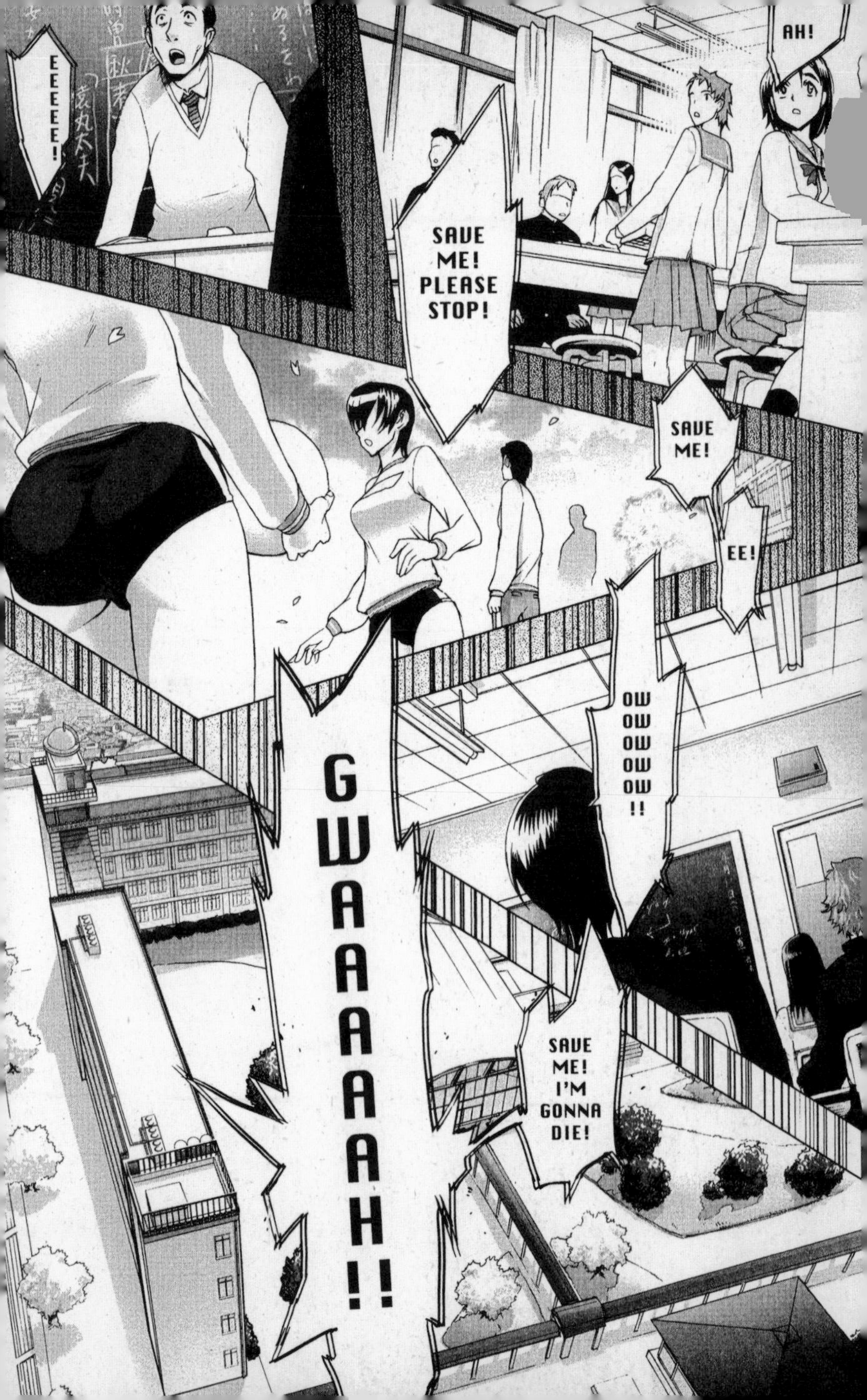
AH!
SAVE ME! PLEASE STOP!
EEEEEE!
SAVE ME!
EE!
OWOWOWOWOW!!
SAVE ME! I'M GONNA DIE!
GWAAAAAH!!

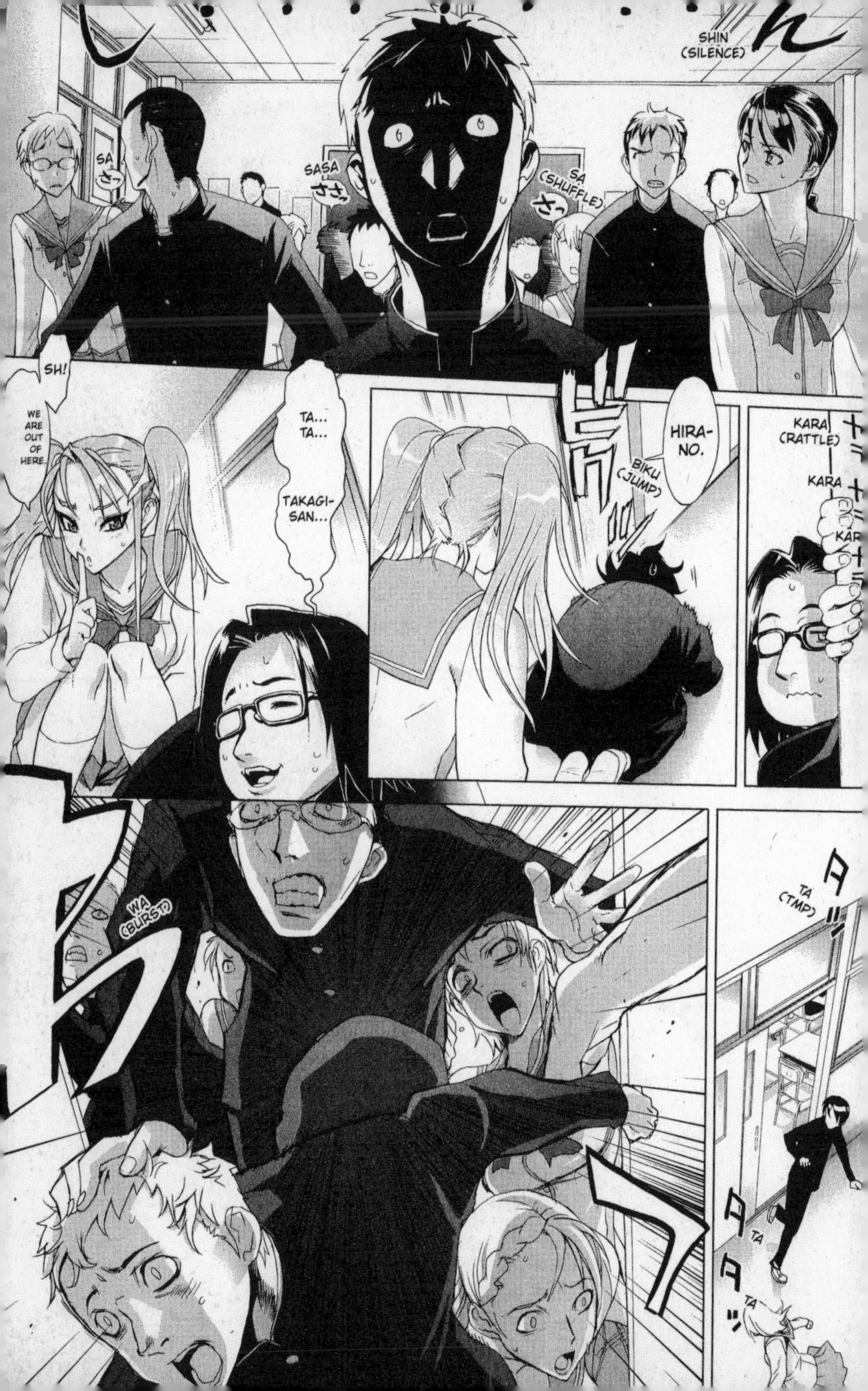
SHIN (SILENCE)
SA (SHUFFLE) さっ
SASA ささっ
SA さっ
KARA (RATTLE)
KARA
KAR
HIRA-NO.
BIKU (JUMP)
TA... TA...
TAKAGI-SAN...
SH!
WE ARE OUT OF HERE.
TA (TMP)
TA
TA
WA (BURST)

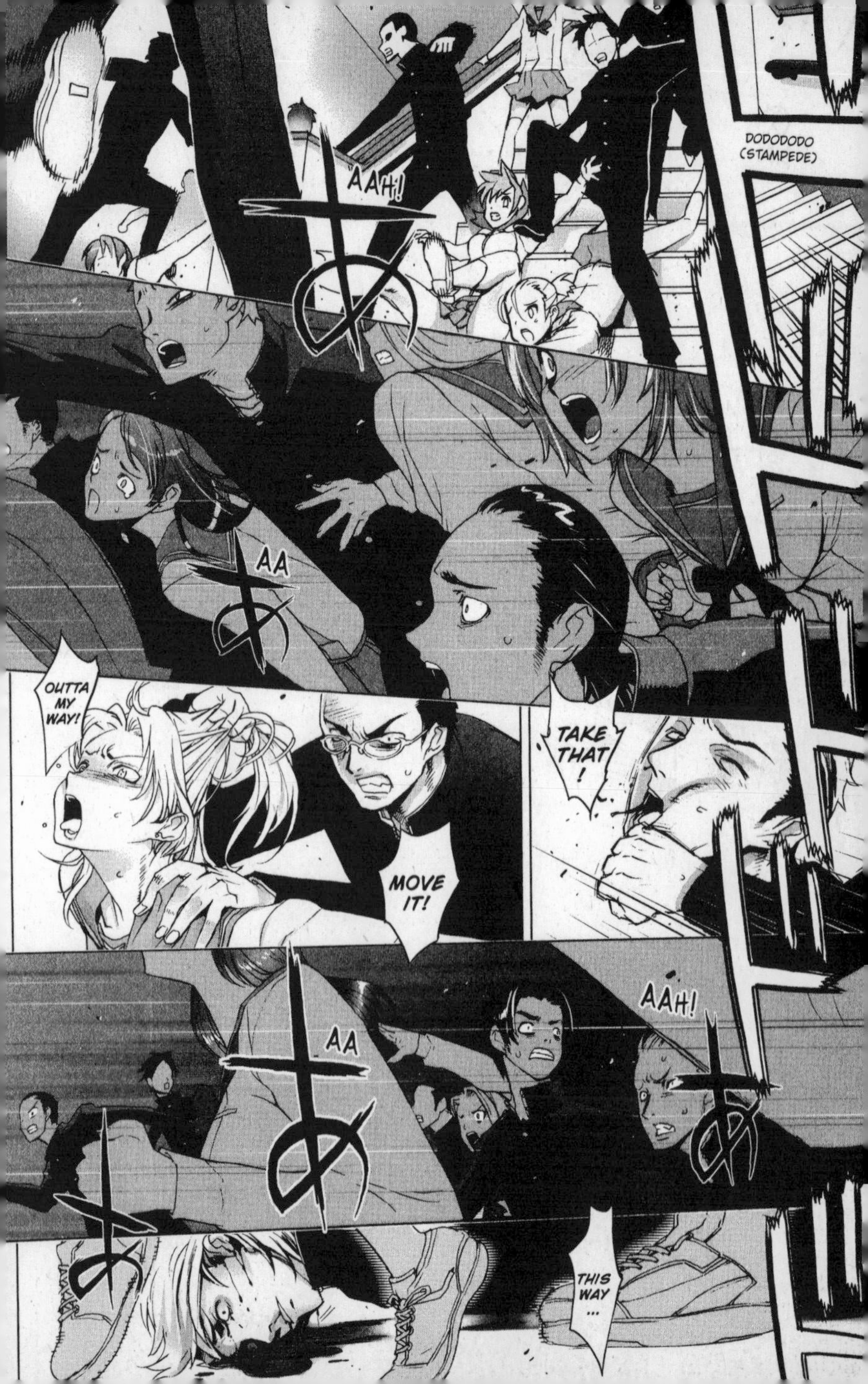
DODODODO (STAMPEDE)
AAH!
AA
TAKE THAT!
OUTTA MY WAY!
MOVE IT!
AAH!
AA
THIS WAY ...

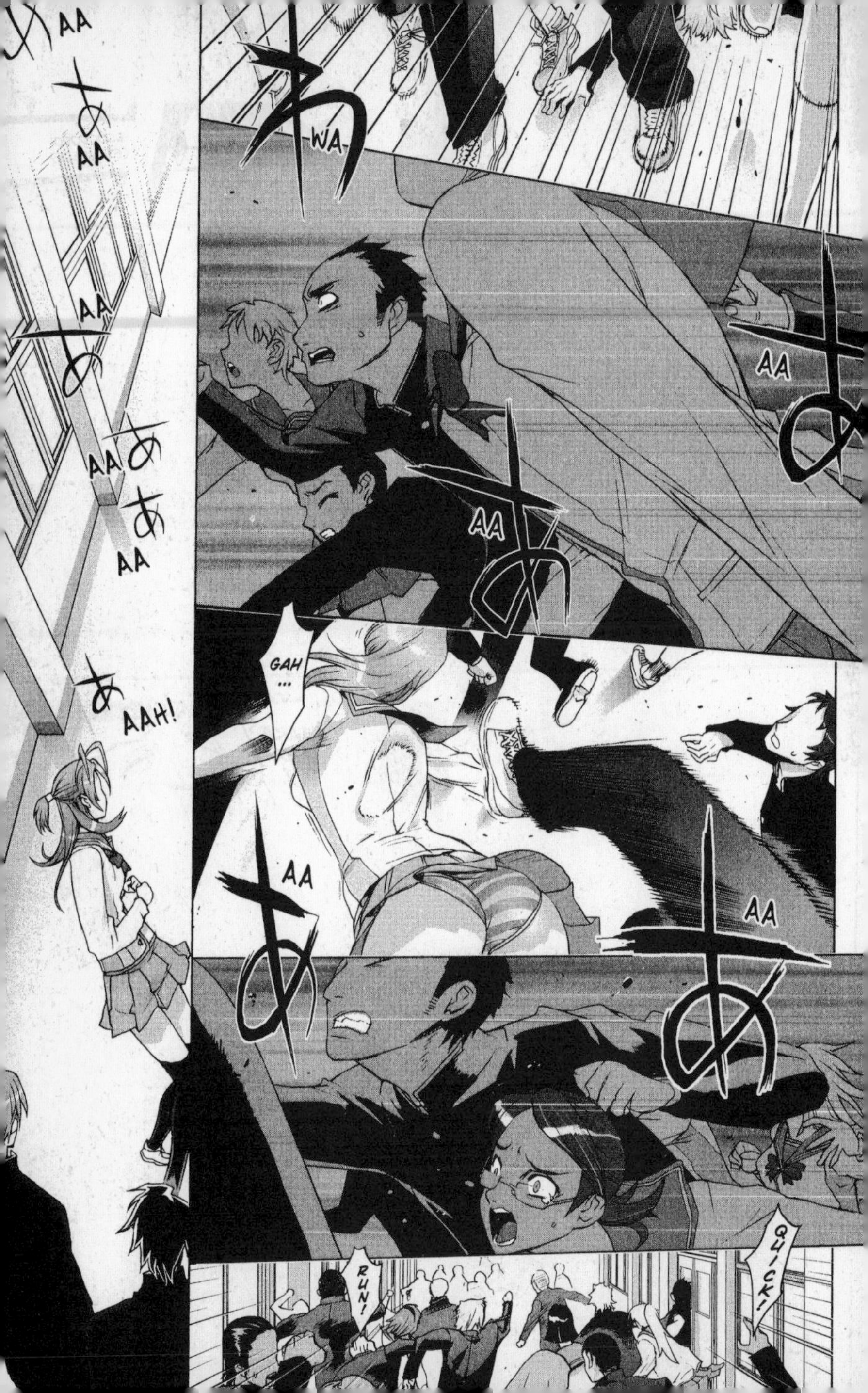

WA
AA
AA
GAH ...
AA
AA
QUICK!
RUN!
AA
AA
AA
AA
AA
AAH!

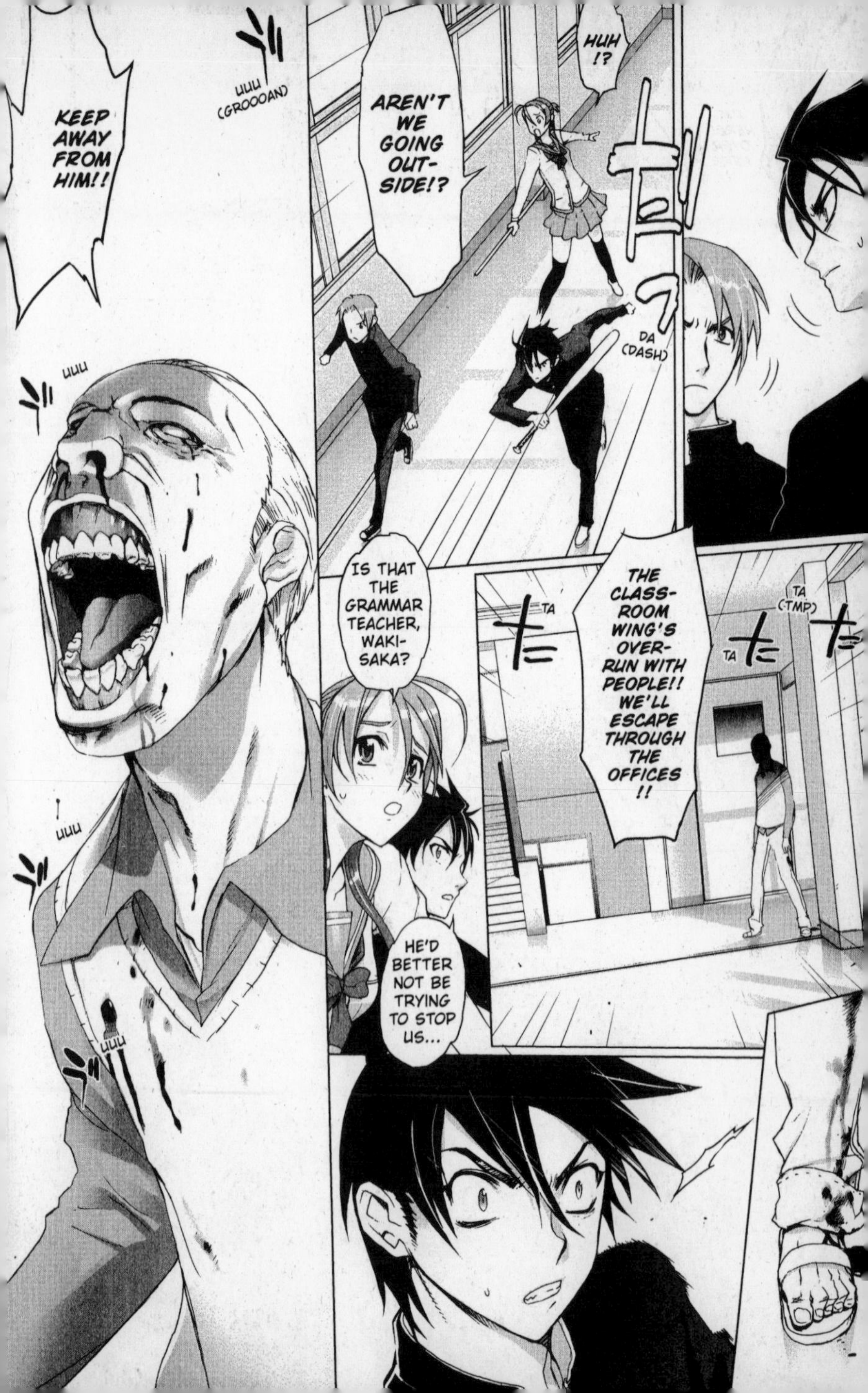
HUH!?
AREN'T WE GOING OUT-SIDE!?
DA (DASH)
TA (TMP)
TA
THE CLASS-ROOM WING'S OVER-RUN WITH PEOPLE!! WE'LL ESCAPE THROUGH THE OFFICES!!
TA
IS THAT THE GRAMMAR TEACHER, WAKI-SAKA?
HE'D BETTER NOT BE TRYING TO STOP US...
KEEP AWAY FROM HIM!!
UUU (GROOOAN)
UUU
!
UUU
UUU

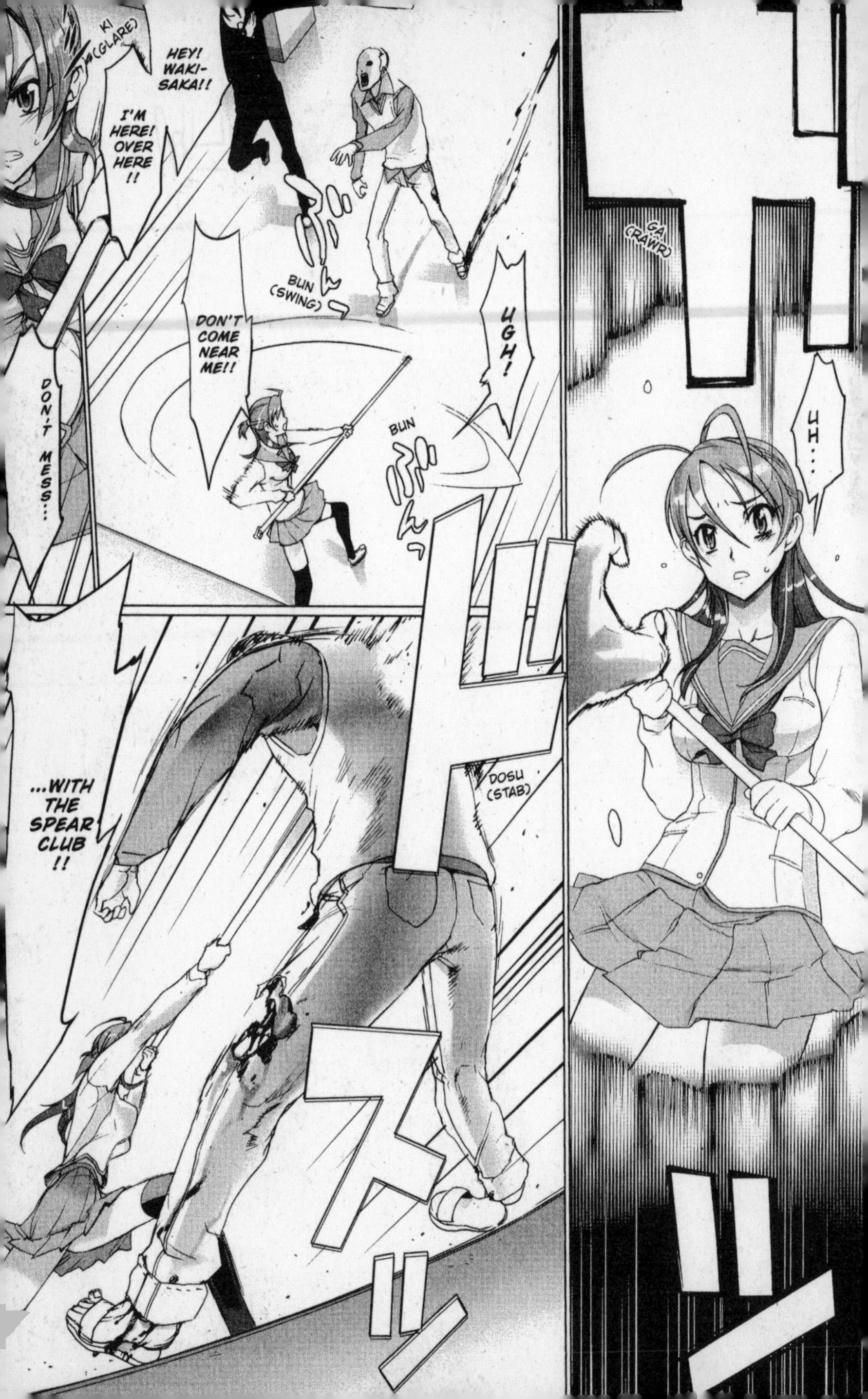
GA (RAWR)
UH...
HEY! WAKI-SAKA!!
KI (GLARE)
I'M HERE! OVER HERE!!
BUN (SWING)
UGH!
DON'T COME NEAR ME!!
BUN
DON'T MESS...
DOSU (STAB)
...WITH THE SPEAR CLUB!!

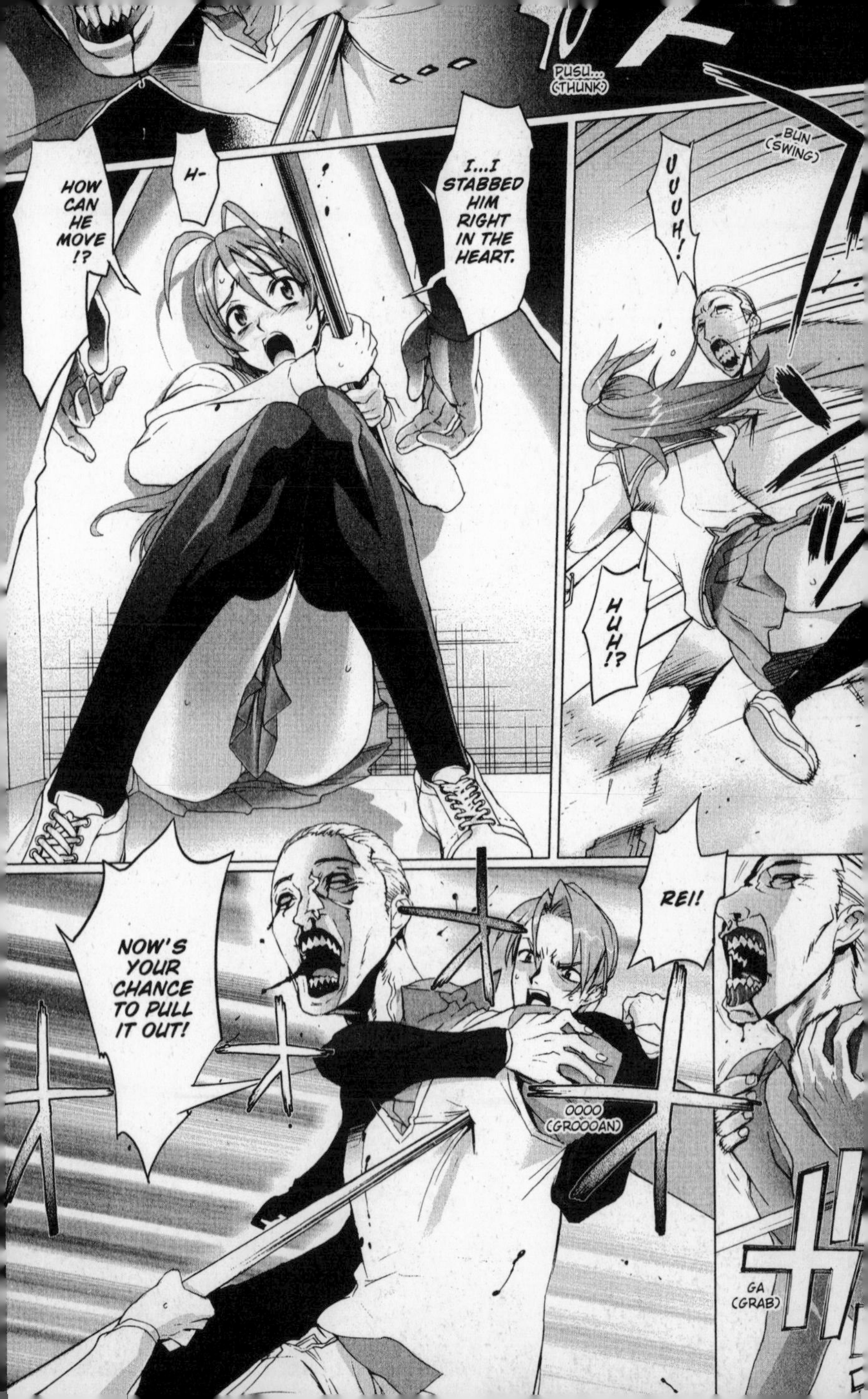

PUSU... (THUNK)
BUN (SWING)
UUUH!
HUH!?
I...I STABBED HIM RIGHT IN THE HEART.
H-
HOW CAN HE MOVE!?
REI!
GA (GRAB)
OOOO (GROOOAN)
NOW'S YOUR CHANCE TO PULL IT OUT!

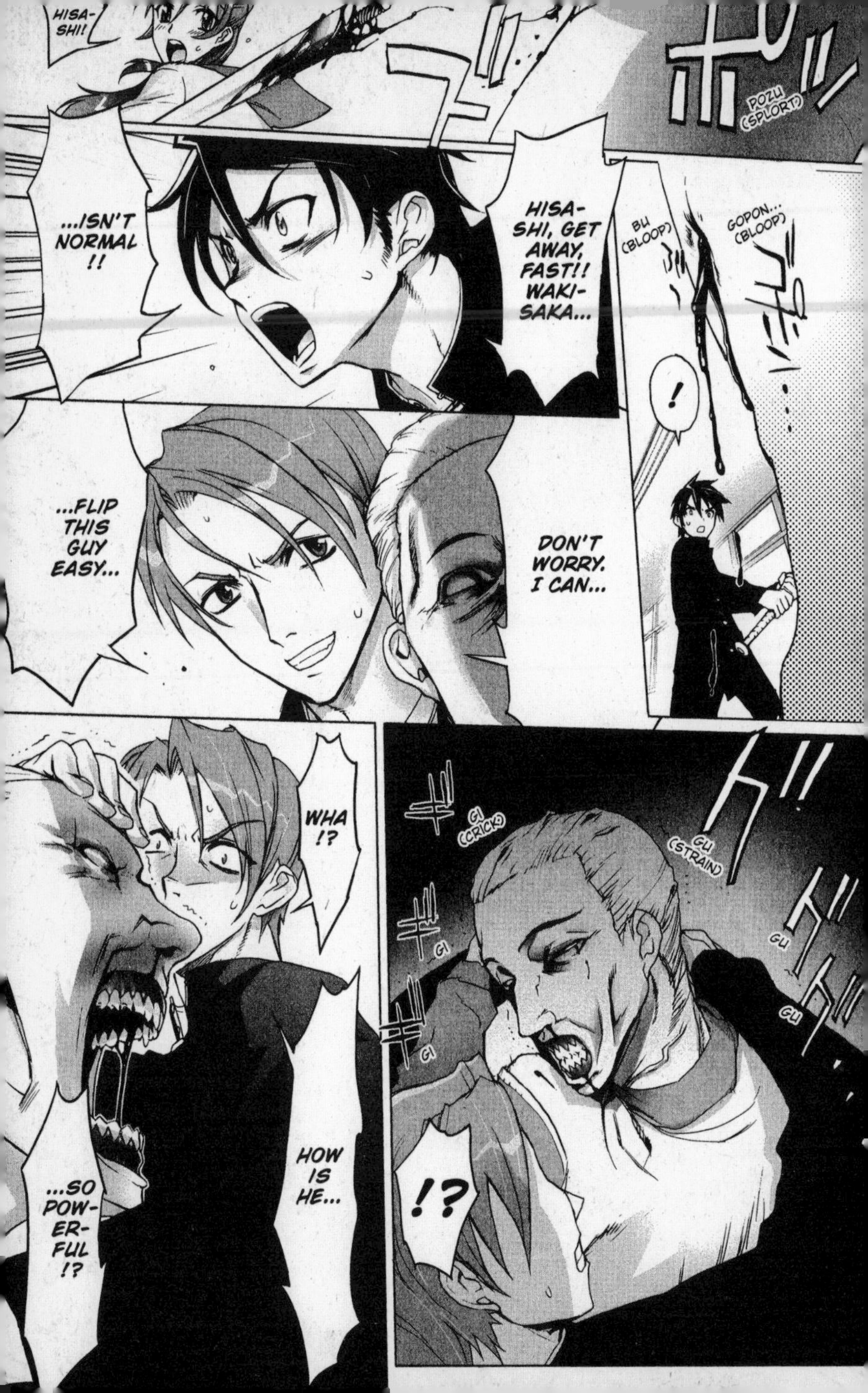
POZU (SPLORT)
HISA-SHI!
GOPON... (BLOOP)
BU (BLOOP)
!
HISA-SHI, GET AWAY, FAST!! WAKI-SAKA...
...ISN'T NORMAL!!
DON'T WORRY. I CAN...
...FLIP THIS GUY EASY...
GU (STRAIN)
GU
GU
GI (CRICK)
GI
GI
!?
WHA!?
HOW IS HE...
...SO POW-ER-FUL!?

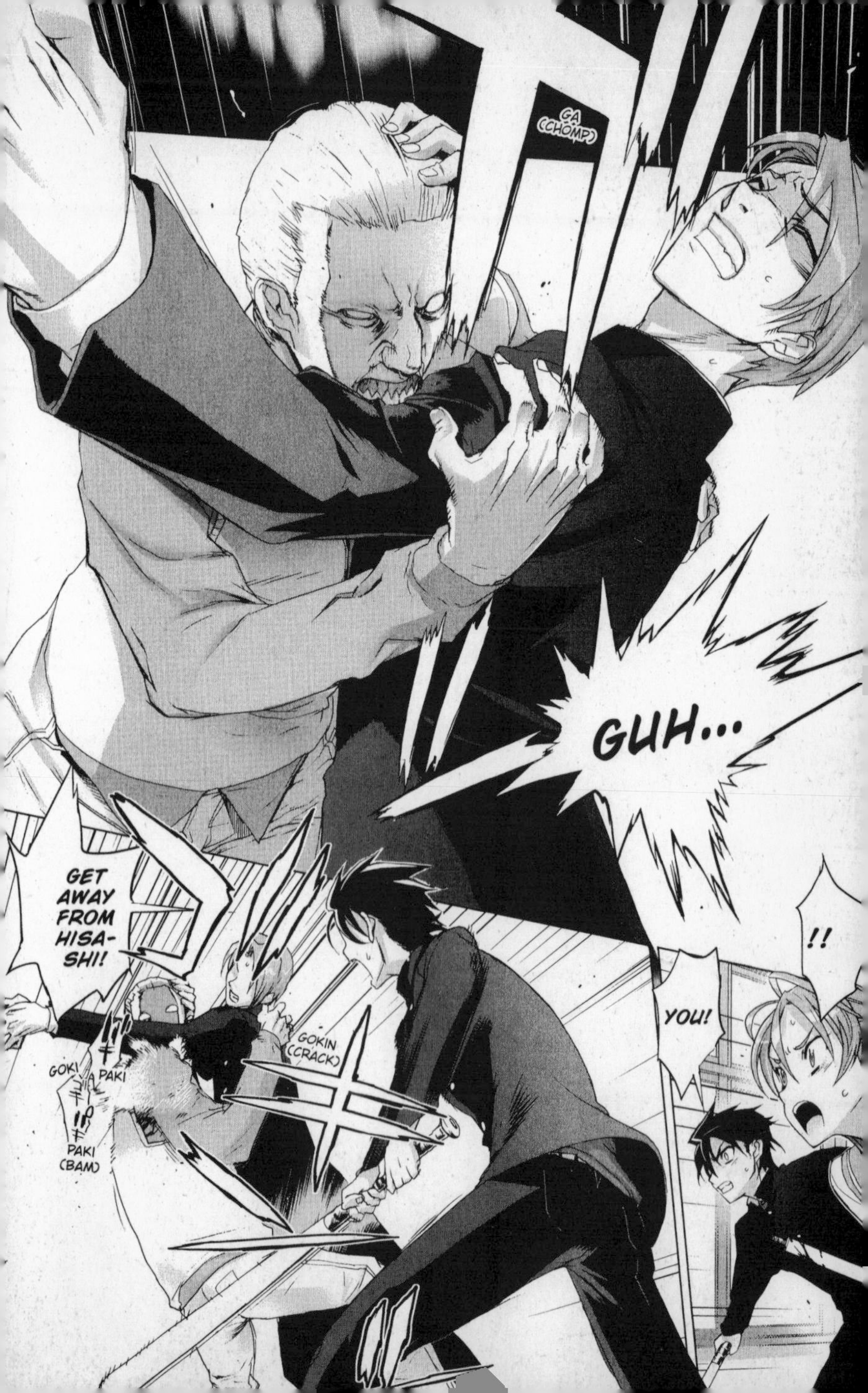
GA (CHOMP)
GUH...
!!
YOU!
GET AWAY FROM HISA-SHI!
GOKIN (CRACK)
GOKI
PAKI
PAKI (BAM)

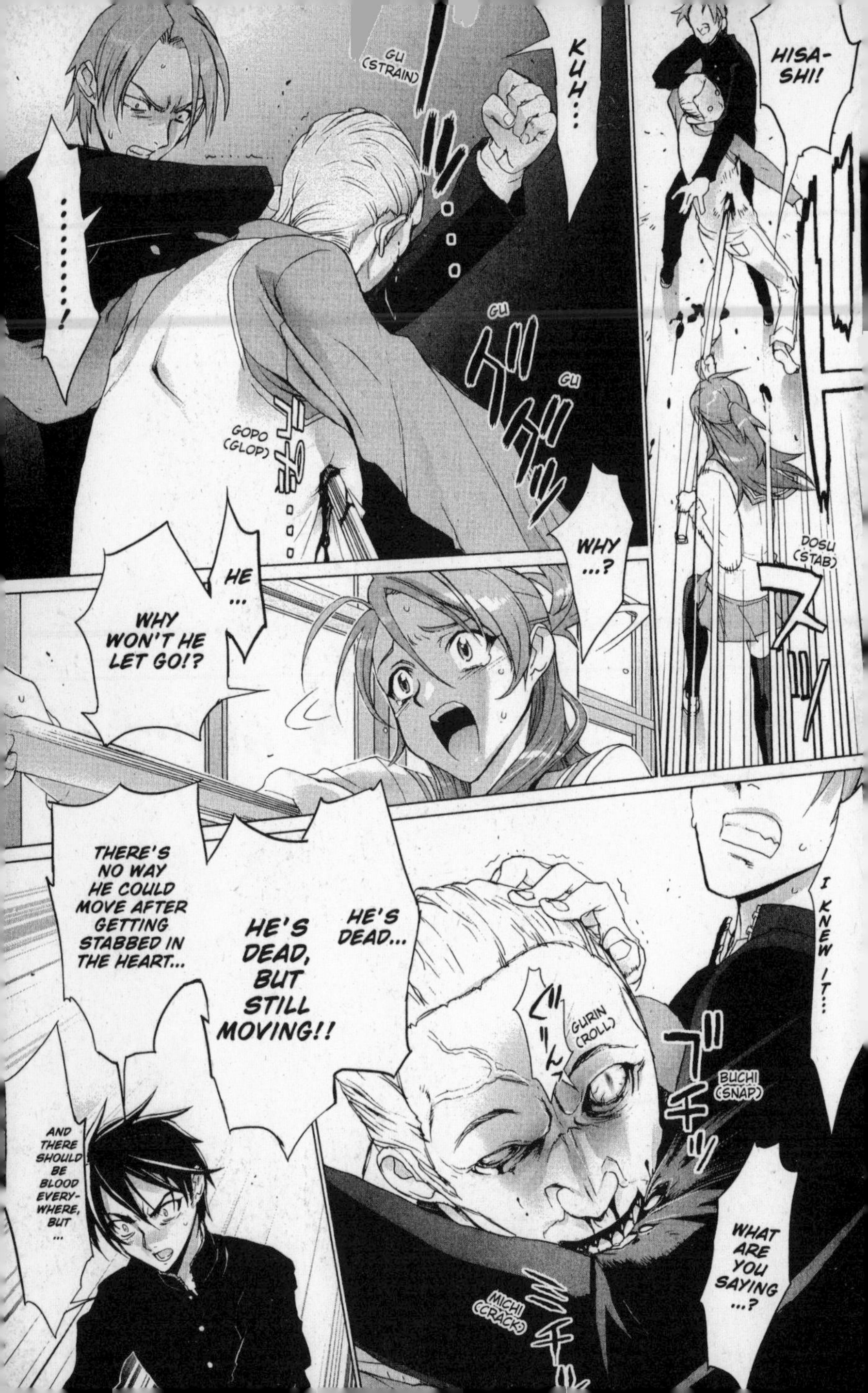
HISA-SHI!
DOSU (STAB)
KUH...
GU (STRAIN)
......!
GU
GU
GOPO (GLOP)
WHY ...?
HE ...
WHY WON'T HE LET GO!?
I KNEW IT...
BUCHI (SNAP)
GURIN (ROLL)
HE'S DEAD...
HE'S DEAD, BUT STILL MOVING!!
THERE'S NO WAY HE COULD MOVE AFTER GETTING STABBED IN THE HEART...
WHAT ARE YOU SAYING ...?
MICHI (CRACK)
AND THERE SHOULD BE BLOOD EVERY-WHERE, BUT ...

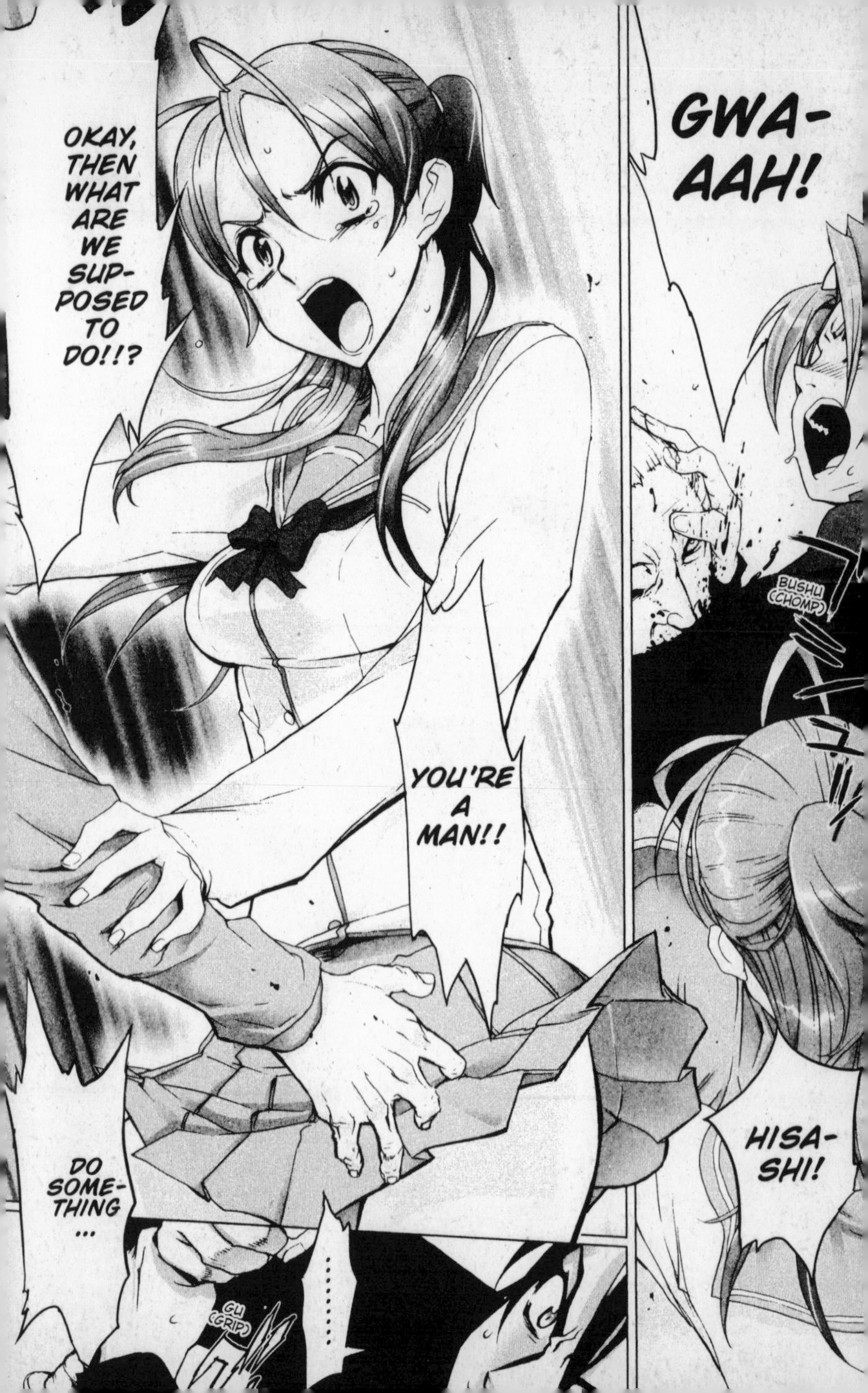
GWA-AAH!
BUSHU (CHOMP)
HISA-SHI!
OKAY, THEN WHAT ARE WE SUP-POSED TO DO!!?
YOU'RE A MAN!!
DO SOME-THING ...
GU (GRIP)

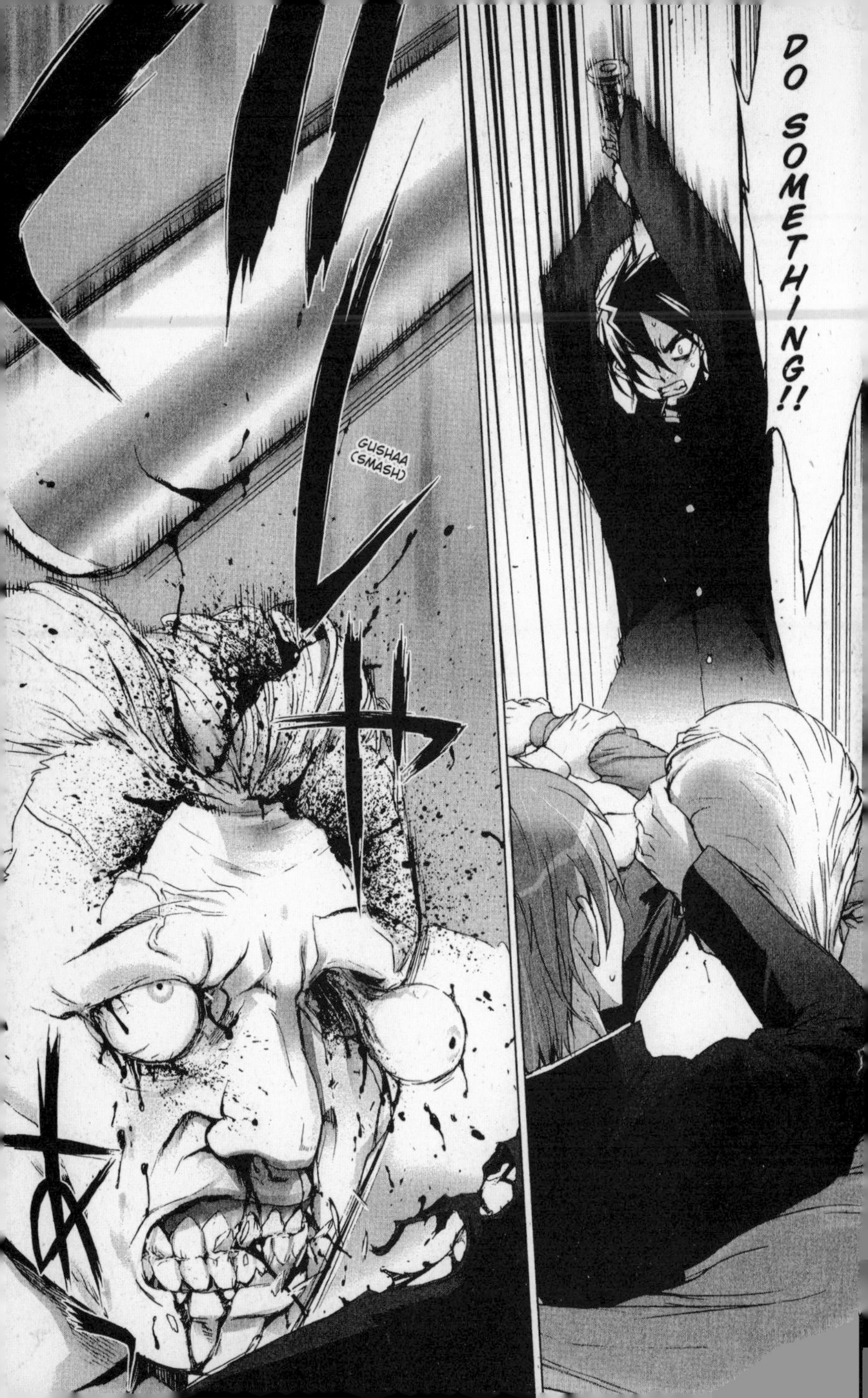
DO SOMETHING!!
GUSHAA (SMASH)

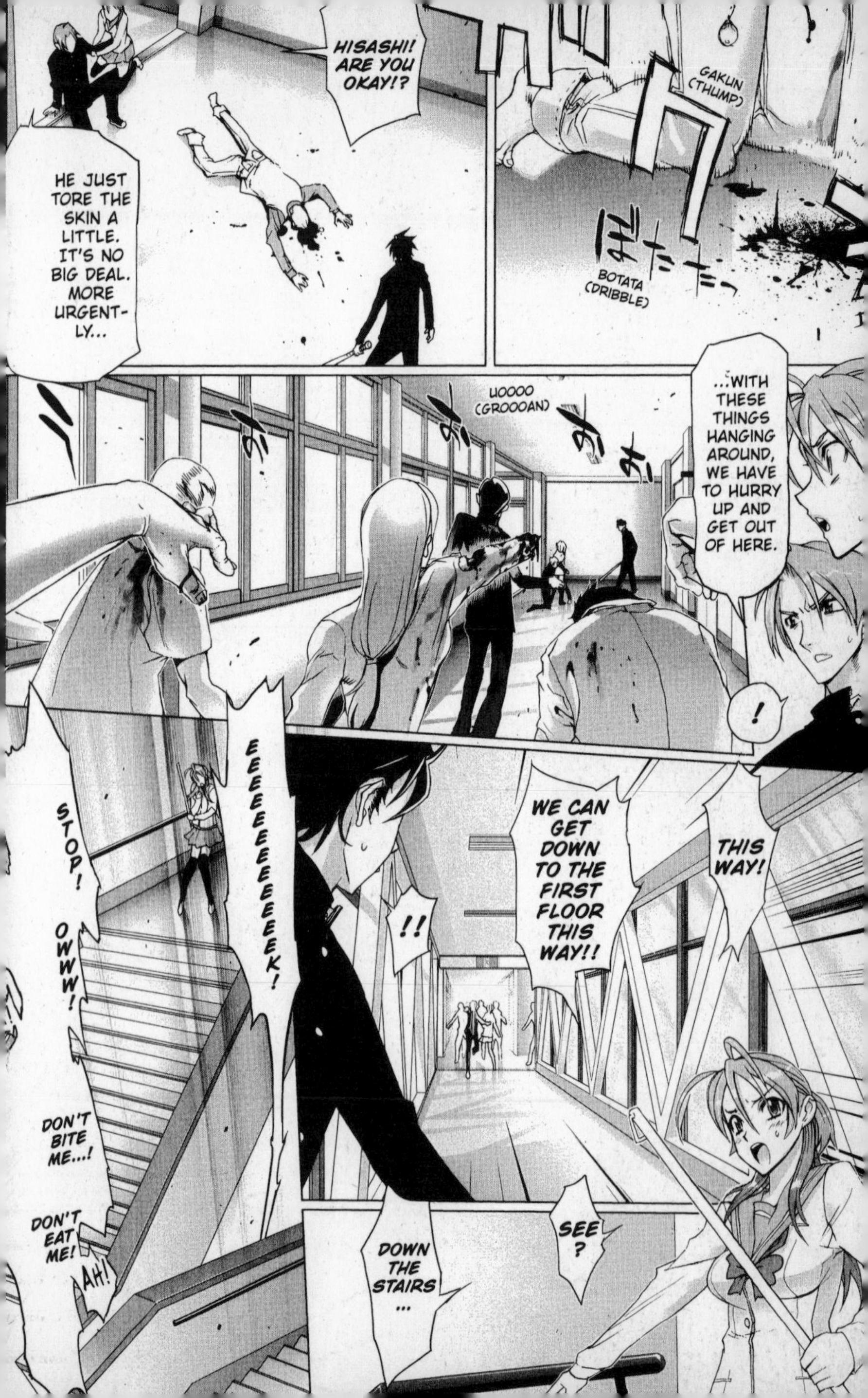
GAKUN (THUMP)
BOTATA (DRIBBLE)
HISASHI! ARE YOU OKAY!?
HE JUST TORE THE SKIN A LITTLE. IT'S NO BIG DEAL. MORE URGENTLY...
...WITH THESE THINGS HANGING AROUND, WE HAVE TO HURRY UP AND GET OUT OF HERE.
UOOOO (GROOOAN)
!
THIS WAY!
WE CAN GET DOWN TO THE FIRST FLOOR THIS WAY!!
!!
EEEEEEEEEEEEEK!
STOP!
OWWW!
DON'T BITE ME...!
DON'T EAT ME!
AH!
SEE?
DOWN THE STAIRS...

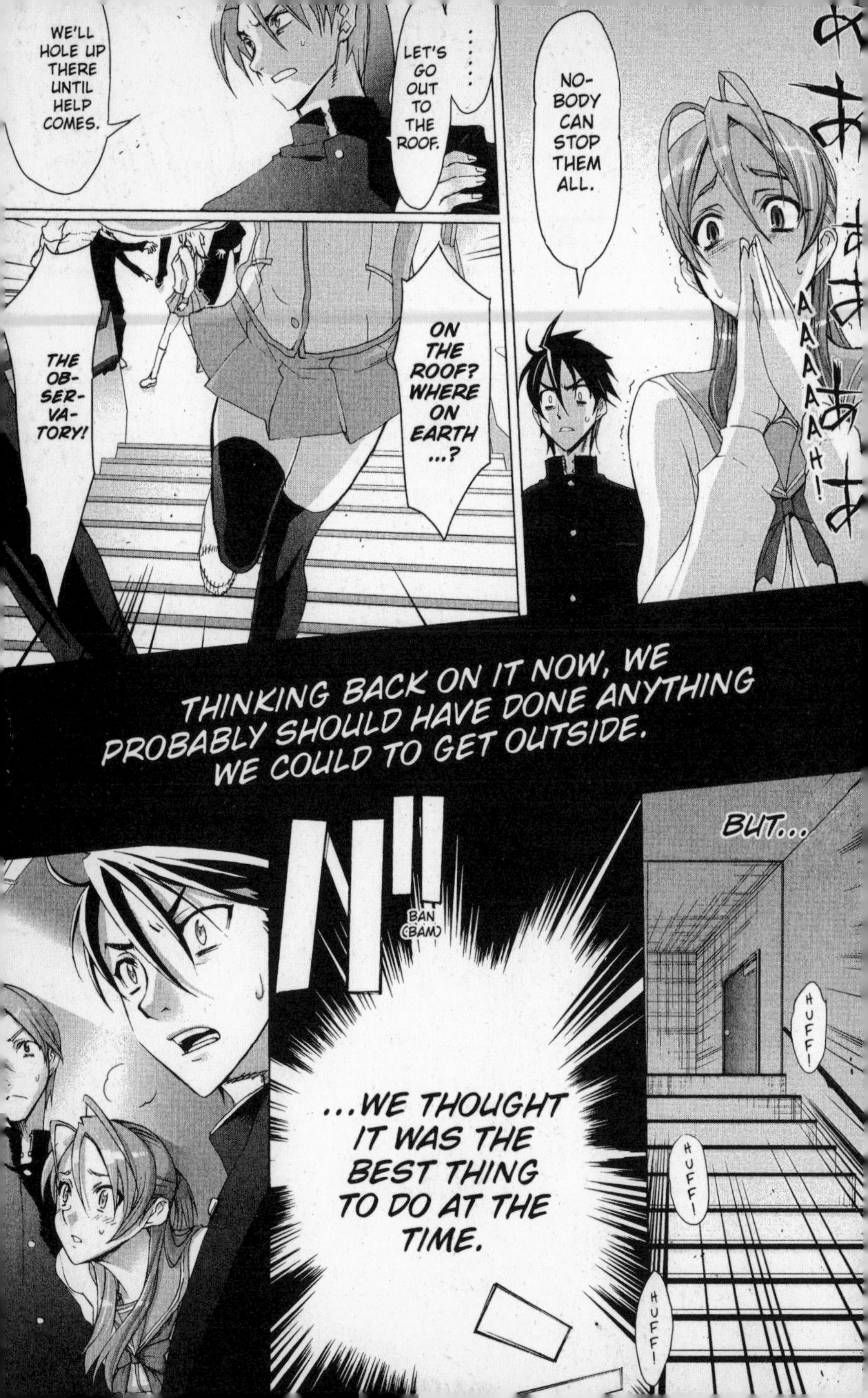
NO-BODY CAN STOP THEM ALL.
AAAAAAH!
......
LET'S GO OUT TO THE ROOF.
WE'LL HOLE UP THERE UNTIL HELP COMES.
ON THE ROOF? WHERE ON EARTH ...?
THE OBSERVATORY!
THINKING BACK ON IT NOW, WE PROBABLY SHOULD HAVE DONE ANYTHING WE COULD TO GET OUTSIDE.
BUT...
HUFF!
HUFF!
HUFF!
BAN (BAM)
...WE THOUGHT IT WAS THE BEST THING TO DO AT THE TIME.

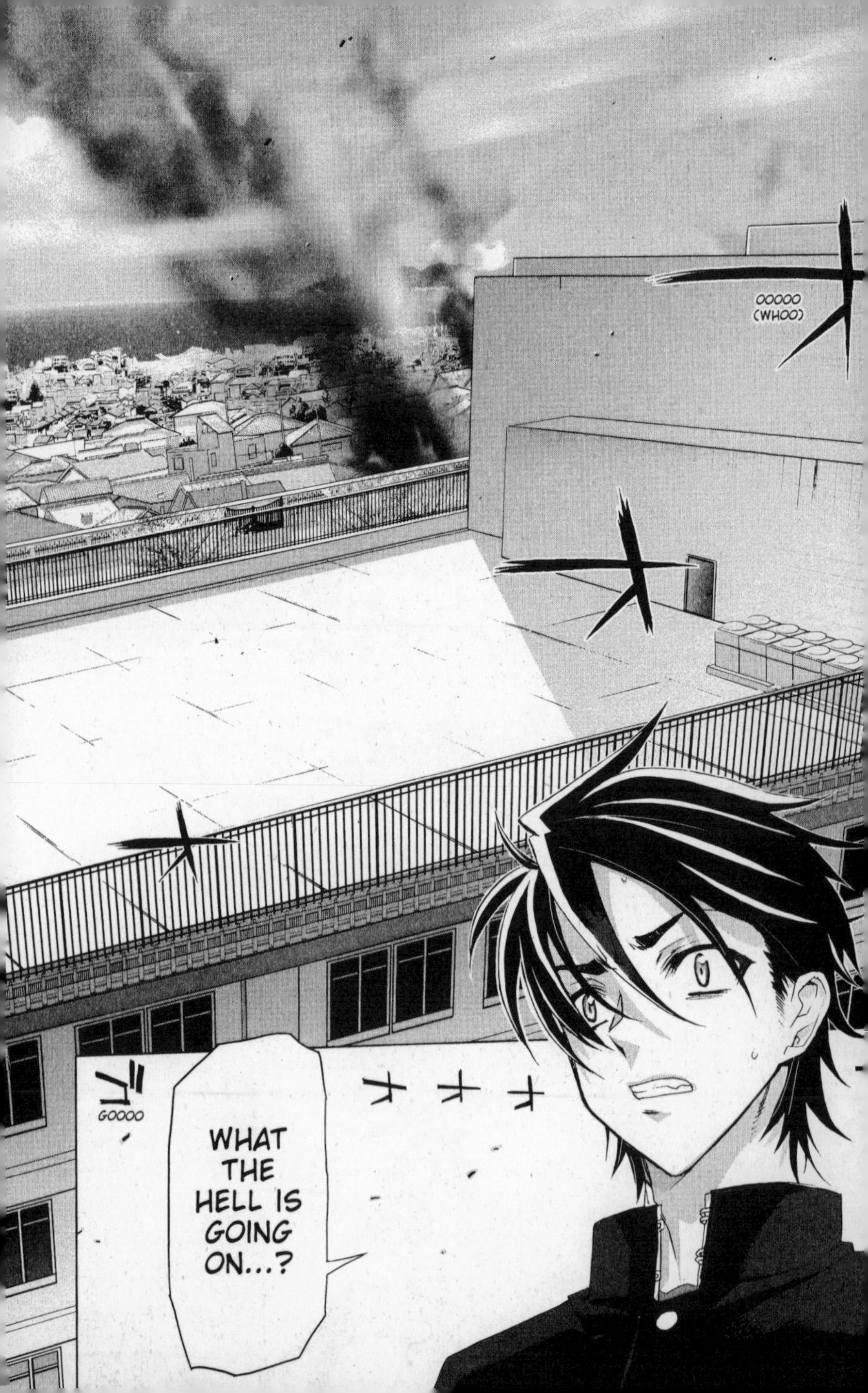
OOOOO (WHOO)
WHAT THE HELL IS GOING ON...?
GOOOO

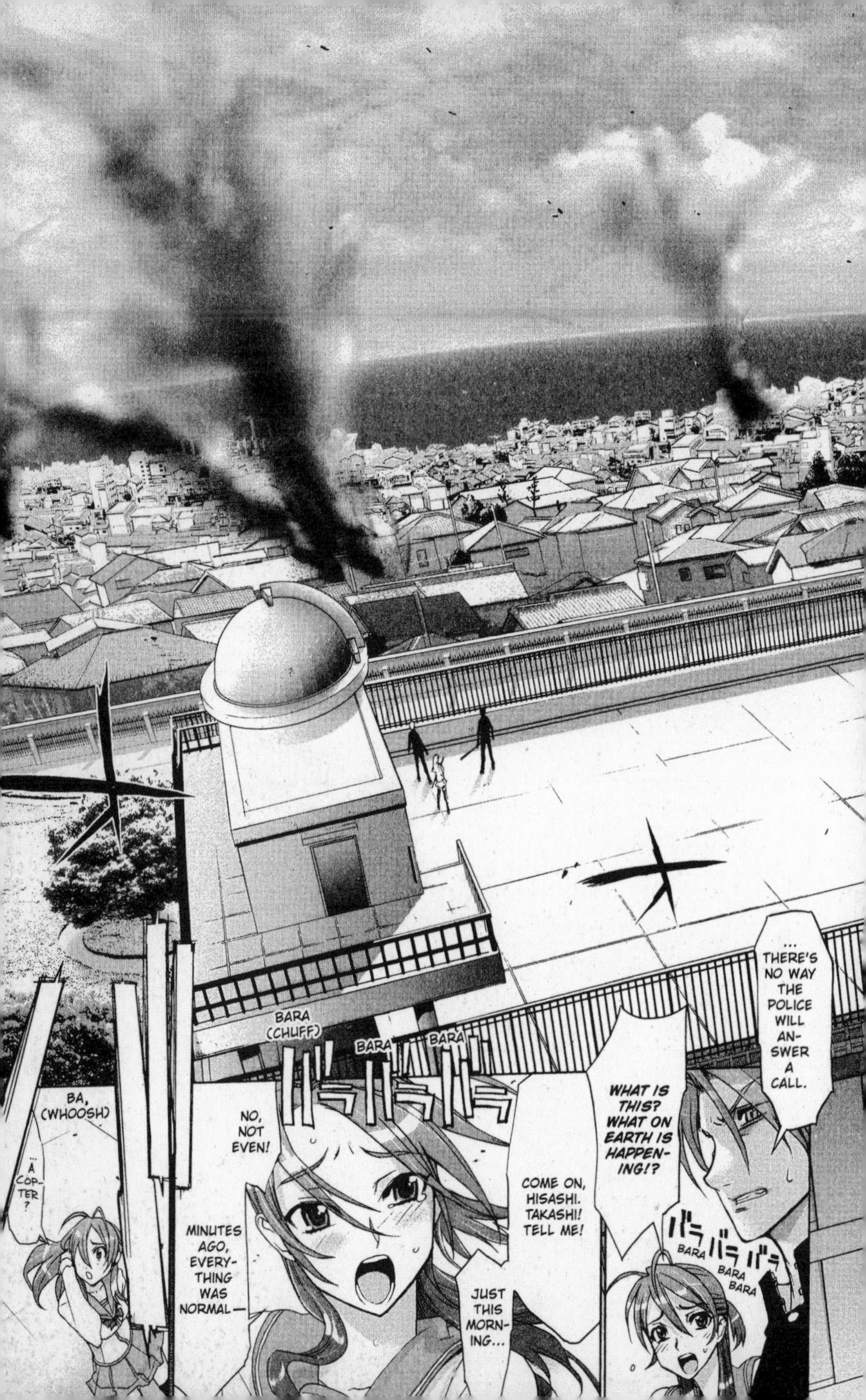

...THERE'S NO WAY THE POLICE WILL ANSWER A CALL.
BARA BARA BARA
WHAT IS THIS? WHAT ON EARTH IS HAPPENING!?
COME ON, HISASHI. TAKASHI! TELL ME!
JUST THIS MORNING...
BARA (CHUFF) BARA BARA
NO, NOT EVEN!
MINUTES AGO, EVERYTHING WAS NORMAL—
BA, (WHOOSH)
...A COPTER?

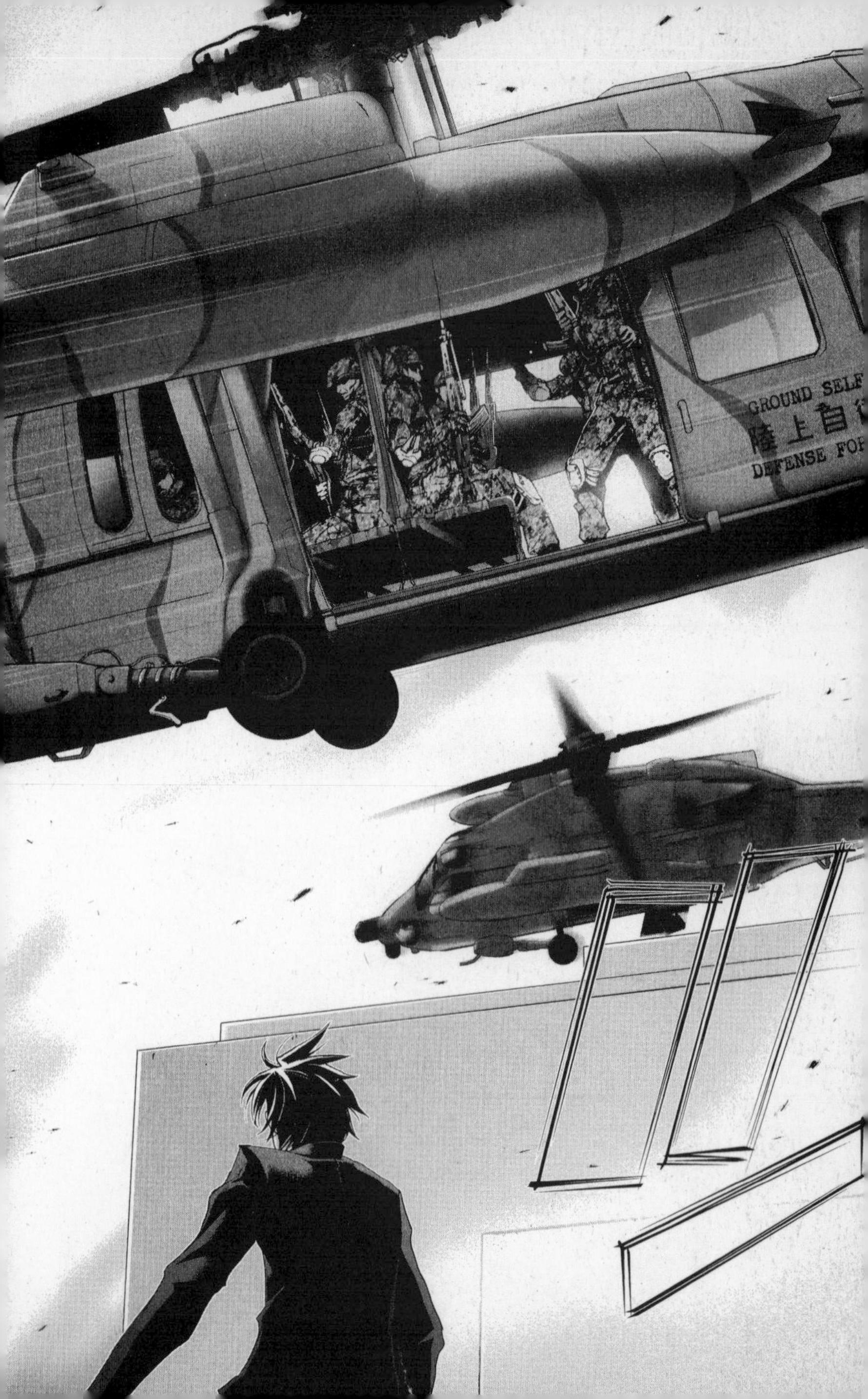
GROUND SELF
陸上自
DEFENSE FO

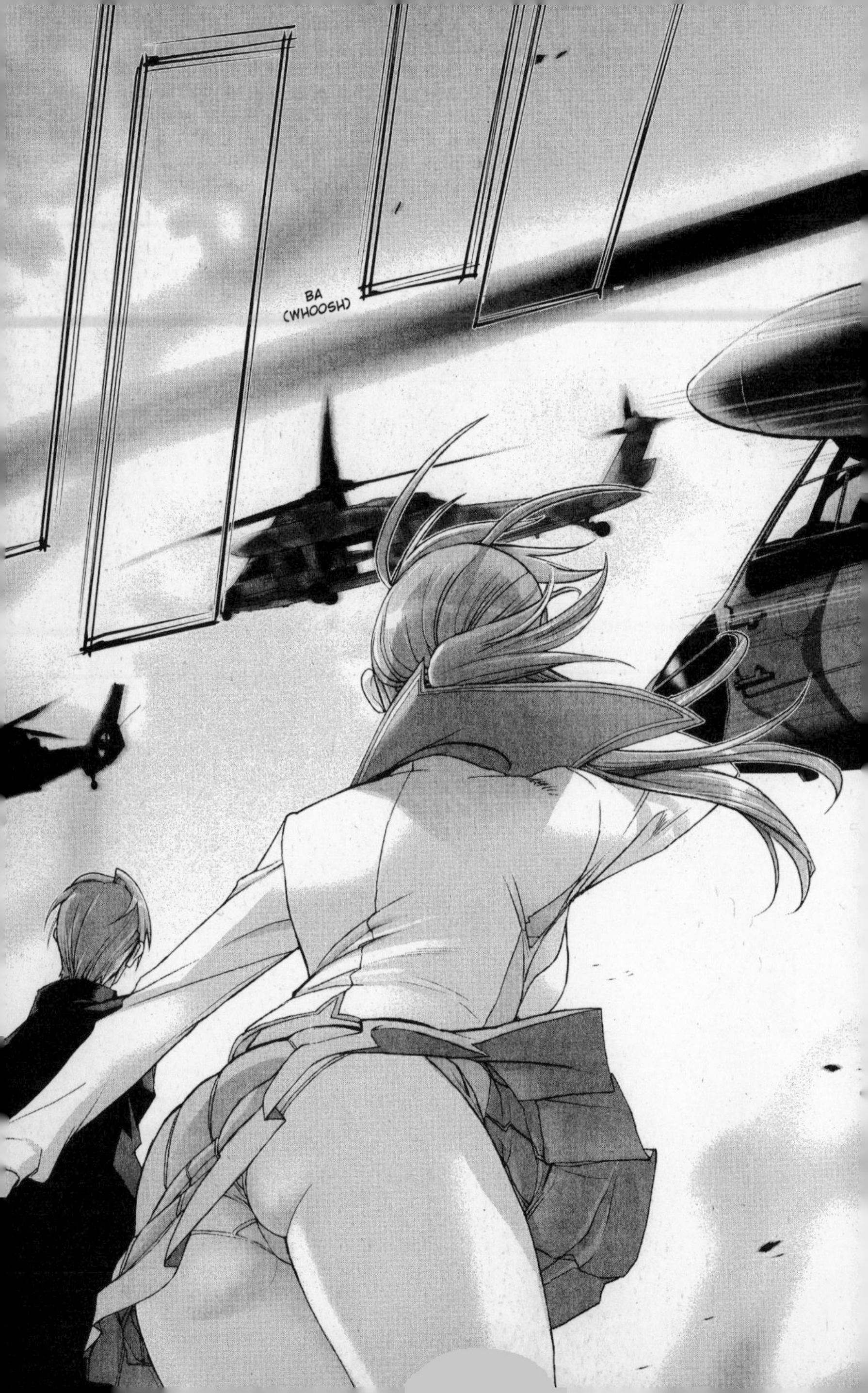
BA
(WHOOSH)

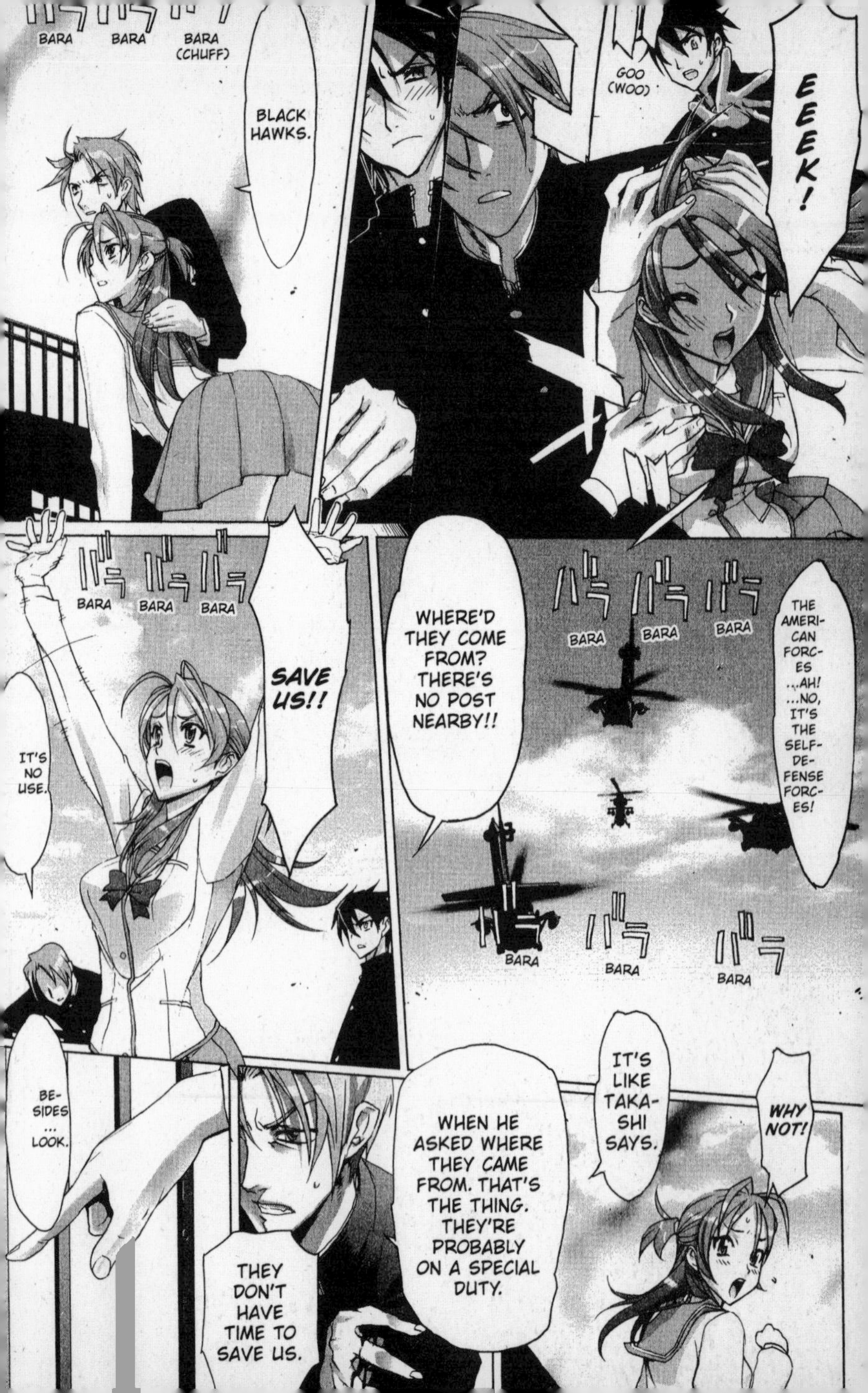

EEEK!
GOO (WOO)
BARA BARA BARA (CHUFF)
BLACK HAWKS.
THE AMERICAN FORCES ...AH! ...NO, IT'S THE SELF-DEFENSE FORCES!
BARA BARA BARA
WHERE'D THEY COME FROM? THERE'S NO POST NEARBY!!
BARA BARA BARA
SAVE US!!
BARA BARA BARA
IT'S NO USE.
WHY NOT!
IT'S LIKE TAKASHI SAYS.
WHEN HE ASKED WHERE THEY CAME FROM. THAT'S THE THING. THEY'RE PROBABLY ON A SPECIAL DUTY.
BESIDES ... LOOK.
THEY DON'T HAVE TIME TO SAVE US.

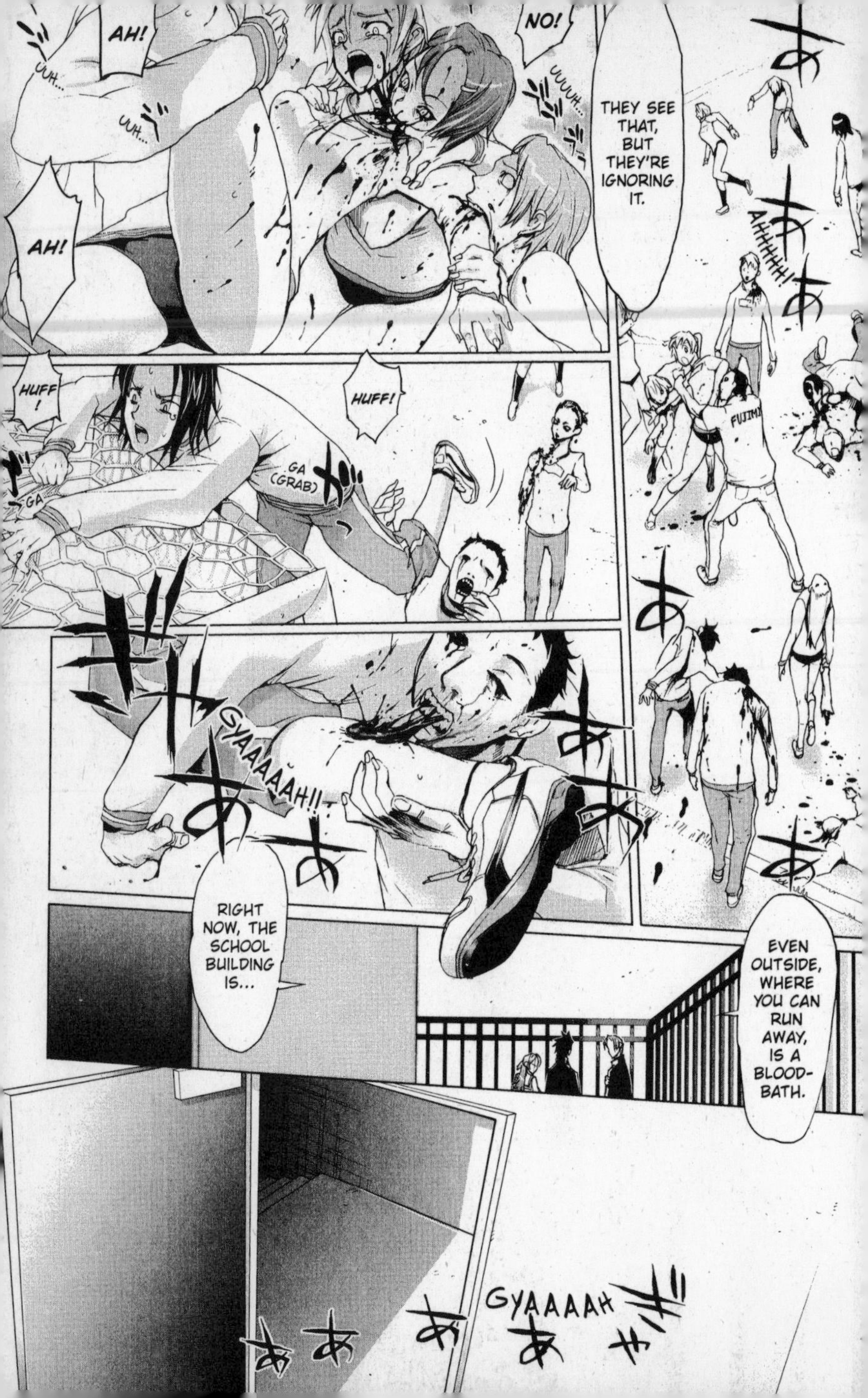
AHHHHHH!
THEY SEE THAT, BUT THEY'RE IGNORING IT.
NO!
UUUUH...
AH!
UUH...
UUH...
AH!
HUFF!
HUFF!
GA (GRAB)
GA
GYAAAAAH!!
RIGHT NOW, THE SCHOOL BUILDING IS...
EVEN OUTSIDE, WHERE YOU CAN RUN AWAY, IS A BLOOD-BATH.
GYAAAAH

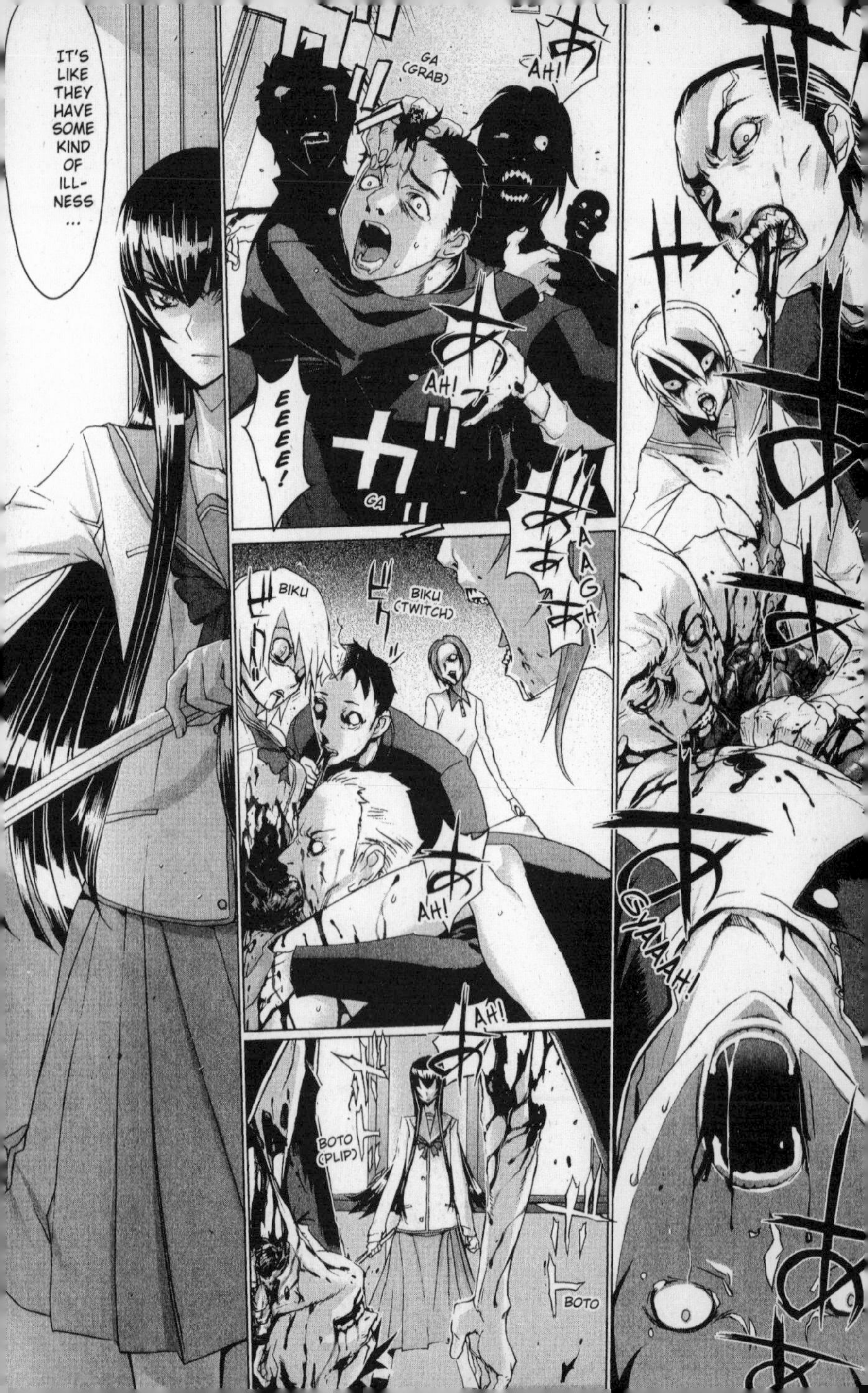
GYAAAAH!
AH!
GA (GRAB)
AH!
EEEEE!
GA
AAGH!
BIKU (TWITCH)
BIKU
AH!
AH!
BOTO (PLIP)
BOTO
IT'S LIKE THEY HAVE SOME KIND OF ILL-NESS...

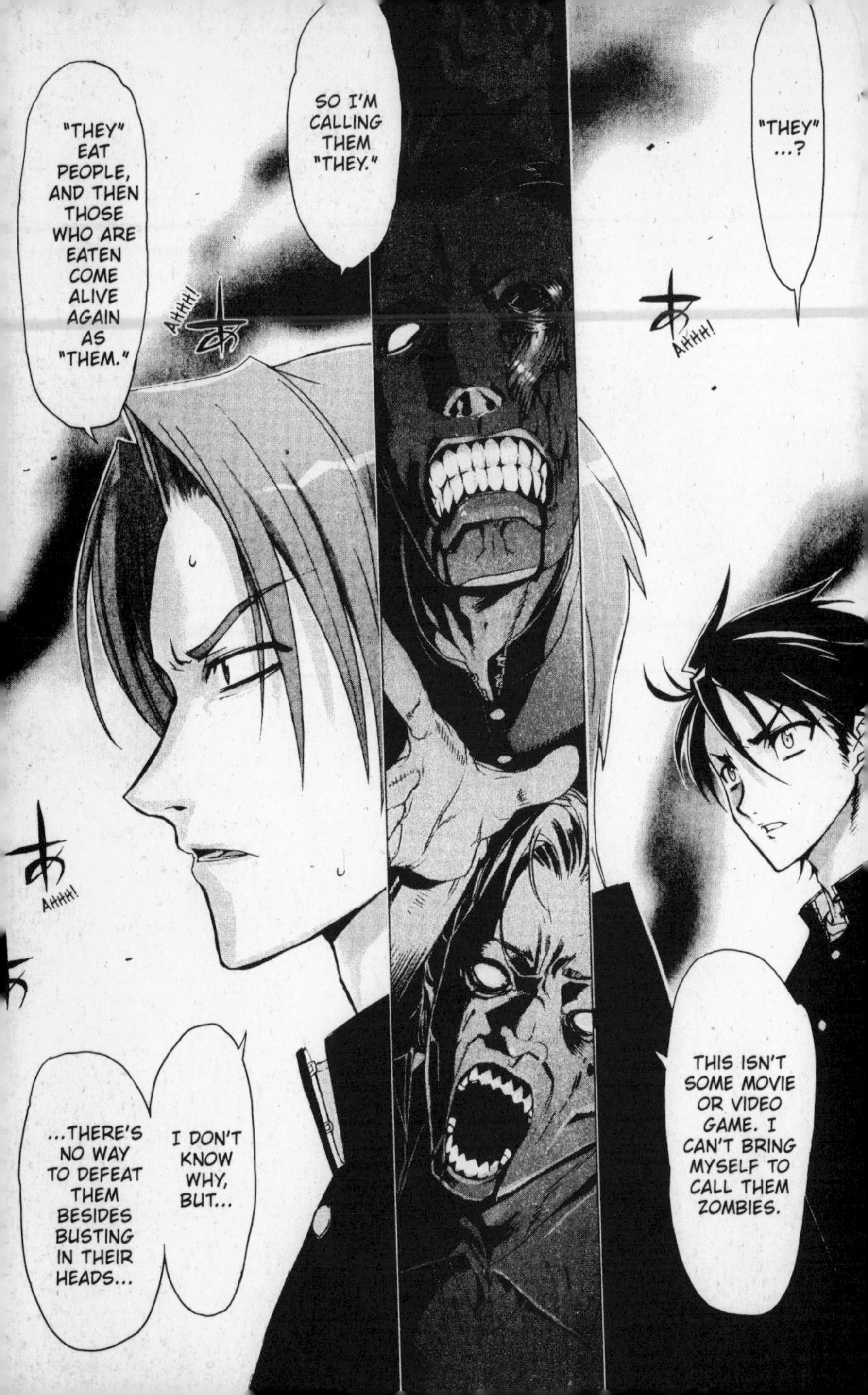
"THEY" ...?
あ AHHH!
THIS ISN'T SOME MOVIE OR VIDEO GAME. I CAN'T BRING MYSELF TO CALL THEM ZOMBIES.
SO I'M CALLING THEM "THEY."
"THEY" EAT PEOPLE, AND THEN THOSE WHO ARE EATEN COME ALIVE AGAIN AS "THEM."
あ AHHH!
あ AHHH!
I DON'T KNOW WHY, BUT...
...THERE'S NO WAY TO DEFEAT THEM BESIDES BUSTING IN THEIR HEADS...

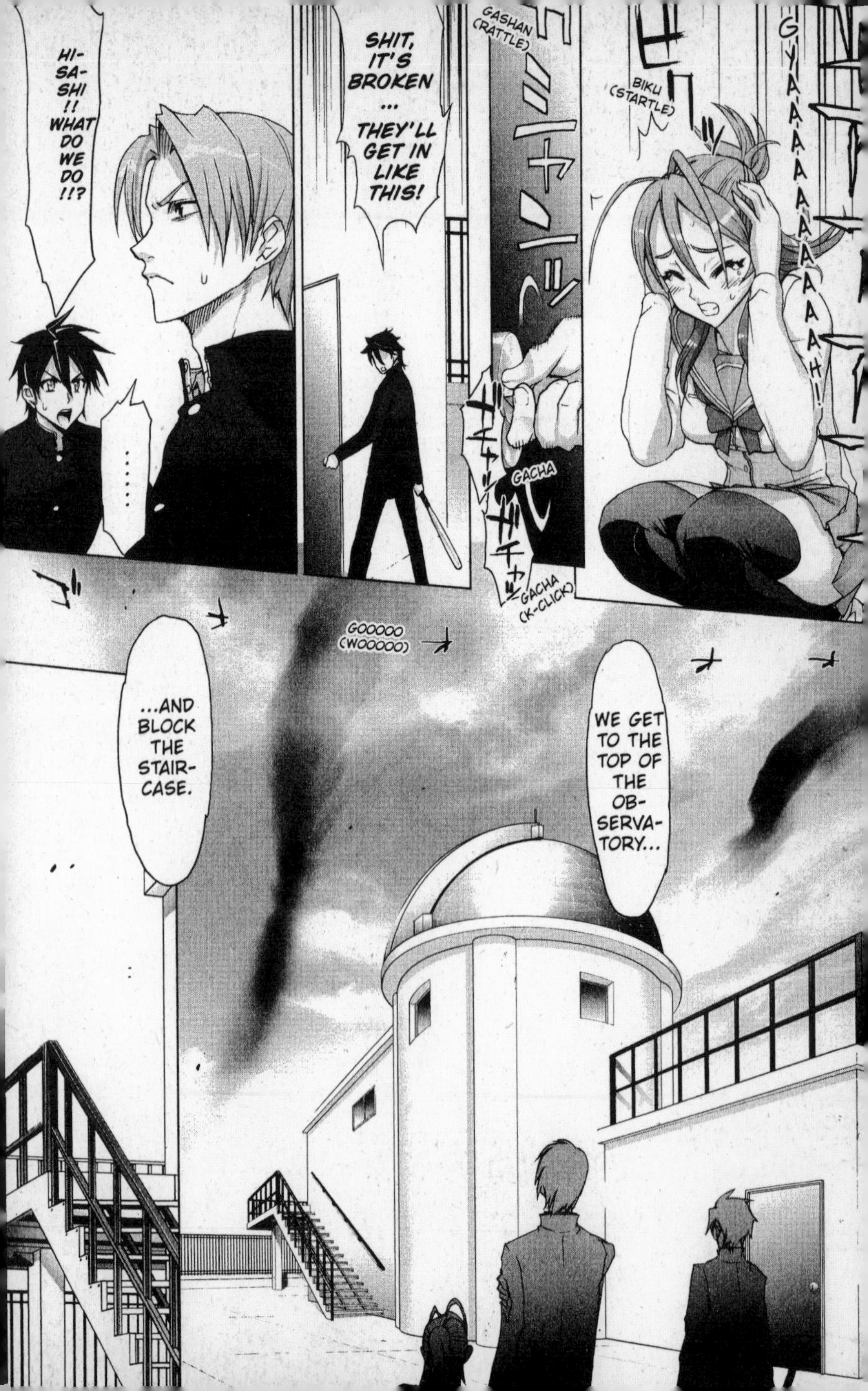
GYAAAAAAAAAAAH!
BIKU (STARTLE)
GASHAN (RATTLE)
GACHA
GACHA (K-CLICK)
SHIT, IT'S BROKEN... THEY'LL GET IN LIKE THIS!
HI-SASHI!! WHAT DO WE DO!!?
......
GOOOOO (WOOOOO)
WE GET TO THE TOP OF THE OB-SERVA-TORY...
...AND BLOCK THE STAIR-CASE.

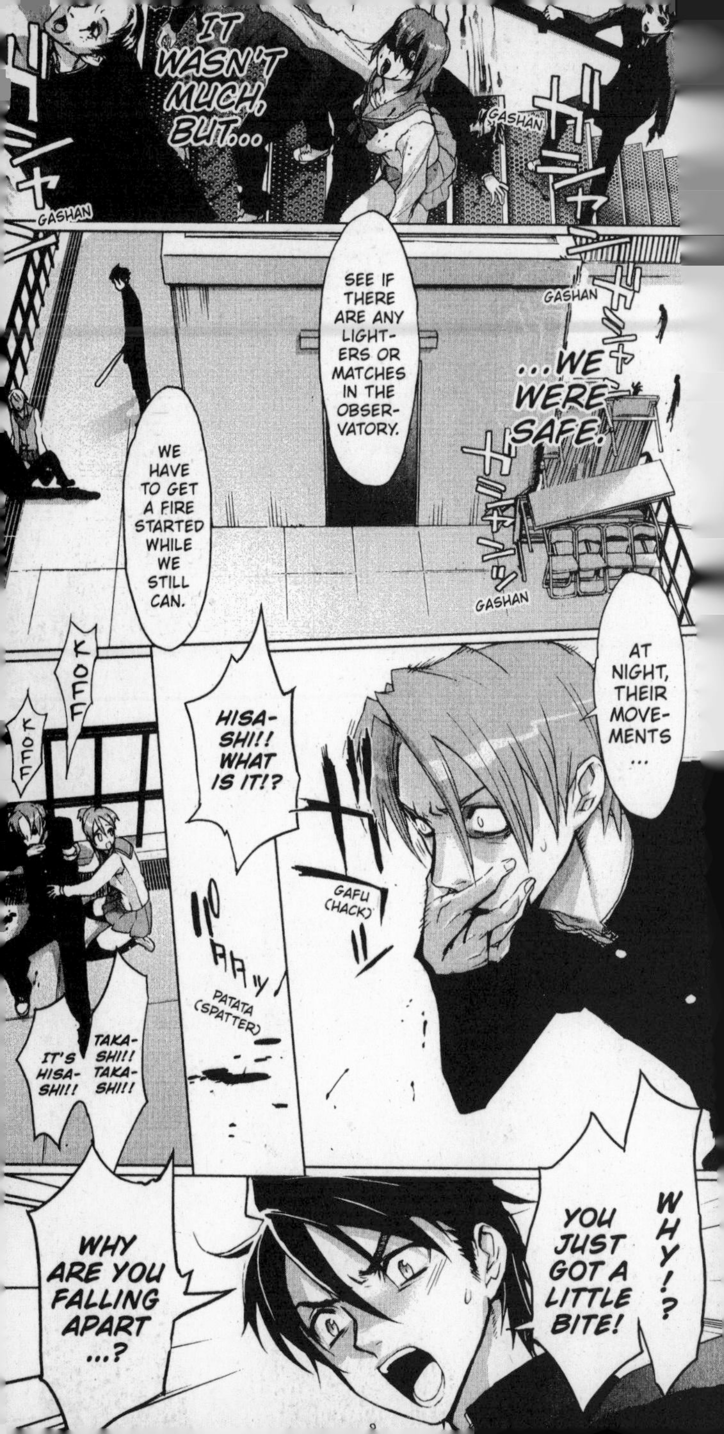
GASHAN
IT WASN'T MUCH, BUT...
GASHAN
GASHAN
...WE WERE SAFE.
GASHAN
SEE IF THERE ARE ANY LIGHTERS OR MATCHES IN THE OBSERVATORY.
WE HAVE TO GET A FIRE STARTED WHILE WE STILL CAN.
AT NIGHT, THEIR MOVEMENTS...
GAFU (HACK)
HISASHI!! WHAT IS IT!?
PATATA (SPATTER)
KOFF
KOFF
TAKASHI!! TAKASHI!!
IT'S HISASHI!!
WHY!?
YOU JUST GOT A LITTLE BITE!
WHY ARE YOU FALLING APART...?

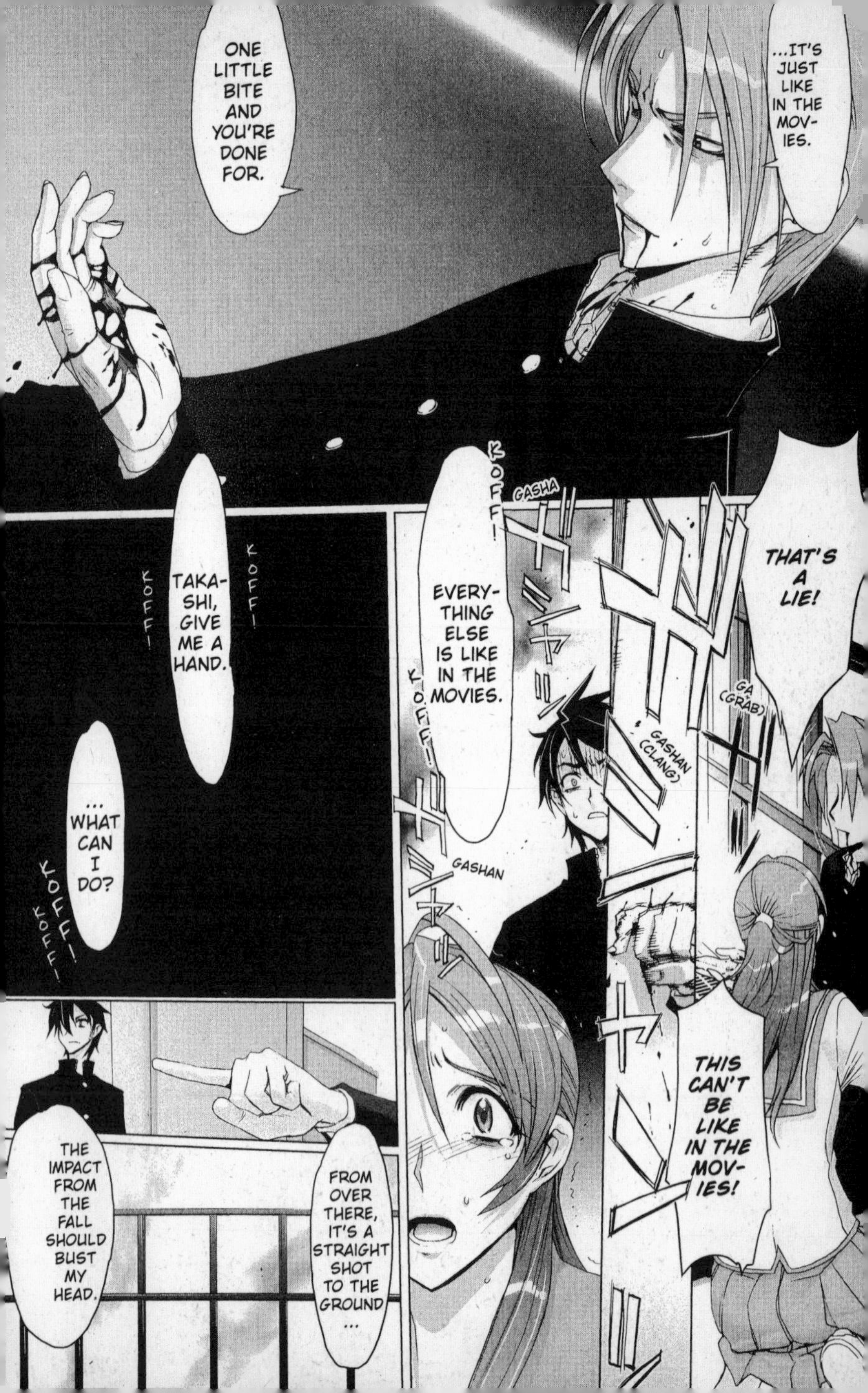

...IT'S JUST LIKE IN THE MOVIES.
ONE LITTLE BITE AND YOU'RE DONE FOR.
THAT'S A LIE!
GA (GRAB)
GASHAN (CLANG)
GASHA
KOFF!
EVERY-THING ELSE IS LIKE IN THE MOVIES.
KOFF!
GASHAN
KOFF!
TAKA-SHI, GIVE ME A HAND.
KOFF!
...WHAT CAN I DO?
KOFF!
KOFF!
THIS CAN'T BE LIKE IN THE MOV-IES!
FROM OVER THERE, IT'S A STRAIGHT SHOT TO THE GROUND...
THE IMPACT FROM THE FALL SHOULD BUST MY HEAD.

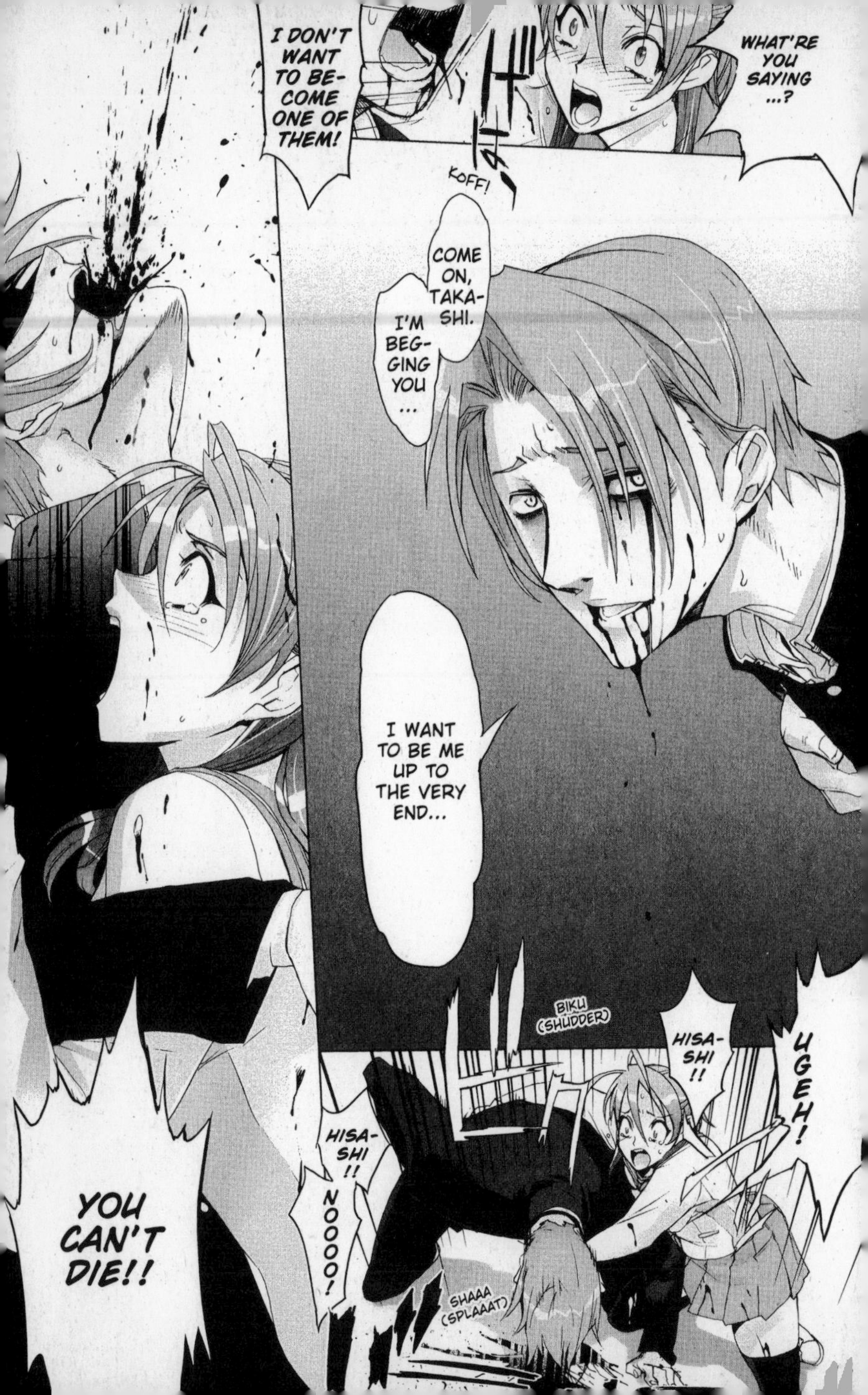
WHAT'RE YOU SAYING ...?
I DON'T WANT TO BECOME ONE OF THEM!
KOFF!
COME ON, TAKASHI.
I'M BEGGING YOU ...
I WANT TO BE ME UP TO THE VERY END...
BIKU (SHUDDER)
HISASHI !!
UGEH!
HISASHI !!
NOOOO!
SHAAA (SPLAAAT)
YOU CAN'T DIE!!

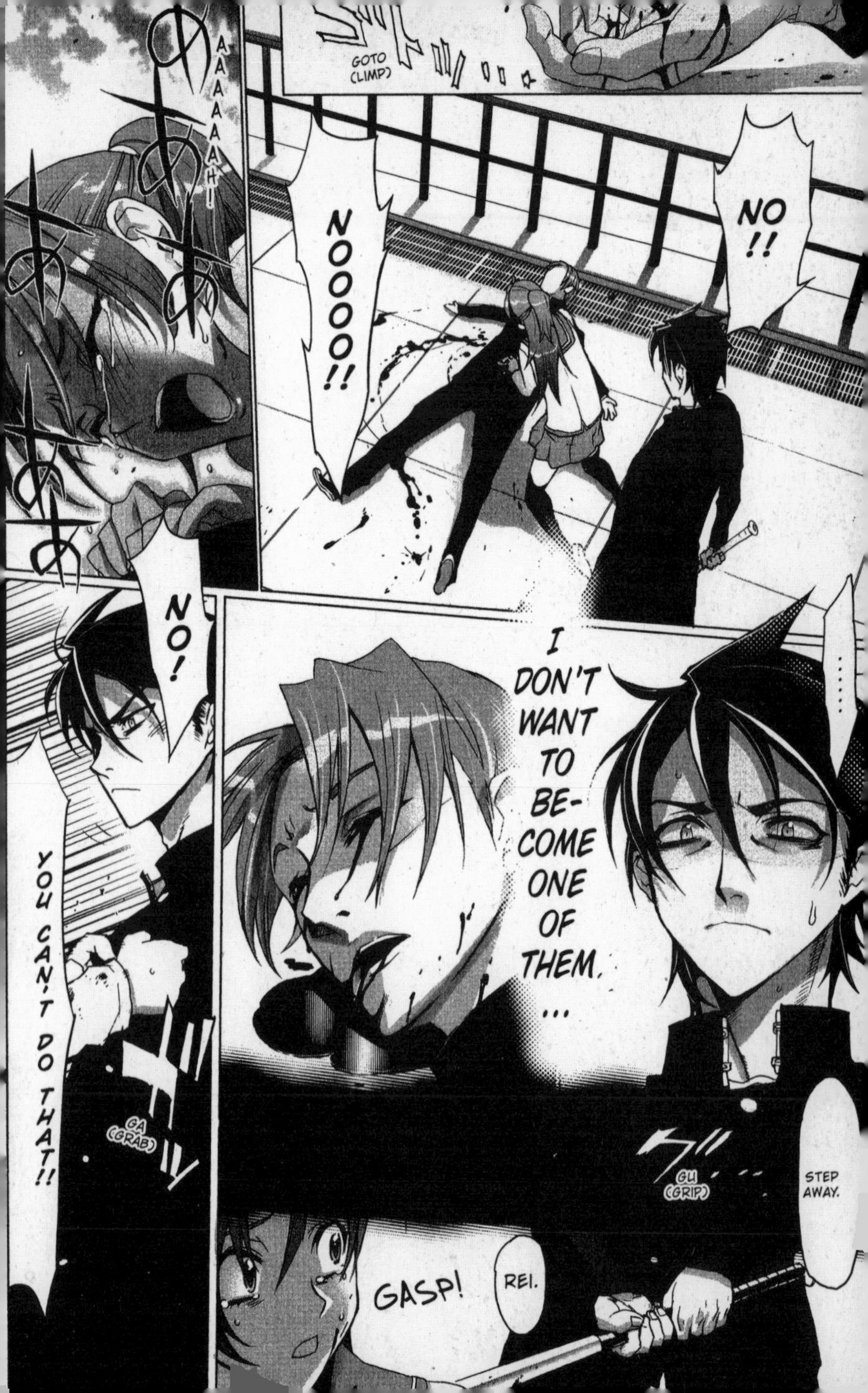
GOTO (LIMP)
NO!!
NOOOOO!!
AAAAAAAH!
......
I DON'T WANT TO BE-COME ONE OF THEM. ...
GU (GRIP)
STEP AWAY.
REI.
GASP!
NO!
YOU CAN'T DO THAT!!
GA (GRAB)

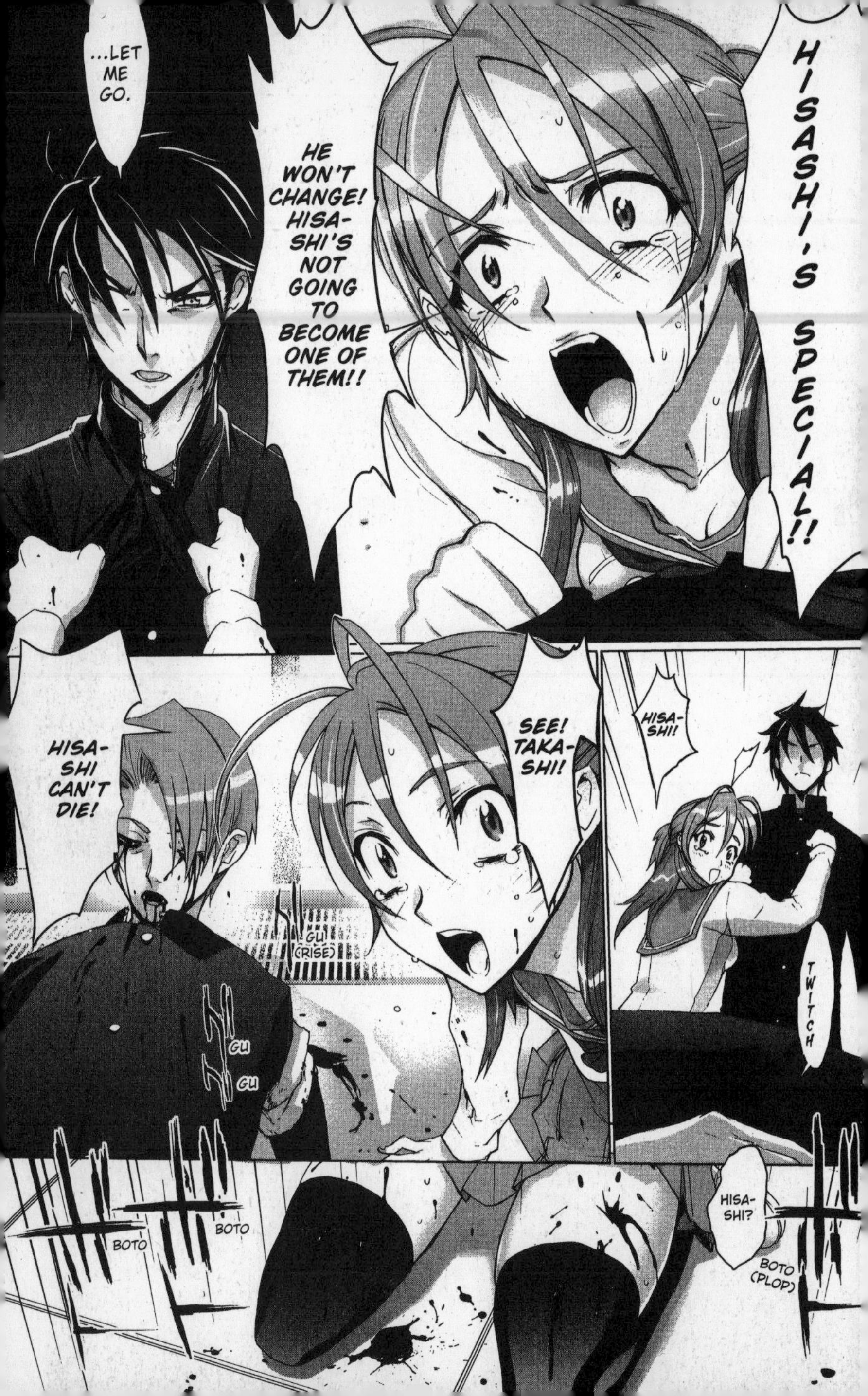
HISASHI'S SPECIAL!!
HE WON'T CHANGE! HISA-SHI'S NOT GOING TO BECOME ONE OF THEM!!
...LET ME GO.
HISA-SHI!
TWITCH
SEE! TAKA-SHI!
GU (RISE)
HISA-SHI CAN'T DIE!
GU
GU
HISA-SHI?
BOTO (PLOP)
BOTO
BOTO

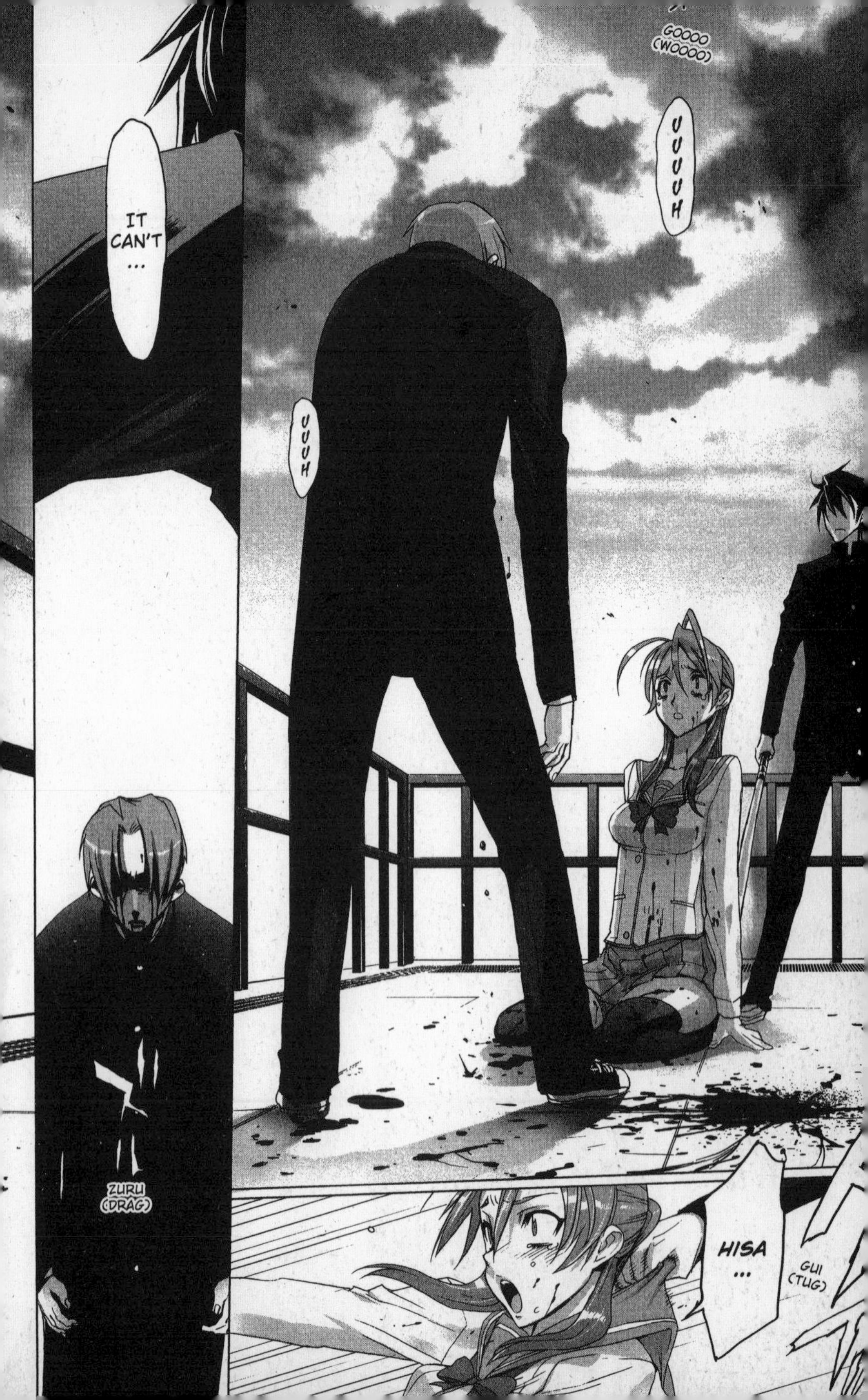
GOOOO (WOOOO)
UUUUH
UUUH
HISA ...
GUI (TUG)
IT CAN'T ...
ZURU (DRAG)

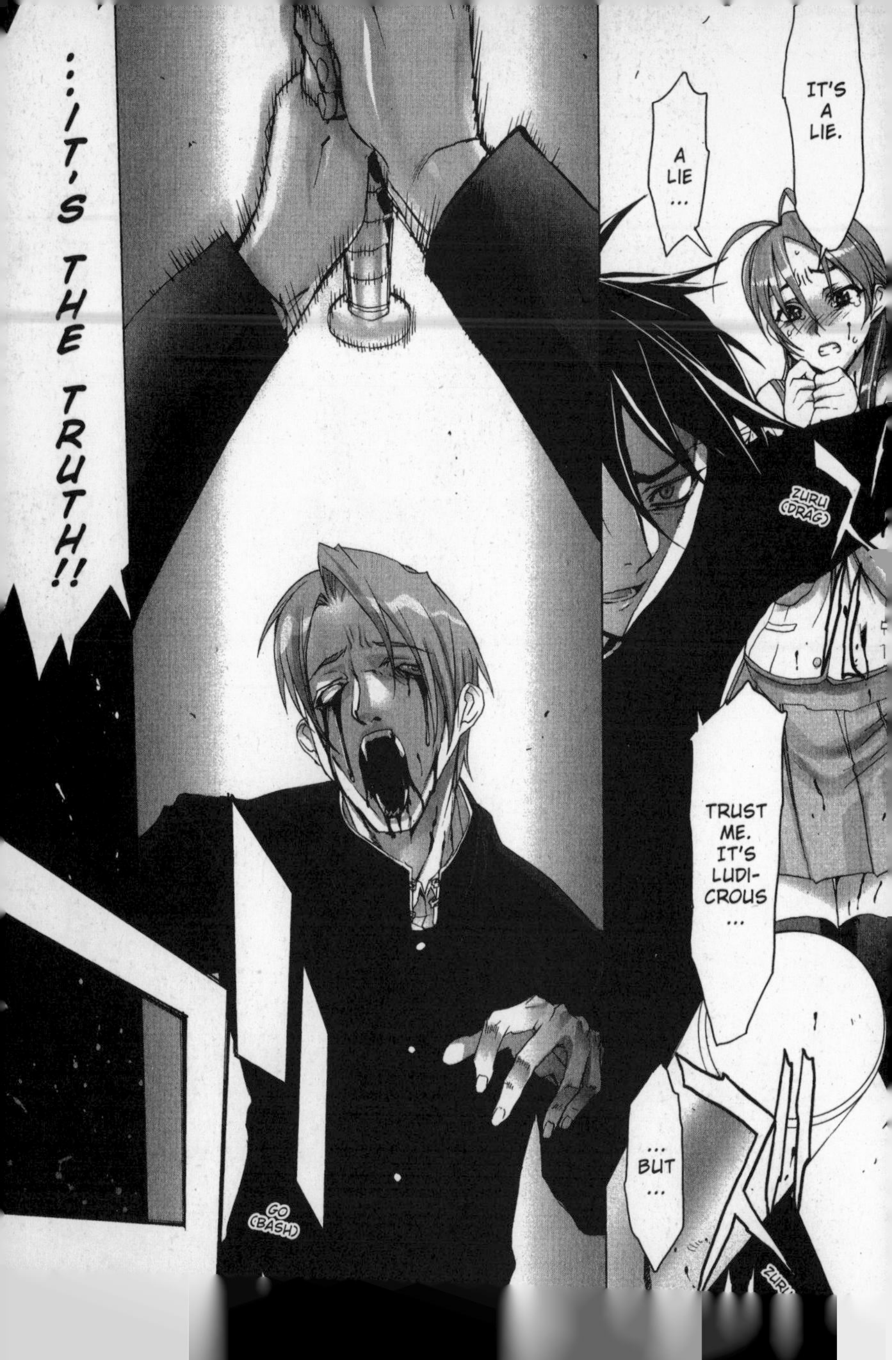

IT'S A LIE.
A LIE ...
ZURU (DRAG)
TRUST ME. IT'S LUDI-CROUS ...
... BUT ...
ZURU
...IT'S THE TRUTH!!
GO (BASH)

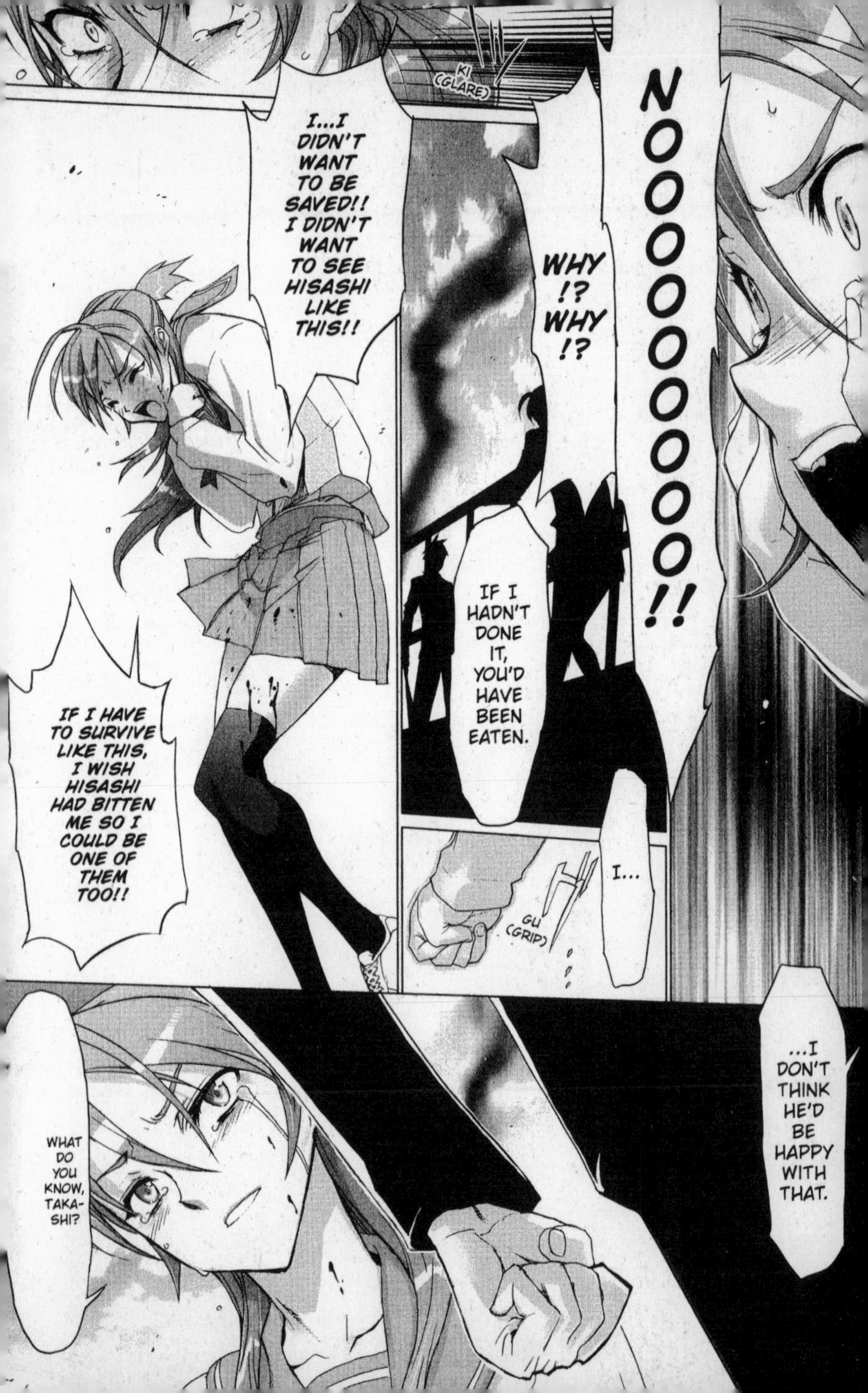
NOOOOOOOOOOOOO!!
KI (GLARE)
WHY!? WHY!?
I...I DIDN'T WANT TO BE SAVED!! I DIDN'T WANT TO SEE HISASHI LIKE THIS!!
IF I HADN'T DONE IT, YOU'D HAVE BEEN EATEN.
I...
GU (GRIP)
IF I HAVE TO SURVIVE LIKE THIS, I WISH HISASHI HAD BITTEN ME SO I COULD BE ONE OF THEM TOO!!
...I DON'T THINK HE'D BE HAPPY WITH THAT.
WHAT DO YOU KNOW, TAKA-SHI?

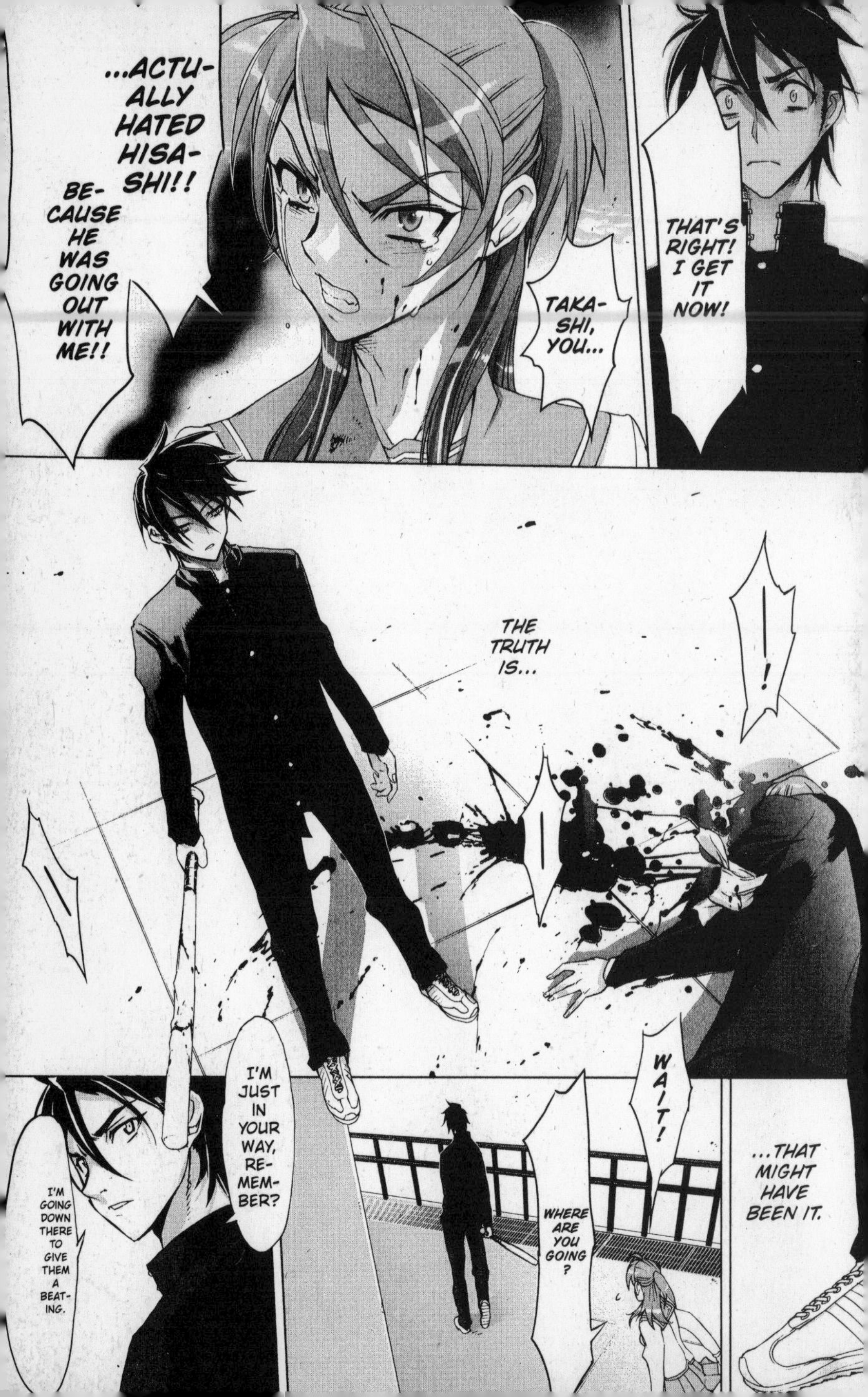
THAT'S RIGHT! I GET IT NOW!
TAKA-SHI, YOU...
...ACTU-ALLY HATED HISA-SHI!!
BE-CAUSE HE WAS GOING OUT WITH ME!!
!
THE TRUTH IS...
!
!
...THAT MIGHT HAVE BEEN IT.
WAIT!
WHERE ARE YOU GOING?
I'M JUST IN YOUR WAY, RE-MEM-BER?
I'M GOING DOWN THERE TO GIVE THEM A BEAT-ING.

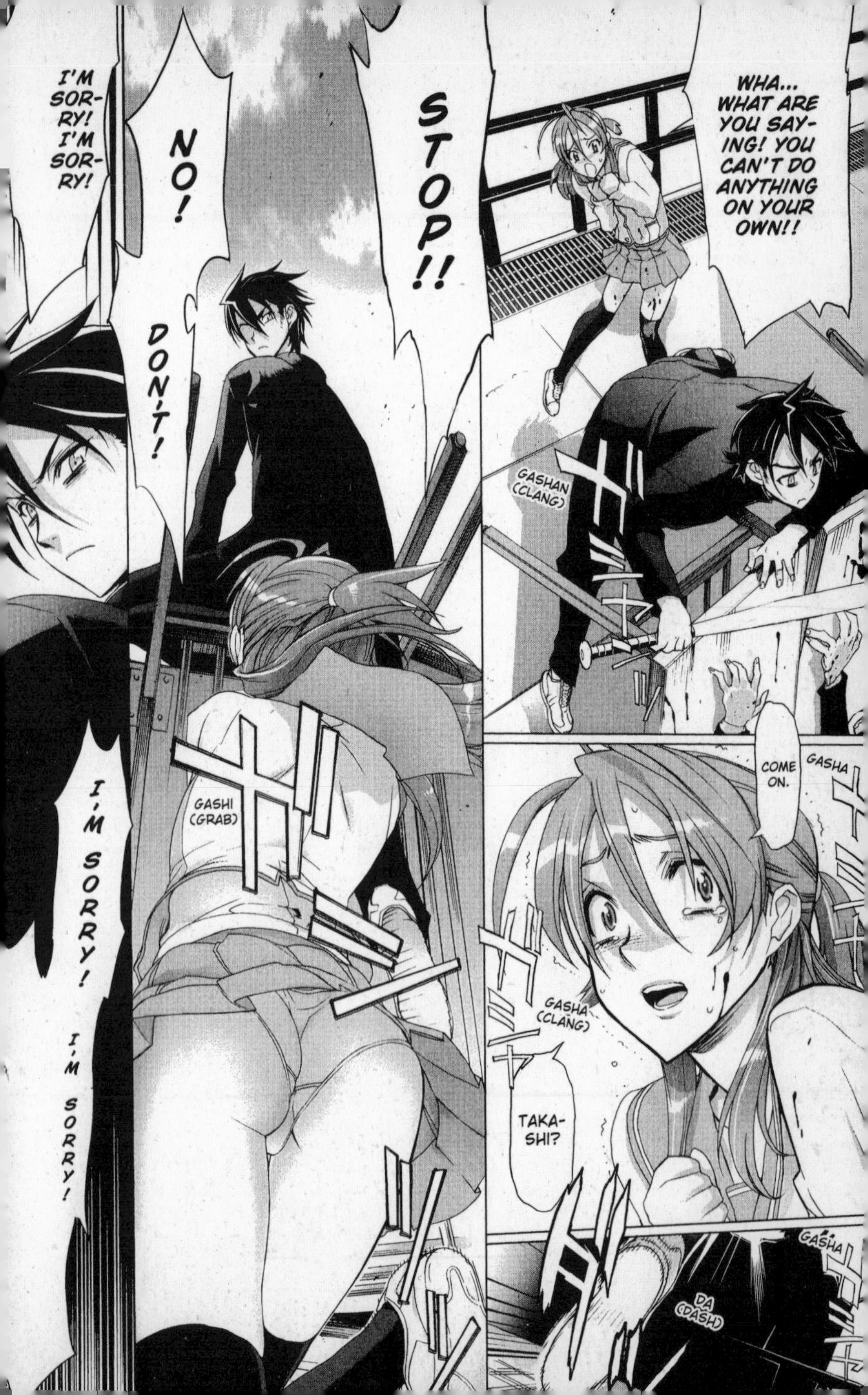
WHA... WHAT ARE YOU SAYING! YOU CAN'T DO ANYTHING ON YOUR OWN!!
GASHAN (CLANG)
COME ON.
GASHA
GASHA (CLANG)
TAKASHI?
GASHA
DA (DASH)
STOP!!
NO!
DON'T!
GASHI (GRAB)
I'M SORRY! I'M SORRY!
I'M SORRY!
I'M SORRY!

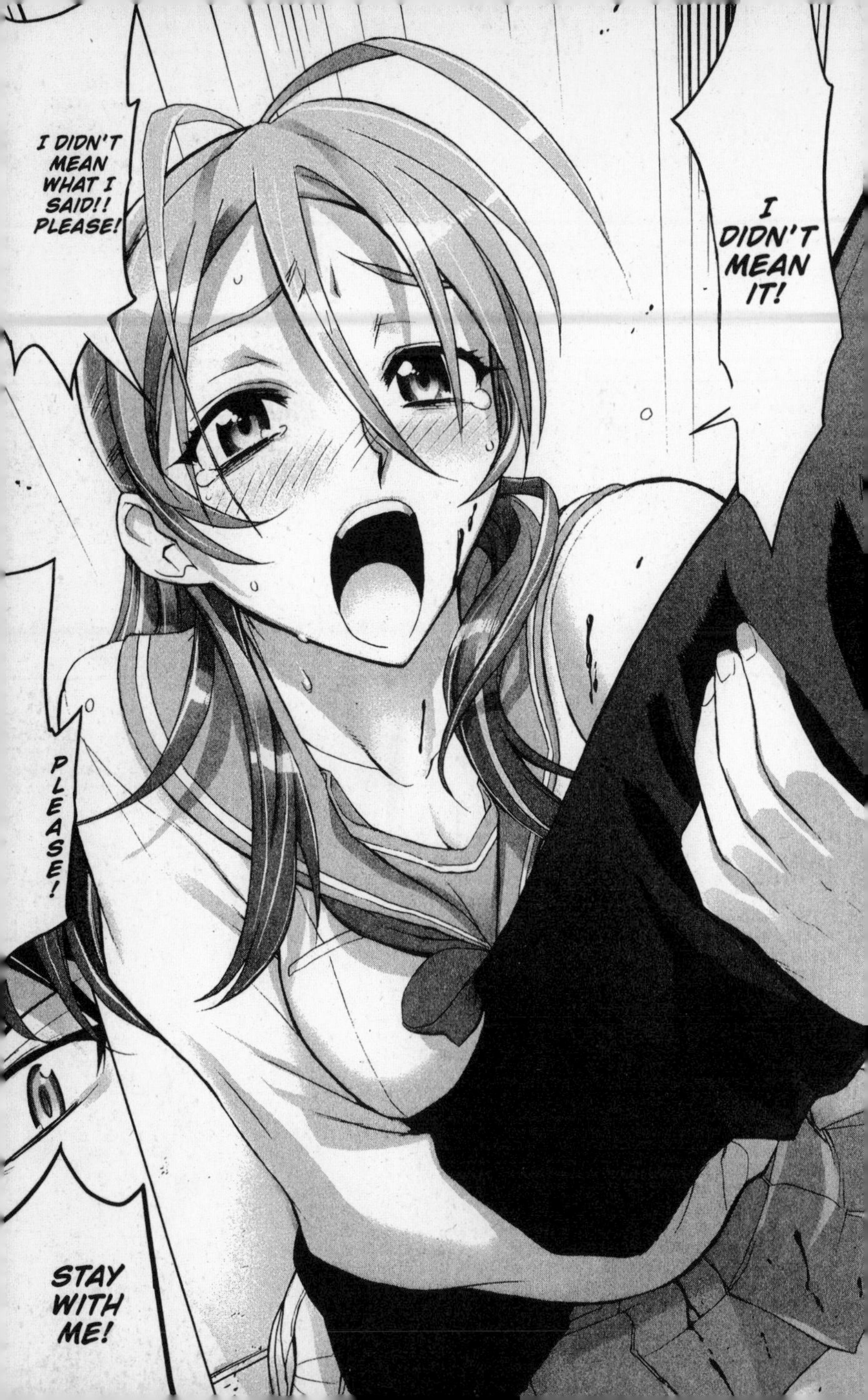
I DIDN'T MEAN IT!
I DIDN'T MEAN WHAT I SAID!! PLEASE!
PLEASE!
STAY WITH ME!

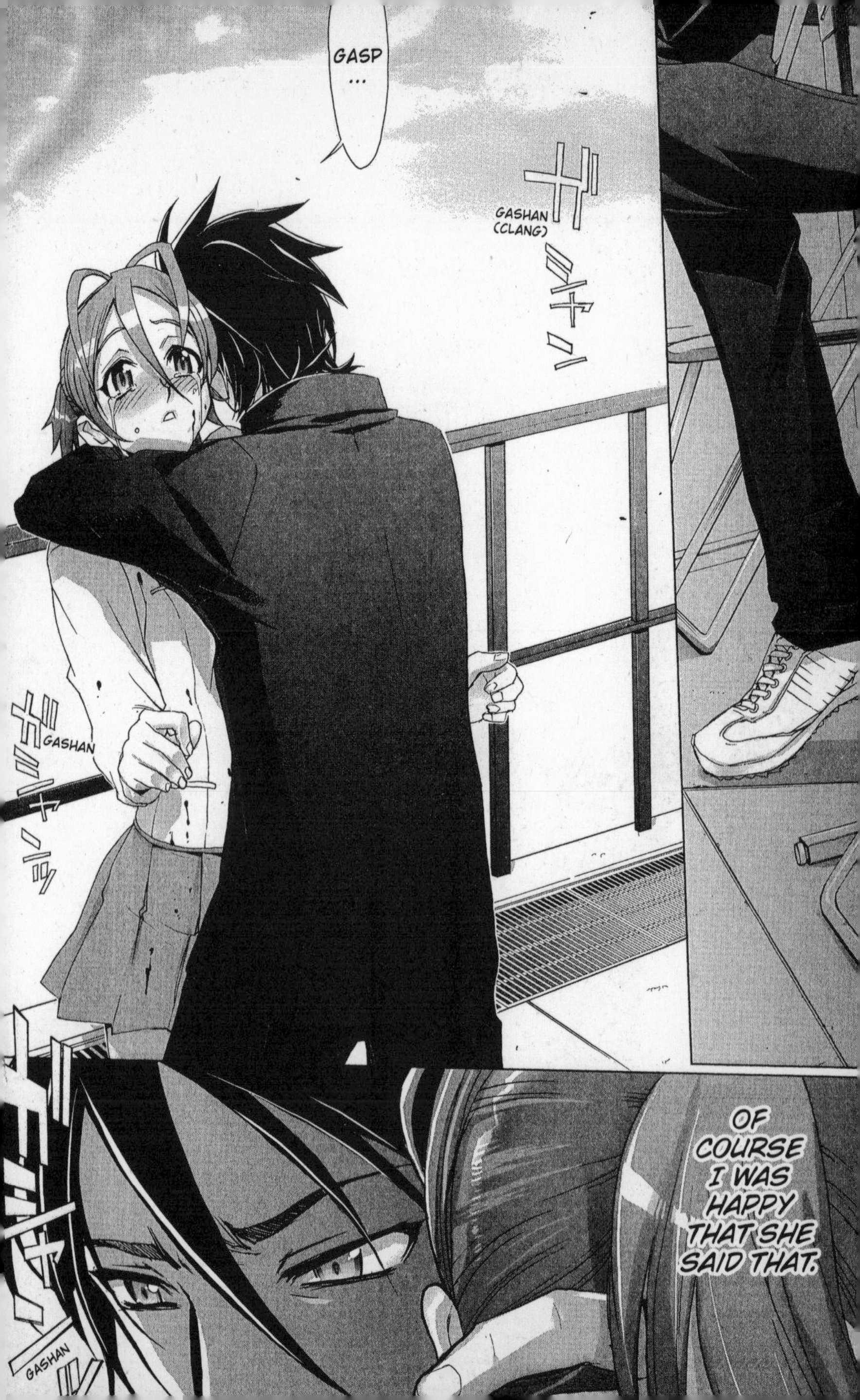
GASP ...
GASHAN (CLANG)
GASHAN
OF COURSE I WAS HAPPY THAT SHE SAID THAT.
GASHAN

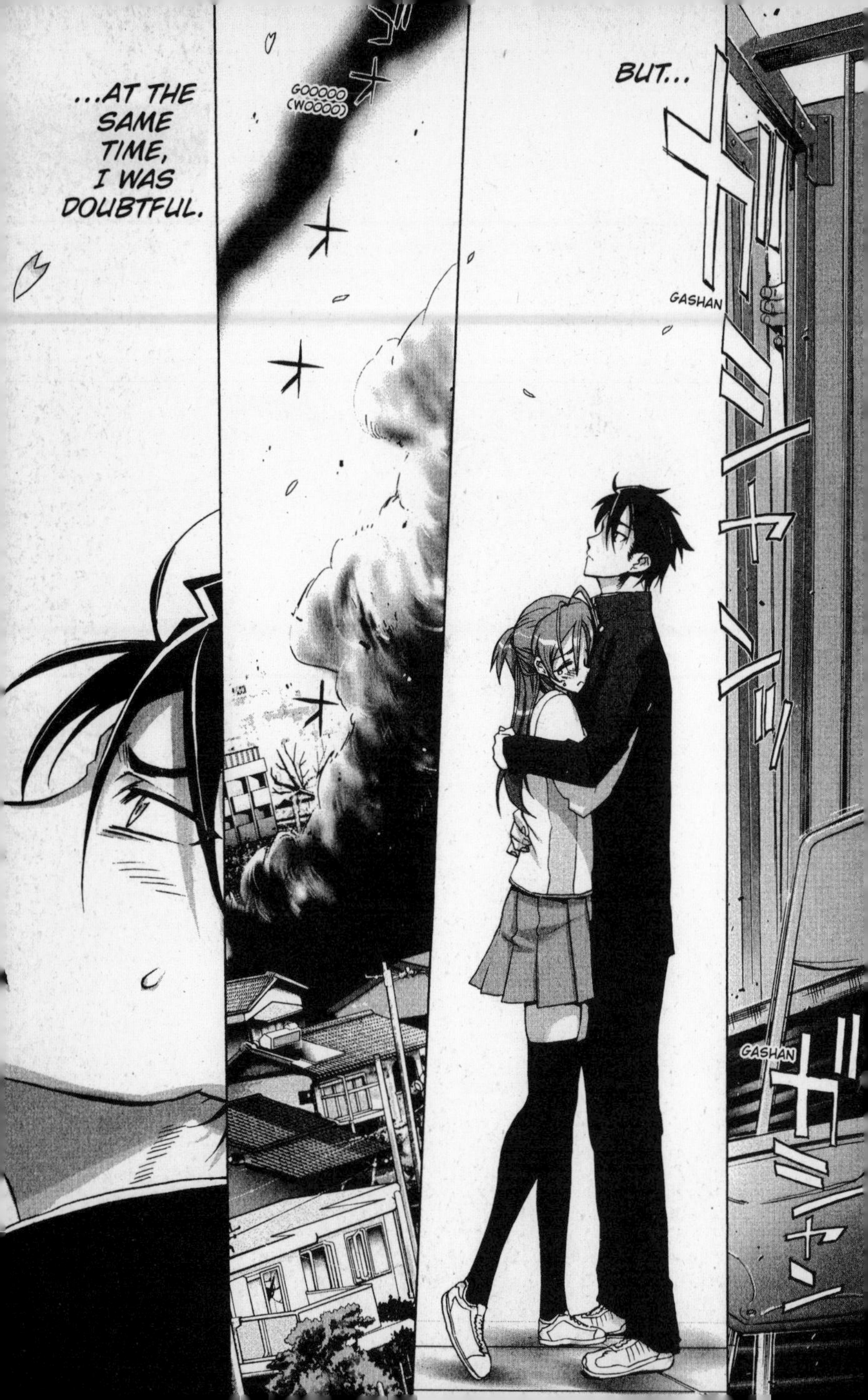
GASHAN
GASHAN
BUT...
GOOOOO (WOOOO)
...AT THE SAME TIME, I WAS DOUBTFUL.

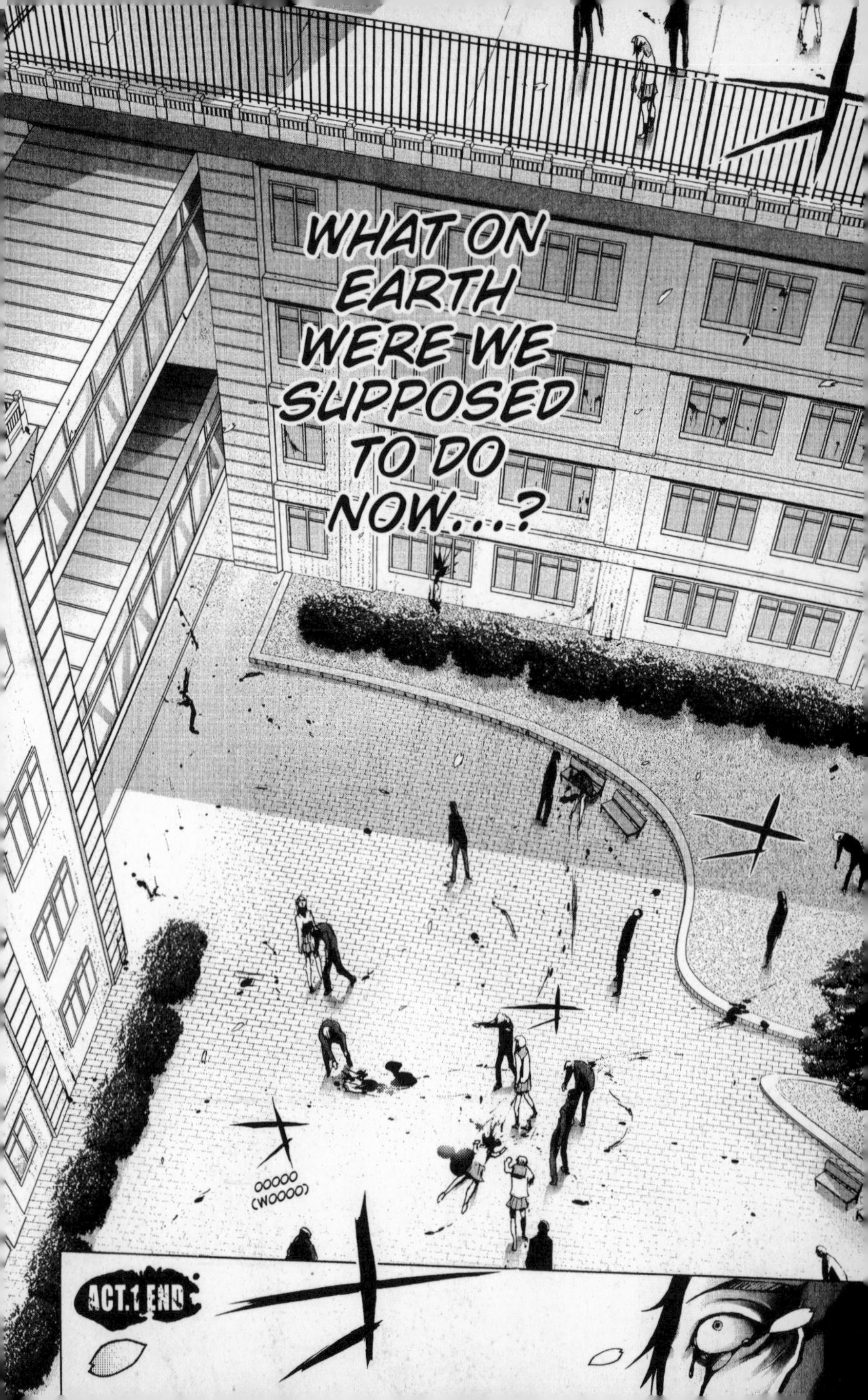
WHAT ON EARTH WERE WE SUPPOSED TO DO NOW...?
OOOOO (WOOOO)
ACT.1 END

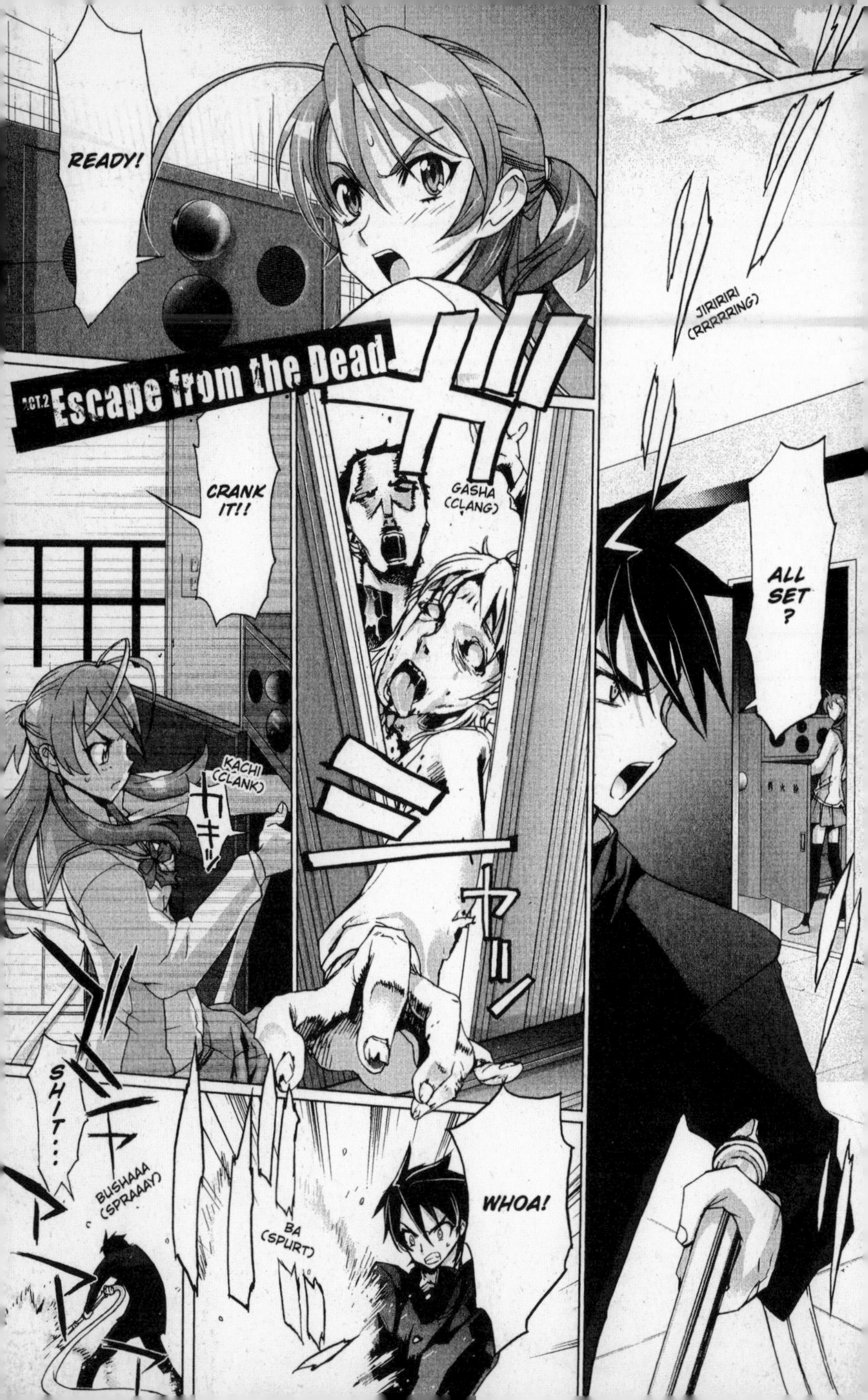
JIRIRIRI (RRRRRING)
ALL SET?
READY!
ACT.2 Escape from the Dead
CRANK IT!!
GASHA (CLANG)
KACHI (CLANK)
WHOA!
BA (SPURT)
BUSHAAA (SPRAAAY)
SHIT...

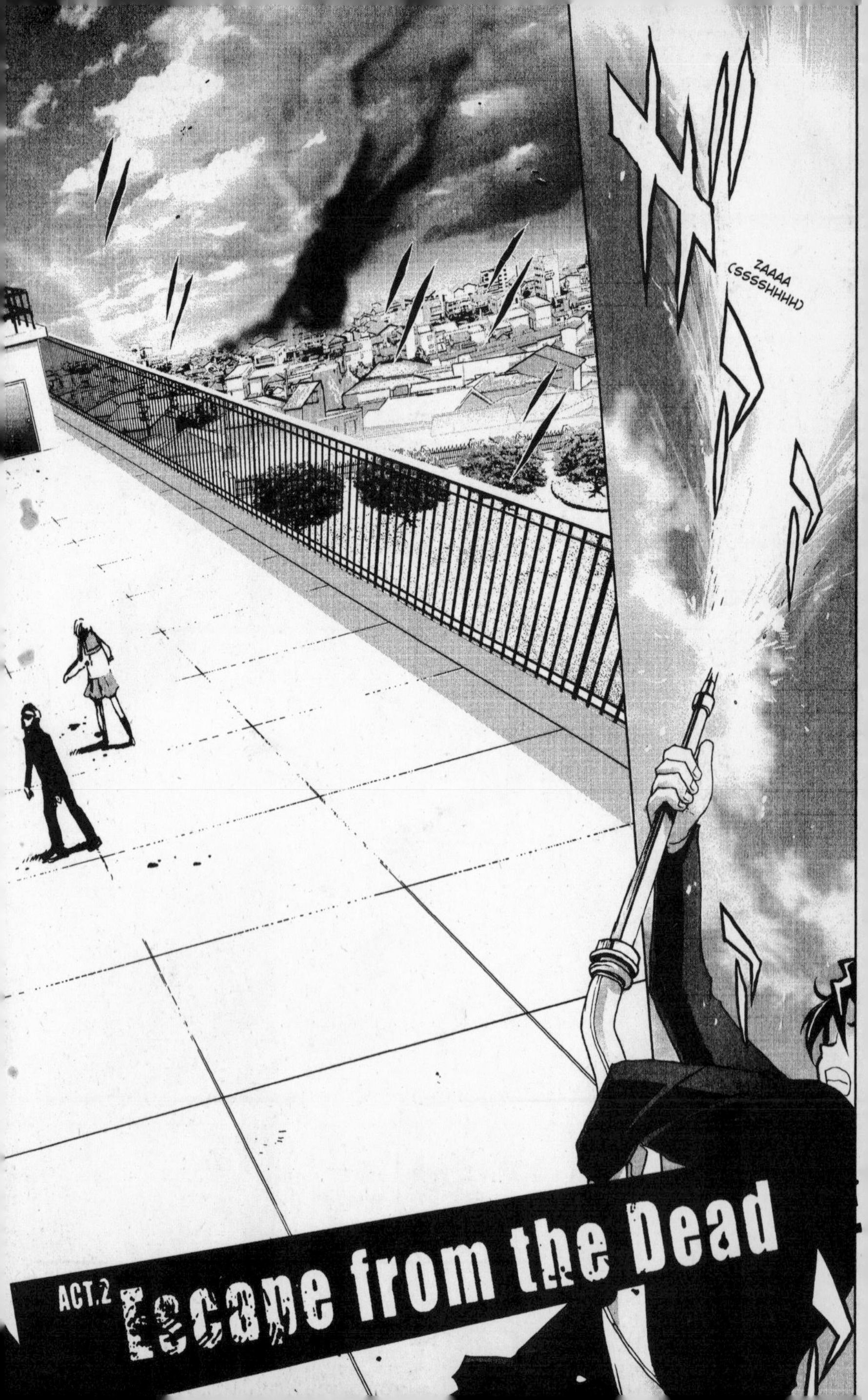
ZAAAA
(SSSSHHHH)
ACT.2
Escape from the Dead

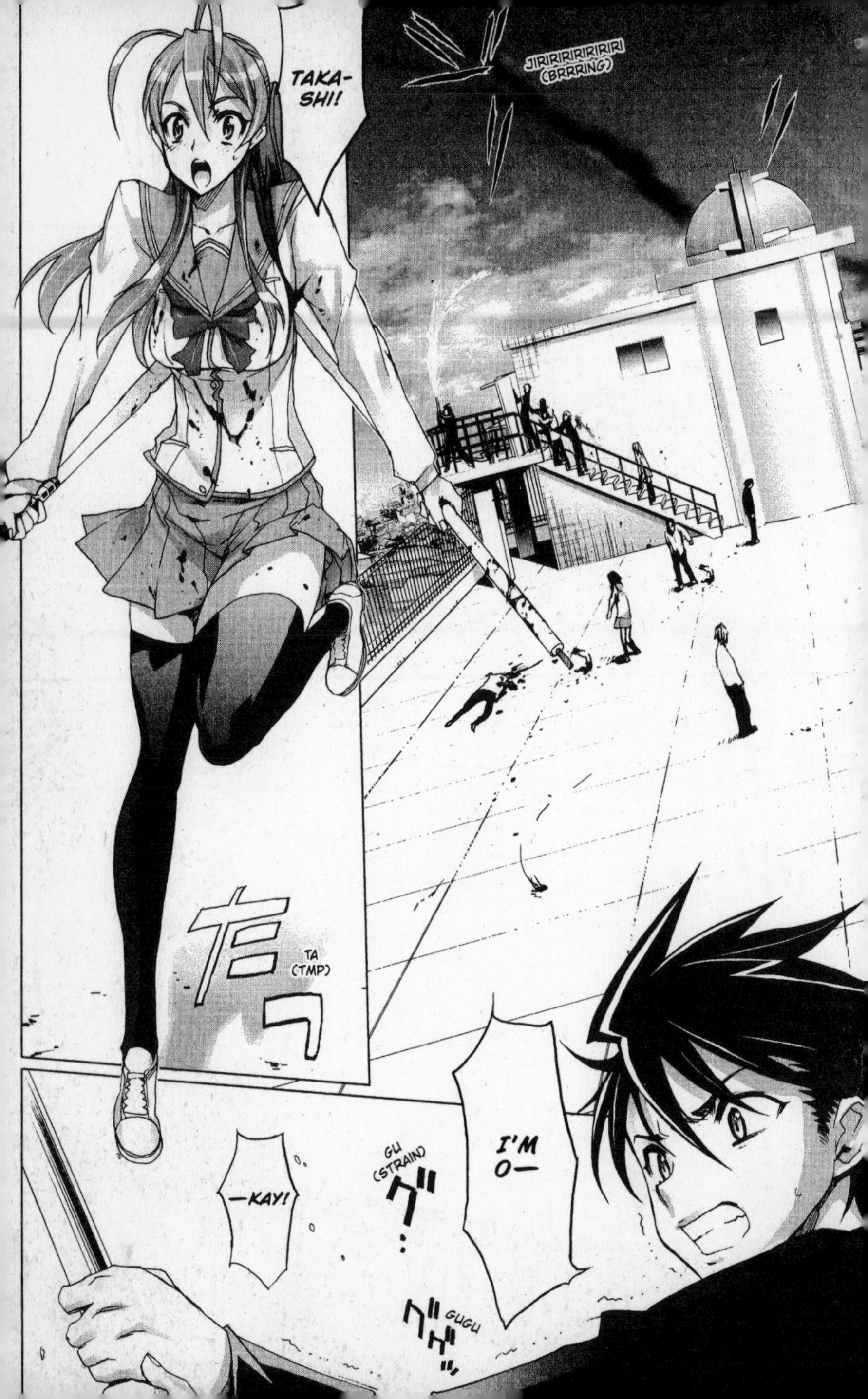
JIRIRIRIRIRIRI
(BRRRING)
TAKA-SHI!
TA
(TMP)
I'M O—
GU
(STRAIN)
GUGU
—KAY!

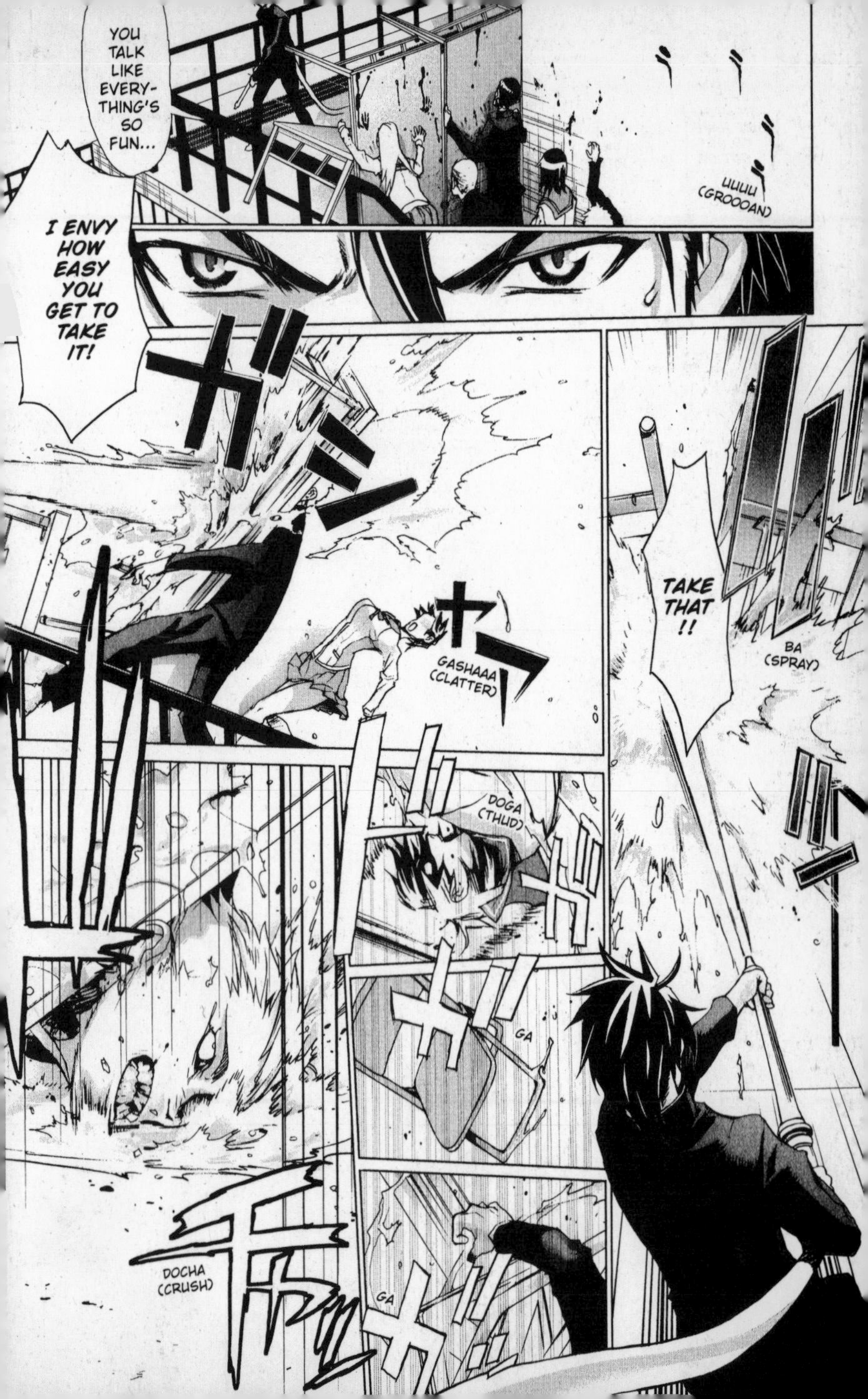
UUUU (GROOOAN)
YOU TALK LIKE EVERY-THING'S SO FUN...
I ENVY HOW EASY YOU GET TO TAKE IT!
TAKE THAT!!
BA (SPRAY)
GASHAAA (CLATTER)
DOGA (THUD)
GA
GA
DOCHA (CRUSH)

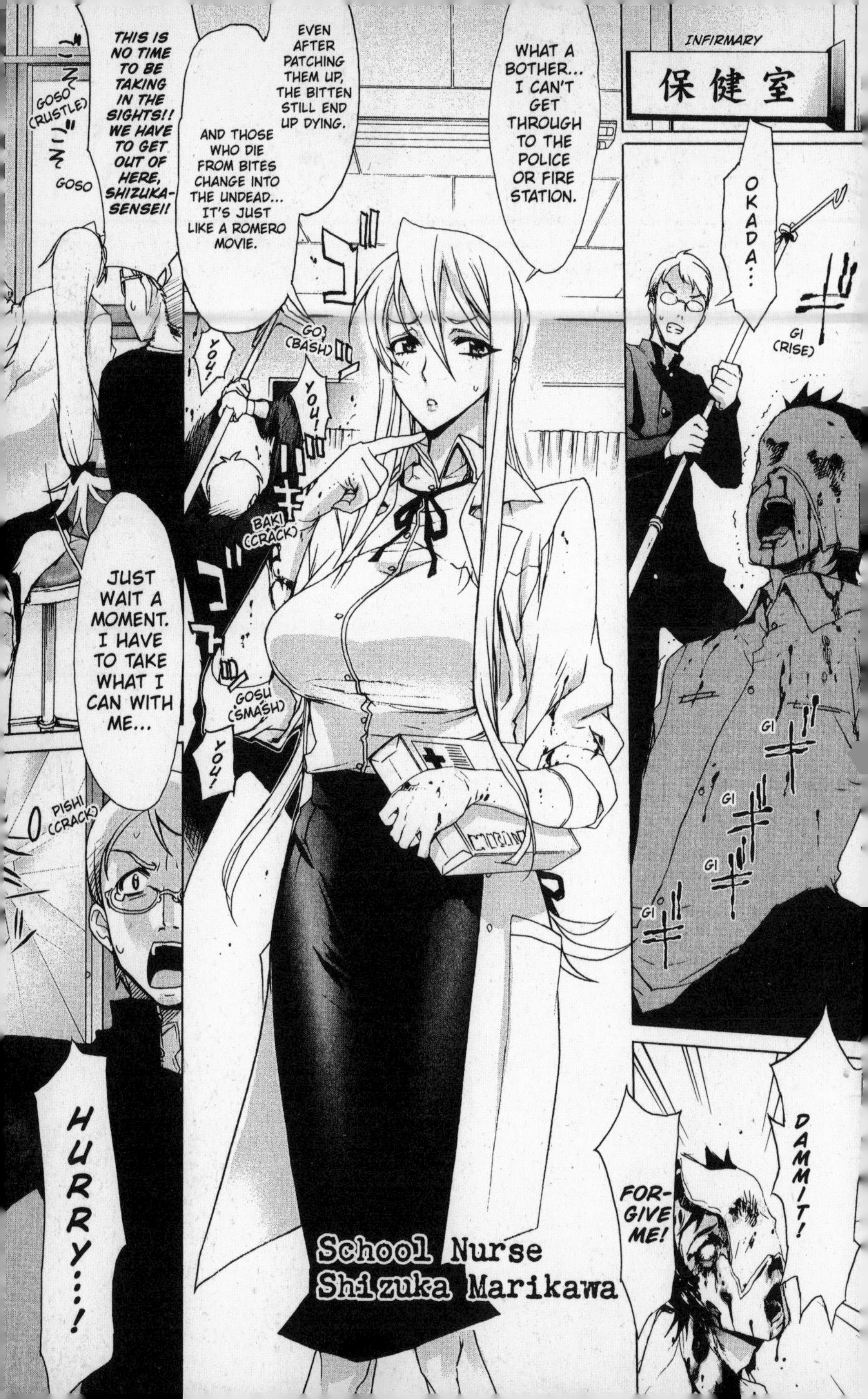
INFIRMARY
保健室
OKADA...
GI (RISE)
GI
GI
GI
GI
DAMMIT!
FOR-GIVE ME!
WHAT A BOTHER... I CAN'T GET THROUGH TO THE POLICE OR FIRE STATION.
EVEN AFTER PATCHING THEM UP, THE BITTEN STILL END UP DYING.
AND THOSE WHO DIE FROM BITES CHANGE INTO THE UNDEAD... IT'S JUST LIKE A ROMERO MOVIE.
GO (BASH)
YOU!
YOU!
BAKI (CRACK)
GOSU (SMASH)
YOU!
School Nurse
Shizuka Marikawa
THIS IS NO TIME TO BE TAKING IN THE SIGHTS!! WE HAVE TO GET OUT OF HERE, SHIZUKA-SENSEI!!
GOSO (RUSTLE)
GOSO
JUST WAIT A MOMENT. I HAVE TO TAKE WHAT I CAN WITH ME...
PISHI (CRACK)
HURRY...!

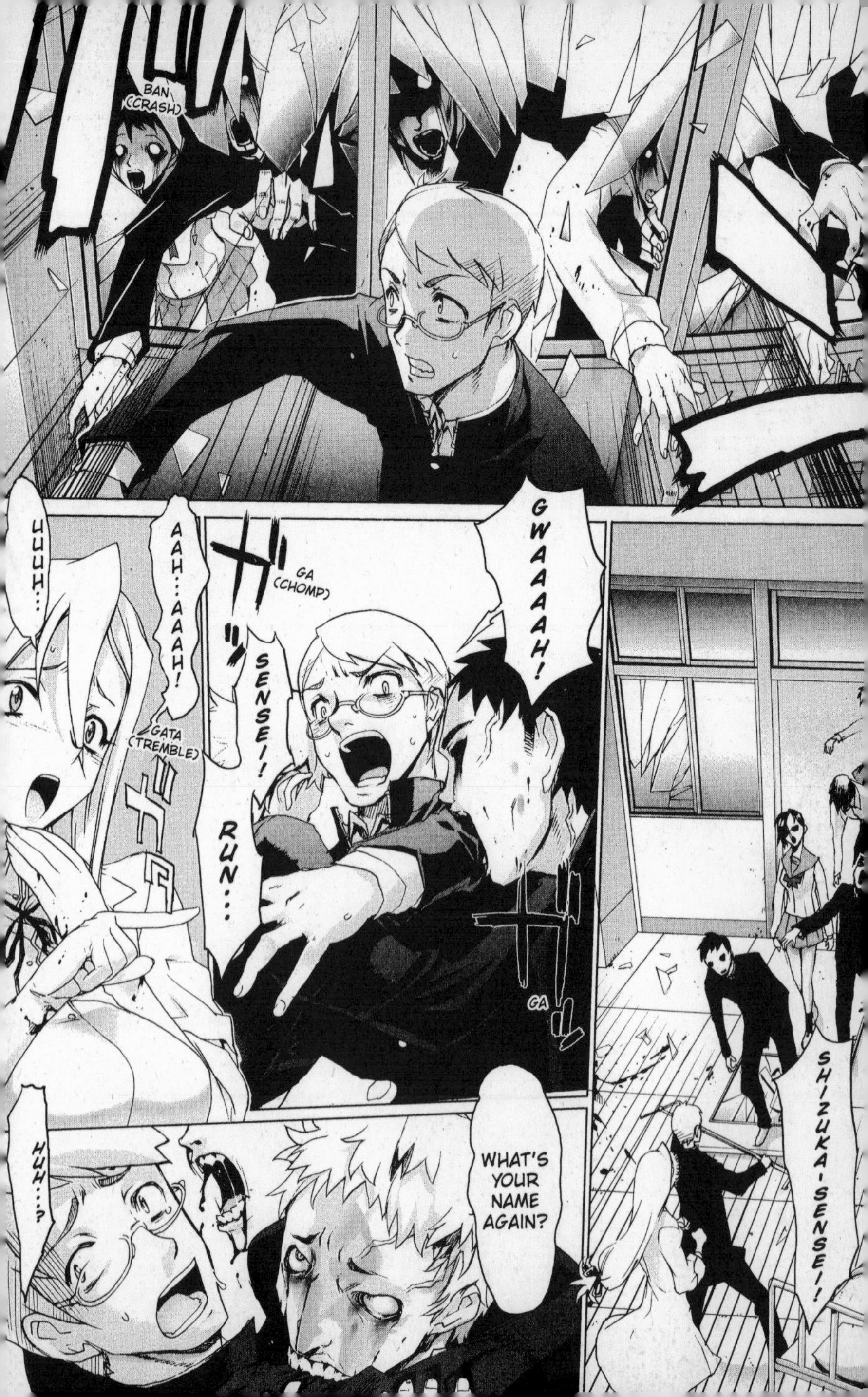
BAN (CRASH)
SHIZUKA-SENSEI!!
GWAAAAAH!
GA (CHOMP)
SENSEI!!
RUN...
GA
AAH...AAAAH!
GATA (TREMBLE)
UUUH...
WHAT'S YOUR NAME AGAIN?
HUH...?

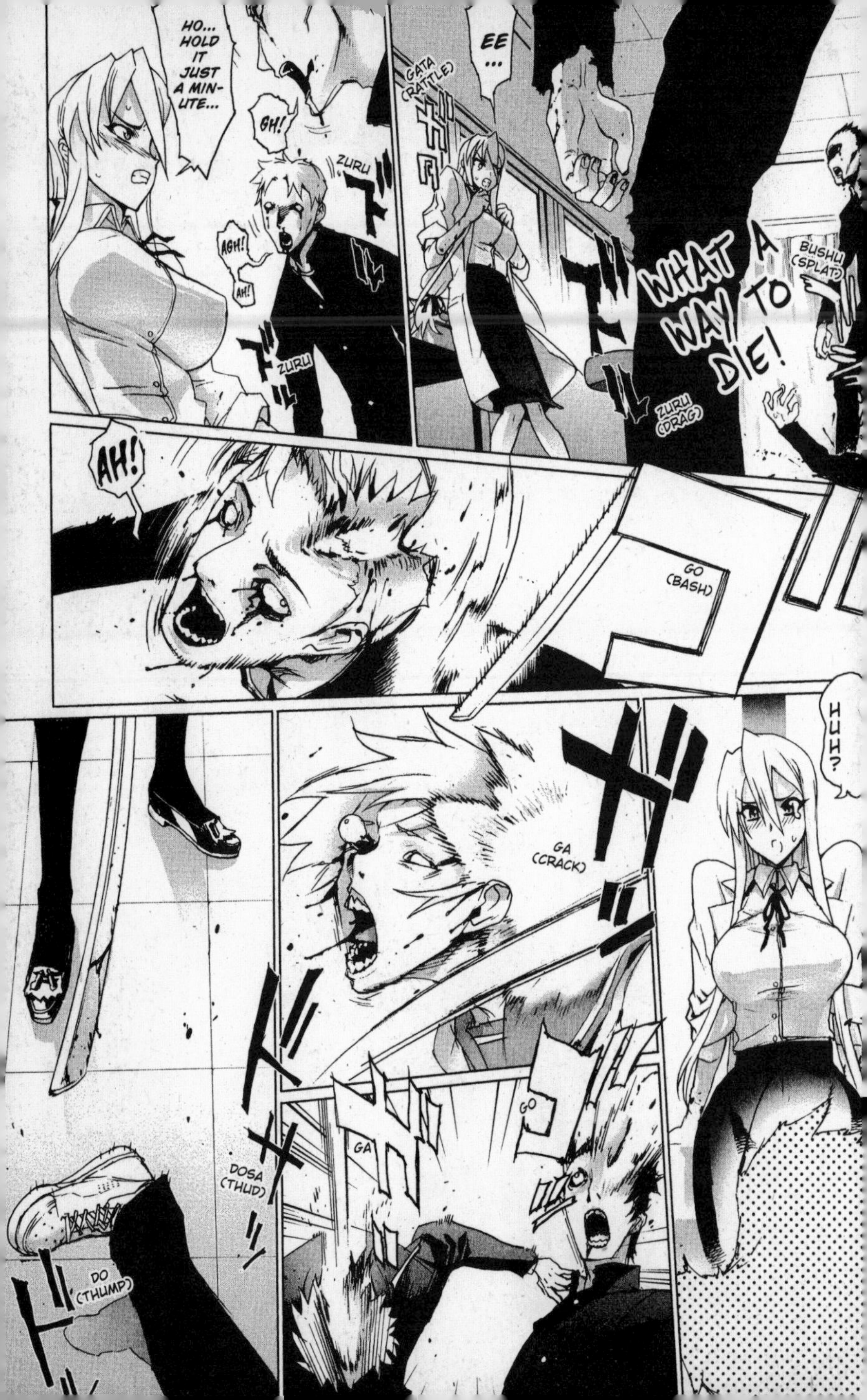
BUSHU (SPLAT)
WHAT A WAY TO DIE!
ZURU (DRAG)
EE ...
GATA (RATTLE)
HO... HOLD IT JUST A MINUTE...
GH!
ZURU
AGH!
AH!
ZURU
AH!
GO (BASH)
HUH?
GA (CRACK)
GO
GA
DOSA (THUD)
DO (THUMP)

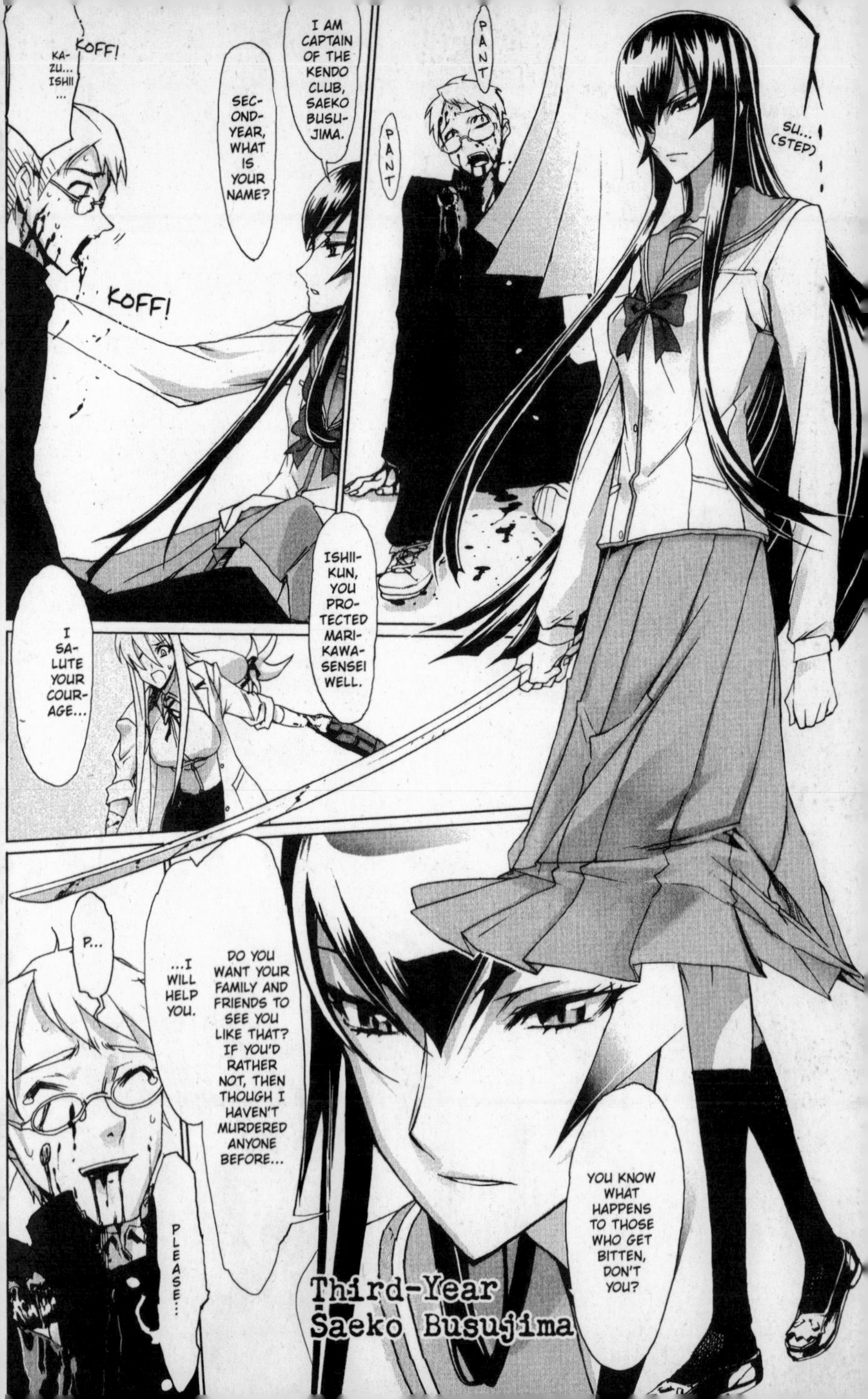
SU... (STEP)
PANT
PANT
I AM CAPTAIN OF THE KENDO CLUB, SAEKO BUSUJIMA.
SEC-OND-YEAR, WHAT IS YOUR NAME?
KOFF!
KA-ZU... ISHII...
KOFF!
ISHII-KUN, YOU PRO-TECTED MARI-KAWA-SENSEI WELL.
I SA-LUTE YOUR COUR-AGE...
YOU KNOW WHAT HAPPENS TO THOSE WHO GET BITTEN, DON'T YOU?
Third-Year Saeko Busujima
DO YOU WANT YOUR FAMILY AND FRIENDS TO SEE YOU LIKE THAT? IF YOU'D RATHER NOT, THEN THOUGH I HAVEN'T MURDERED ANYONE BEFORE...
...I WILL HELP YOU.
P...
PLEASE...

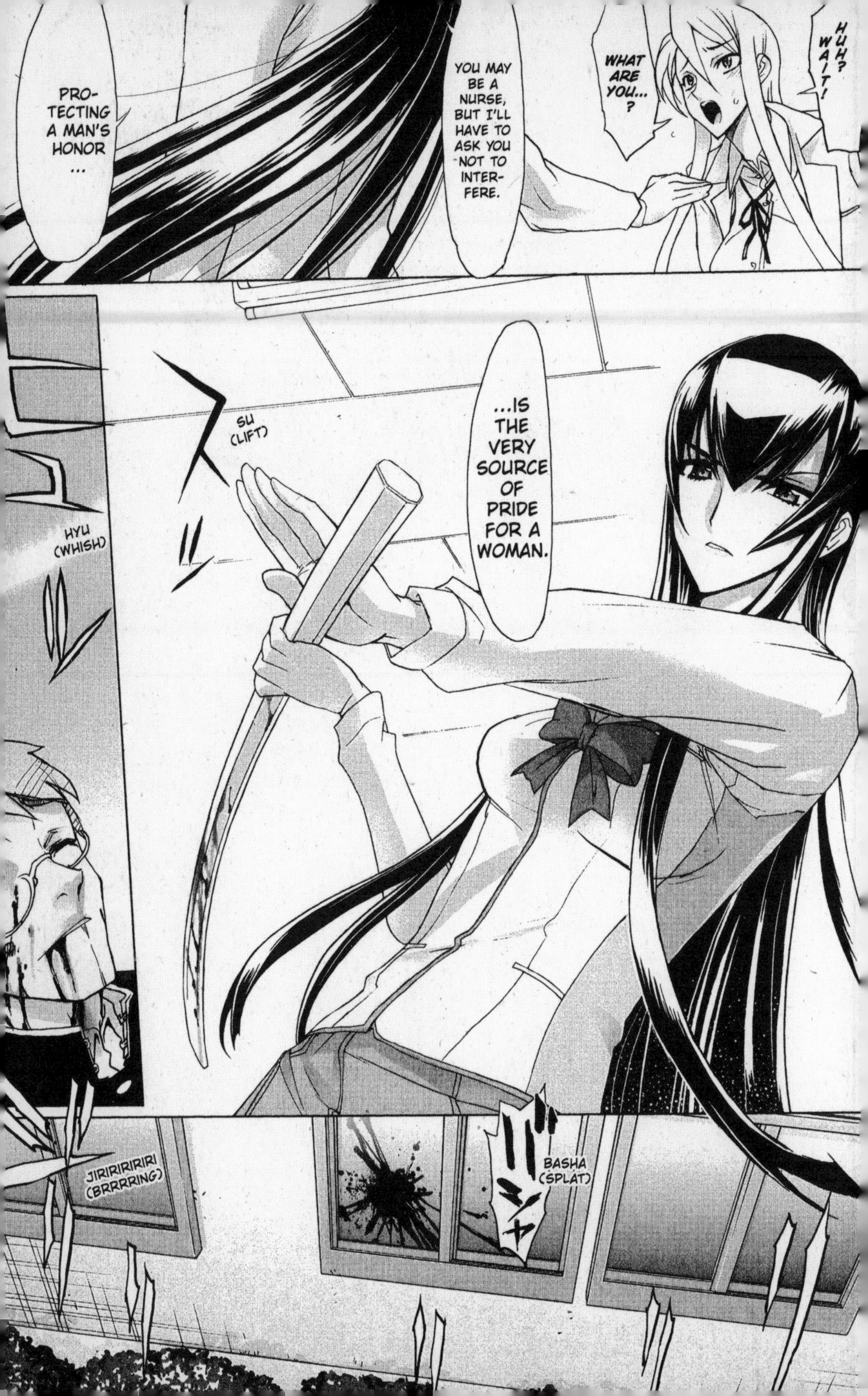
HUH? WAIT!
WHAT ARE YOU...?
YOU MAY BE A NURSE, BUT I'LL HAVE TO ASK YOU NOT TO INTERFERE.
PRO-TECTING A MAN'S HONOR...
...IS THE VERY SOURCE OF PRIDE FOR A WOMAN.
SU (LIFT)
HYU (WHISH)
BASHA (SPLAT)
JIRIRIRIRIRI (BRRRRING)

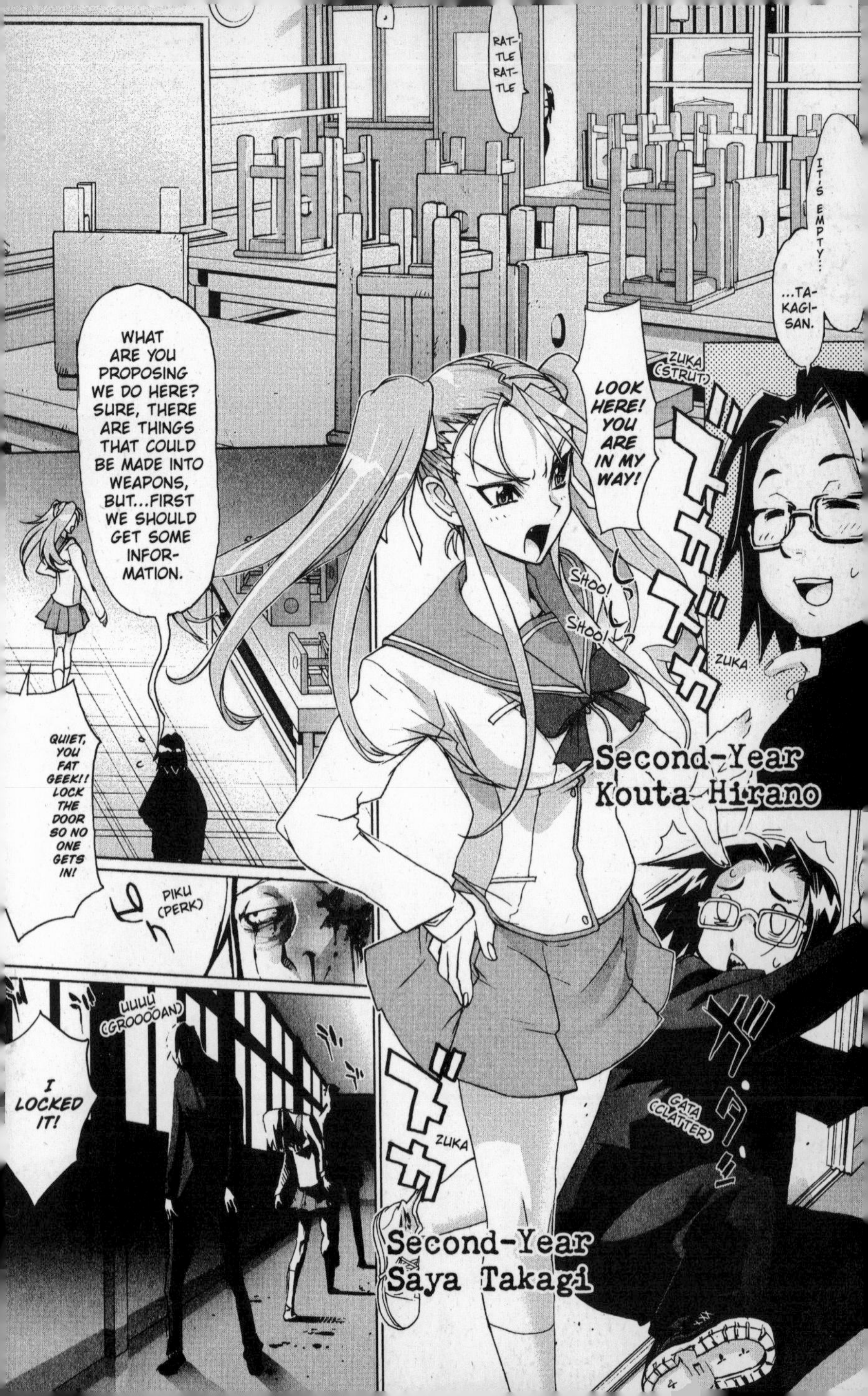

RAT-TLE RAT-TLE
IT'S EMPTY... ...TA-KAGI-SAN.
ZUKA (STRUT)
LOOK HERE! YOU ARE IN MY WAY!
WHAT ARE YOU PROPOSING WE DO HERE? SURE, THERE ARE THINGS THAT COULD BE MADE INTO WEAPONS, BUT...FIRST WE SHOULD GET SOME INFOR-MATION.
SHOO! SHOO!
ZUKA
Second-Year Kouta Hirano
QUIET, YOU FAT GEEK!! LOCK THE DOOR SO NO ONE GETS IN!
GATA (CLATTER)
ZUKA
Second-Year Saya Takagi
PIKU (PERK)
UUUU (GROOOOAN)
I LOCKED IT!

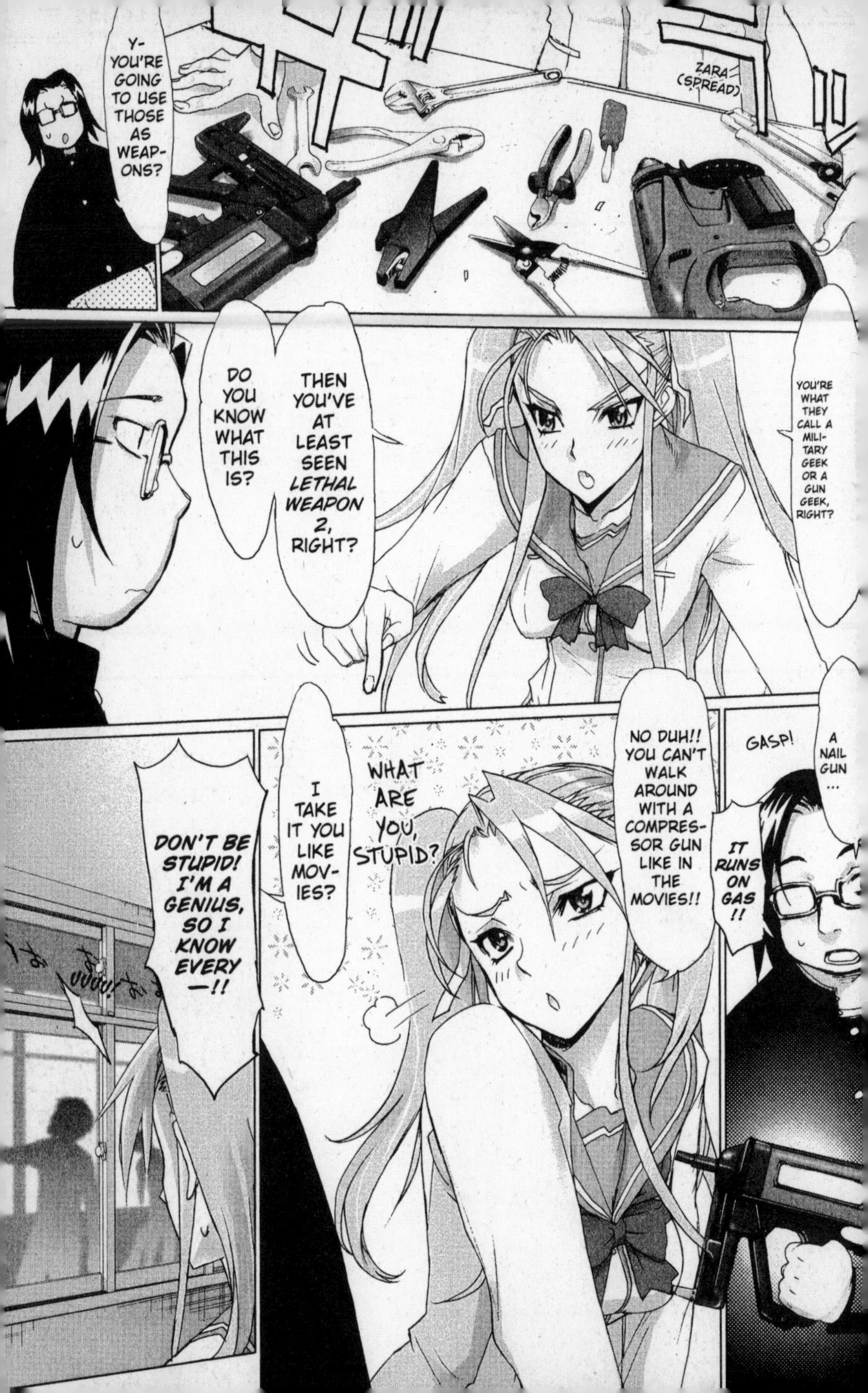
ZARA (SPREAD)
Y-YOU'RE GOING TO USE THOSE AS WEAPONS?
YOU'RE WHAT THEY CALL A MILITARY GEEK OR A GUN GEEK, RIGHT?
THEN YOU'VE AT LEAST SEEN *LETHAL WEAPON 2*, RIGHT?
DO YOU KNOW WHAT THIS IS?
A NAIL GUN...
GASP!
IT RUNS ON GAS!!
NO DUH!! YOU CAN'T WALK AROUND WITH A COMPRESSOR GUN LIKE IN THE MOVIES!!
WHAT ARE YOU, STUPID?
I TAKE IT YOU LIKE MOVIES?
DON'T BE STUPID! I'M A GENIUS, SO I KNOW EVERY—!!

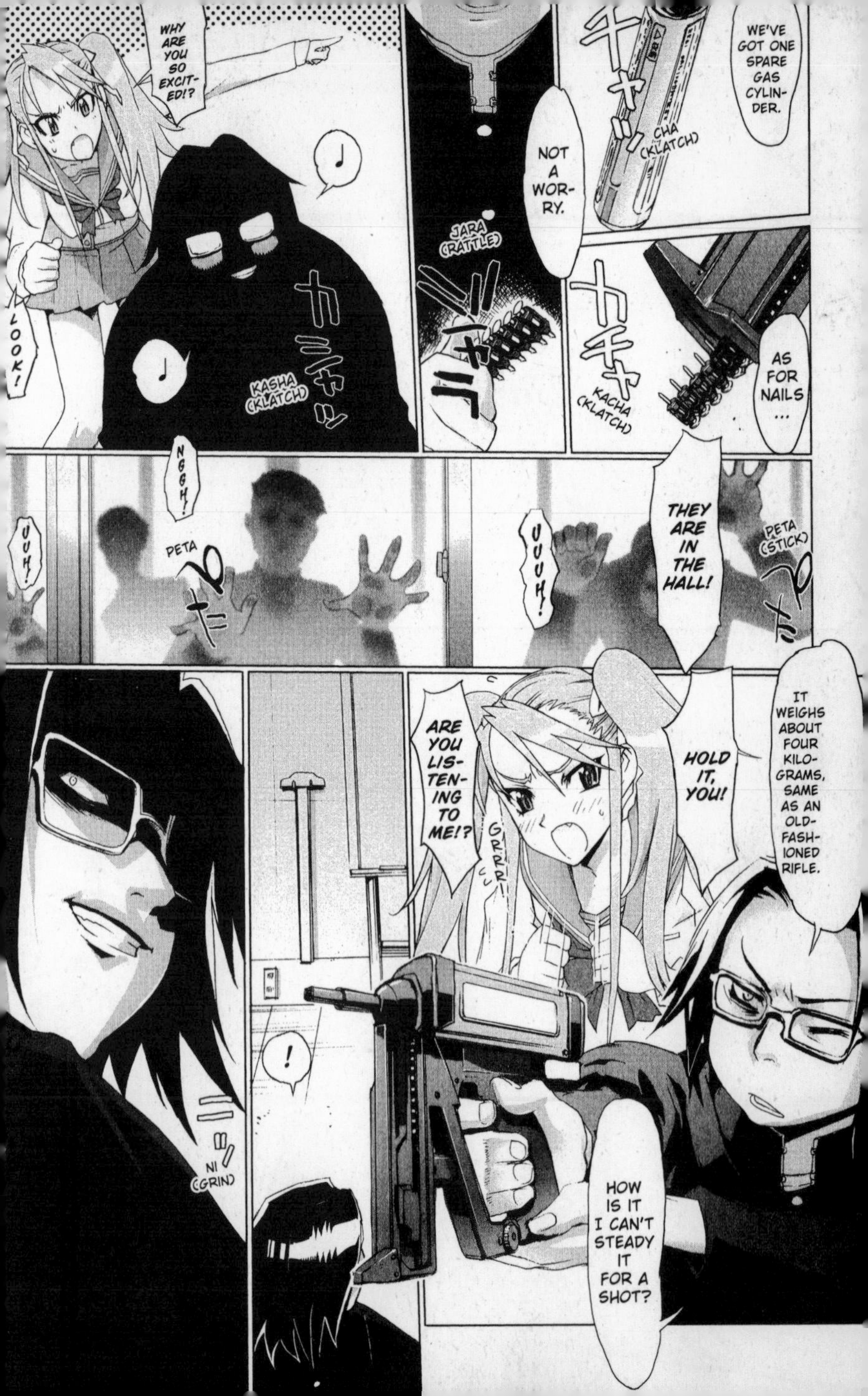
WE'VE GOT ONE SPARE GAS CYLINDER.
CHA (KLATCH)
AS FOR NAILS...
KACHA (KLATCH)
NOT A WORRY.
JARA (RATTLE)
WHY ARE YOU SO EXCITED!?
♪
♪
KASHA (KLATCH)
LOOK!
THEY ARE IN THE HALL!
PETA (STICK)
UUUH!
NGGH!
PETA
UUH!
IT WEIGHS ABOUT FOUR KILOGRAMS, SAME AS AN OLD-FASHIONED RIFLE.
HOLD IT, YOU!
ARE YOU LISTENING TO ME!?
GRRR!
HOW IS IT I CAN'T STEADY IT FOR A SHOT?
!
NI (GRIN)

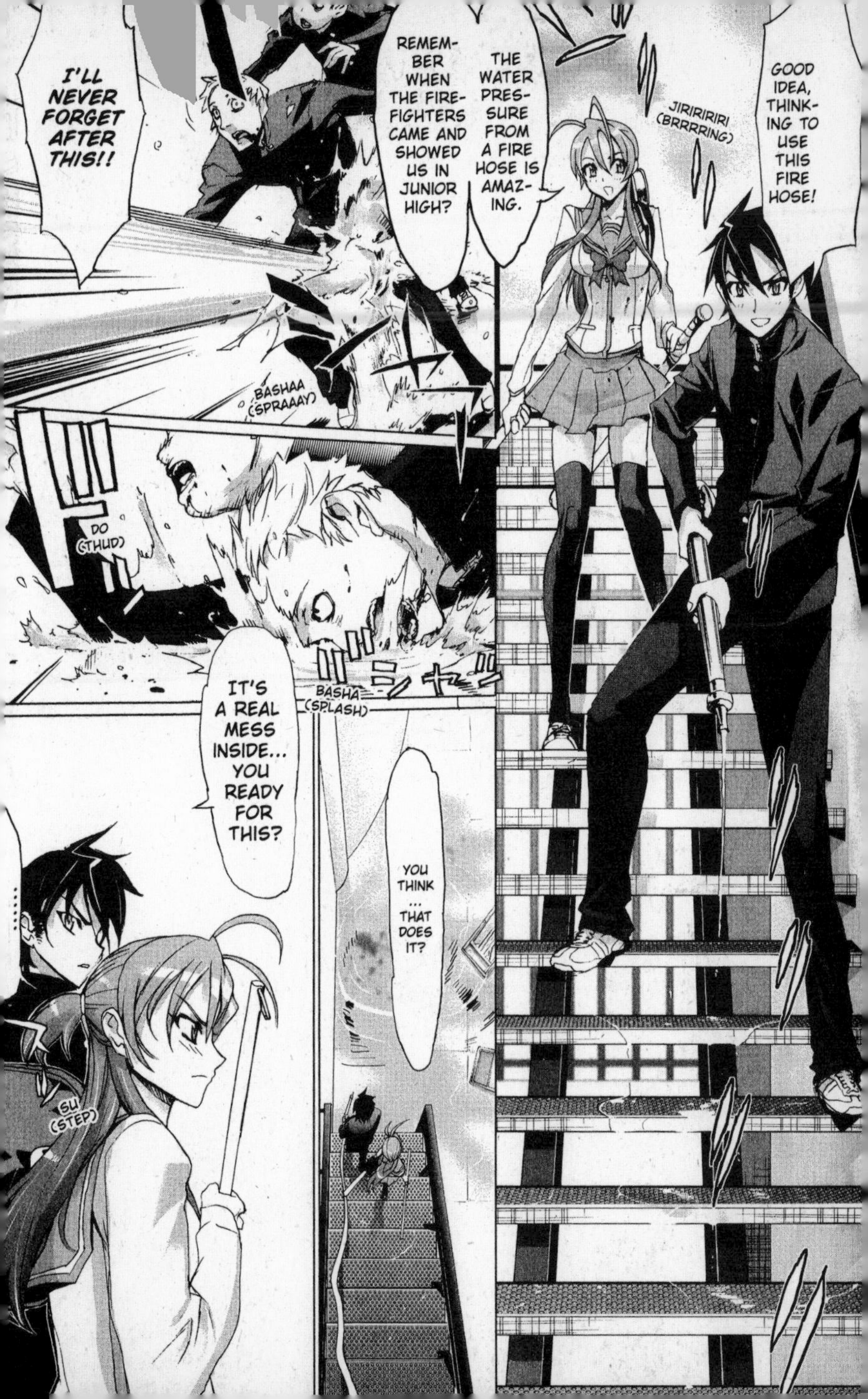
GOOD IDEA, THINKING TO USE THIS FIRE HOSE!
JIRIRIRIRI (BRRRRING)
THE WATER PRESSURE FROM A FIRE HOSE IS AMAZING.
REMEMBER WHEN THE FIREFIGHTERS CAME AND SHOWED US IN JUNIOR HIGH?
I'LL NEVER FORGET AFTER THIS!!
BASHAA (SPRAAAY)
DO (THUD)
BASHA (SPLASH)
YOU THINK ... THAT DOES IT?
IT'S A REAL MESS INSIDE... YOU READY FOR THIS?
SU (STEP)

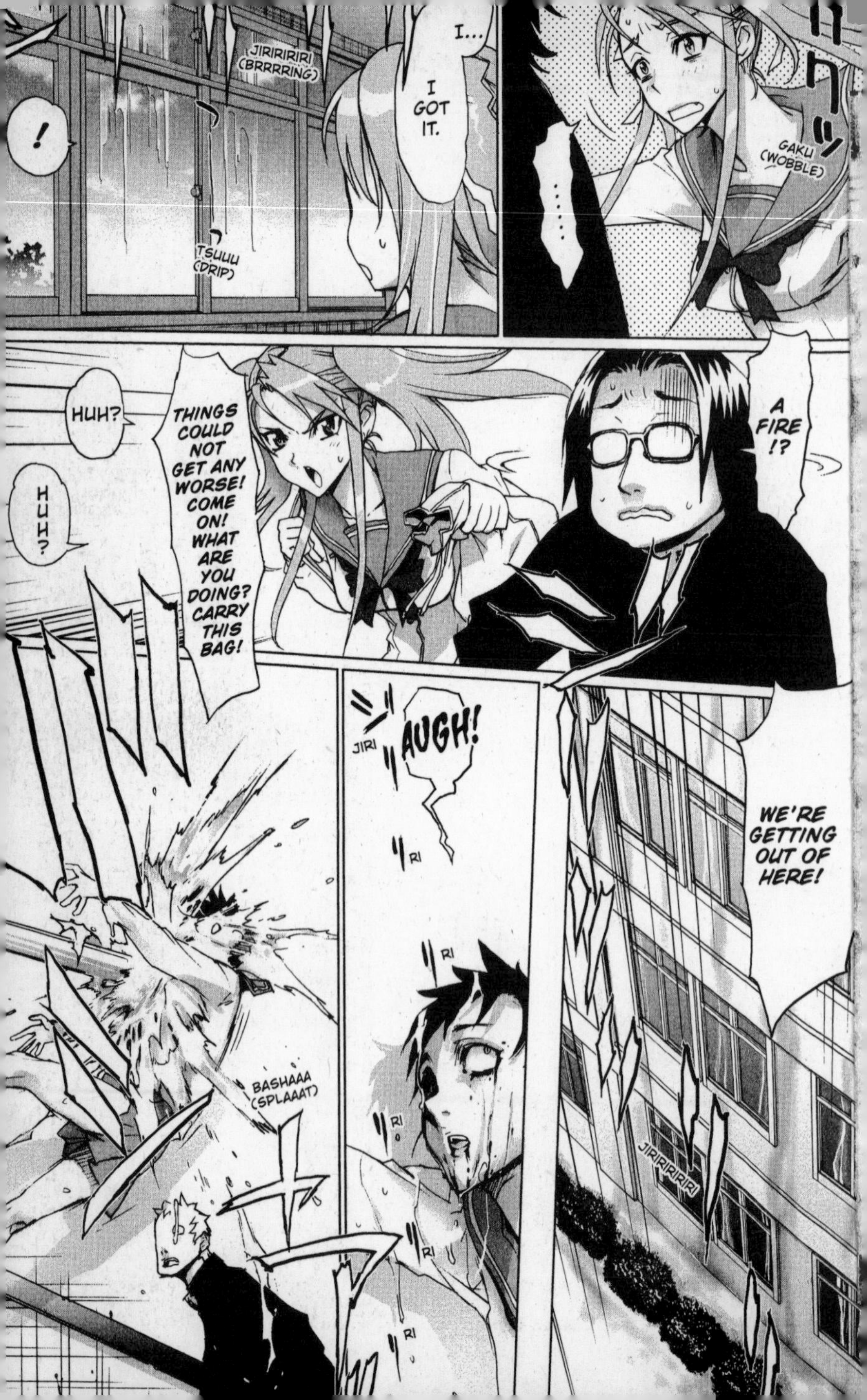
GAKU (WOBBLE)
......
I...
I GOT IT.
JIRIRIRIRI (BRRRRING)
!
TSUUU (DRIP)
A FIRE!?
THINGS COULD NOT GET ANY WORSE! COME ON! WHAT ARE YOU DOING? CARRY THIS BAG!
HUH?
HUH?
WE'RE GETTING OUT OF HERE!
JIRIRIRIRIRI
JIRI
AUGH!
RI
RI
RI
RI
RI
BASHAAA (SPLAAAT)

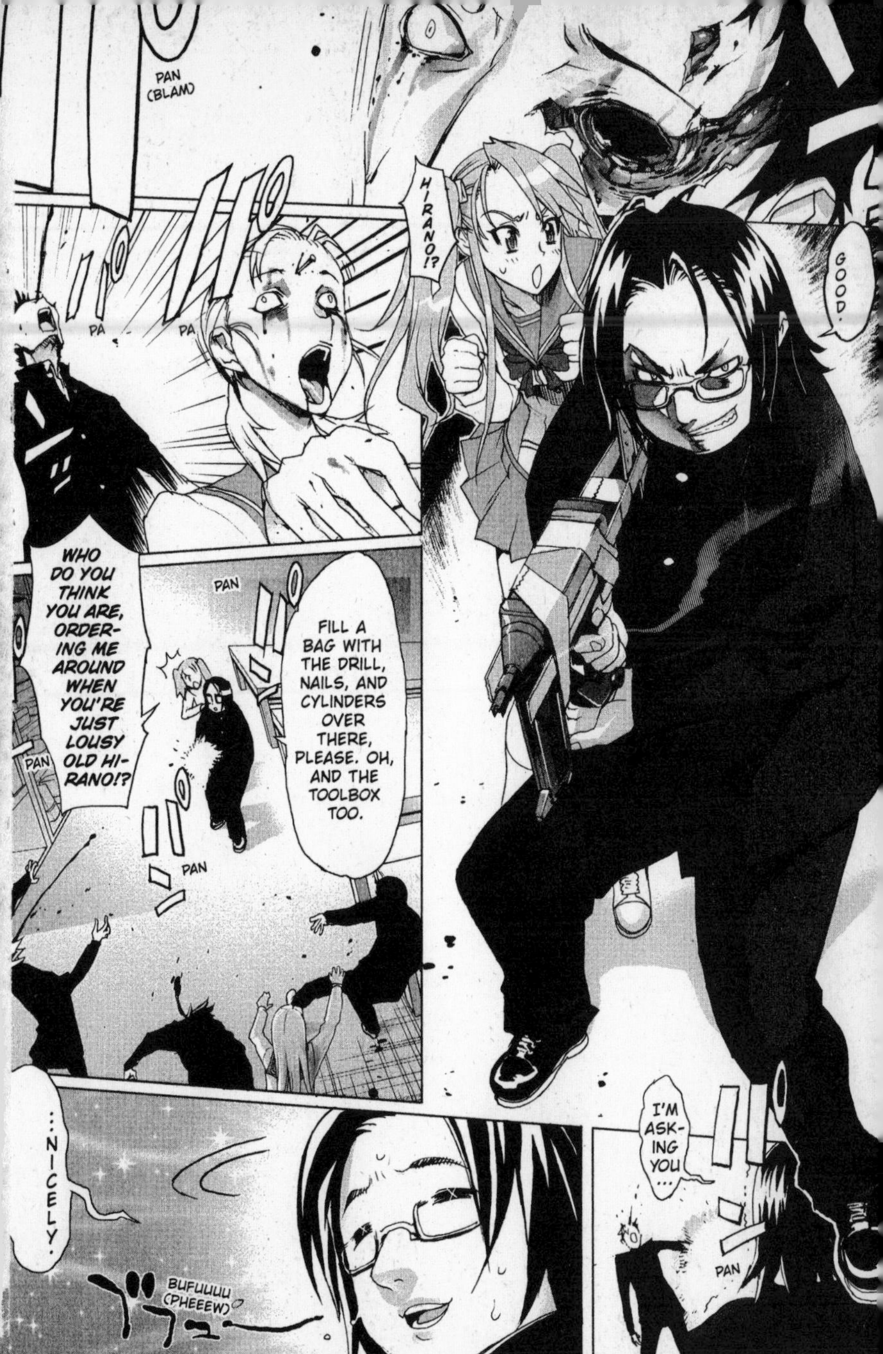
HIRANO!?
GOOD.
PAN
(BLAM)
PA
PA
FILL A BAG WITH THE DRILL, NAILS, AND CYLINDERS OVER THERE, PLEASE. OH, AND THE TOOLBOX TOO.
PAN
WHO DO YOU THINK YOU ARE, ORDERING ME AROUND WHEN YOU'RE JUST LOUSY OLD HIRANO!?
PAN
PAN
I'M ASKING YOU...
PAN
...NICELY.
BUFUUUU
(PHEEEW)

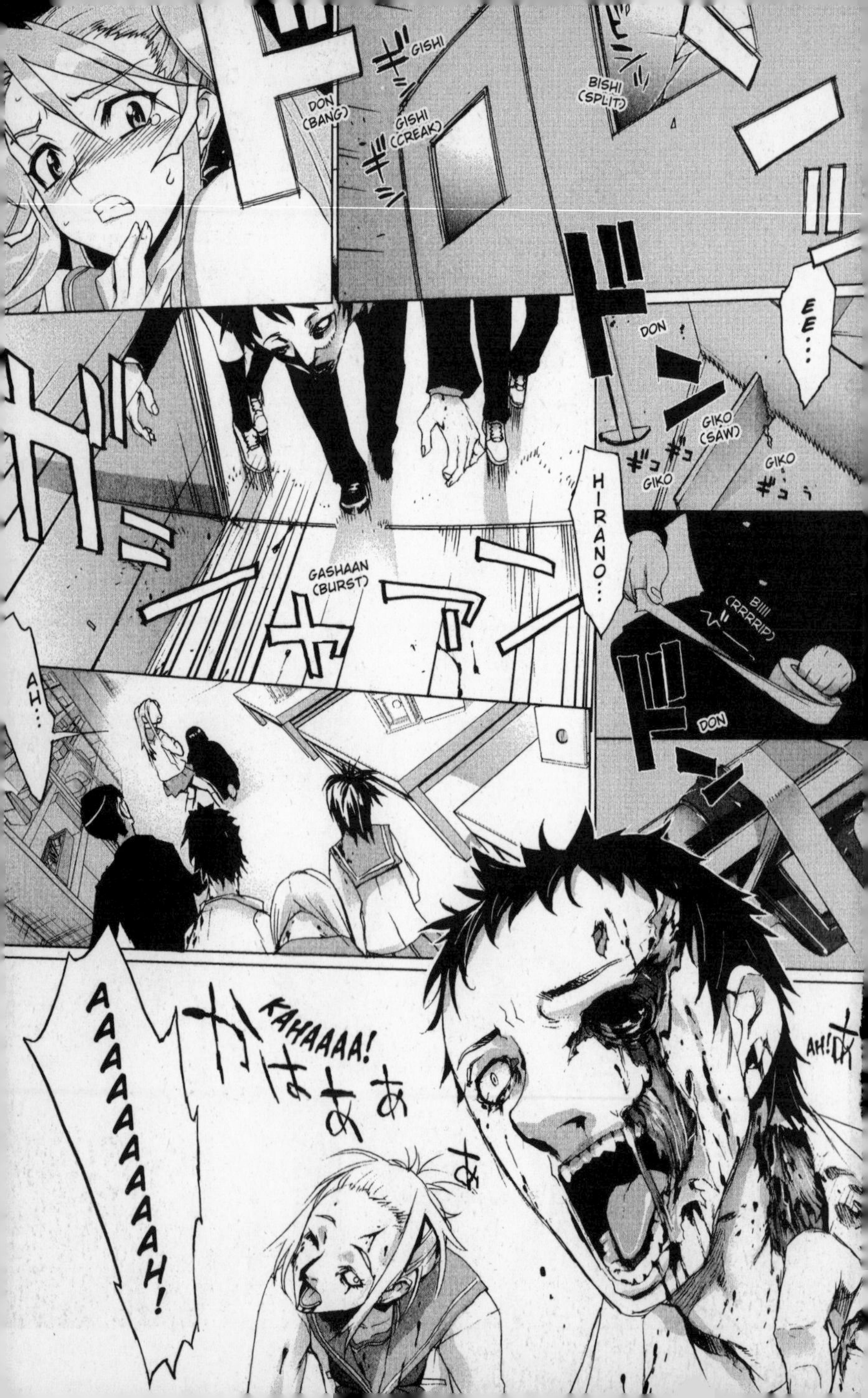

BISHI (SPLIT)
EE...
GISHI
GISHI (CREAK)
DON (BANG)
DON
GIKO (SAW)
GIKO
GIKO
HIRANO...
BIIII (RRRRIP)
DON
GASHAAN (BURST)
AH...
AH!
KAHAAAAA!
AAAAAAAAAAAH!

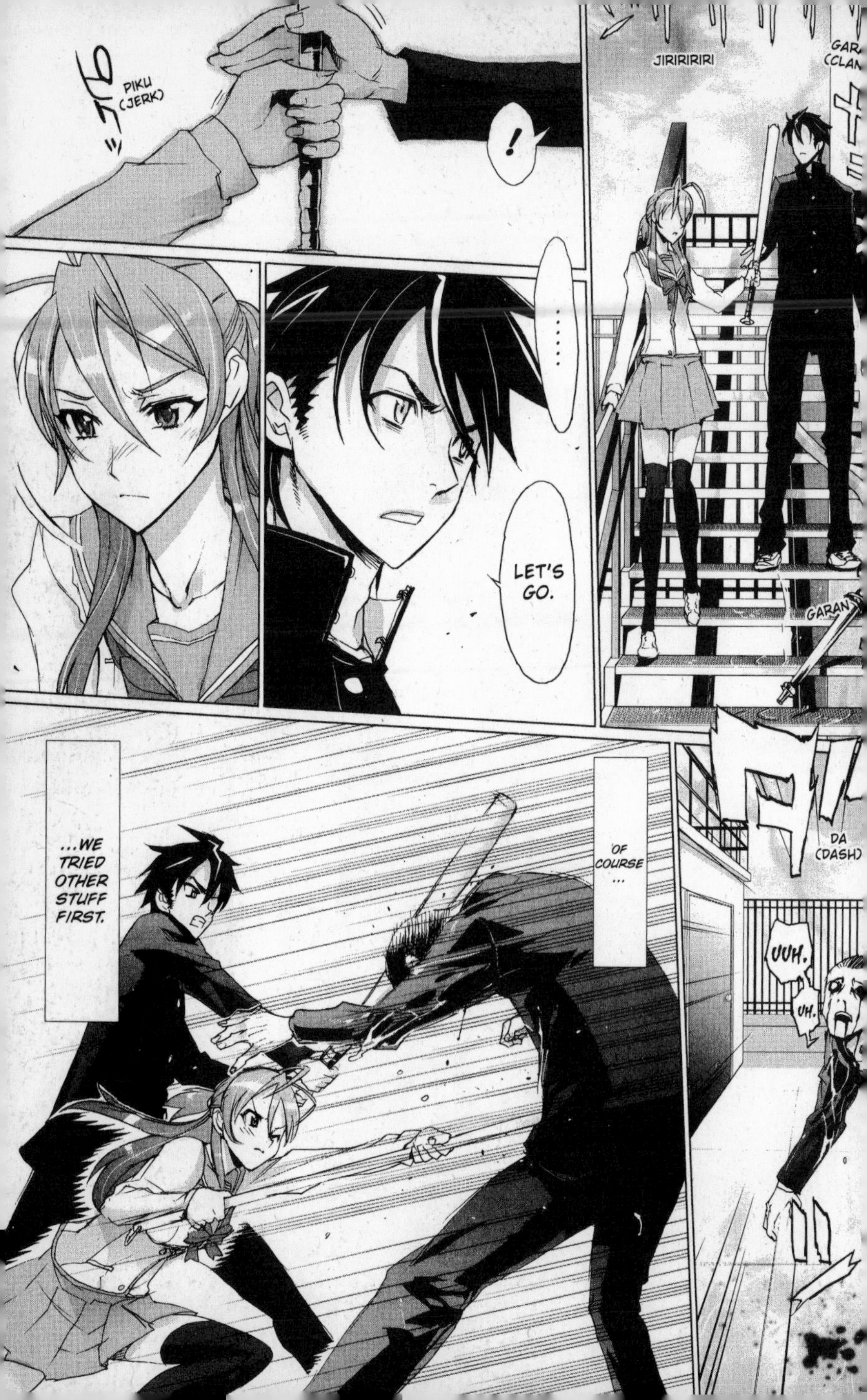

JIRIRIRIRI
GARA
(CLAN
GARAN
PIKU (JERK)
!
......
LET'S GO.
DA (DASH)
UUH.
UH.
OF COURSE ...
...WE TRIED OTHER STUFF FIRST.

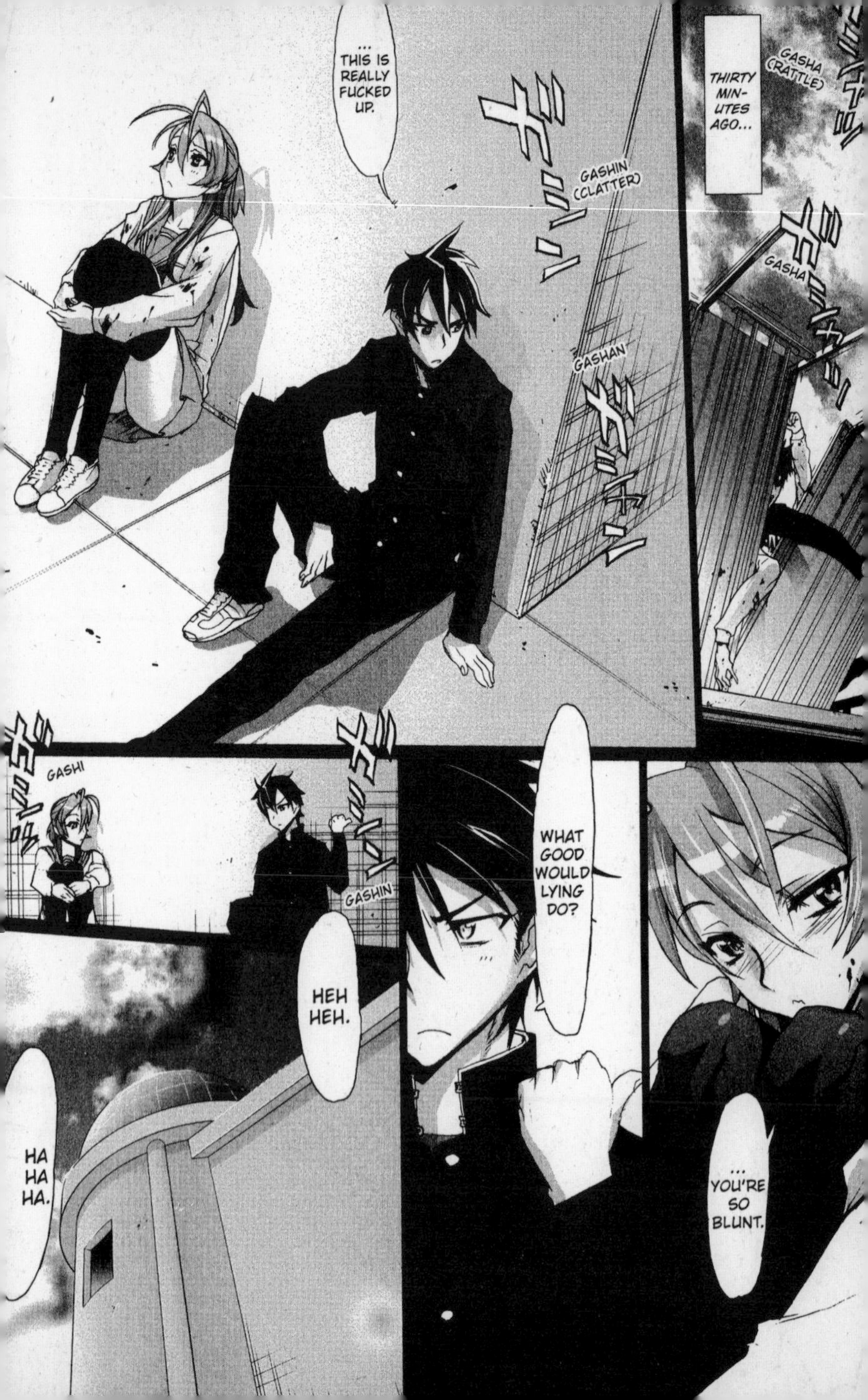
THIRTY MIN-UTES AGO...
GASHA (RATTLE)
GASHA
... THIS IS REALLY FUCKED UP.
GASHIN (CLATTER)
GASHAN
... YOU'RE SO BLUNT.
WHAT GOOD WOULD LYING DO?
GASHIN
GASHI
HEH HEH.
HA HA HA.

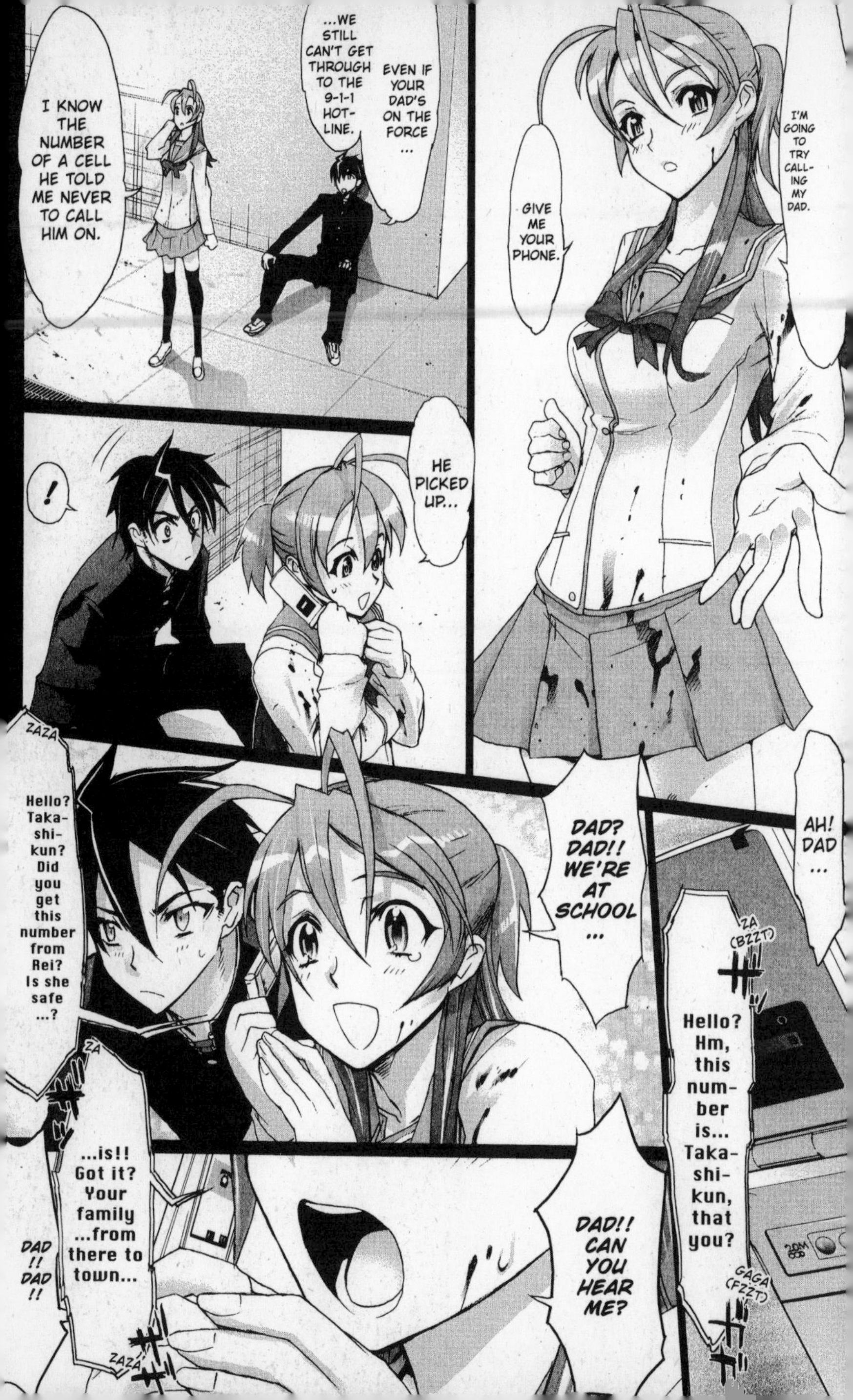
I'M GOING TO TRY CALLING MY DAD.
GIVE ME YOUR PHONE.
EVEN IF YOUR DAD'S ON THE FORCE ...
...WE STILL CAN'T GET THROUGH TO THE 9-1-1 HOT-LINE.
I KNOW THE NUMBER OF A CELL HE TOLD ME NEVER TO CALL HIM ON.
HE PICKED UP...
!
AH! DAD ...
ZA (BZZT)
Hello? Hm, this number is... Takashi-kun, that you?
GAGA (FZZT)
DAD? DAD!! WE'RE AT SCHOOL ...
ZAZA
Hello? Takashi-kun? Did you get this number from Rei? Is she safe ...?
ZA
DAD!! CAN YOU HEAR ME?
...is!! Got it? Your family ...from there to town...
DAD!! DAD!!
ZAZA

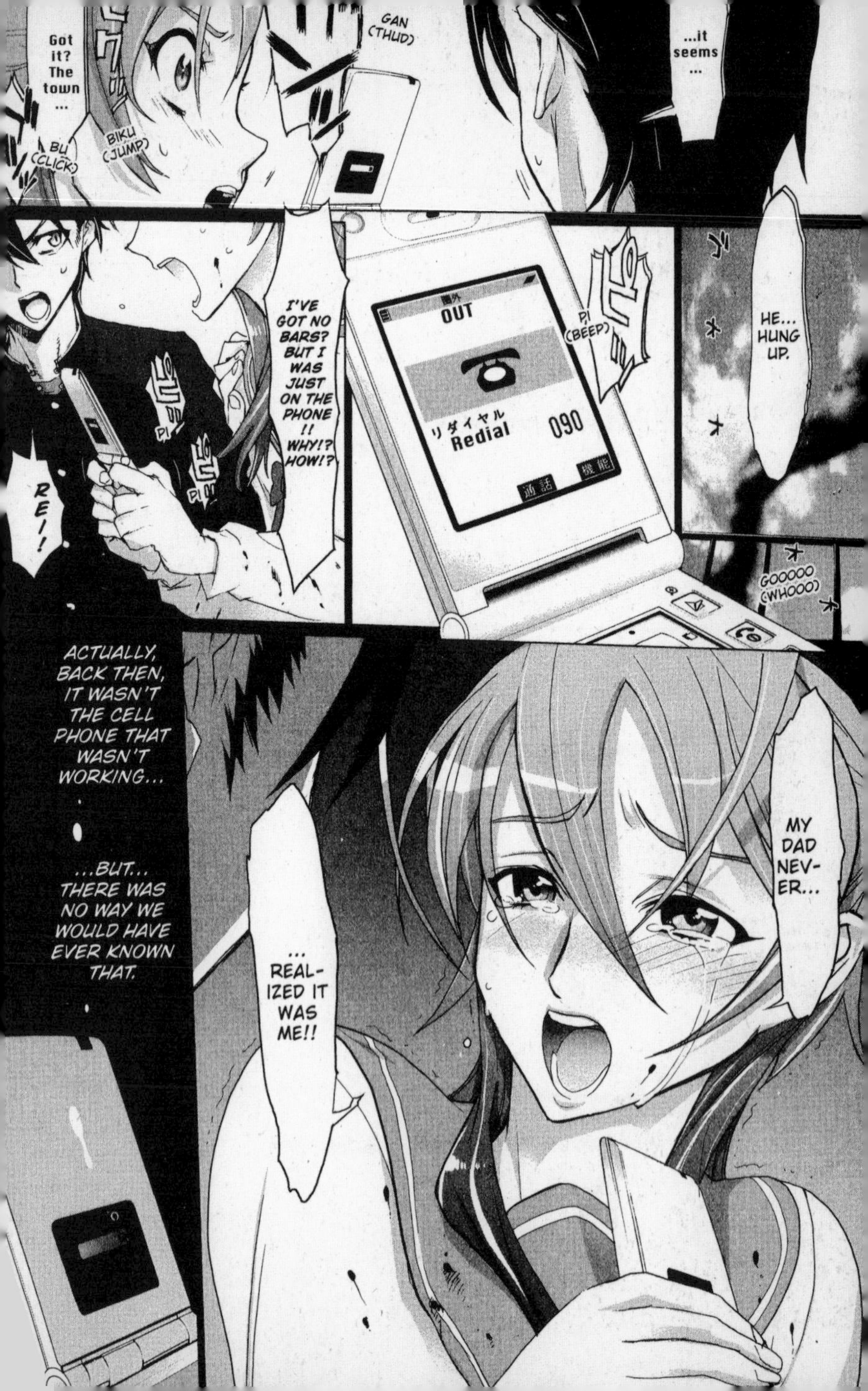

...it seems...
GAN (THUD)
Got it? The town...
BIKU (JUMP)
BU (CLICK)
HE... HUNG UP.
GOOOOO (WHOOO)
PI (BEEP)
圏外
OUT
リダイヤル
Redial
090
通話
機能
I'VE GOT NO BARS? BUT I WAS JUST ON THE PHONE!! WHY!? HOW!?
RE I!!
MY DAD NEVER...
...REALIZED IT WAS ME!!
ACTUALLY, BACK THEN, IT WASN'T THE CELL PHONE THAT WASN'T WORKING...
...BUT... THERE WAS NO WAY WE WOULD HAVE EVER KNOWN THAT.

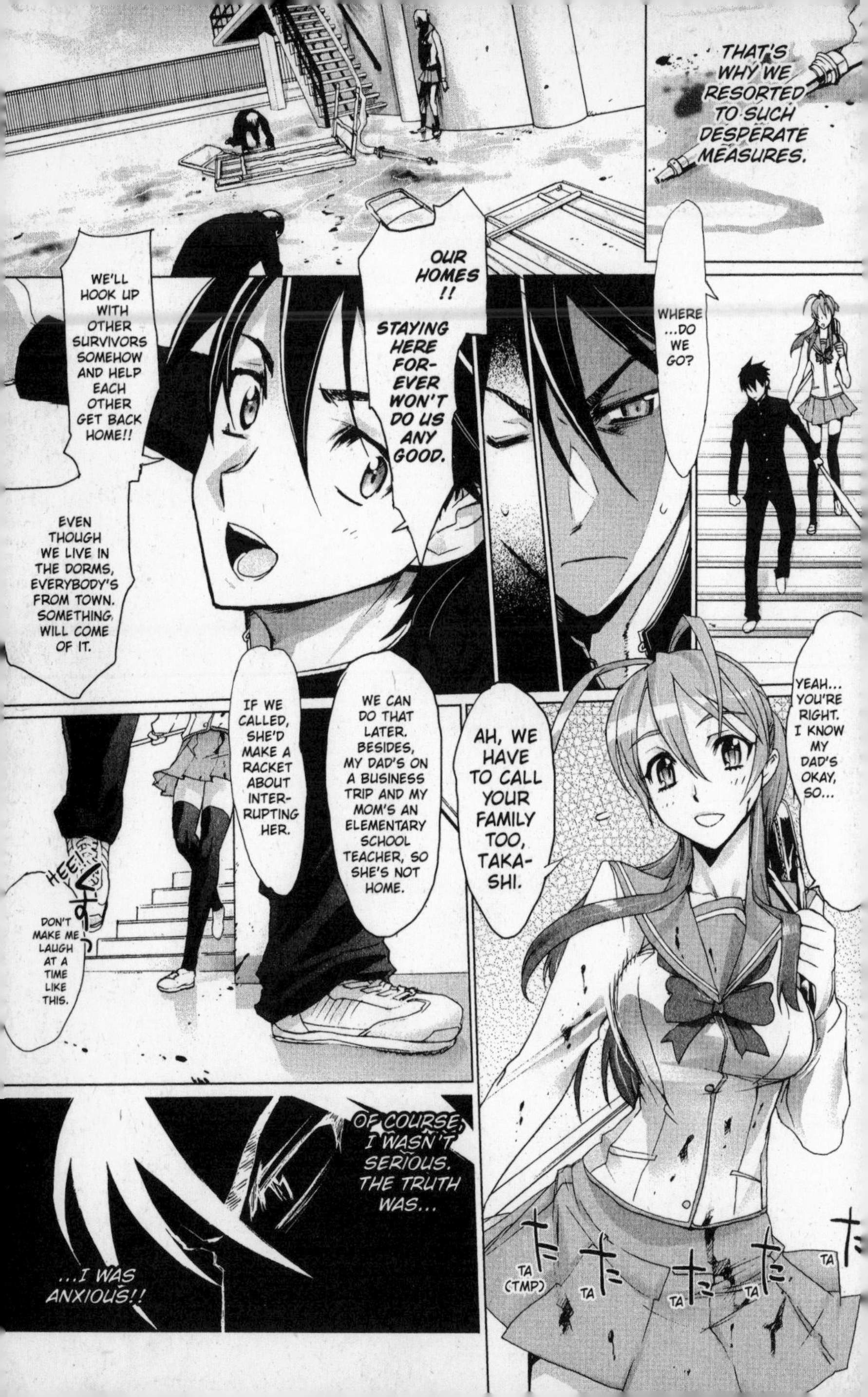
THAT'S WHY WE RESORTED TO SUCH DESPERATE MEASURES.
WHERE ...DO WE GO?
OUR HOMES!!
STAYING HERE FOREVER WON'T DO US ANY GOOD.
WE'LL HOOK UP WITH OTHER SURVIVORS SOMEHOW AND HELP EACH OTHER GET BACK HOME!!
EVEN THOUGH WE LIVE IN THE DORMS, EVERYBODY'S FROM TOWN. SOMETHING WILL COME OF IT.
YEAH... YOU'RE RIGHT. I KNOW MY DAD'S OKAY, SO...
AH, WE HAVE TO CALL YOUR FAMILY TOO, TAKASHI.
TA (TMP) TA TA TA TA
WE CAN DO THAT LATER. BESIDES, MY DAD'S ON A BUSINESS TRIP AND MY MOM'S AN ELEMENTARY SCHOOL TEACHER, SO SHE'S NOT HOME.
IF WE CALLED, SHE'D MAKE A RACKET ABOUT INTERRUPTING HER.
HEE!!
DON'T MAKE ME LAUGH AT A TIME LIKE THIS.
...
OF COURSE, I WASN'T SERIOUS. THE TRUTH WAS...
...I WAS ANXIOUS!!

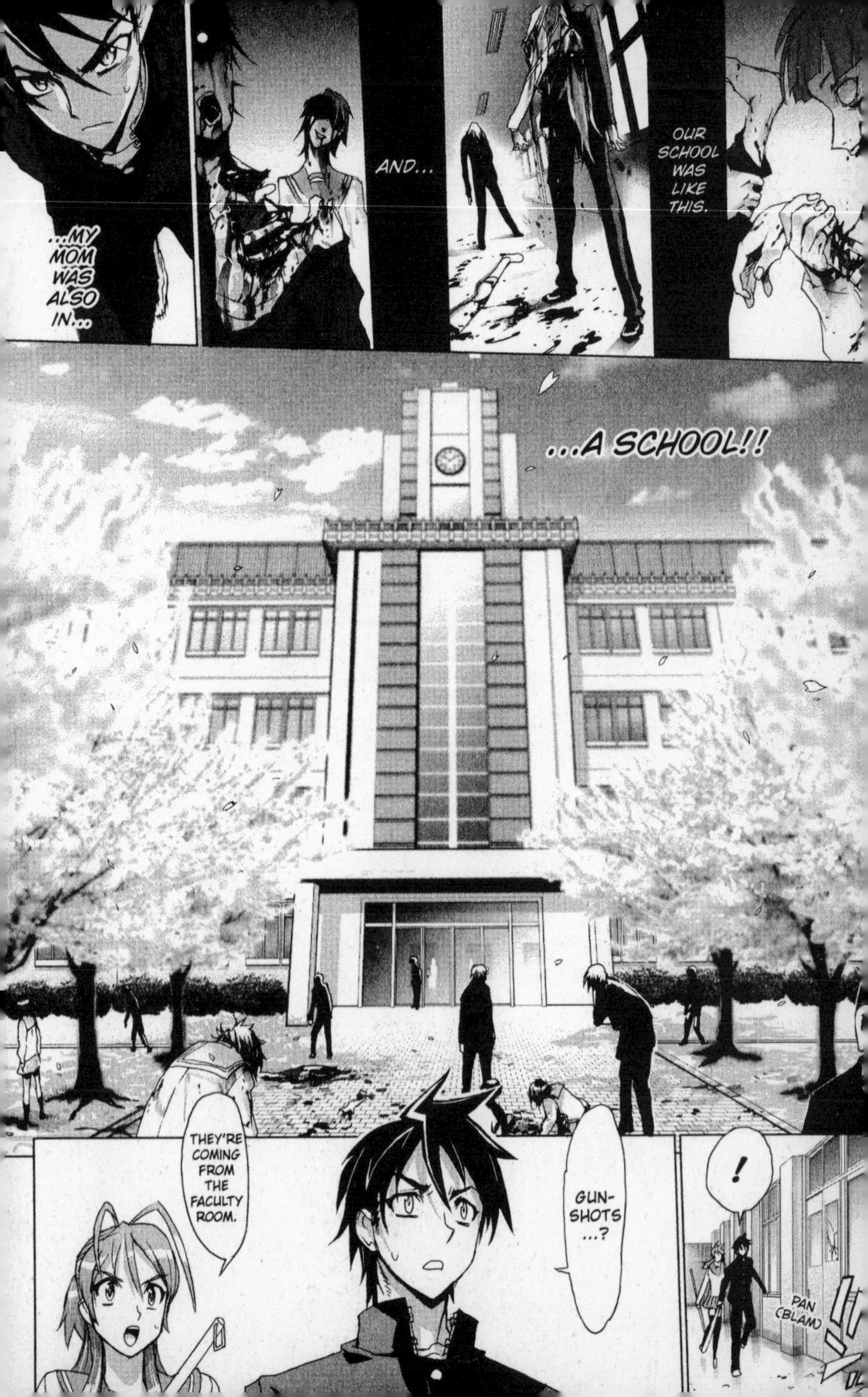
OUR SCHOOL WAS LIKE THIS.
AND...
...MY MOM WAS ALSO IN...
...A SCHOOL!!
!
PAN (BLAM)
GUN-SHOTS ...?
THEY'RE COMING FROM THE FACULTY ROOM.

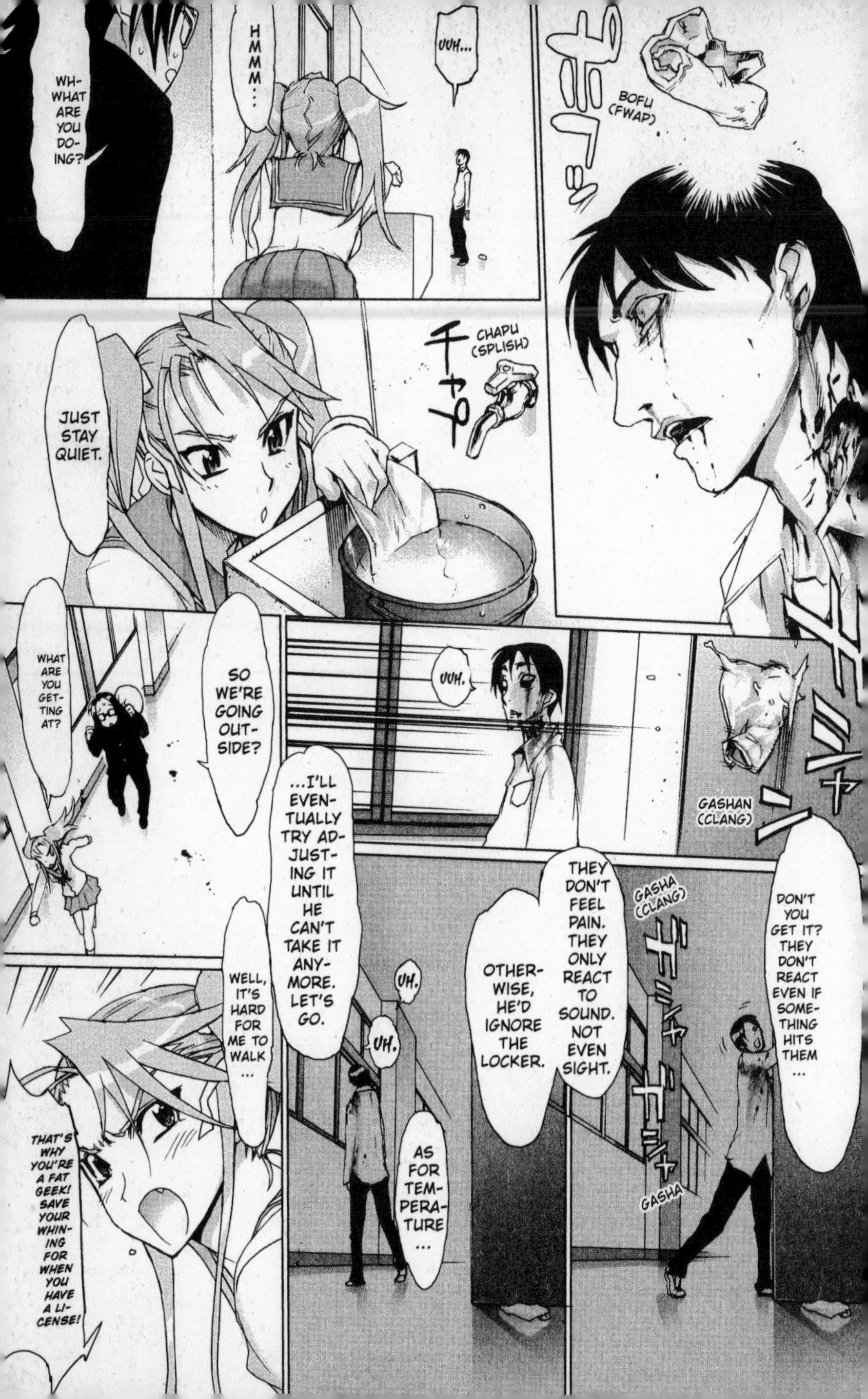

BOFU (FWAP)
UUH...
HMMM...
WH-WHAT ARE YOU DOING?
CHAPU (SPLISH)
JUST STAY QUIET.
GASHAN (CLANG)
UUH.
DON'T YOU GET IT? THEY DON'T REACT EVEN IF SOMETHING HITS THEM...
GASHA (CLANG)
GASHA
THEY DON'T FEEL PAIN. THEY ONLY REACT TO SOUND. NOT EVEN SIGHT.
OTHERWISE, HE'D IGNORE THE LOCKER.
UH.
UH.
AS FOR TEMPERATURE...
...I'LL EVENTUALLY TRY ADJUSTING IT UNTIL HE CAN'T TAKE IT ANYMORE. LET'S GO.
SO WE'RE GOING OUTSIDE?
WHAT ARE YOU GETTING AT?
WELL, IT'S HARD FOR ME TO WALK...
THAT'S WHY YOU'RE A FAT GEEK! SAVE YOUR WHINING FOR WHEN YOU HAVE A LICENSE!

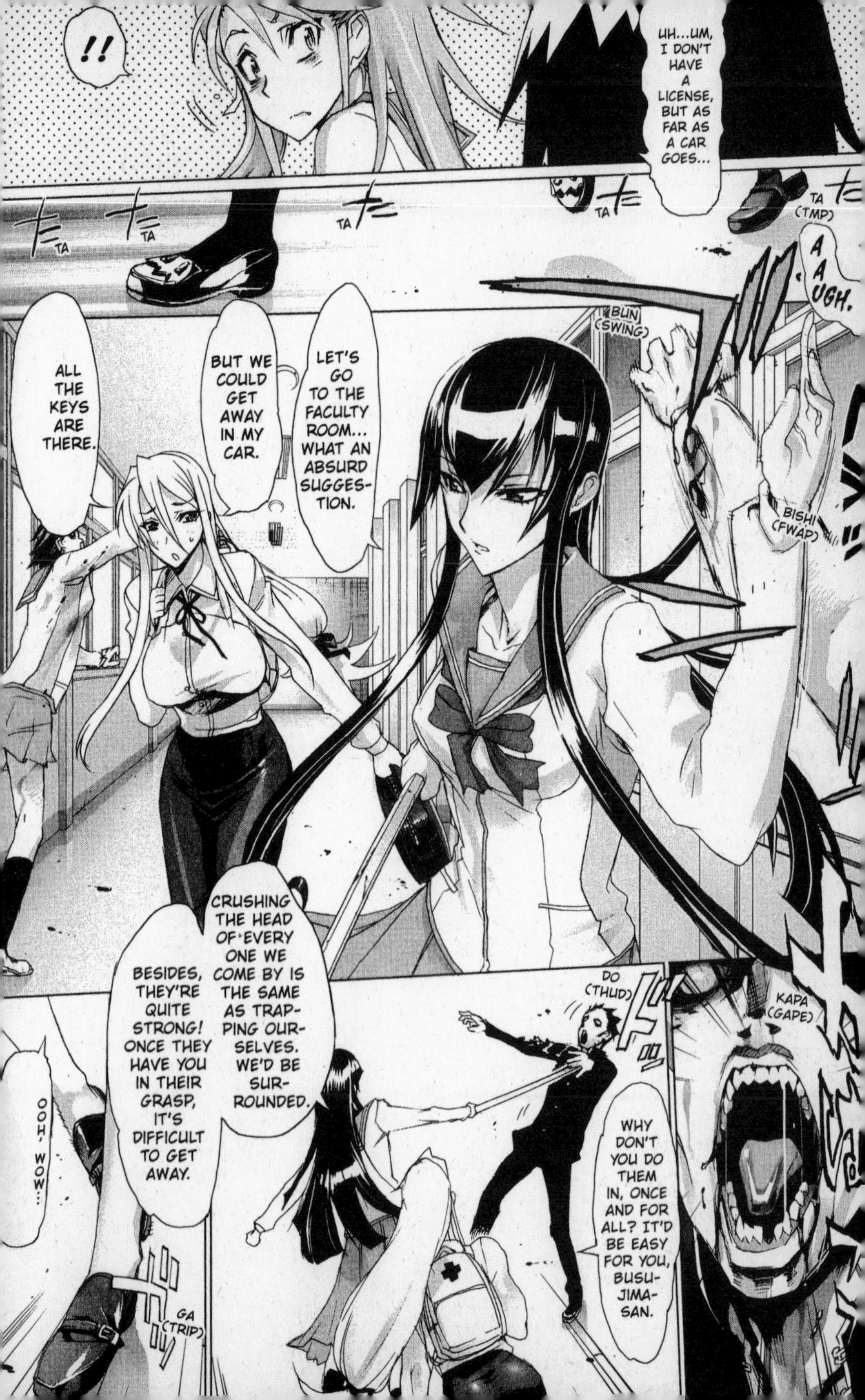
UH...UM, I DON'T HAVE A LICENSE, BUT AS FAR AS A CAR GOES...
!!
TA (TMP)
TA
TA
TA
TA
A A A UGH.
BUN (SWING)
BISHI (FWAP)
LET'S GO TO THE FACULTY ROOM... WHAT AN ABSURD SUGGESTION.
BUT WE COULD GET AWAY IN MY CAR.
ALL THE KEYS ARE THERE.
KAPA (GAPE)
DO (THUD)
WHY DON'T YOU DO THEM IN, ONCE AND FOR ALL? IT'D BE EASY FOR YOU, BUSUJIMA-SAN.
CRUSHING THE HEAD OF EVERY ONE WE COME BY IS THE SAME AS TRAPPING OURSELVES. WE'D BE SURROUNDED.
BESIDES, THEY'RE QUITE STRONG! ONCE THEY HAVE YOU IN THEIR GRASP, IT'S DIFFICULT TO GET AWAY.
GA (TRIP)
OOH, WOW...

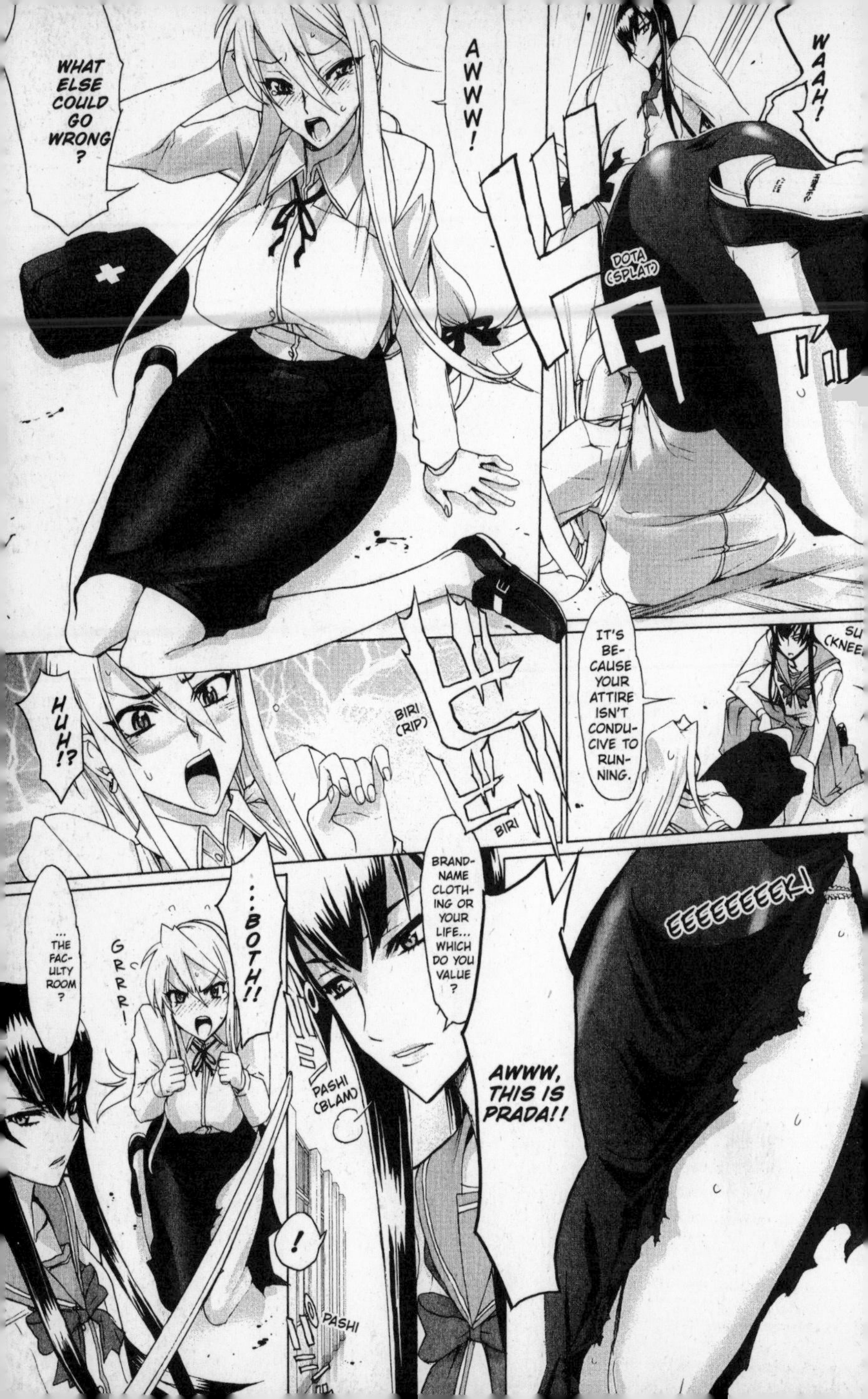

WAAH!
DOTA (SPLAT)
AWWW!
WHAT ELSE COULD GO WRONG?
SU (KNEE
IT'S BECAUSE YOUR ATTIRE ISN'T CONDUCIVE TO RUNNING.
BIRI (RIP)
BIRI
HUH!?
EEEEEEEEK!
AWWW, THIS IS PRADA!!
BRAND-NAME CLOTHING OR YOUR LIFE... WHICH DO YOU VALUE?
PASHI (BLAM)
!
PASHI
...BOTH!!
GRRR!
...THE FACULTY ROOM?

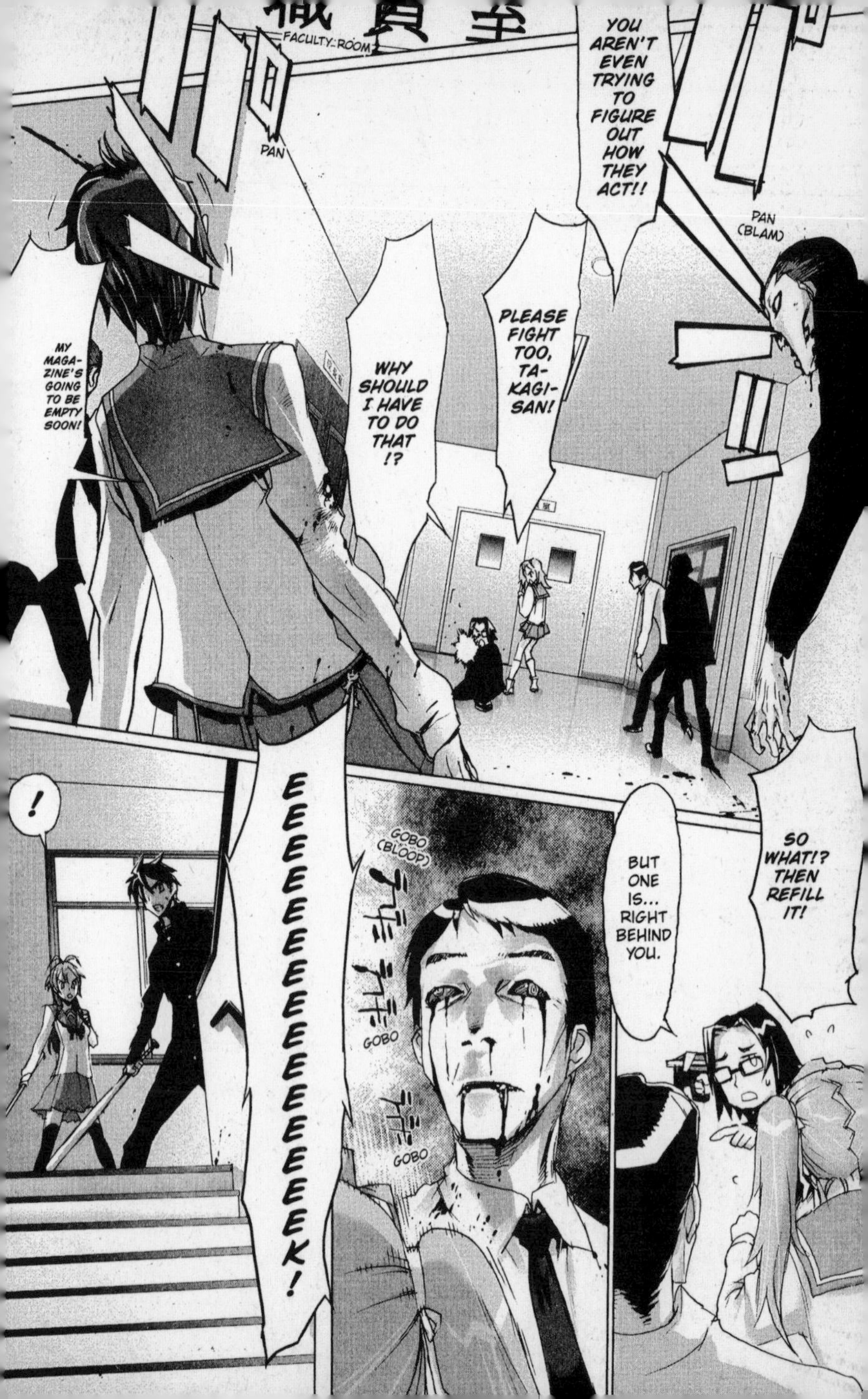
FACULTY ROOM
YOU AREN'T EVEN TRYING TO FIGURE OUT HOW THEY ACT!!
PAN (BLAM)
PAN
PLEASE FIGHT TOO, TA-KAGI-SAN!
WHY SHOULD I HAVE TO DO THAT!?
MY MAGA-ZINE'S GOING TO BE EMPTY SOON!
SO WHAT!? THEN REFILL IT!
BUT ONE IS... RIGHT BEHIND YOU.
GOBO (BLOOP)
GOBO
GOBO
EEEEEEEEEEEEEK!
!

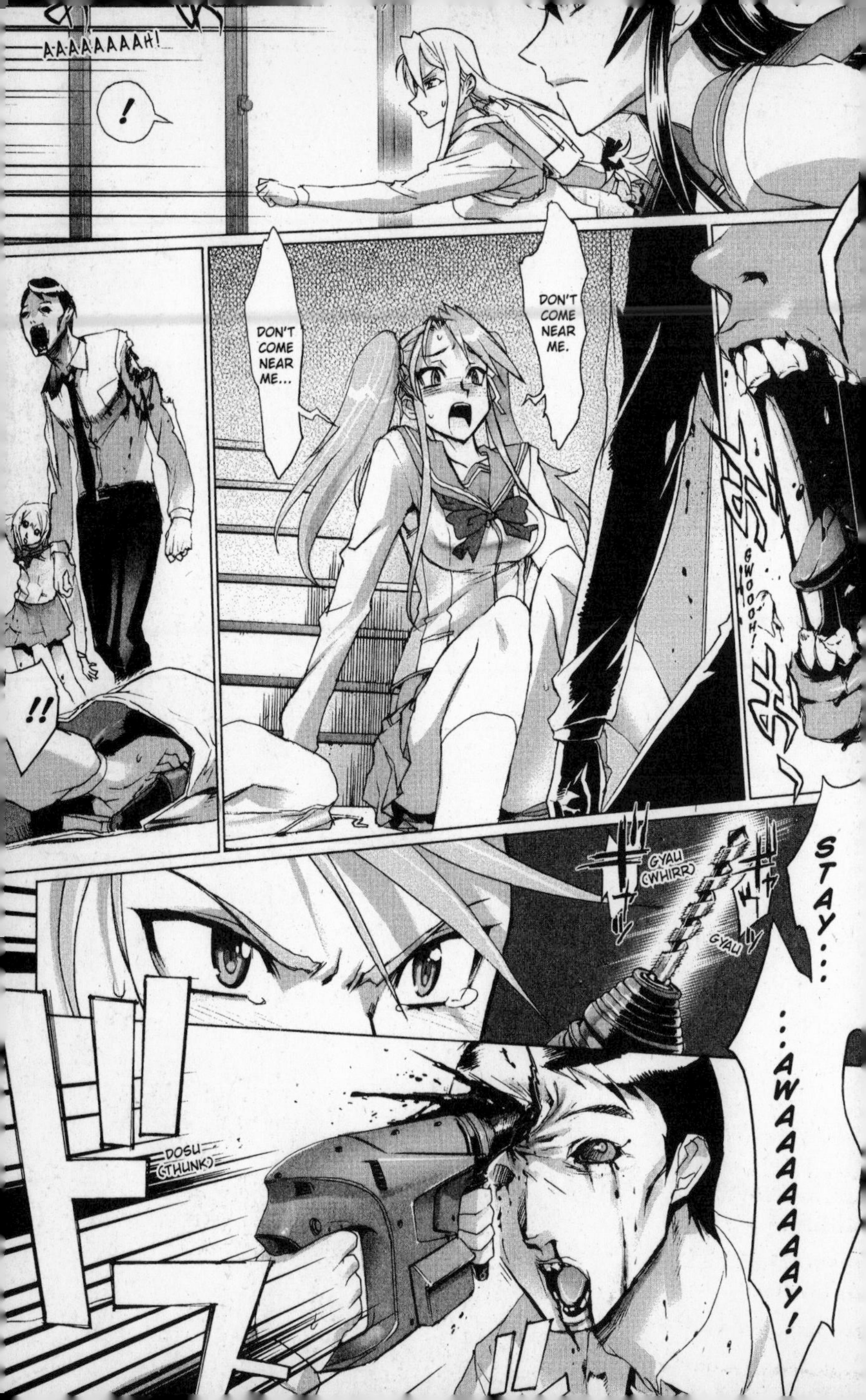
A-A-A-A-A-A-A-AH!
!
DON'T COME NEAR ME.
DON'T COME NEAR ME...
GWOOOH!
!!
STAY...
GYAU (WHIRR)
GYAU
...AWAAAAAAAAAY!
DOSU (THUNK)

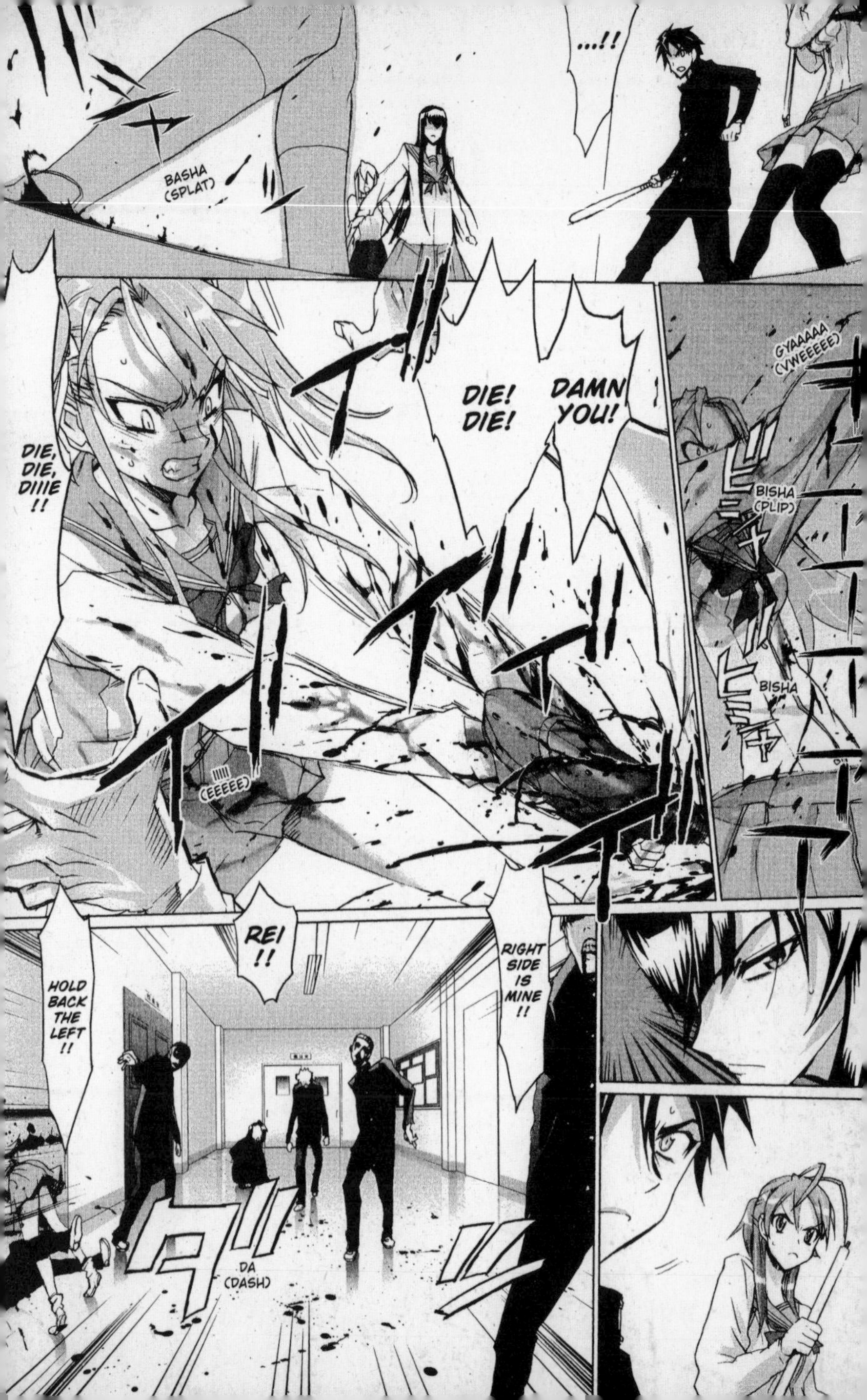
...!!
BASHA (SPLAT)
GYAAAAA (VWEEEEEE)
BISHA (PLIP)
BISHA
DAMN YOU!
DIE! DIE!
DIE, DIE, DIIIE !!
IIIII (EEEEE)
RIGHT SIDE IS MINE !!
REI !!
HOLD BACK THE LEFT !!
DA (DASH)

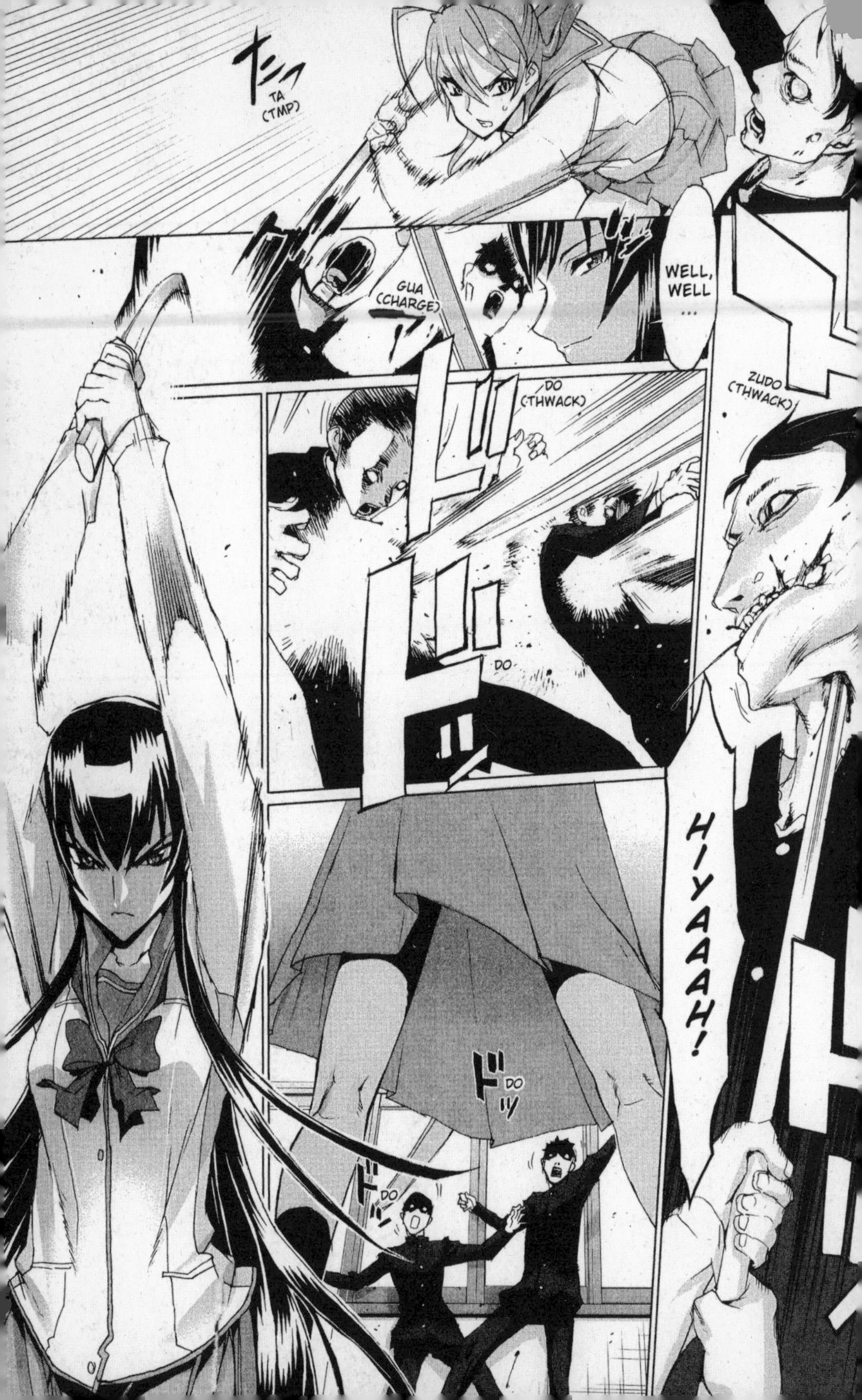
ZUDO (THWACK)
HIYAAAAH!
TA (TMP)
WELL, WELL ...
GUA (CHARGE)
DO (THWACK)
DO
DO
DO

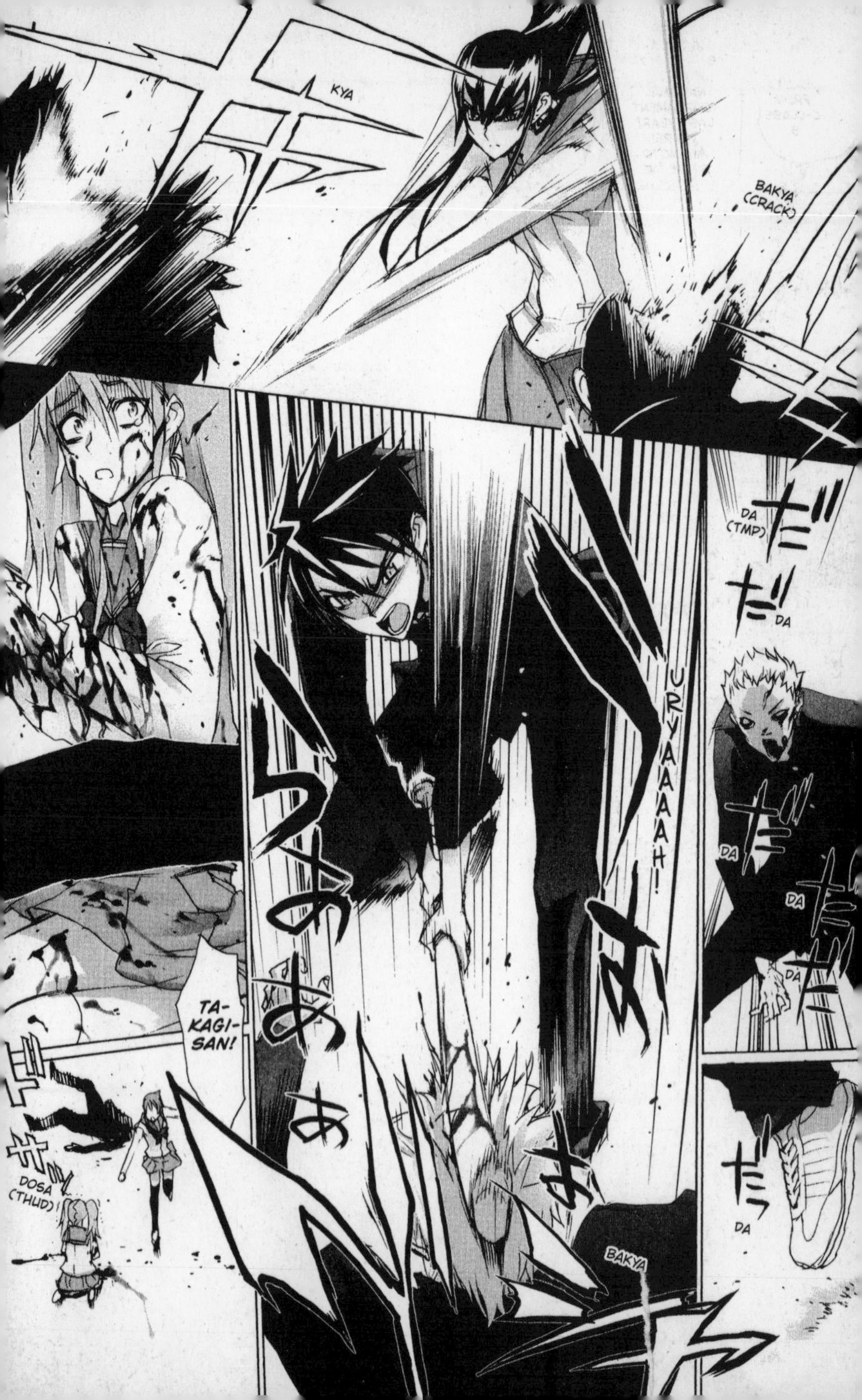

BAKYA (CRACK)
KYA
DA (TMP)
DA
DA
DA
DA
DA
URYAAAAAAH!
BAKYA
TA-KAGI-SAN!
DOSA (THUD)!

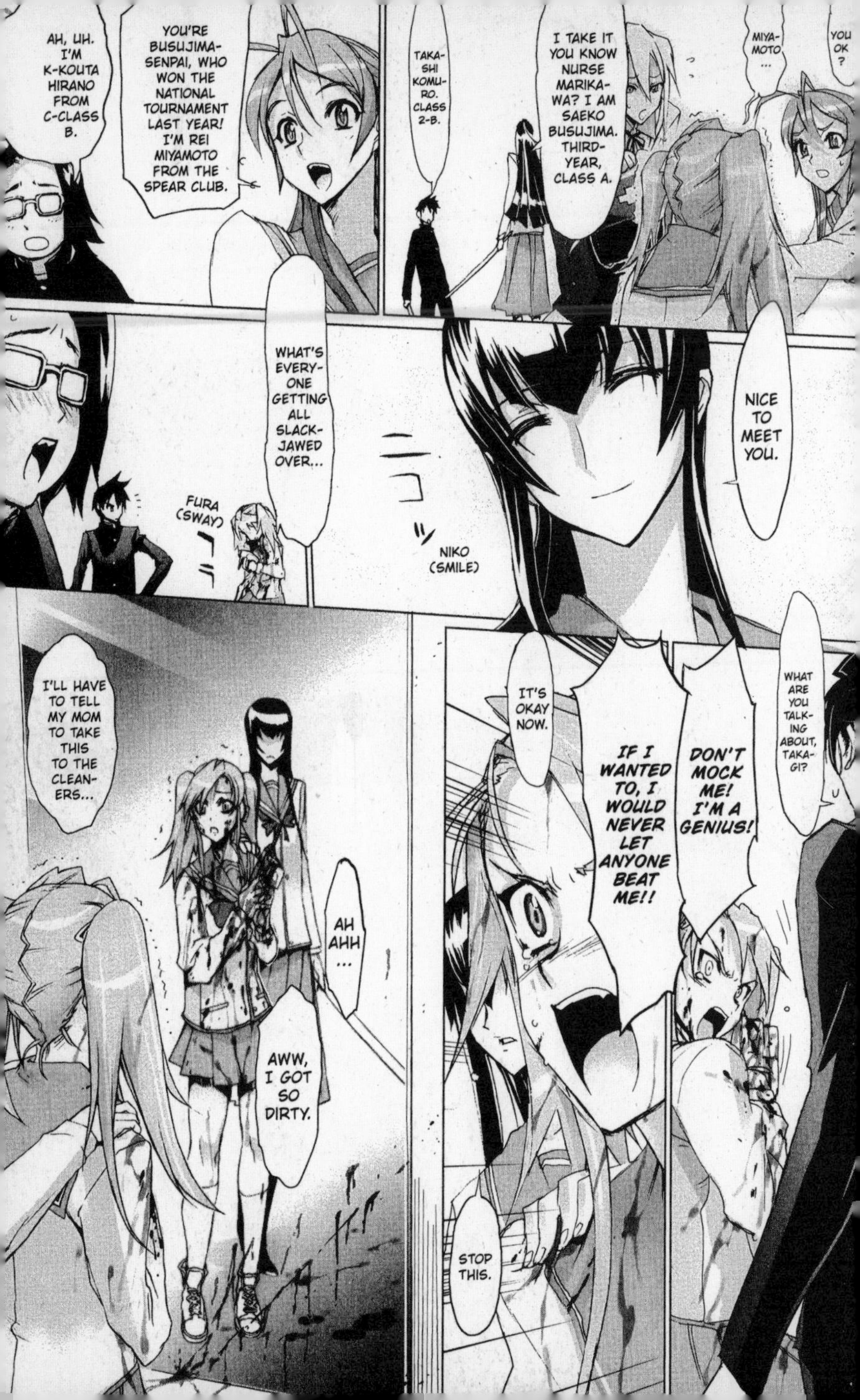

YOU OK?
MIYAMOTO...
I TAKE IT YOU KNOW NURSE MARIKAWA? I AM SAEKO BUSUJIMA. THIRD-YEAR, CLASS A.
TAKASHI KOMURO. CLASS 2-B.
YOU'RE BUSUJIMA-SENPAI, WHO WON THE NATIONAL TOURNAMENT LAST YEAR! I'M REI MIYAMOTO FROM THE SPEAR CLUB.
AH, UH. I'M K-KOUTA HIRANO FROM C-CLASS B.
NICE TO MEET YOU.
NIKO (SMILE)
WHAT'S EVERYONE GETTING ALL SLACK-JAWED OVER...
FURA (SWAY)
WHAT ARE YOU TALKING ABOUT, TAKAGI?
DON'T MOCK ME! I'M A GENIUS!
IF I WANTED TO, I WOULD NEVER LET ANYONE BEAT ME!!
IT'S OKAY NOW.
STOP THIS.
AH AHH...
AWW, I GOT SO DIRTY.
I'LL HAVE TO TELL MY MOM TO TAKE THIS TO THE CLEANERS...

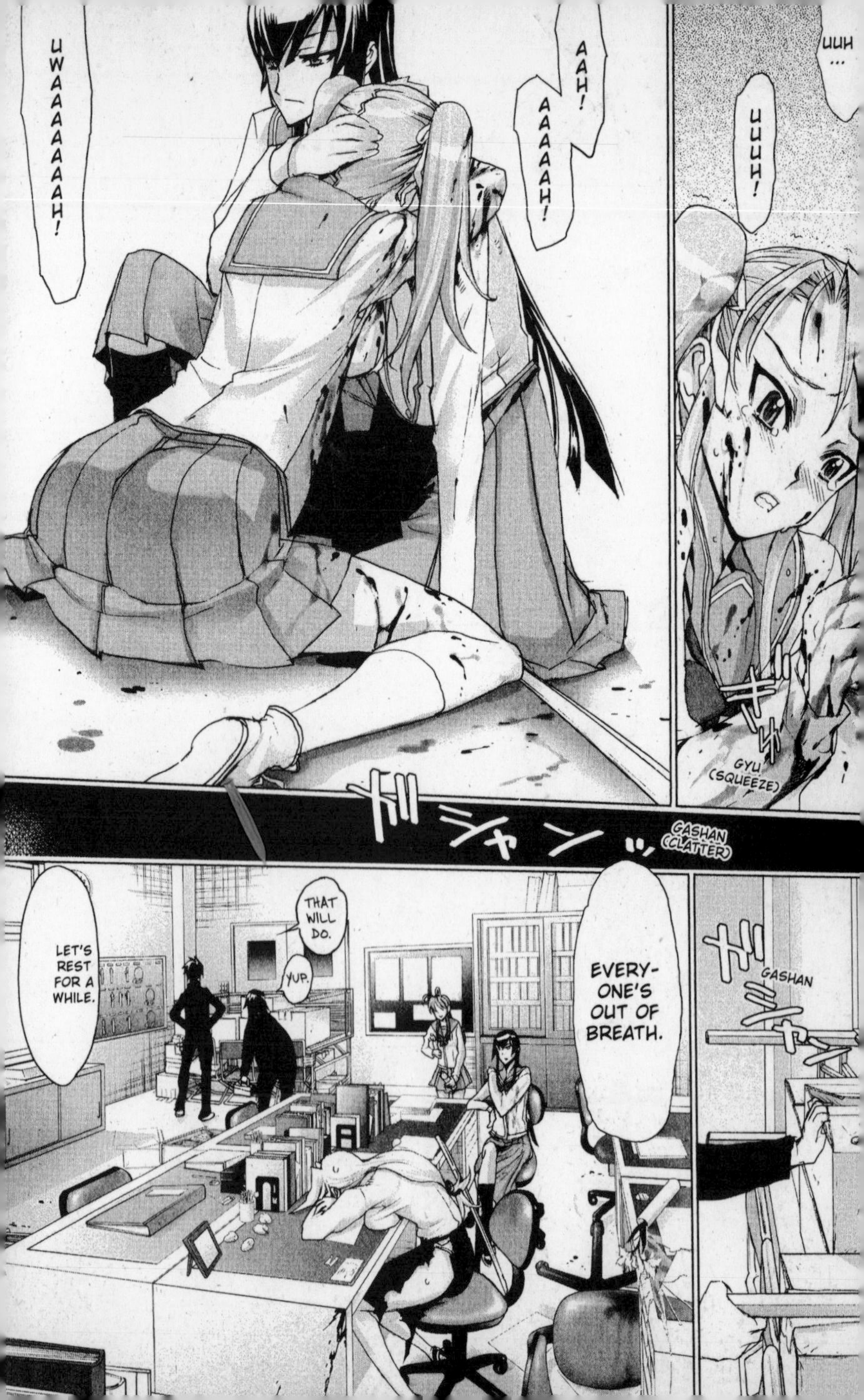
UUH ...
UUUH!
GYU (SQUEEZE)
AAH! AAAAAAH!
UWAAAAAAAAAAH!
GASHAN (CLATTER)
GASHAN
EVERY-ONE'S OUT OF BREATH.
THAT WILL DO.
YUP.
LET'S REST FOR A WHILE.

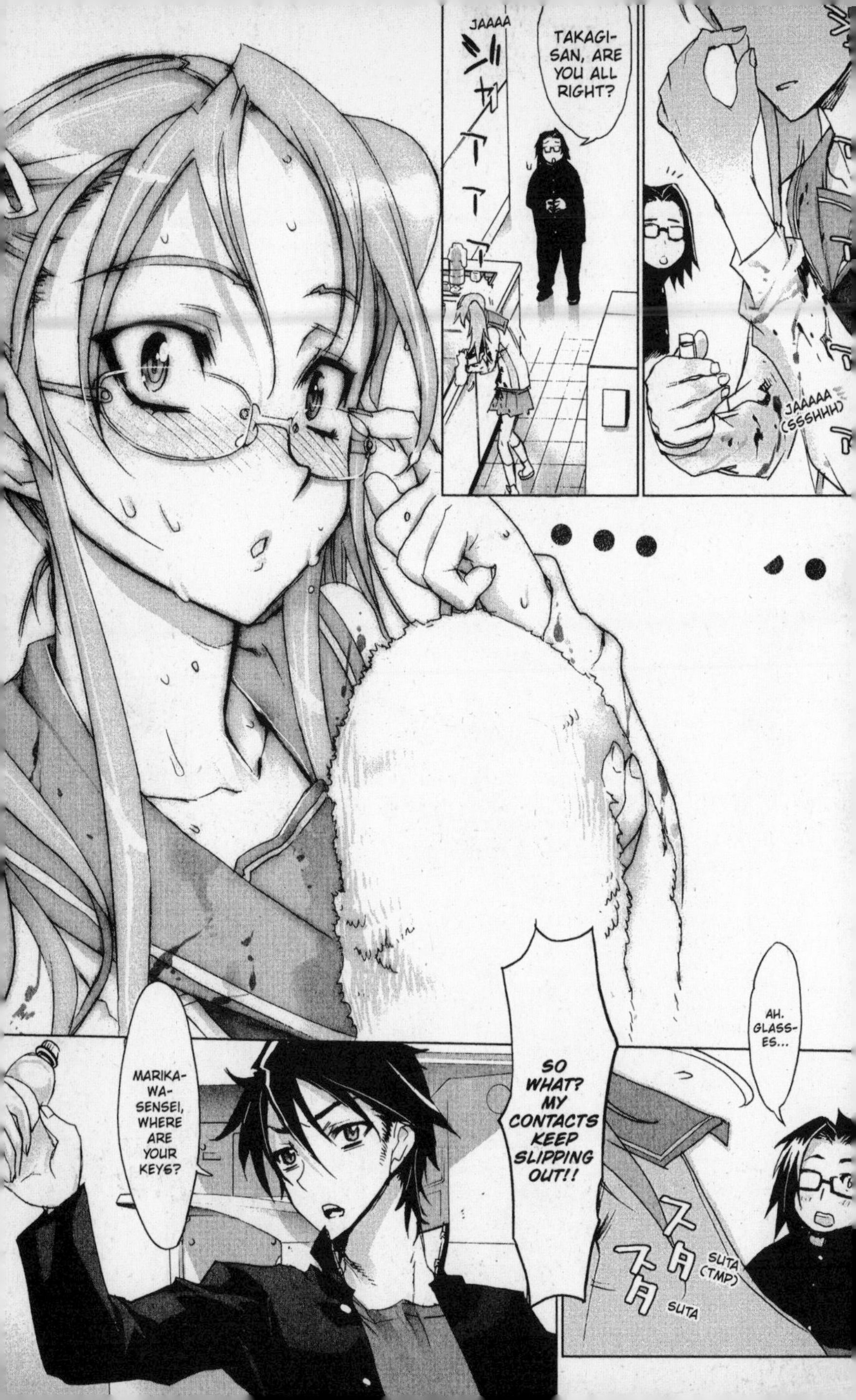
JAAAAA (SSSHHH)
TAKAGI-SAN, ARE YOU ALL RIGHT?
JAAAA
AH. GLASSES...
SO WHAT? MY CONTACTS KEEP SLIPPING OUT!!
SUTA (TMP)
SUTA
MARIKAWA-SENSEI, WHERE ARE YOUR KEYS?

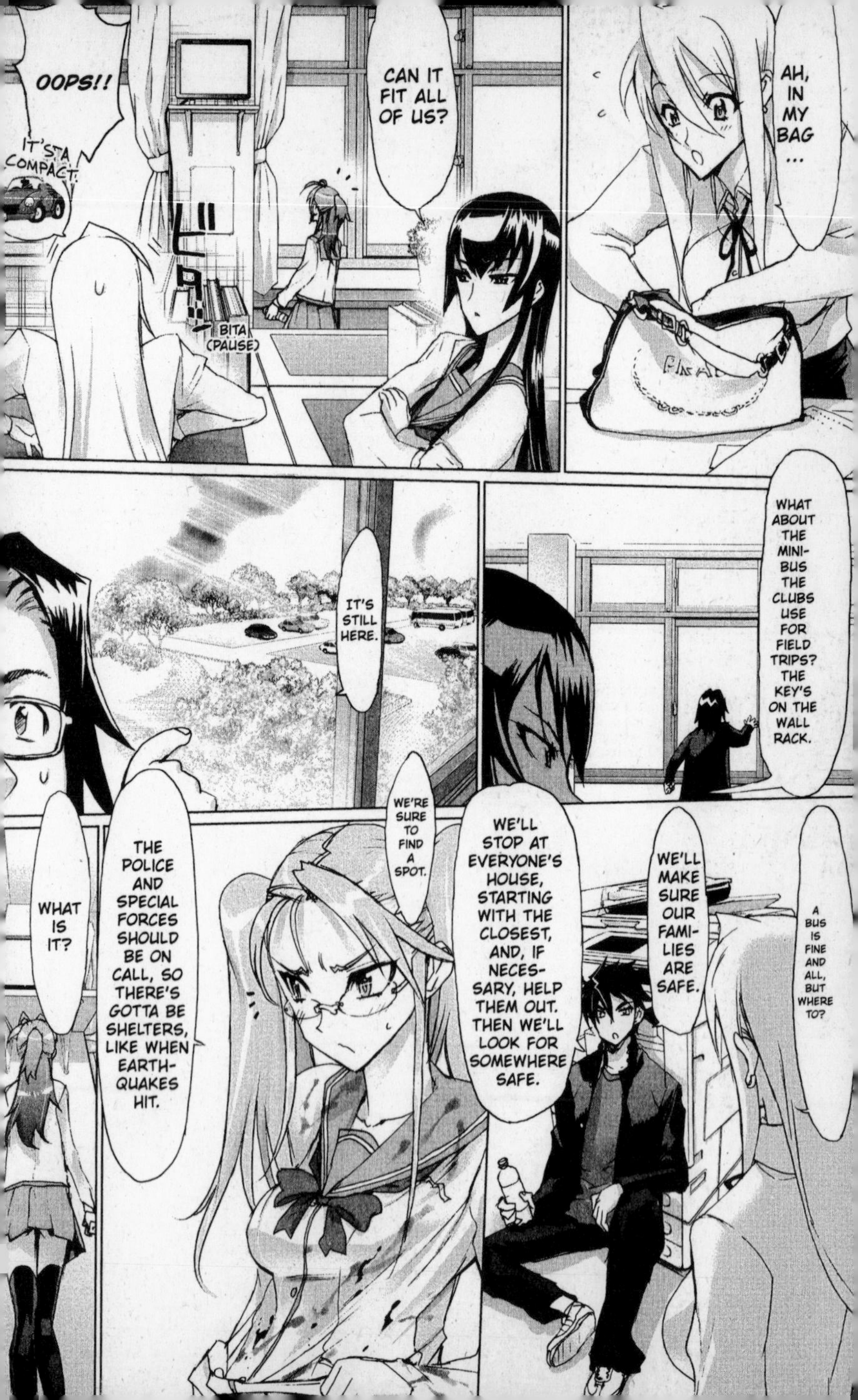
AH, IN MY BAG...
CAN IT FIT ALL OF US?
OOPS!!
IT'S A COMPACT.
BITA (PAUSE)
WHAT ABOUT THE MINI-BUS THE CLUBS USE FOR FIELD TRIPS? THE KEY'S ON THE WALL RACK.
IT'S STILL HERE.
A BUS IS FINE AND ALL, BUT WHERE TO?
WE'LL MAKE SURE OUR FAMILIES ARE SAFE.
WE'LL STOP AT EVERYONE'S HOUSE, STARTING WITH THE CLOSEST, AND, IF NECESSARY, HELP THEM OUT. THEN WE'LL LOOK FOR SOMEWHERE SAFE.
WE'RE SURE TO FIND A SPOT.
THE POLICE AND SPECIAL FORCES SHOULD BE ON CALL, SO THERE'S GOTTA BE SHELTERS, LIKE WHEN EARTHQUAKES HIT.
WHAT IS IT?

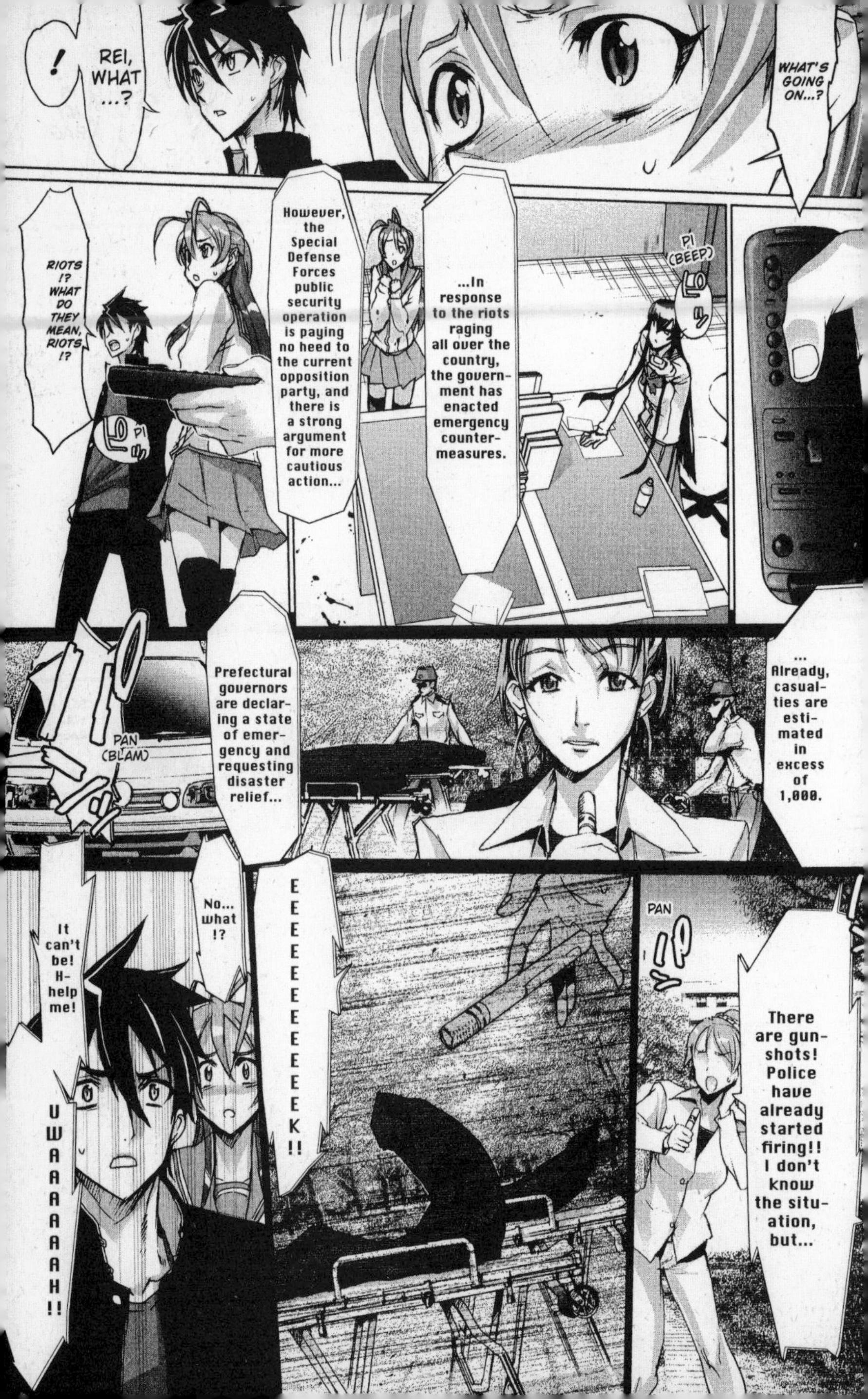
WHAT'S GOING ON...?
!
REI, WHAT ...?
PI (BEEP)
...In response to the riots raging all over the country, the government has enacted emergency counter-measures.
However, the Special Defense Forces public security operation is paying no heed to the current opposition party, and there is a strong argument for more cautious action...
RIOTS!? WHAT DO THEY MEAN, RIOTS!?
PI
...Already, casualties are estimated in excess of 1,000.
Prefectural governors are declaring a state of emergency and requesting disaster relief...
PAN (BLAM)
PAN
There are gunshots! Police have already started firing!! I don't know the situation, but...
EEEEEEEEEEEEEEEEK!!
No... what!?
It can't be! H-help me!
UWAAAAAAAAAH!!

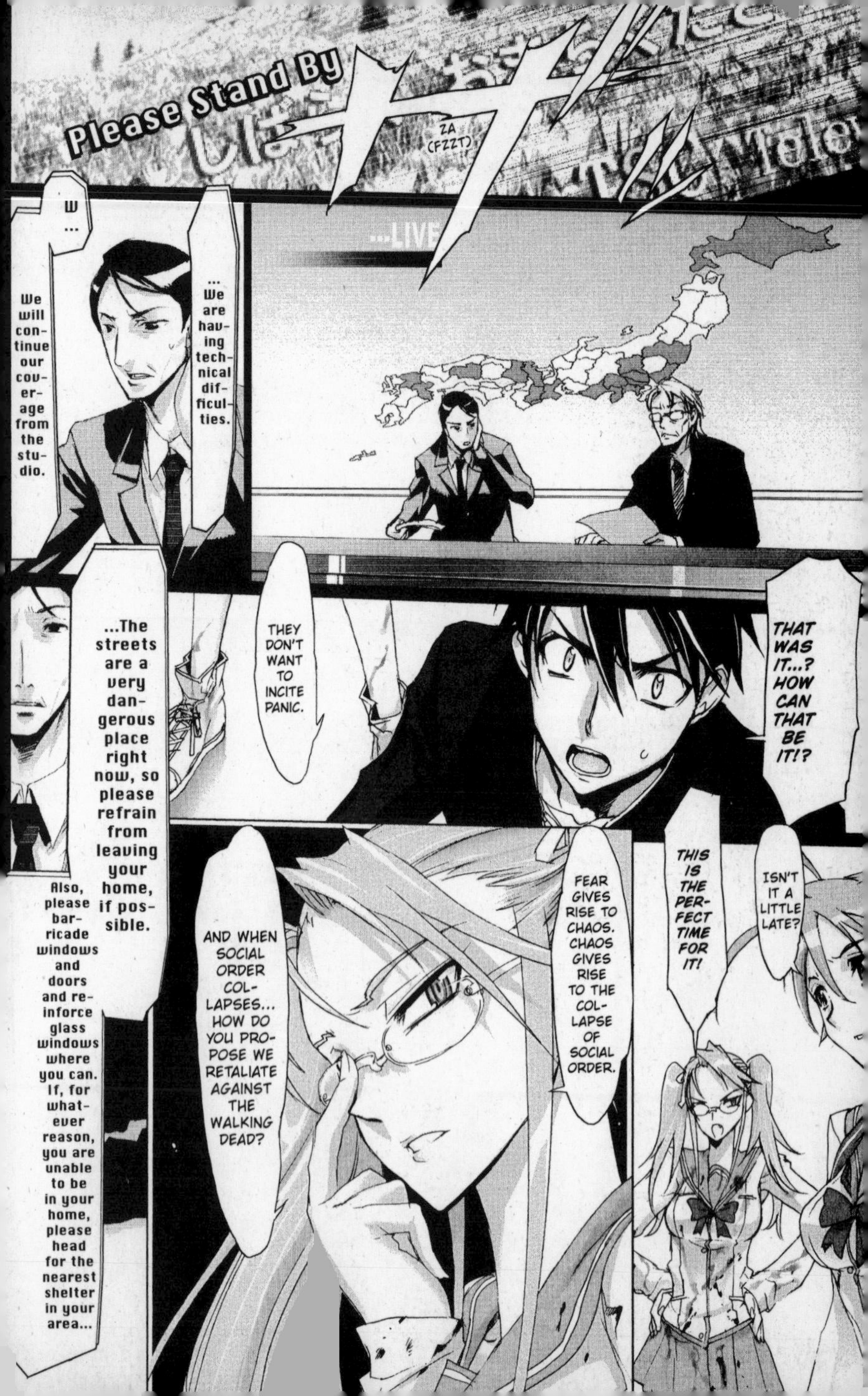
Please Stand By
ZA (FZZT)
...LIVE
W...
...We are having technical difficulties.
We will continue our coverage from the studio.
THAT WAS IT...? HOW CAN THAT BE IT!?
THEY DON'T WANT TO INCITE PANIC.
...The streets are a very dangerous place right now, so please refrain from leaving your home, if possible.
ISN'T IT A LITTLE LATE?
THIS IS THE PERFECT TIME FOR IT!
FEAR GIVES RISE TO CHAOS. CHAOS GIVES RISE TO THE COLLAPSE OF SOCIAL ORDER.
AND WHEN SOCIAL ORDER COLLAPSES... HOW DO YOU PROPOSE WE RETALIATE AGAINST THE WALKING DEAD?
Also, please barricade windows and doors and reinforce glass windows where you can. If, for whatever reason, you are unable to be in your home, please head for the nearest shelter in your area...

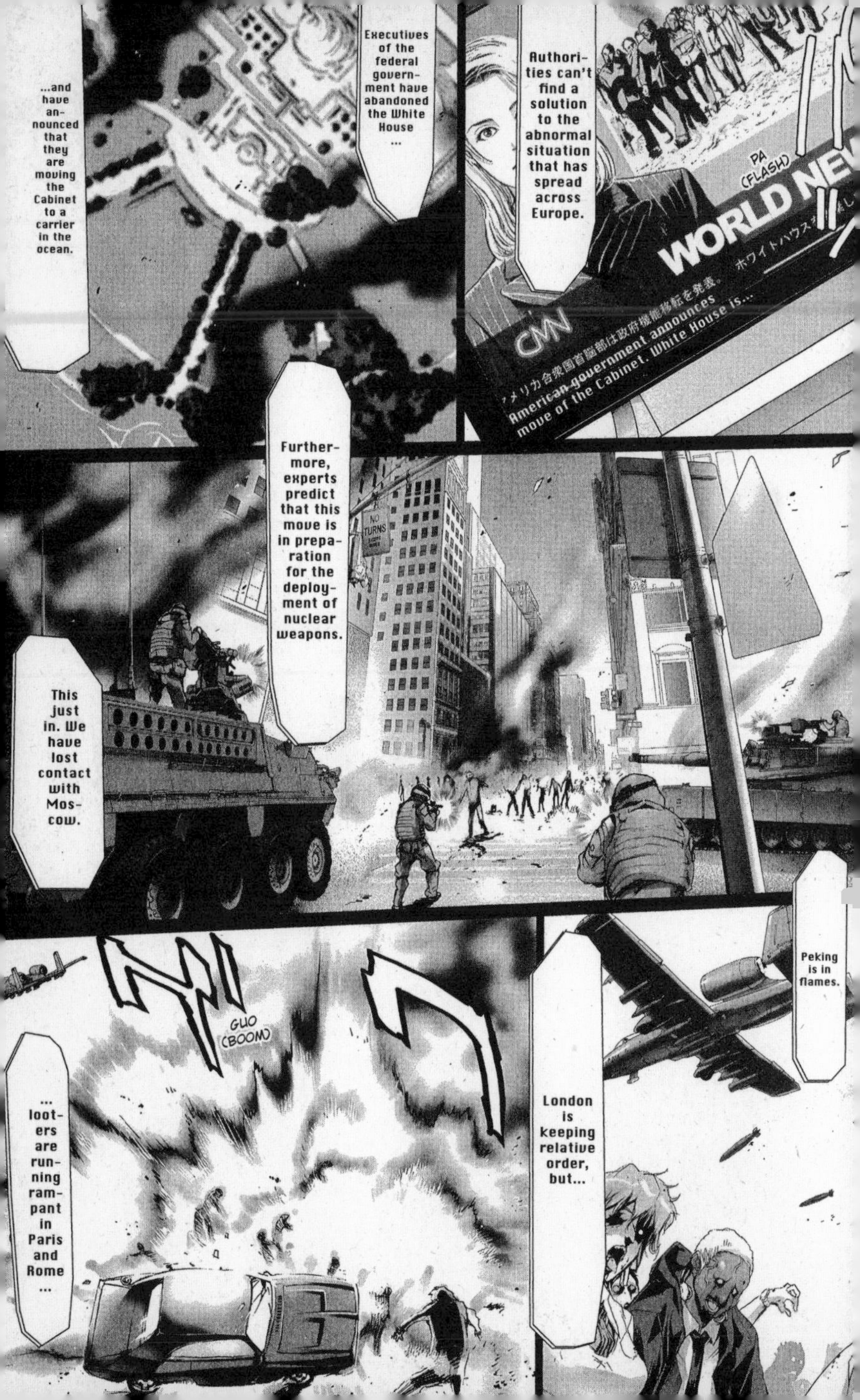
Authorities can't find a solution to the abnormal situation that has spread across Europe.
PA (FLASH)
CNN
アメリカ合衆国首脳部は政府機能移転を発表。
American government announces move of the Cabinet. White House is...
Executives of the federal government have abandoned the White House ...
...and have announced that they are moving the Cabinet to a carrier in the ocean.
Furthermore, experts predict that this move is in preparation for the deployment of nuclear weapons.
NO TURNS
This just in. We have lost contact with Moscow.
Peking is in flames.
London is keeping relative order, but...
GUO (BOOM)
... looters are running rampant in Paris and Rome ...

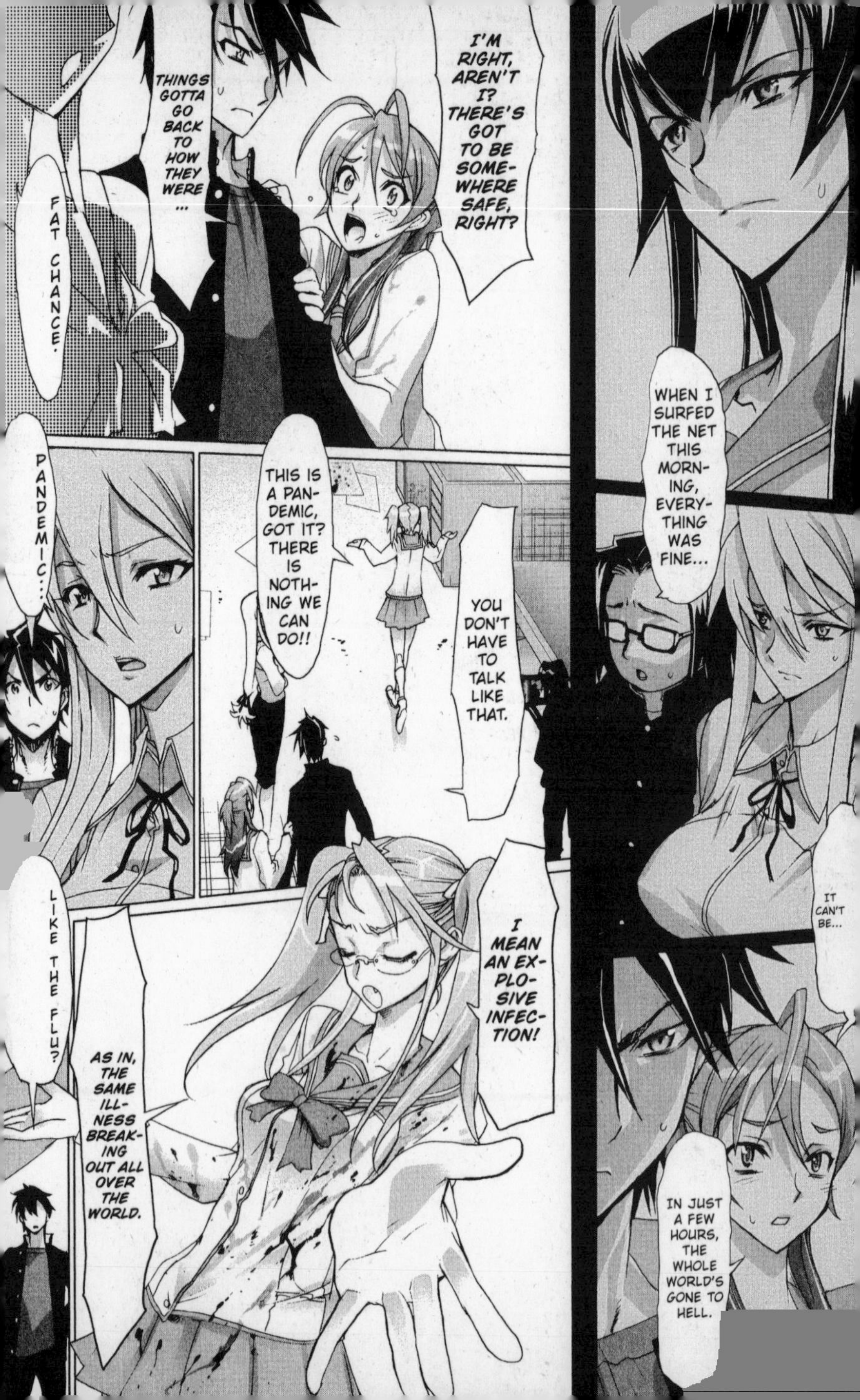
WHEN I SURFED THE NET THIS MORNING, EVERYTHING WAS FINE...
IT CAN'T BE...
IN JUST A FEW HOURS, THE WHOLE WORLD'S GONE TO HELL.
I'M RIGHT, AREN'T I? THERE'S GOT TO BE SOMEWHERE SAFE, RIGHT?
THINGS GOTTA GO BACK TO HOW THEY WERE...
FAT CHANCE.
THIS IS A PANDEMIC, GOT IT? THERE IS NOTHING WE CAN DO!!
YOU DON'T HAVE TO TALK LIKE THAT.
PANDEMIC...
LIKE THE FLU?
I MEAN AN EXPLOSIVE INFECTION!
AS IN, THE SAME ILLNESS BREAKING OUT ALL OVER THE WORLD.

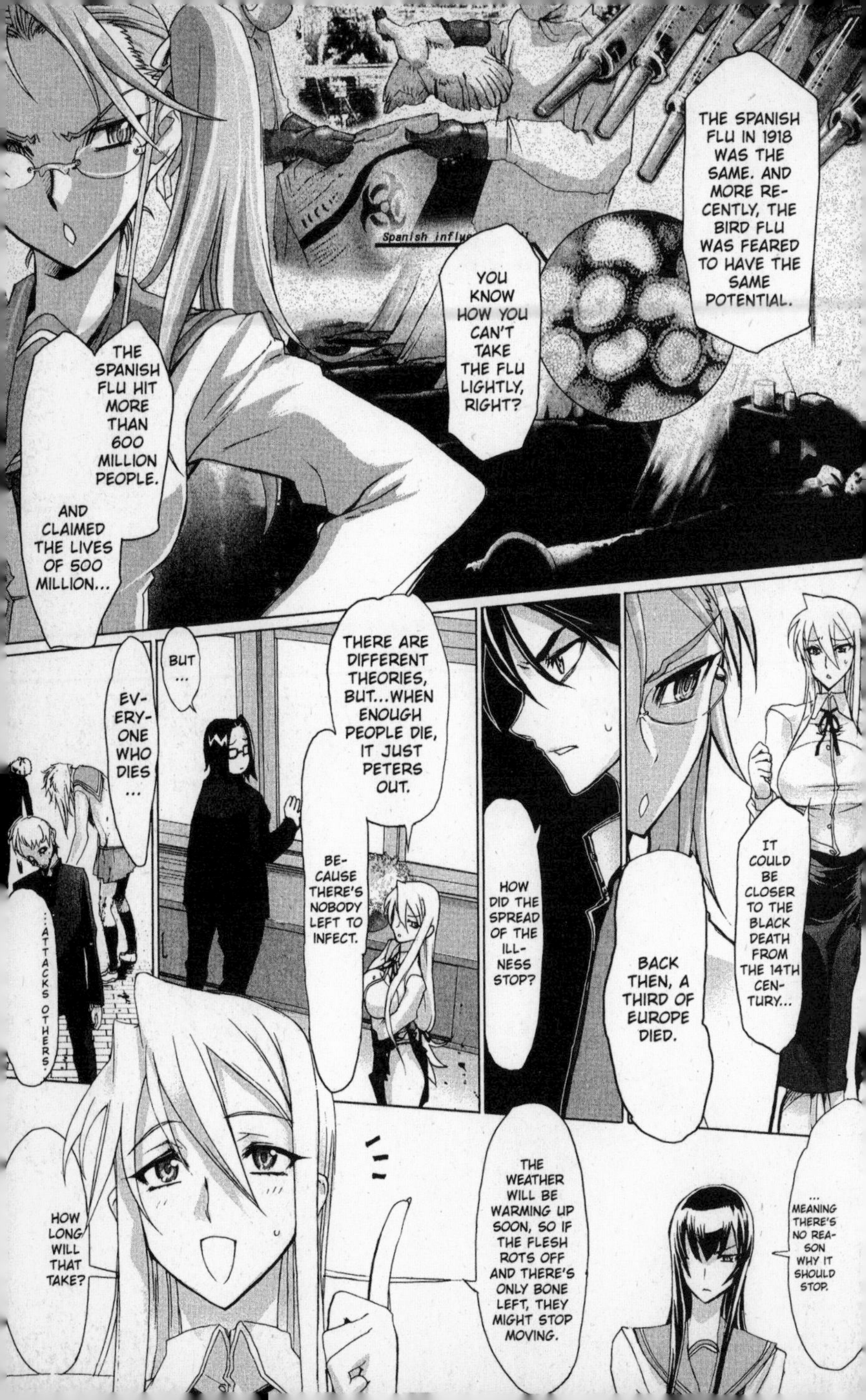

THE SPANISH FLU IN 1918 WAS THE SAME. AND MORE RE-CENTLY, THE BIRD FLU WAS FEARED TO HAVE THE SAME POTENTIAL.
YOU KNOW HOW YOU CAN'T TAKE THE FLU LIGHTLY, RIGHT?
THE SPANISH FLU HIT MORE THAN 600 MILLION PEOPLE.
AND CLAIMED THE LIVES OF 500 MILLION...
IT COULD BE CLOSER TO THE BLACK DEATH FROM THE 14TH CEN-TURY...
BACK THEN, A THIRD OF EUROPE DIED.
HOW DID THE SPREAD OF THE ILL-NESS STOP?
THERE ARE DIFFERENT THEORIES, BUT...WHEN ENOUGH PEOPLE DIE, IT JUST PETERS OUT.
BE-CAUSE THERE'S NOBODY LEFT TO INFECT.
BUT...
EV-ERY-ONE WHO DIES...
...ATTACKS OTHERS.
...MEANING THERE'S NO REA-SON WHY IT SHOULD STOP.
THE WEATHER WILL BE WARMING UP SOON, SO IF THE FLESH ROTS OFF AND THERE'S ONLY BONE LEFT, THEY MIGHT STOP MOVING.
HOW LONG WILL THAT TAKE?

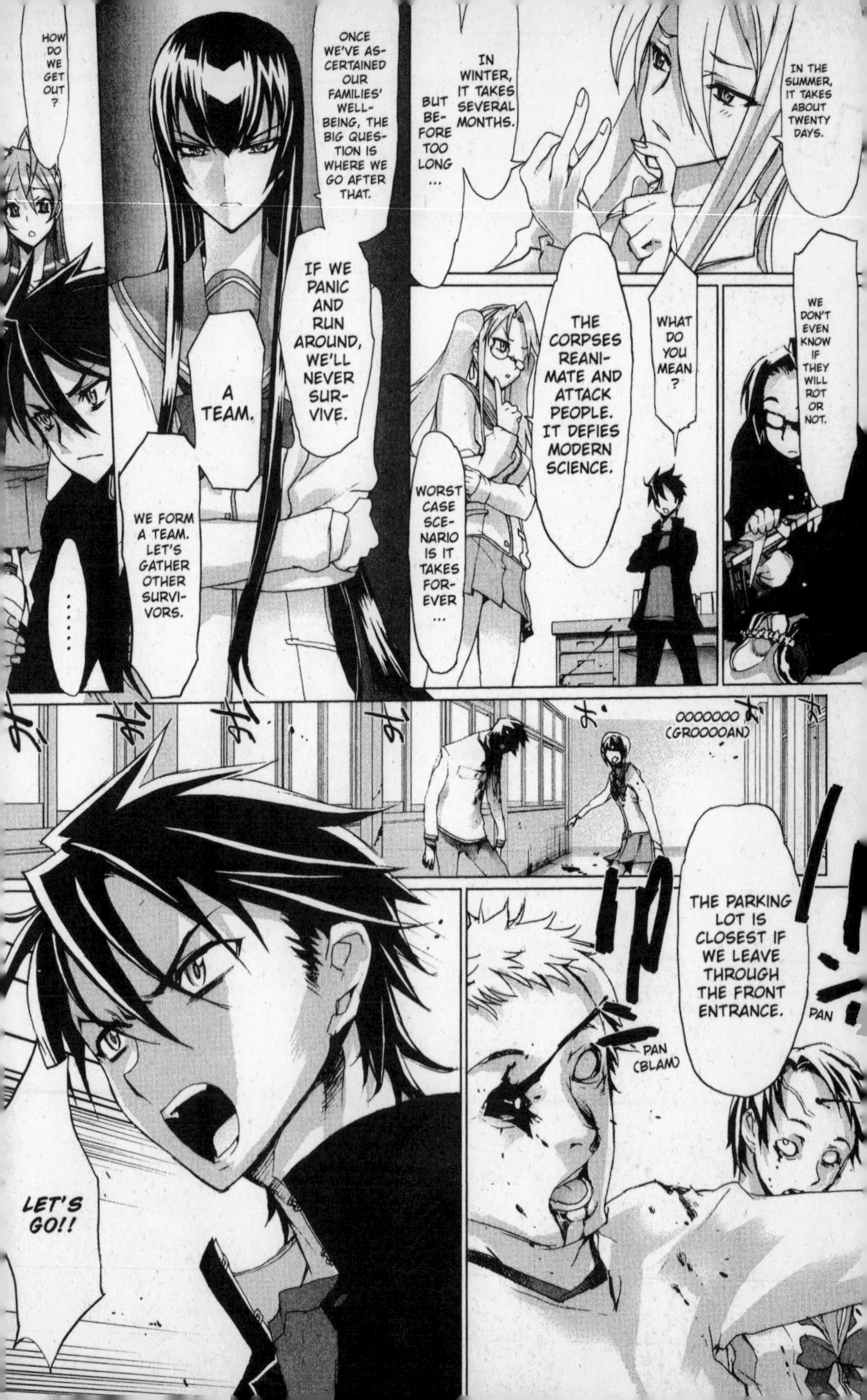
IN THE SUMMER, IT TAKES ABOUT TWENTY DAYS.
IN WINTER, IT TAKES SEVERAL MONTHS.
BUT BEFORE TOO LONG ...
WE DON'T EVEN KNOW IF THEY WILL ROT OR NOT.
WHAT DO YOU MEAN?
THE CORPSES REANIMATE AND ATTACK PEOPLE. IT DEFIES MODERN SCIENCE.
WORST CASE SCENARIO IS IT TAKES FOREVER ...
ONCE WE'VE ASCERTAINED OUR FAMILIES' WELL-BEING, THE BIG QUESTION IS WHERE WE GO AFTER THAT.
HOW DO WE GET OUT?
IF WE PANIC AND RUN AROUND, WE'LL NEVER SURVIVE.
A TEAM.
WE FORM A TEAM. LET'S GATHER OTHER SURVIVORS.
......
OOOOOOO (GROOOOAN)
THE PARKING LOT IS CLOSEST IF WE LEAVE THROUGH THE FRONT ENTRANCE.
PAN
PAN (BLAM)
LET'S GO!!

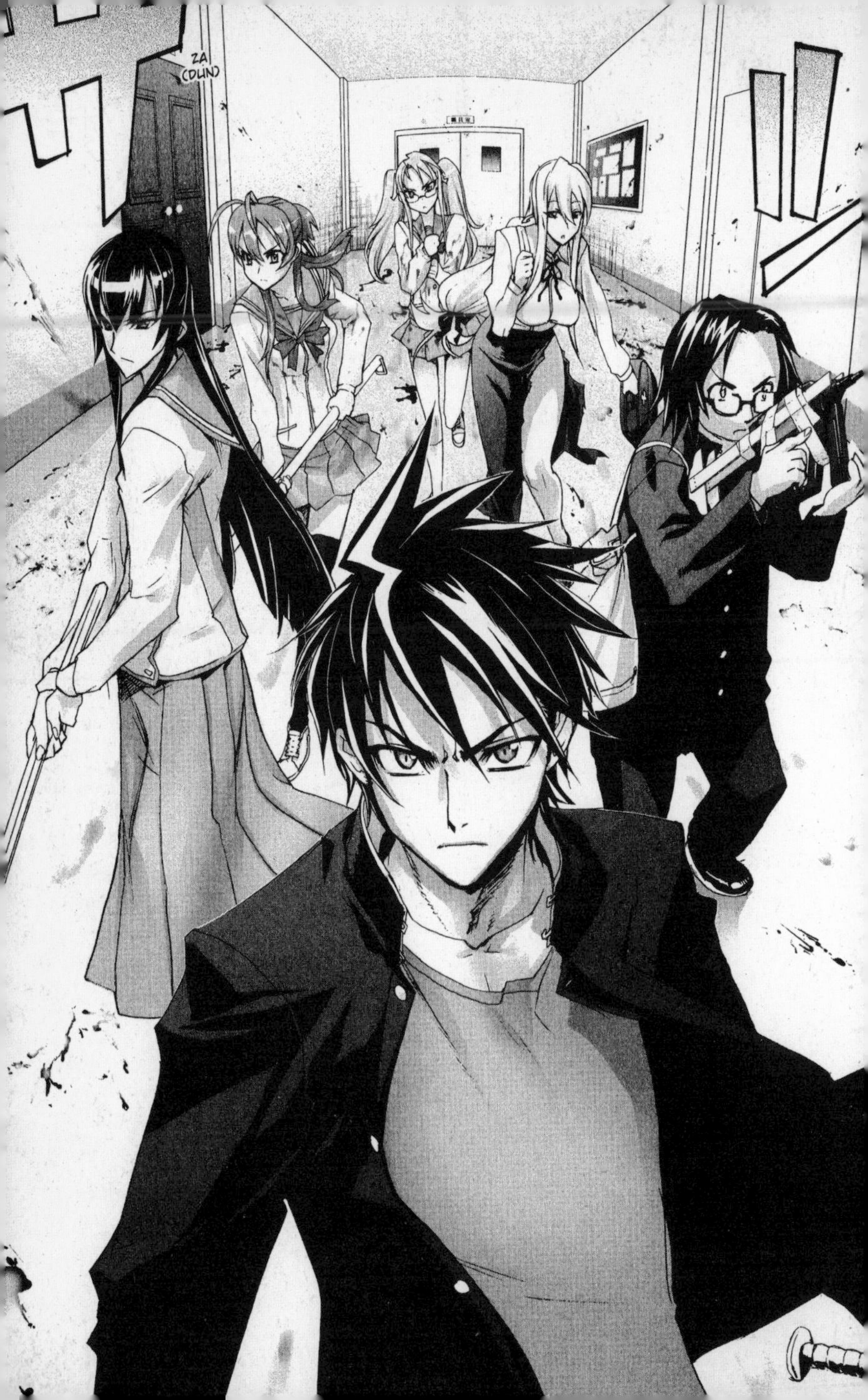
ZA
(DUN)

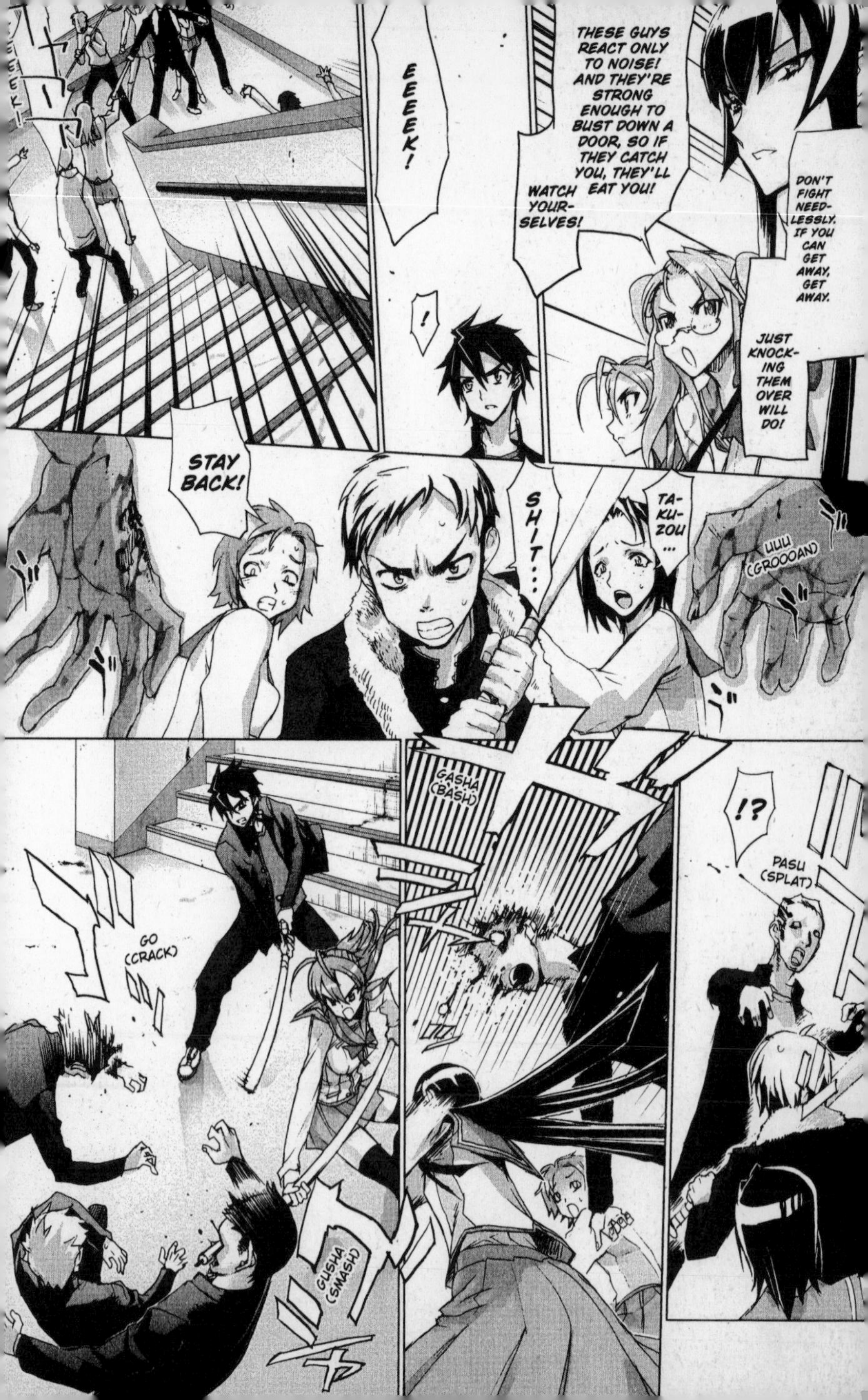
DON'T FIGHT NEEDLESSLY. IF YOU CAN GET AWAY, GET AWAY.
JUST KNOCKING THEM OVER WILL DO!
THESE GUYS REACT ONLY TO NOISE! AND THEY'RE STRONG ENOUGH TO BUST DOWN A DOOR, SO IF THEY CATCH YOU, THEY'LL EAT YOU!
WATCH YOURSELVES!
EEEEK!
!
EEEEK!
UUU (GROOOAN)
TA-KU-ZOU...
SHIT...
STAY BACK!
!?
PASU (SPLAT)
GASHA (BASH)
GO (CRACK)
GUSHA (SMASH)

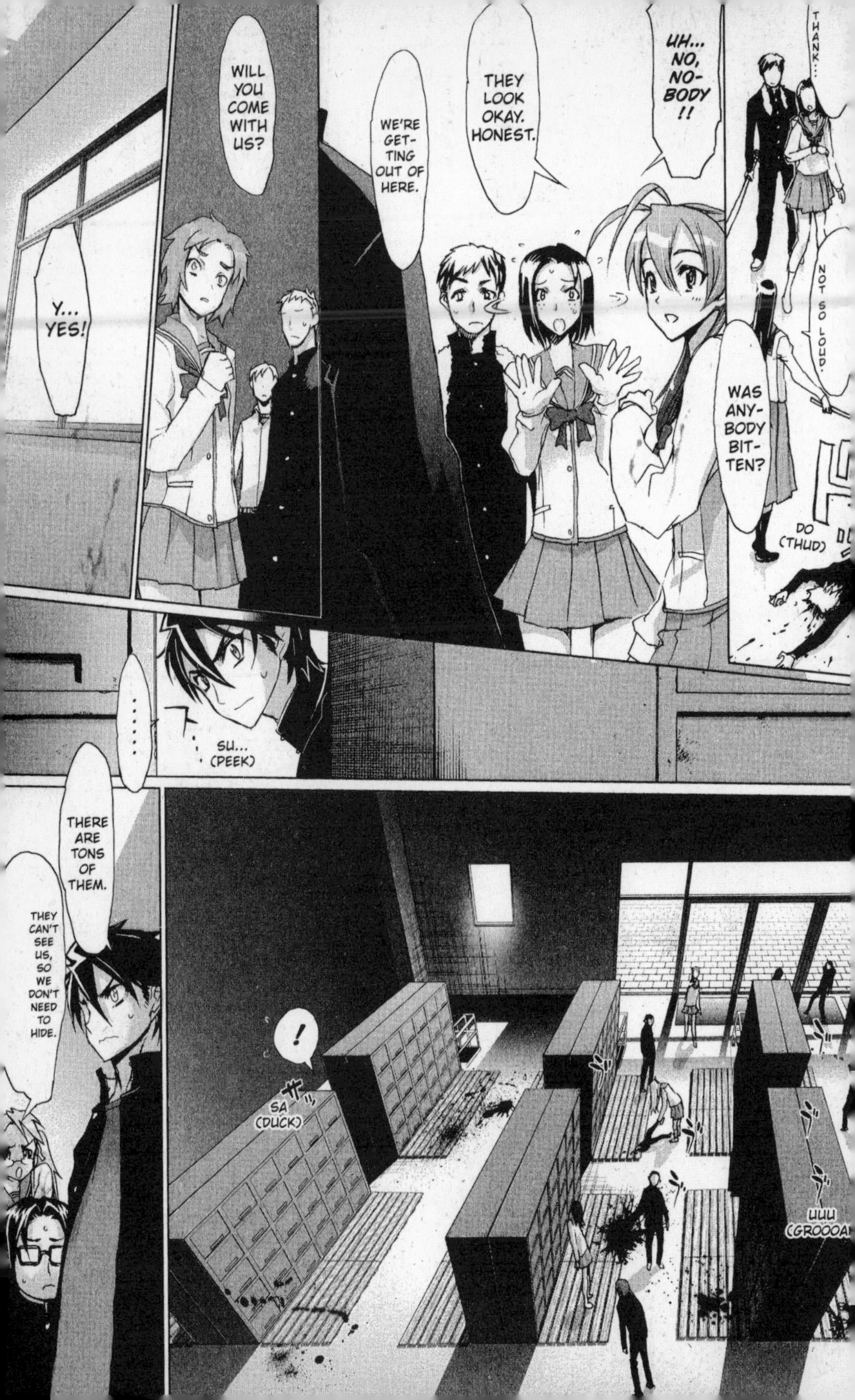
THANK...
NOT SO LOUD.
WAS ANYBODY BITTEN?
DO (THUD)
UH... NO, NOBODY!!
THEY LOOK OKAY. HONEST.
WE'RE GETTING OUT OF HERE.
WILL YOU COME WITH US?
Y... YES!
SU... (PEEK)
......
UUU (GROOOA
SA (DUCK)
!
THERE ARE TONS OF THEM.
THEY CAN'T SEE US, SO WE DON'T NEED TO HIDE.

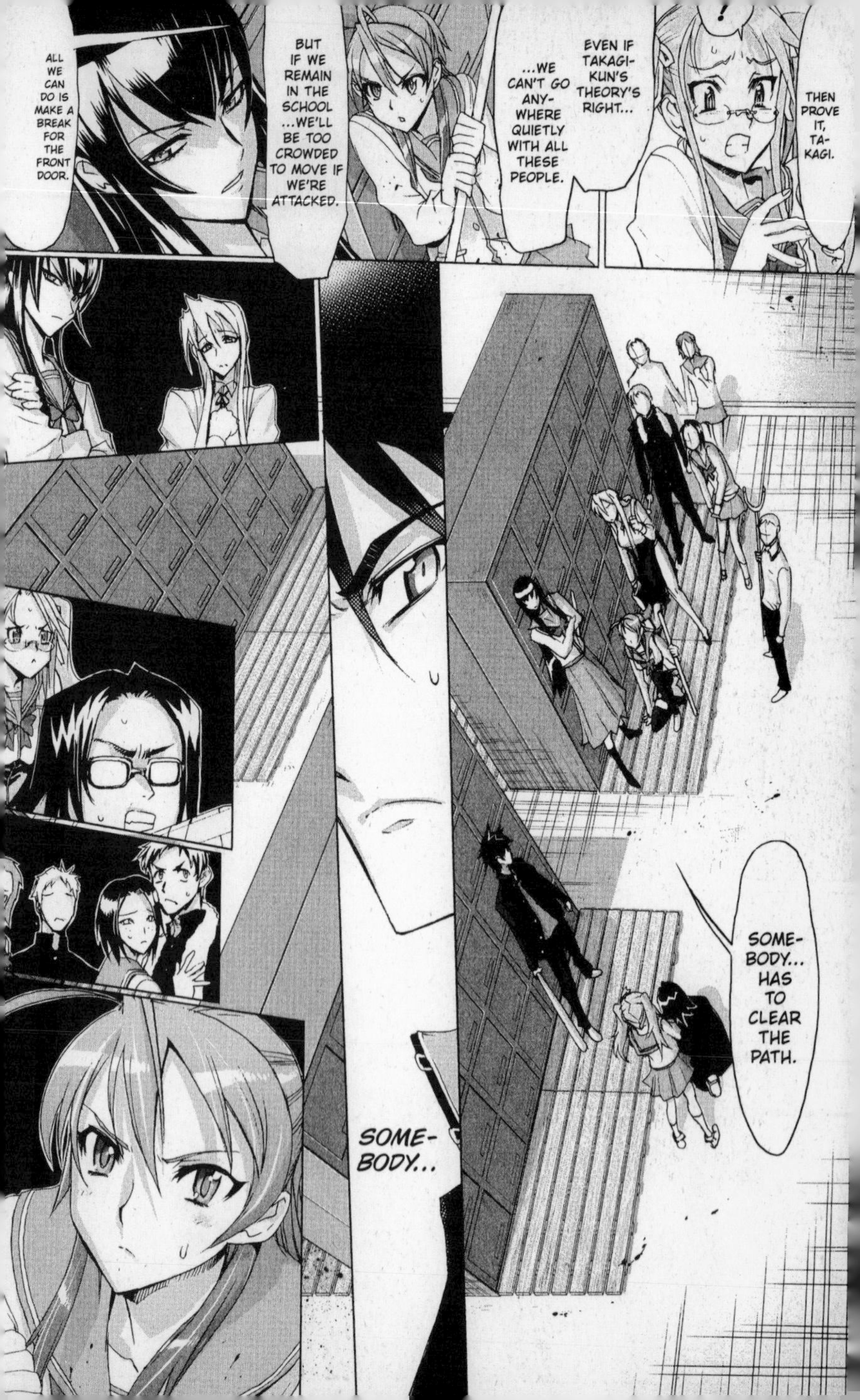
!
THEN PROVE IT, TA-KAGI.
EVEN IF TAKAGI-KUN'S THEORY'S RIGHT...
...WE CAN'T GO ANY-WHERE QUIETLY WITH ALL THESE PEOPLE.
BUT IF WE REMAIN IN THE SCHOOL ...WE'LL BE TOO CROWDED TO MOVE IF WE'RE ATTACKED.
ALL WE CAN DO IS MAKE A BREAK FOR THE FRONT DOOR.
SOME-BODY... HAS TO CLEAR THE PATH.
SOME-BODY...

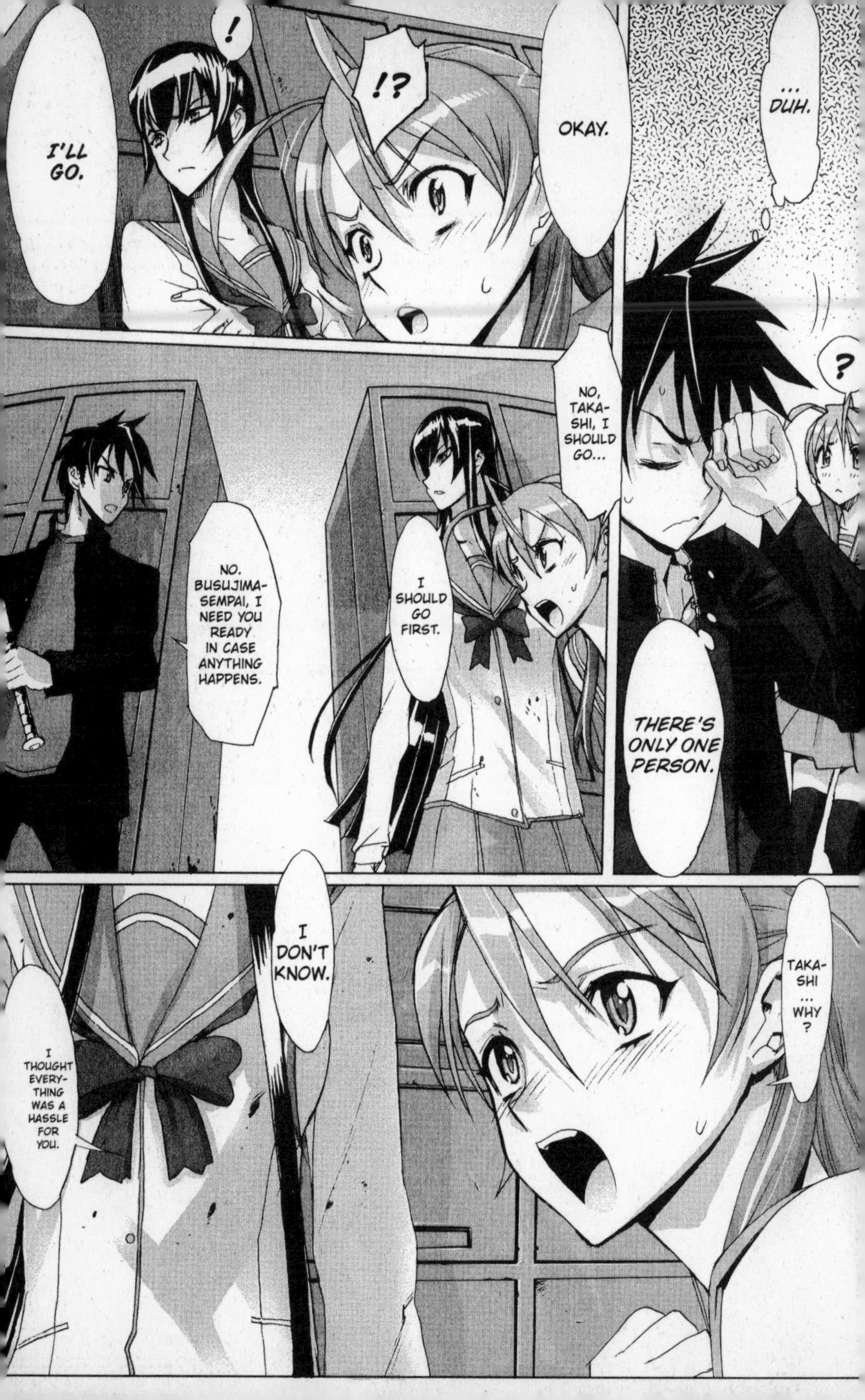
... DUH.
?
NO, TAKASHI, I SHOULD GO...
THERE'S ONLY ONE PERSON.
OKAY.
!?
!
I'LL GO.
I SHOULD GO FIRST.
NO. BUSUJIMA-SEMPAI, I NEED YOU READY IN CASE ANYTHING HAPPENS.
TAKASHI ... WHY?
I DON'T KNOW.
I THOUGHT EVERYTHING WAS A HASSLE FOR YOU.

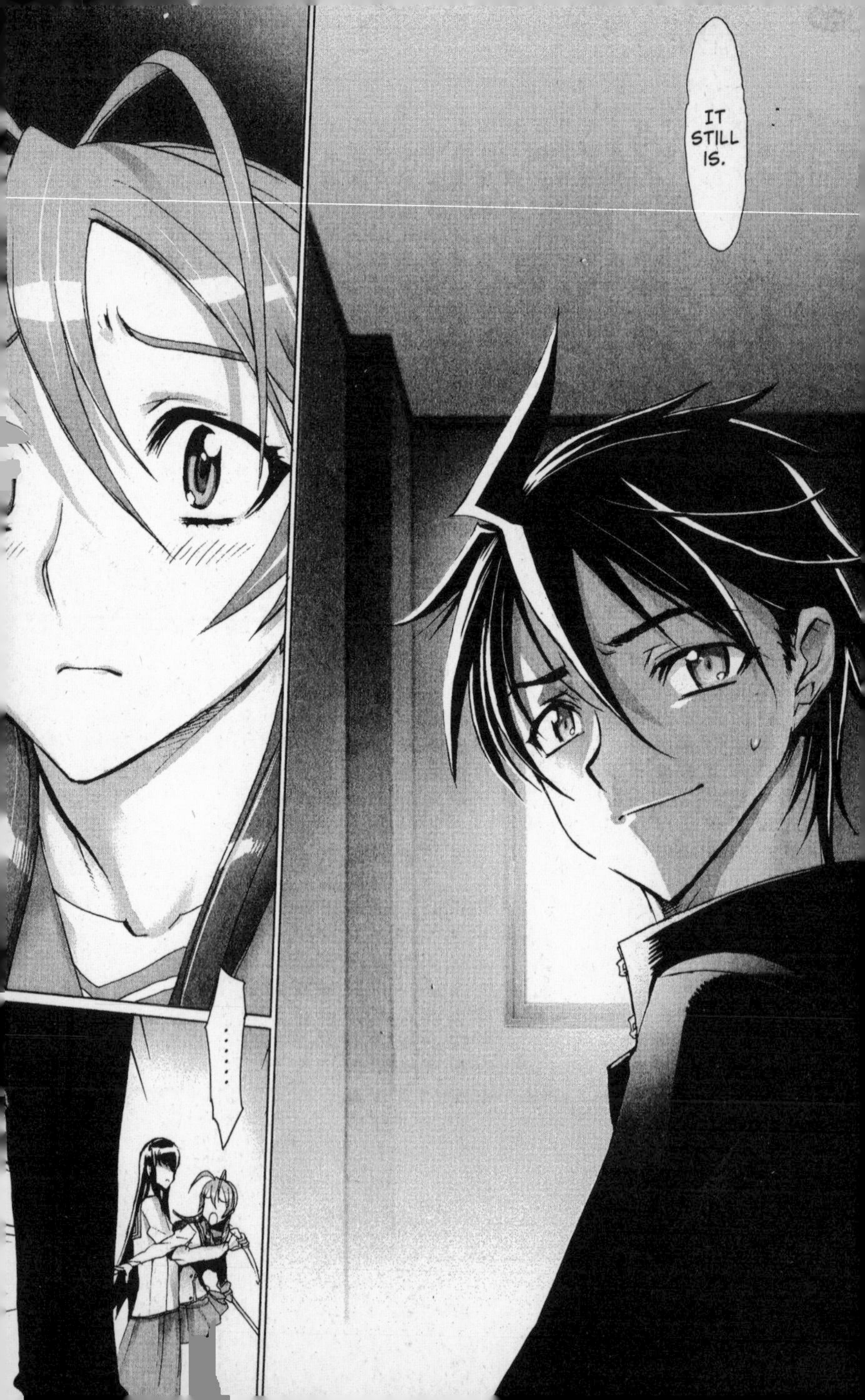
IT STILL IS.
......

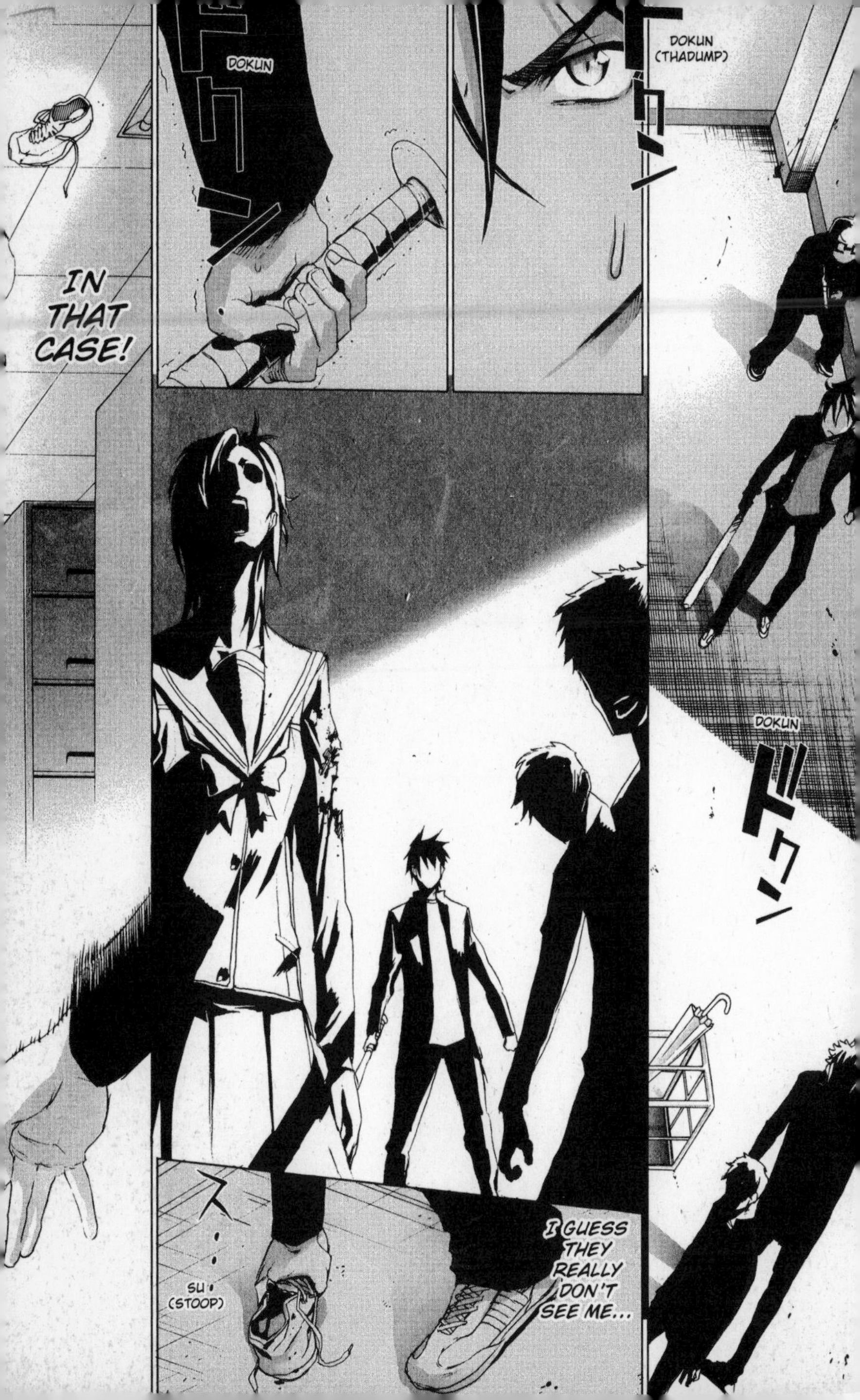
DOKUN (THADUMP)
ドクン
DOKUN
ドクン
IN THAT CASE!
DOKUN
ドクン
I GUESS THEY REALLY DON'T SEE ME...
ス
SU (STOOP)

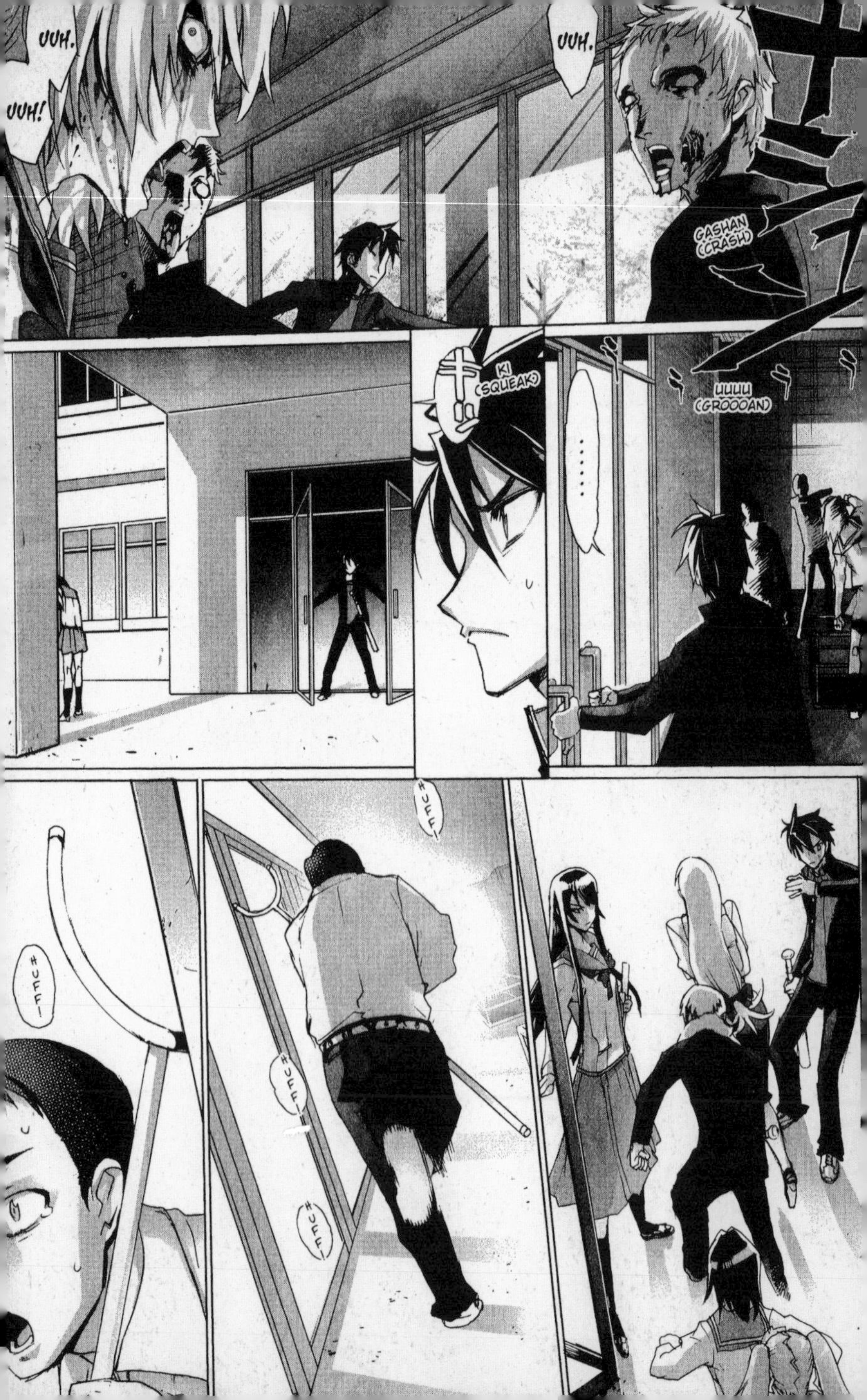
UUH.
GASHAN (CRASH)
UUH.
UUH!
UUUU (GROOOAN)
......
KI (SQUEAK)
HUFF!
HUFF!
HUFF!
HUFF!

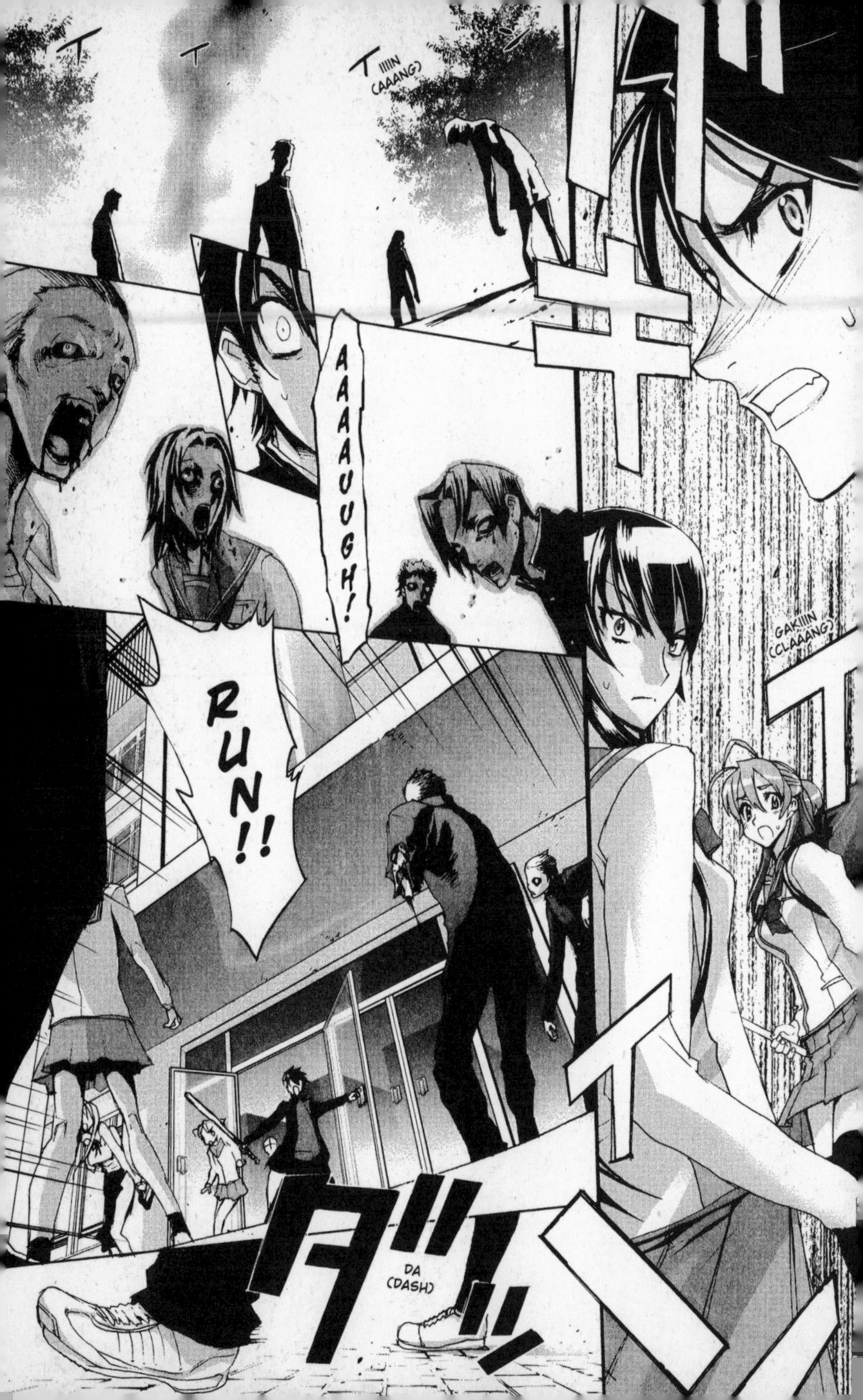
T T TIIIIN (AAANG)
AAAAAUUGH!
GAKIIIN (CLAAANG)
RUN!!
DA (DASH)

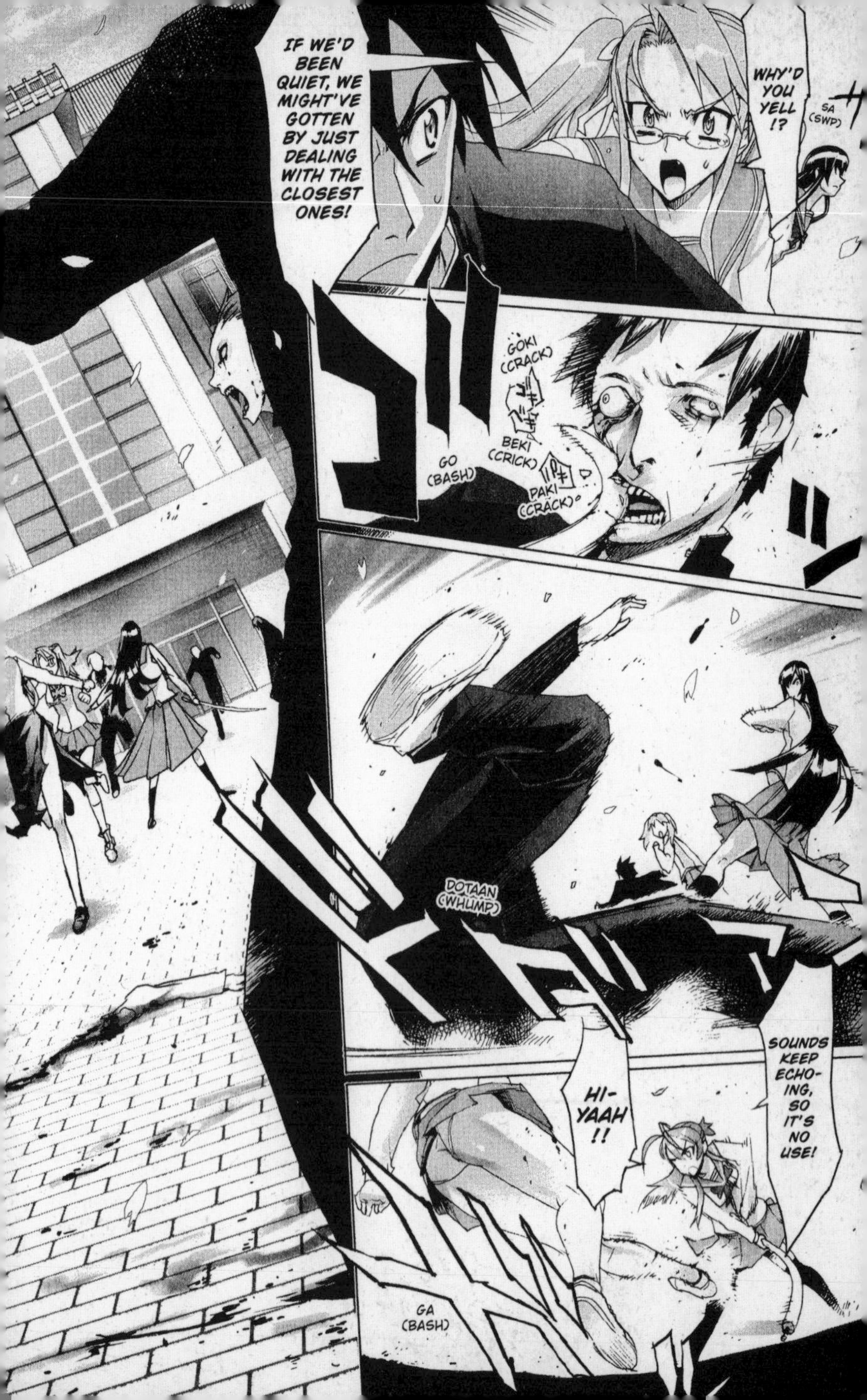
WHY'D YOU YELL !?
SA (SWP)
IF WE'D BEEN QUIET, WE MIGHT'VE GOTTEN BY JUST DEALING WITH THE CLOSEST ONES!
GOKI (CRACK)
BEKI (CRICK)
GO (BASH)
PAKI (CRACK)
DOTAAN (WHUMP)
SOUNDS KEEP ECHOING, SO IT'S NO USE!
HI-YAAH !!
GA (BASH)

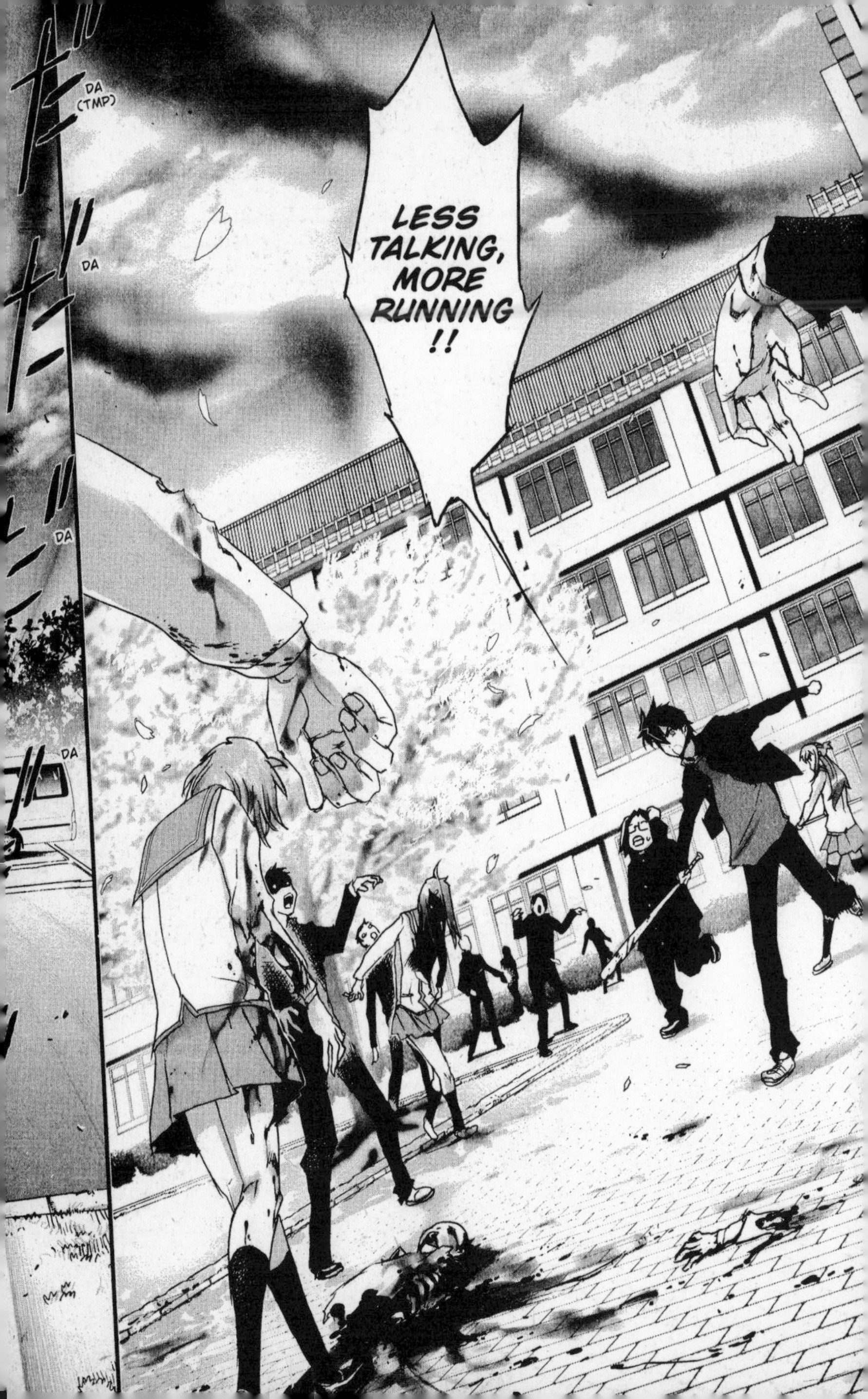
LESS TALKING, MORE RUNNING!!
DA (TMP)
DA
DA
DA

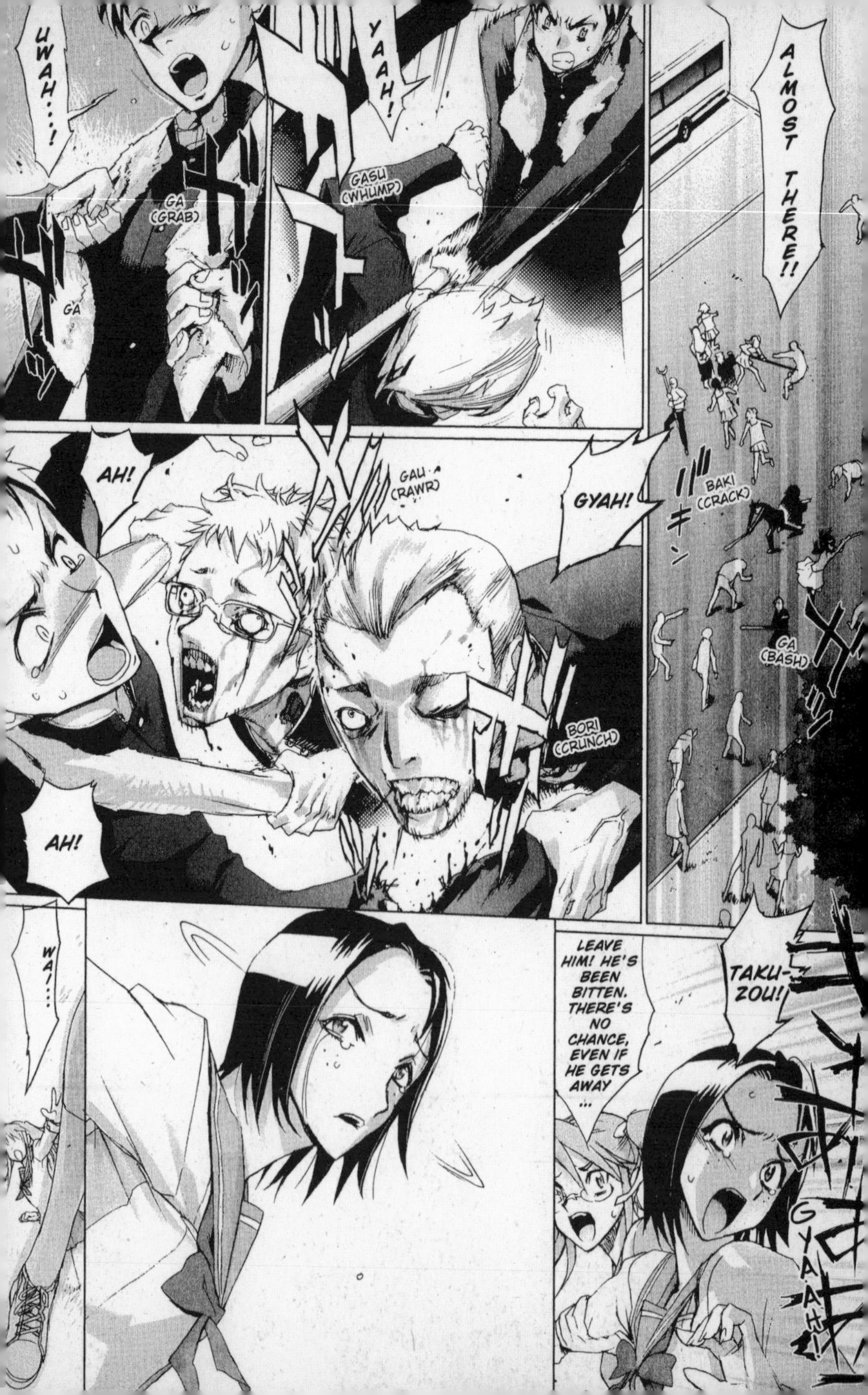
ALMOST THERE!!
BAKI (CRACK)
GA (BASH)
YAAAH!
GASU (WHUMP)
UWAH...!
GA (GRAB)
GA
GYAH!
GAU (RAWR)
BORI (CRUNCH)
AH!
AH!
TAKU-ZOU!
LEAVE HIM! HE'S BEEN BITTEN. THERE'S NO CHANCE, EVEN IF HE GETS AWAY...
GYAAAH!
WA!...

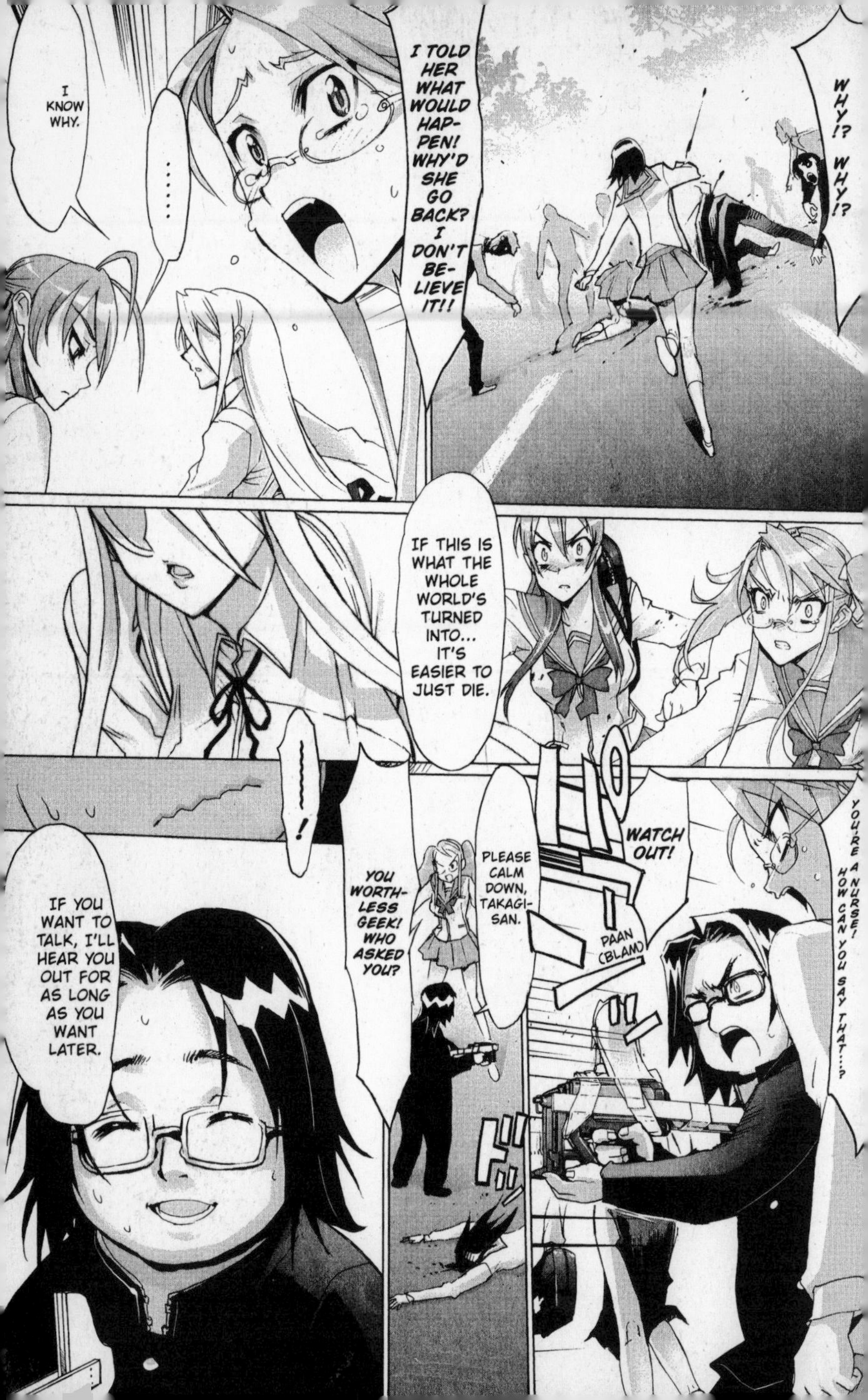

WHY!? WHY!?
I TOLD HER WHAT WOULD HAP-PEN! WHY'D SHE GO BACK? I DON'T BE-LIEVE IT!!
......
I KNOW WHY.
IF THIS IS WHAT THE WHOLE WORLD'S TURNED INTO... IT'S EASIER TO JUST DIE.
......!
YOU'RE A NURSE! HOW CAN YOU SAY THAT...?
WATCH OUT!
PAAN (BLAM)
PLEASE CALM DOWN, TAKAGI-SAN.
YOU WORTHLESS GEEK! WHO ASKED YOU?
IF YOU WANT TO TALK, I'LL HEAR YOU OUT FOR AS LONG AS YOU WANT LATER.

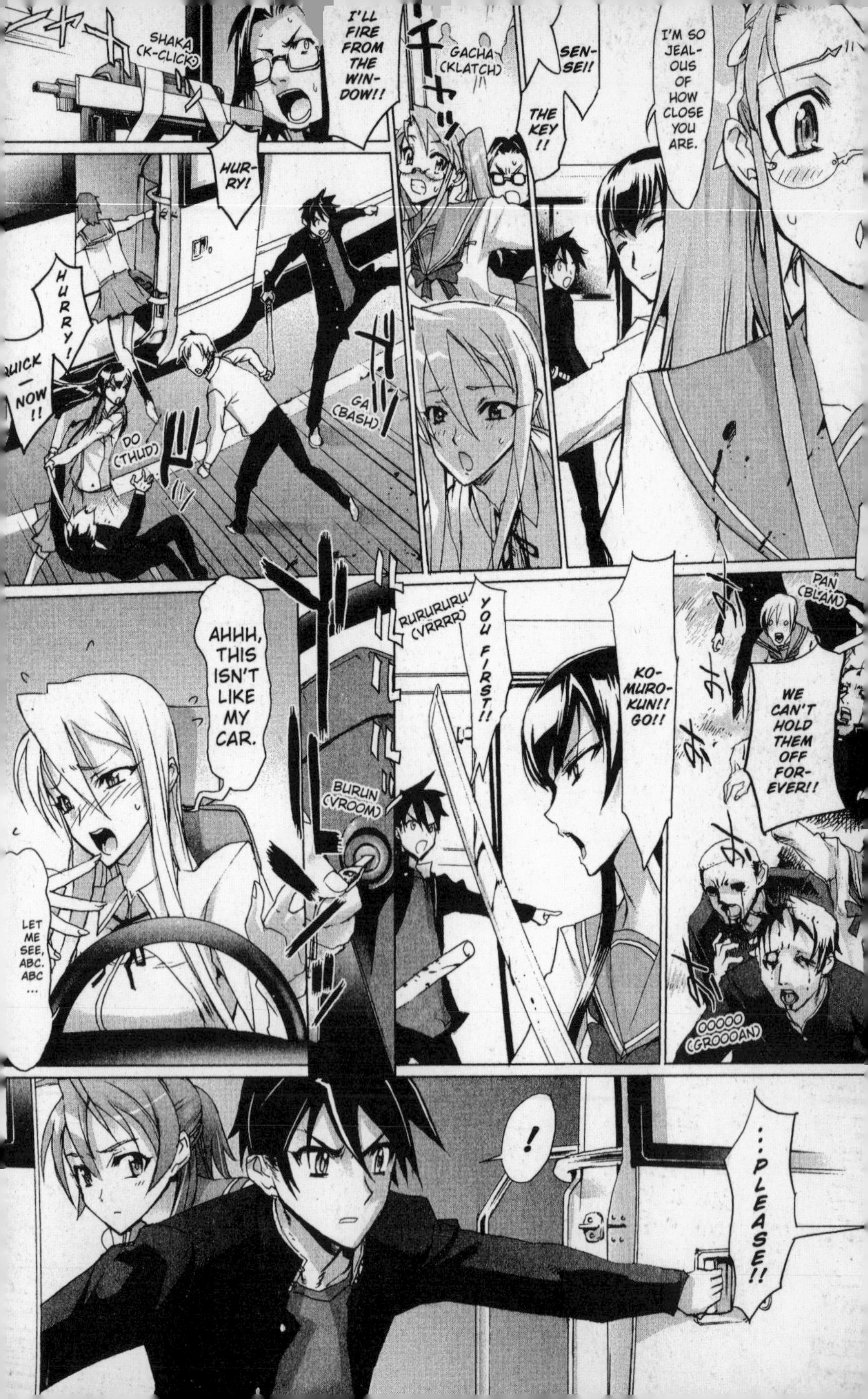
I'M SO JEALOUS OF HOW CLOSE YOU ARE.
SEN-SEI!!
THE KEY!!
GACHA (KLATCH)
GA (BASH)
I'LL FIRE FROM THE WIN-DOW!!
SHAKA (K-CLICK)
HUR-RY!
HURRY!
QUICK — NOW!!
DO (THUD)
PAN (BLAM)
WE CAN'T HOLD THEM OFF FOR-EVER!!
OOOOO (GROOOAN)
KO-MURO-KUN!! GO!!
YOU FIRST!!
RURURURU (VRRRR)
BURUN (VROOM)
AHHH, THIS ISN'T LIKE MY CAR.
LET ME SEE, ABC. ABC...
...PLEASE!!
!

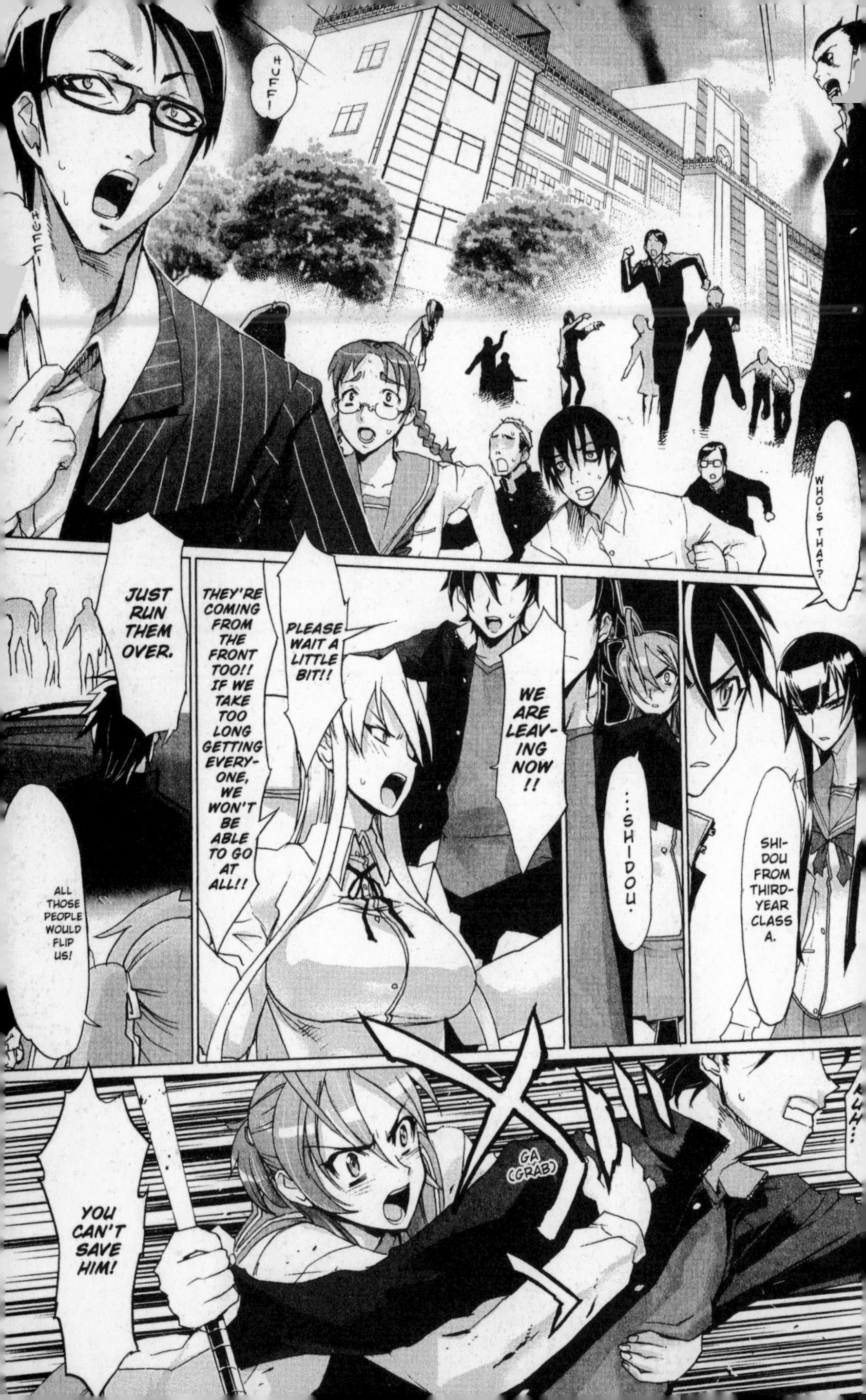
HUFF!
HUFF!
WHO'S THAT?
SHI-DOU FROM THIRD-YEAR CLASS A.
...SHIDOU.
WE ARE LEAVING NOW!!
PLEASE WAIT A LITTLE BIT!!
THEY'RE COMING FROM THE FRONT TOO!! IF WE TAKE TOO LONG GETTING EVERYONE, WE WON'T BE ABLE TO GO AT ALL!!
JUST RUN THEM OVER.
ALL THOSE PEOPLE WOULD FLIP US!
RUH...
GA (GRAB)
YOU CAN'T SAVE HIM!

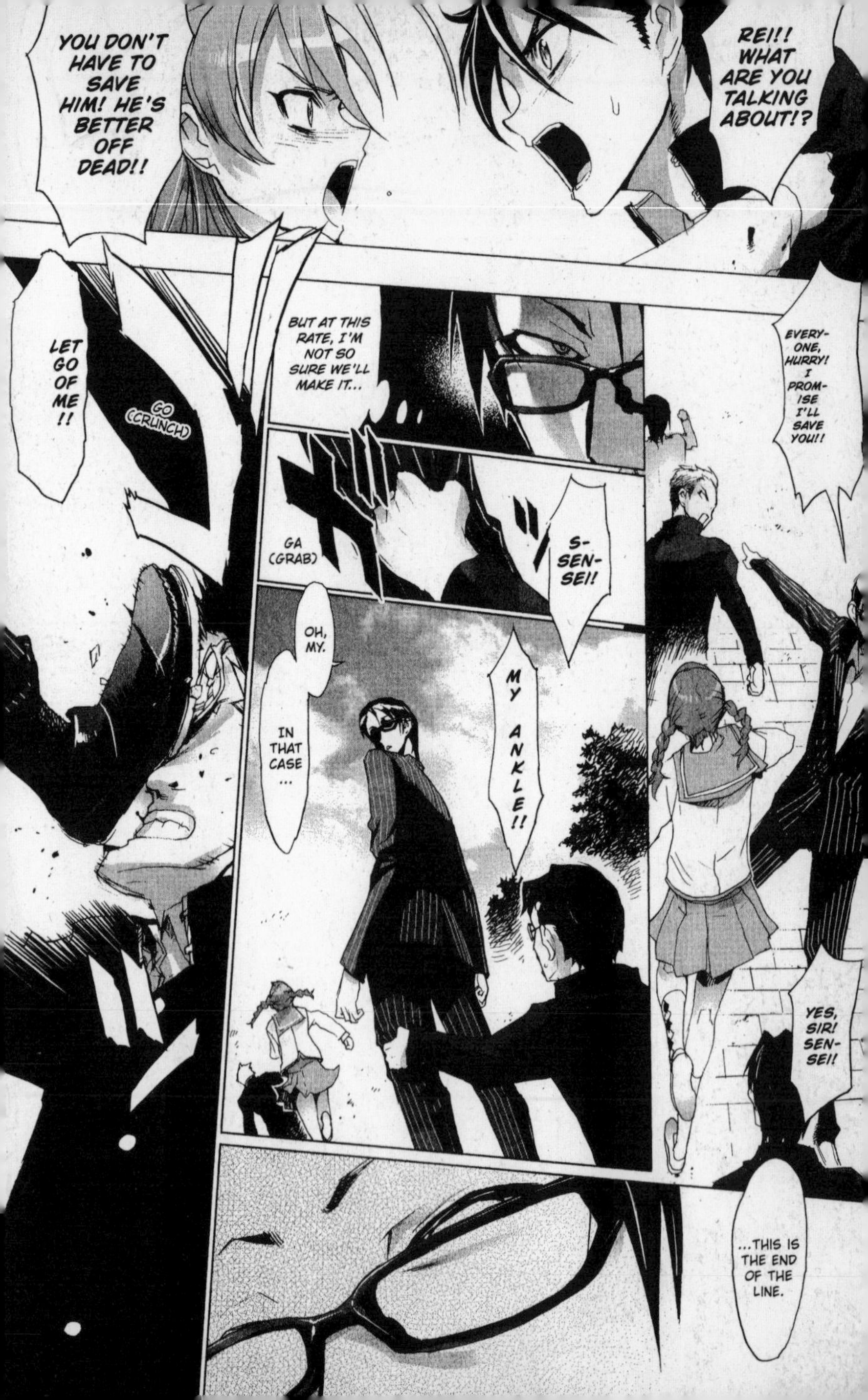
REI!! WHAT ARE YOU TALKING ABOUT!?
YOU DON'T HAVE TO SAVE HIM! HE'S BETTER OFF DEAD!!
EVERY-ONE, HURRY! I PROM-ISE I'LL SAVE YOU!!
YES, SIR! SEN-SEI!
BUT AT THIS RATE, I'M NOT SO SURE WE'LL MAKE IT...
S-SEN-SEI!
GA (GRAB)
MY ANKLE!!
OH, MY.
IN THAT CASE...
...THIS IS THE END OF THE LINE.
LET GO OF ME!!
GO (CRUNCH)

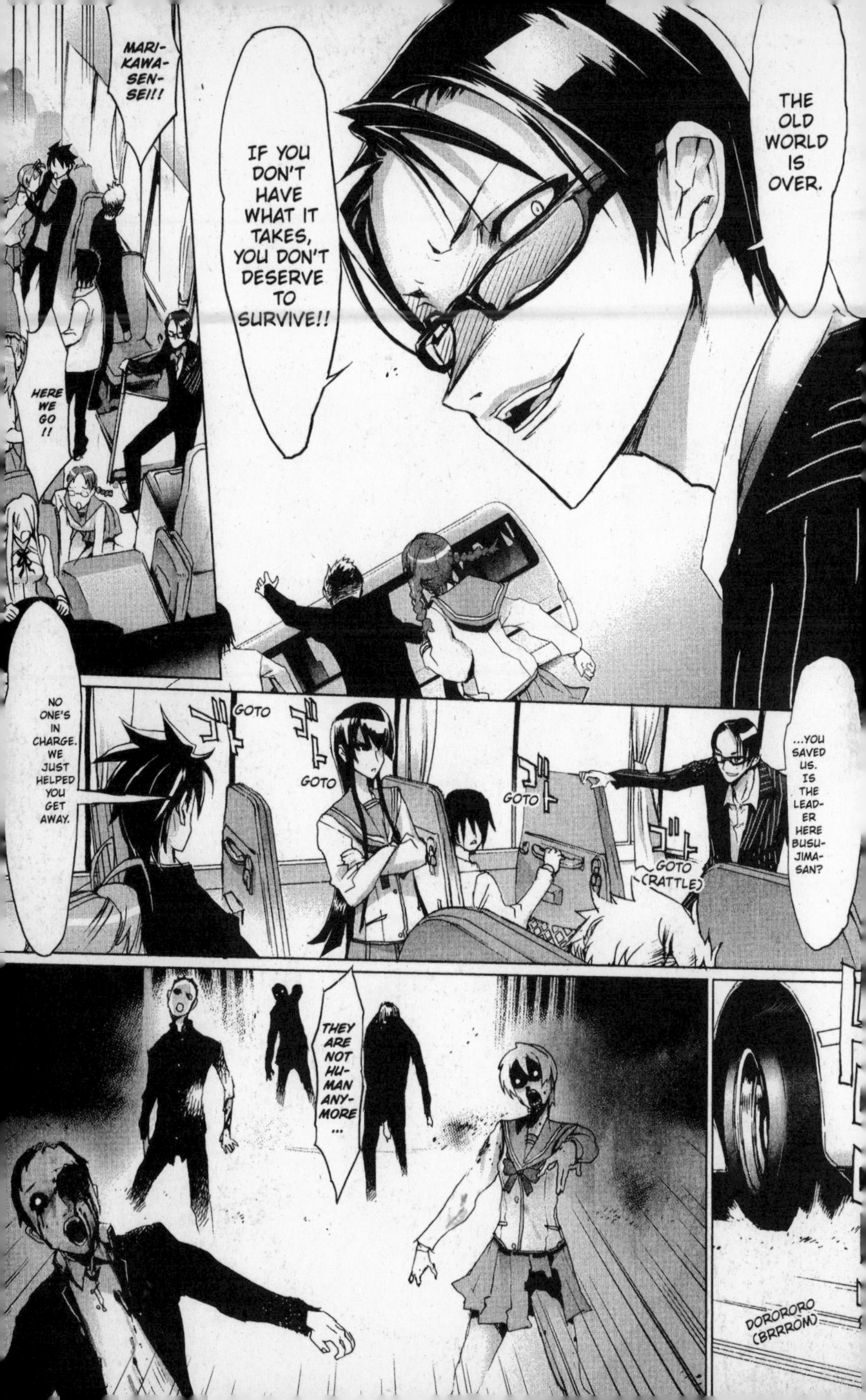
THE OLD WORLD IS OVER.
IF YOU DON'T HAVE WHAT IT TAKES, YOU DON'T DESERVE TO SURVIVE!!
MARI-KAWA-SEN-SEI!!
HERE WE GO!!
...YOU SAVED US. IS THE LEADER HERE BUSUJIMA-SAN?
GOTO (RATTLE)
GOTO
GOTO
GOTO
NO ONE'S IN CHARGE. WE JUST HELPED YOU GET AWAY.
DOROROROR (BRRROM)
THEY ARE NOT HU-MAN ANY-MORE...

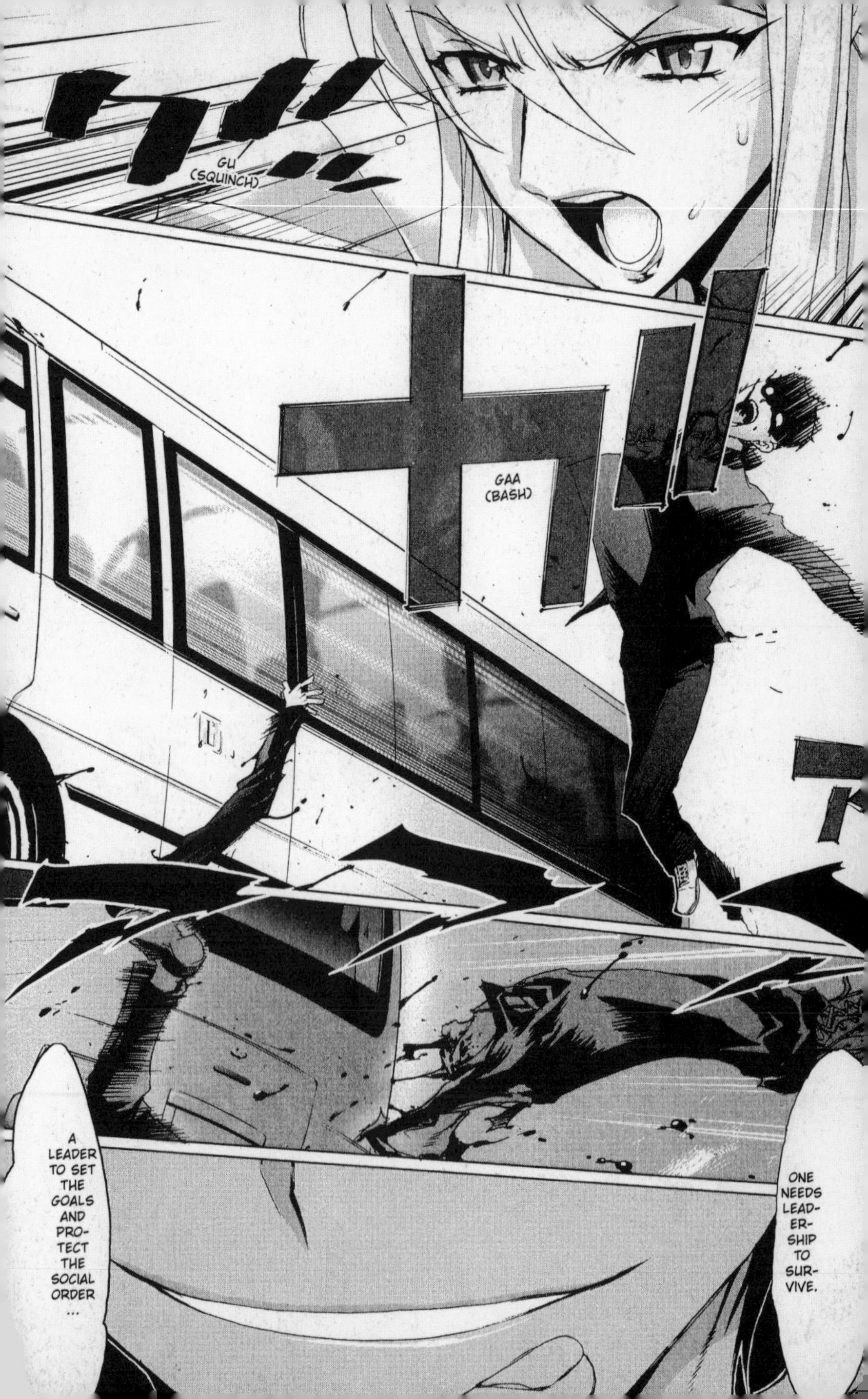
GU (SQUINCH)
GAA (BASH)
ONE NEEDS LEADERSHIP TO SURVIVE.
A LEADER TO SET THE GOALS AND PROTECT THE SOCIAL ORDER ...

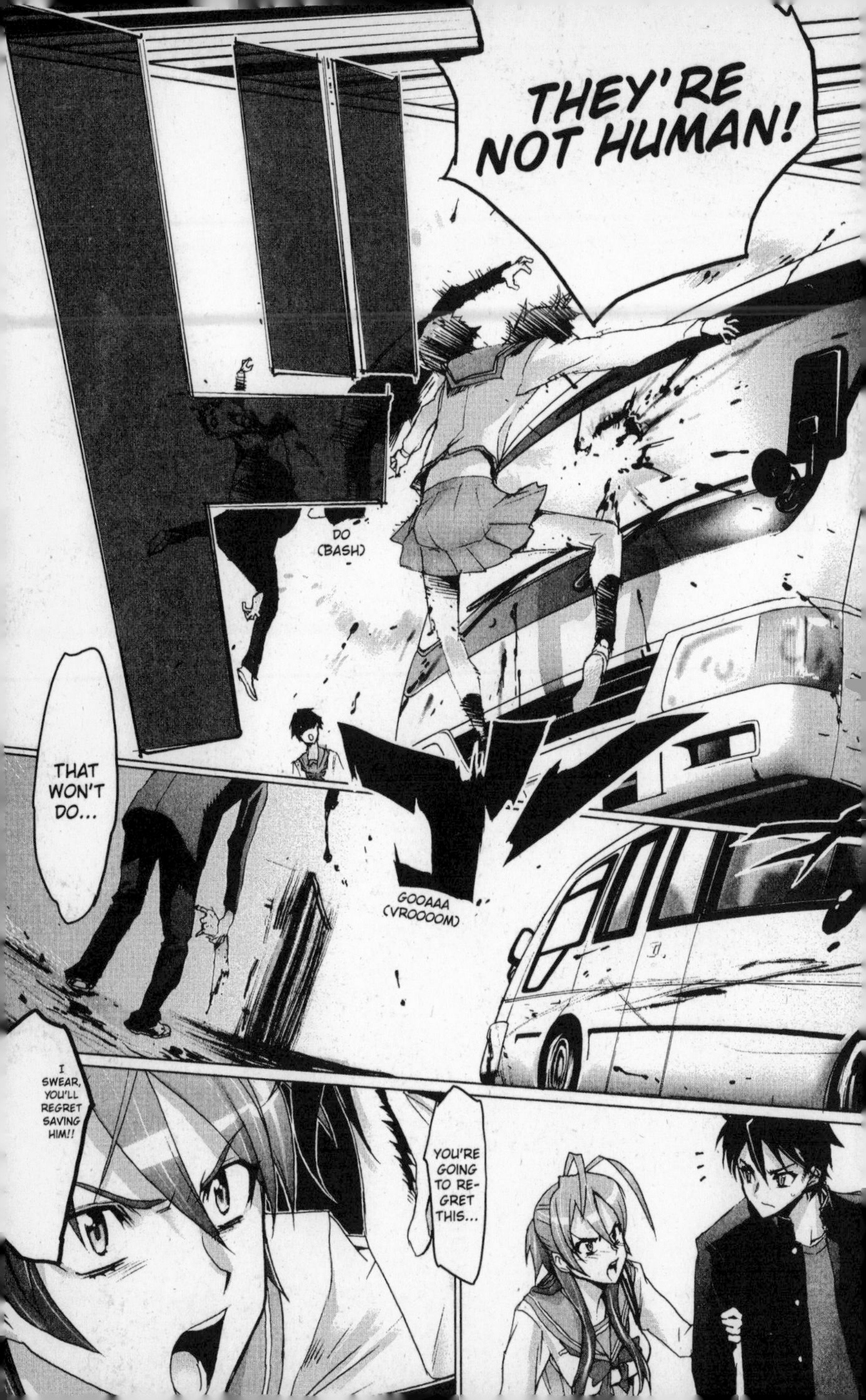
THEY'RE NOT HUMAN!
DO (BASH)
THAT WON'T DO...
GOOAAA (VROOOOM)
YOU'RE GOING TO RE-GRET THIS...
I SWEAR, YOU'LL REGRET SAVING HIM!!

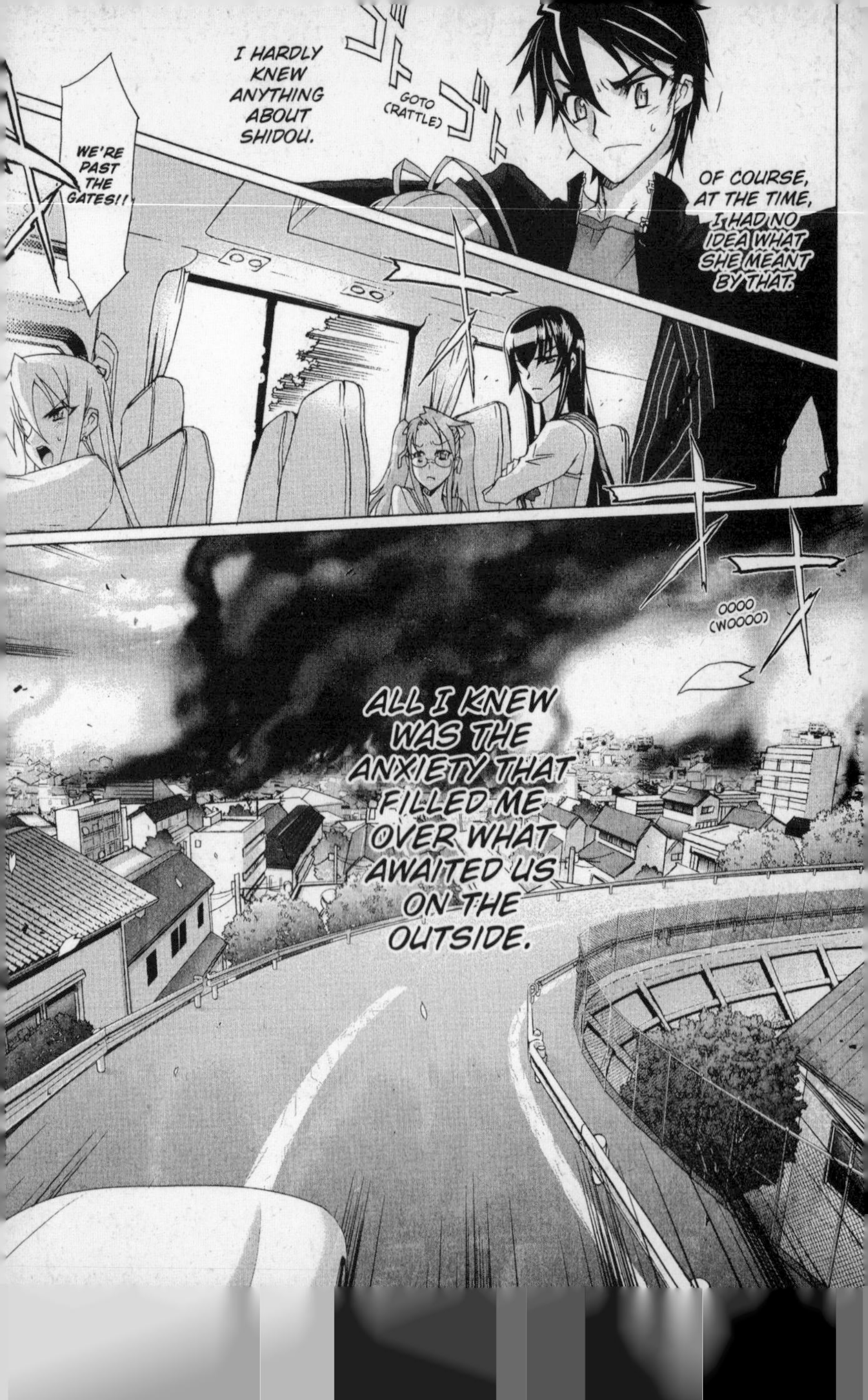
I HARDLY KNEW ANYTHING ABOUT SHIDOU.
GOTO (RATTLE)
OF COURSE, AT THE TIME, I HAD NO IDEA WHAT SHE MEANT BY THAT.
WE'RE PAST THE GATES!!
OOOO (WOOOO)
ALL I KNEW WAS THE ANXIETY THAT FILLED ME OVER WHAT AWAITED US ON THE OUTSIDE.

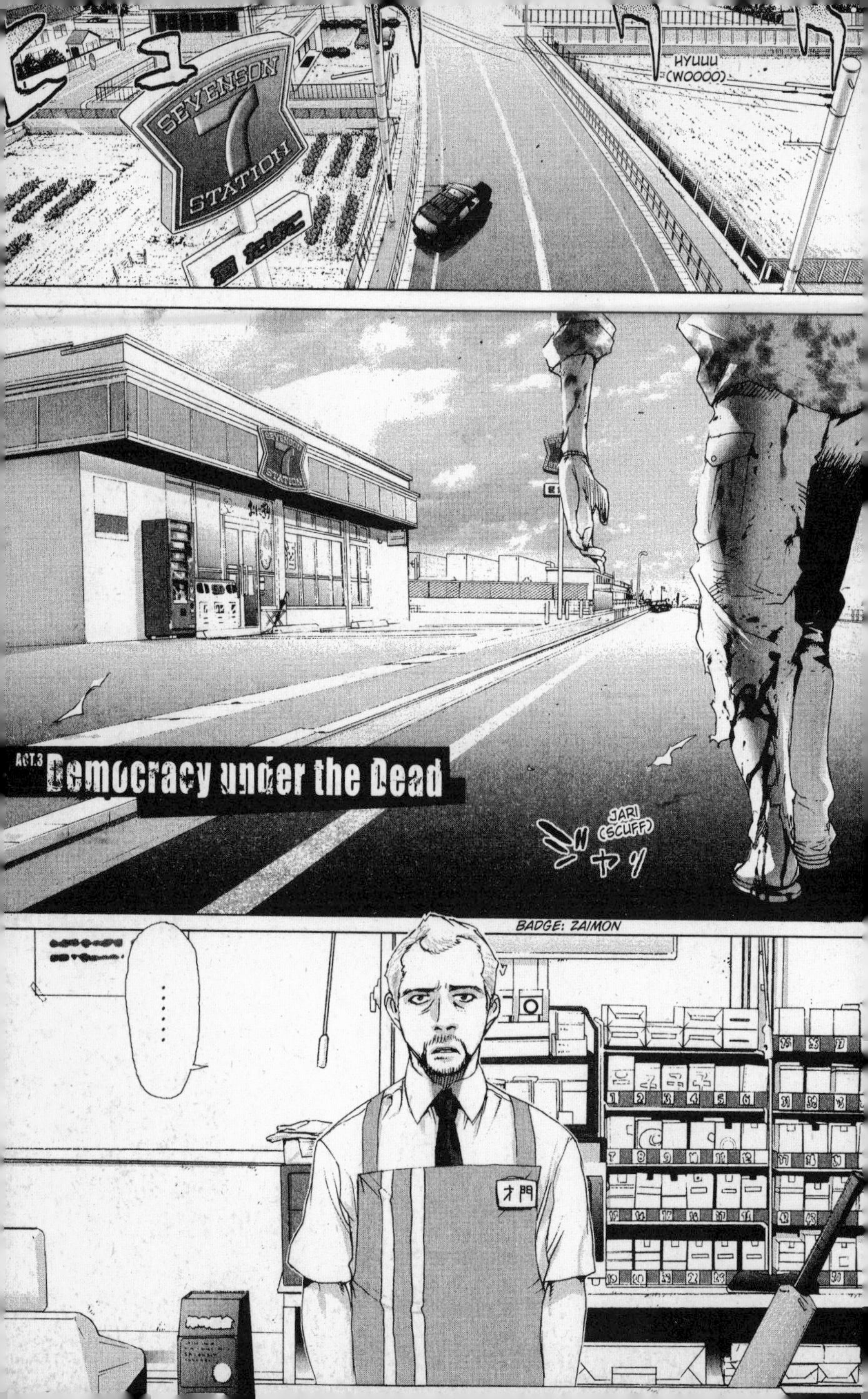
SEVENSON 7 STATION
HYUUU (WOOOO)
ACT.3 Democracy under the Dead
JARI (SCUFF)
BADGE: ZAIMON
......

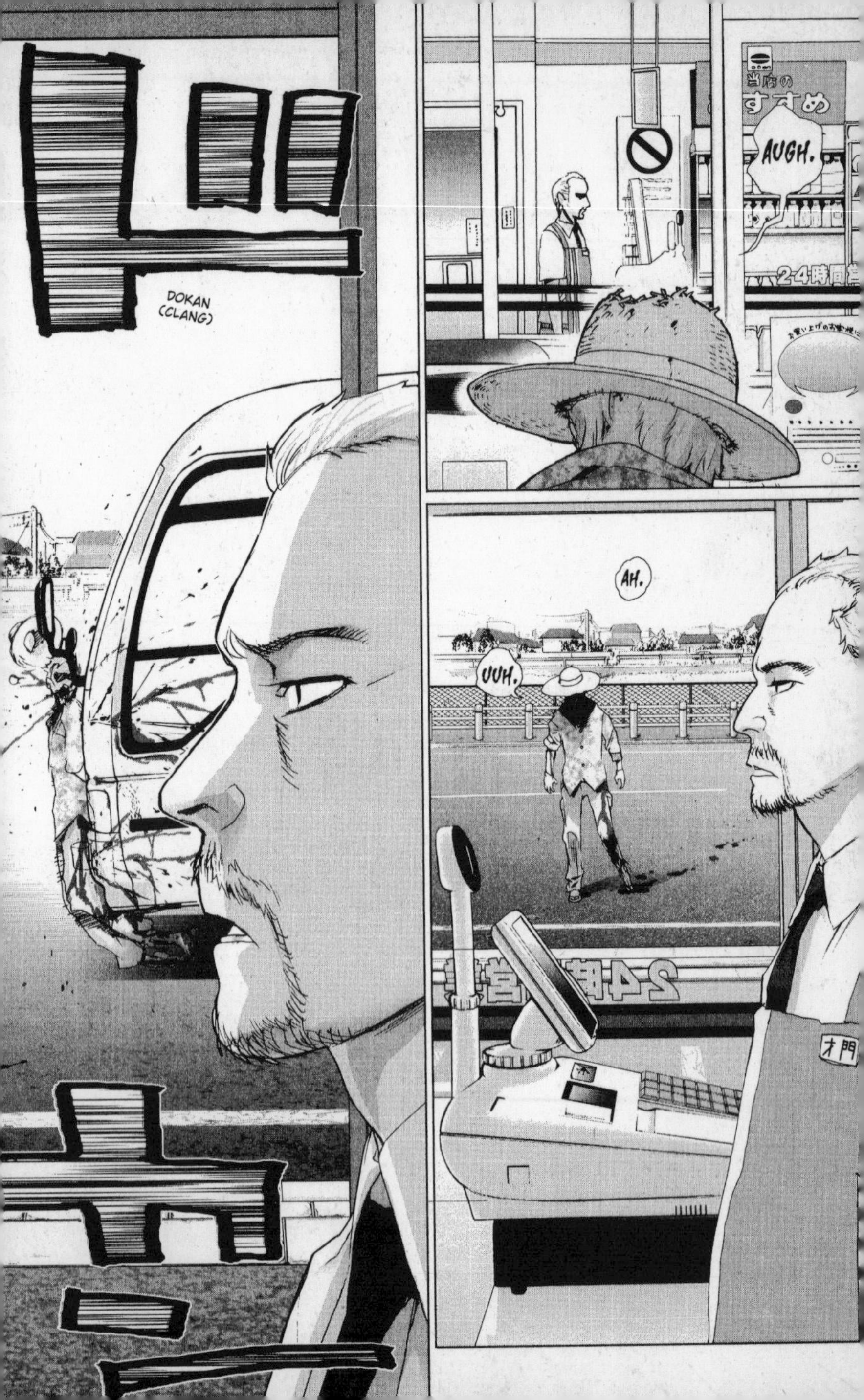
AUGH.
AH.
UUH.
DOKAN
(CLANG)

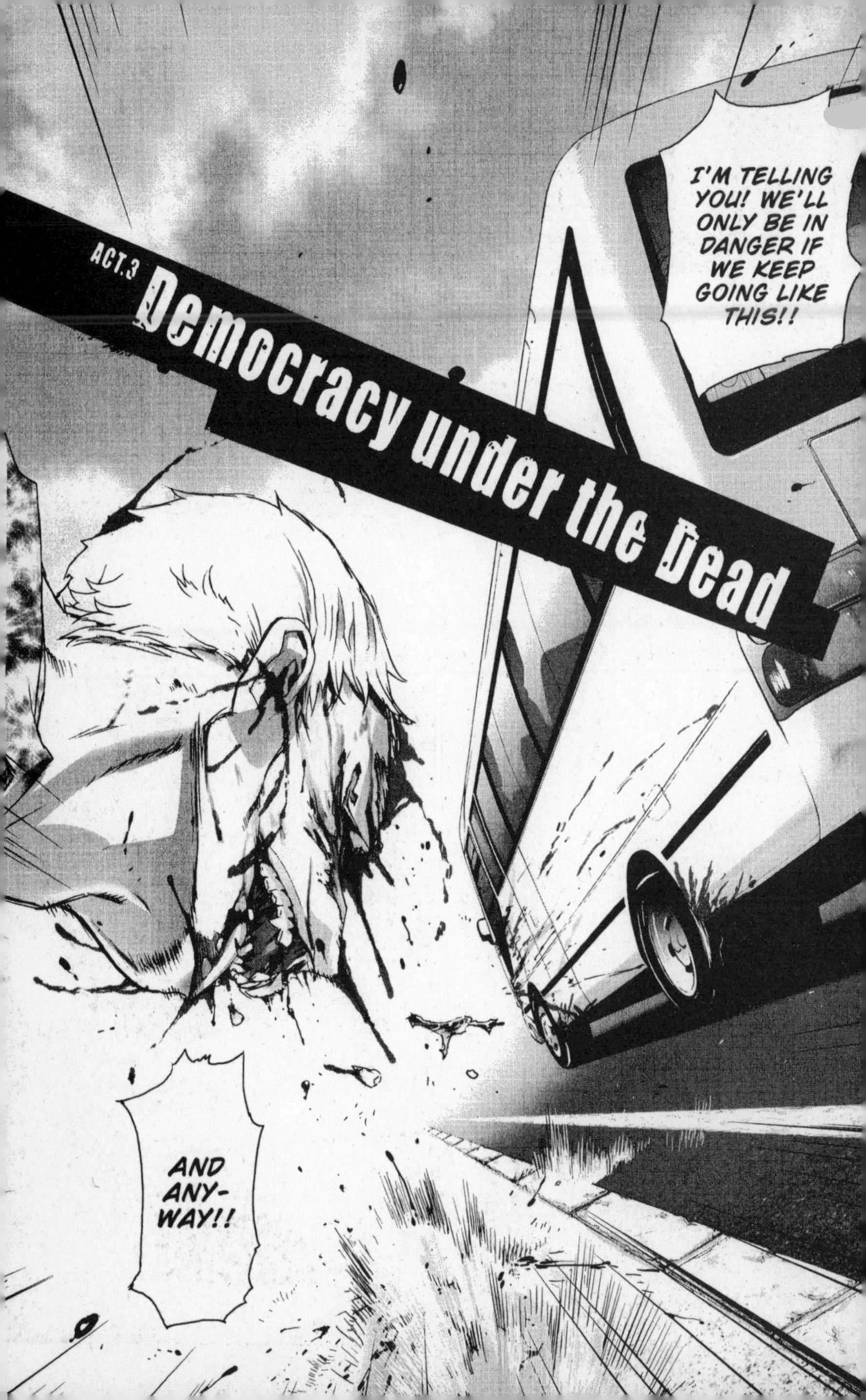
I'M TELLING YOU! WE'LL ONLY BE IN DANGER IF WE KEEP GOING LIKE THIS!!
ACT.3
Democracy under the Dead
AND ANY-WAY!!

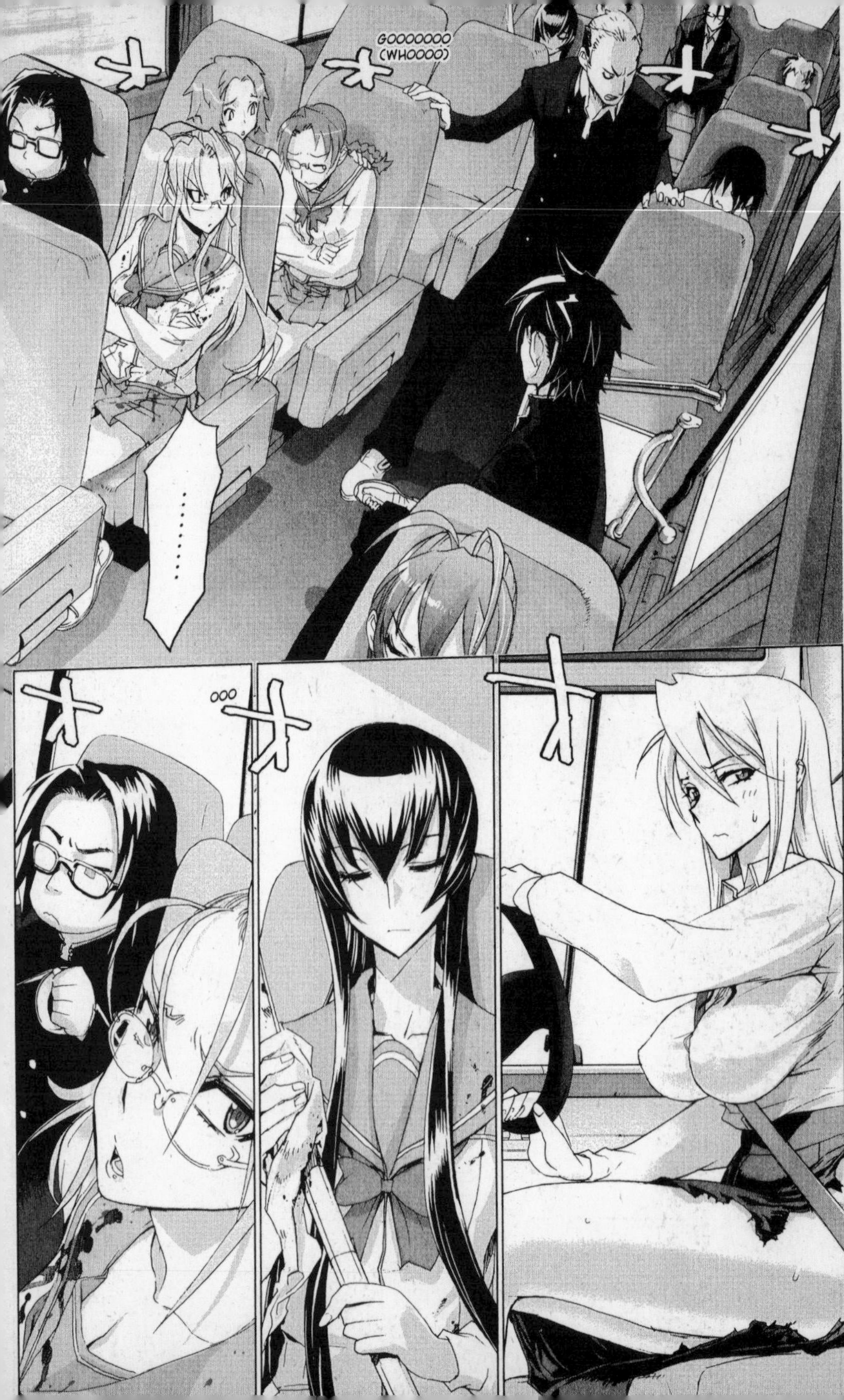
GOOOOOOO
(WHOOOO)
......
ooo

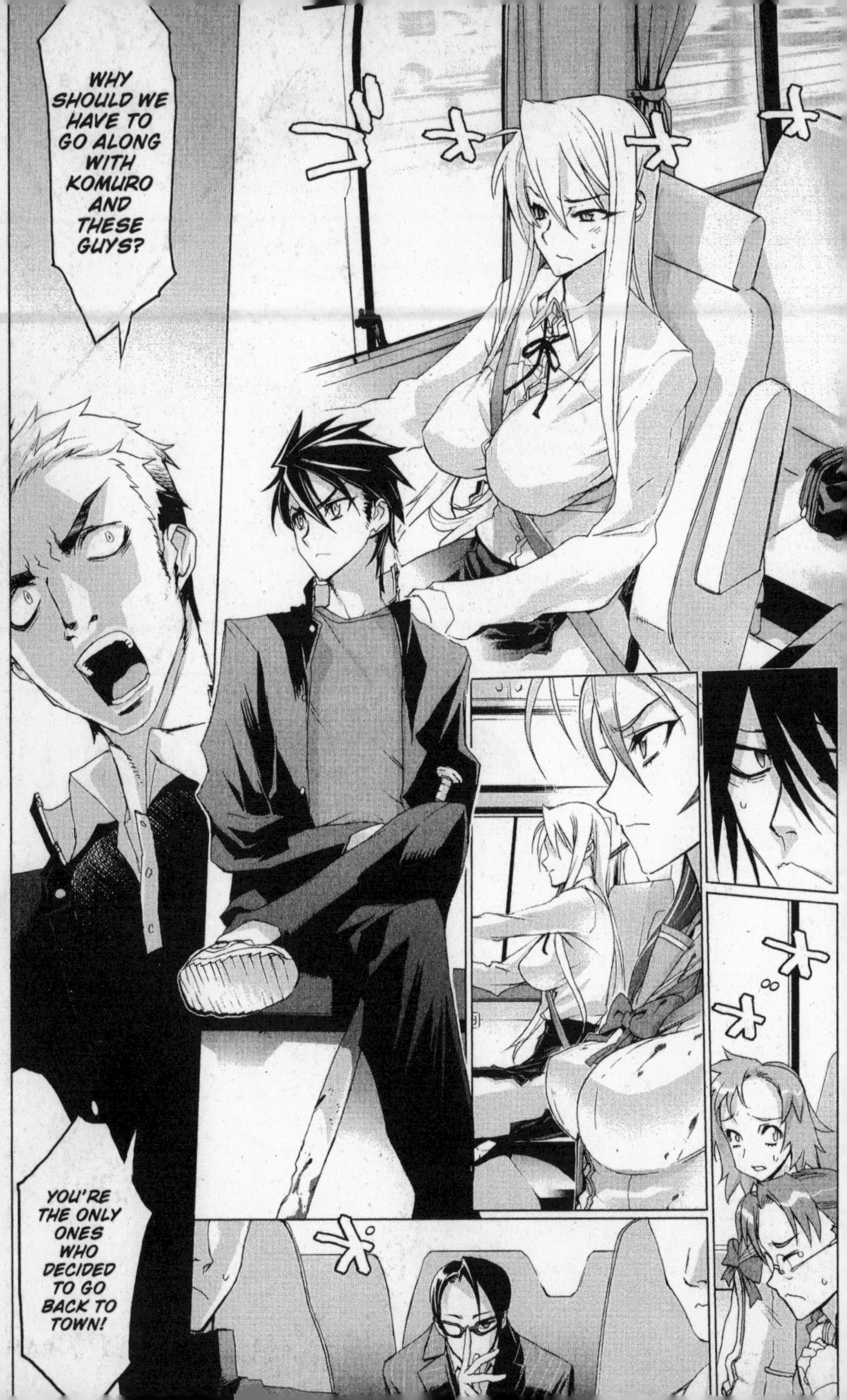
WHY SHOULD WE HAVE TO GO ALONG WITH KOMURO AND THESE GUYS?
YOU'RE THE ONLY ONES WHO DECIDED TO GO BACK TO TOWN!

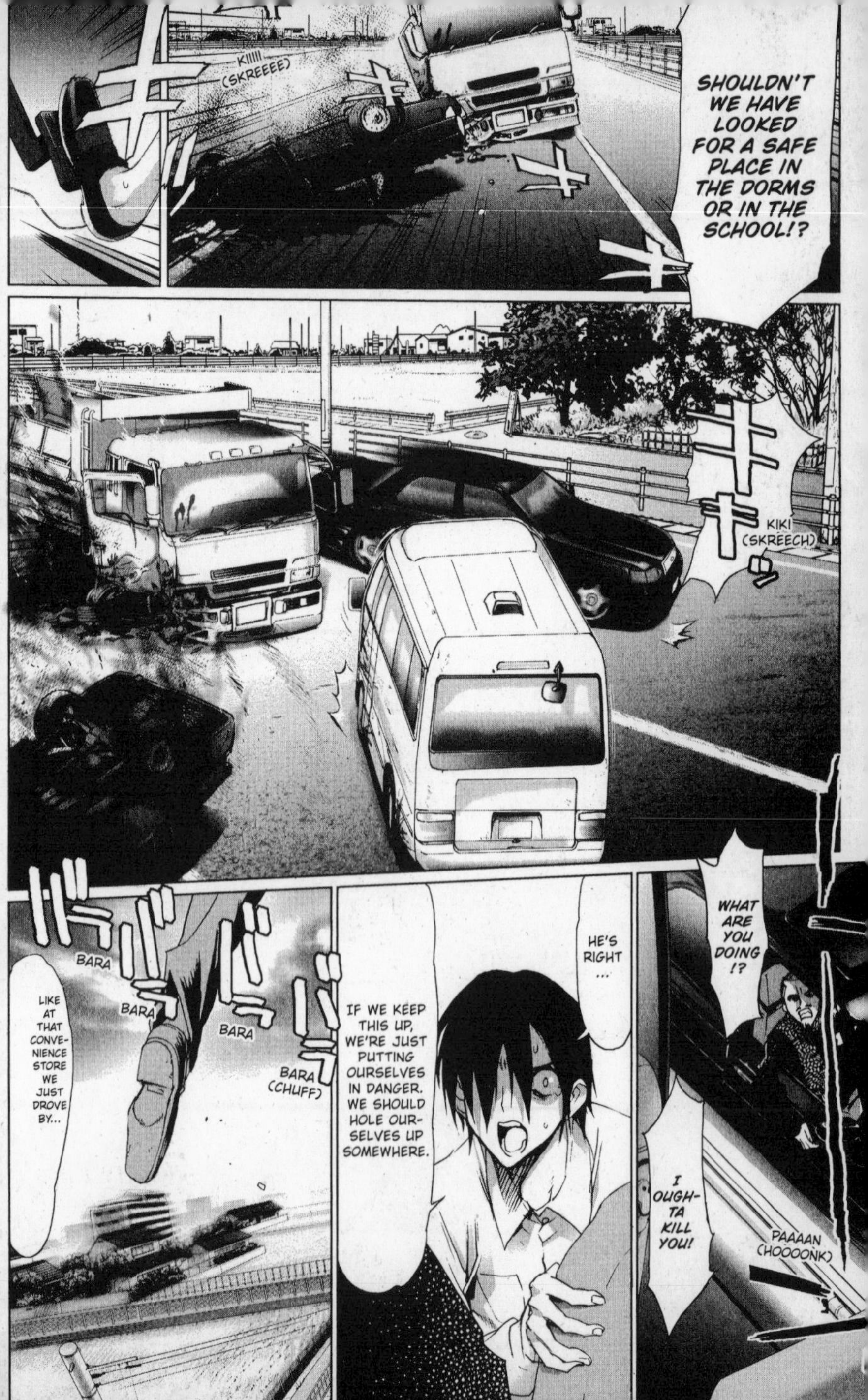
SHOULDN'T WE HAVE LOOKED FOR A SAFE PLACE IN THE DORMS OR IN THE SCHOOL!?
KIIIII (SKREEEE)
KIKI (SKREECH)
WHAT ARE YOU DOING!?
I OUGHT-TA KILL YOU!
PAAAAN (HOOOONK)
HE'S RIGHT...
IF WE KEEP THIS UP, WE'RE JUST PUTTING OURSELVES IN DANGER. WE SHOULD HOLE OUR-SELVES UP SOMEWHERE.
BARA
BARA
BARA
BARA (CHUFF)
LIKE AT THAT CONVE-NIENCE STORE WE JUST DROVE BY...

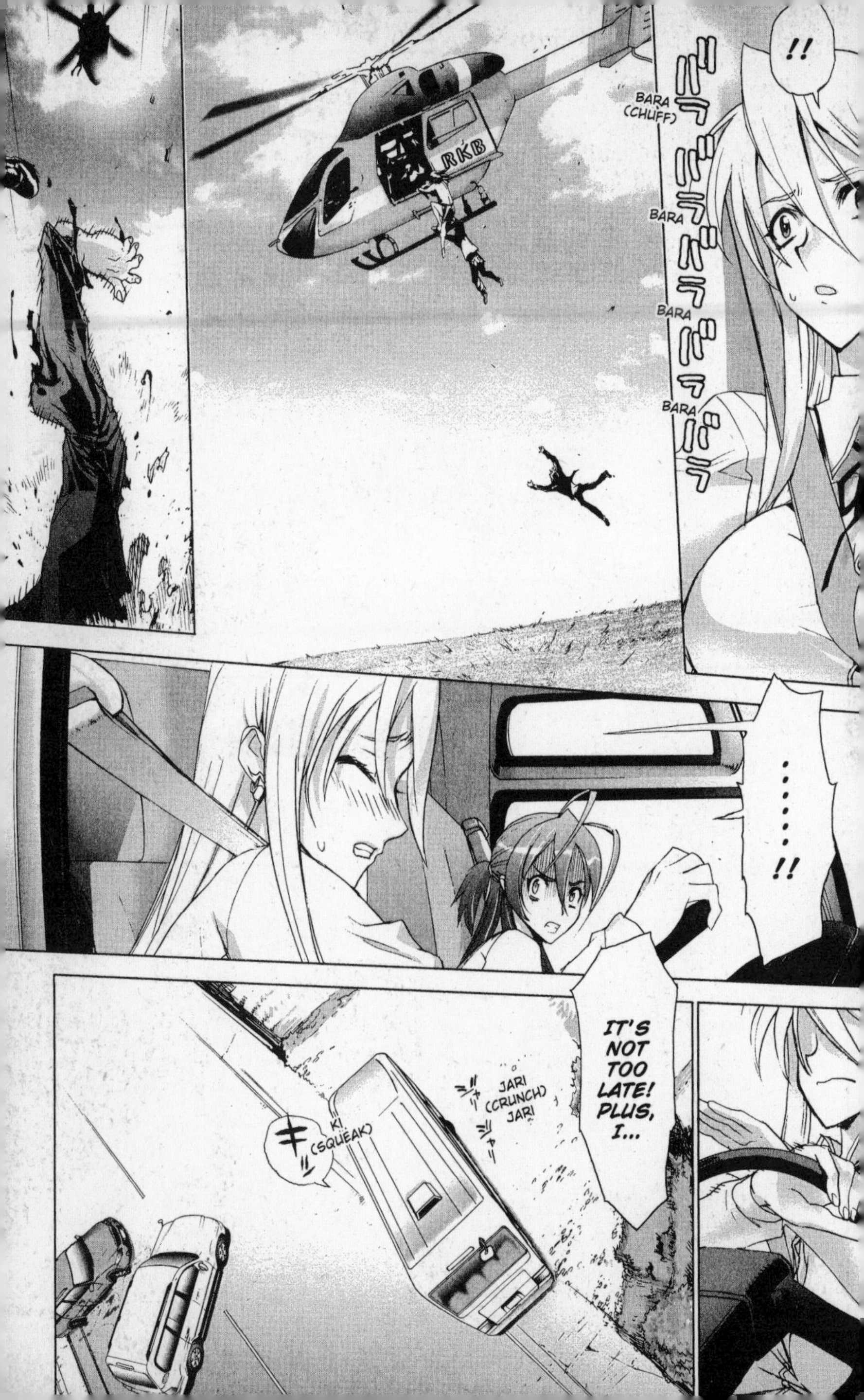
!!
BARA (CHUFF)
BARA
BARA
BARA
......!!
IT'S NOT TOO LATE! PLUS, I...
JARI (CRUNCH) JARI
KI (SQUEAK)

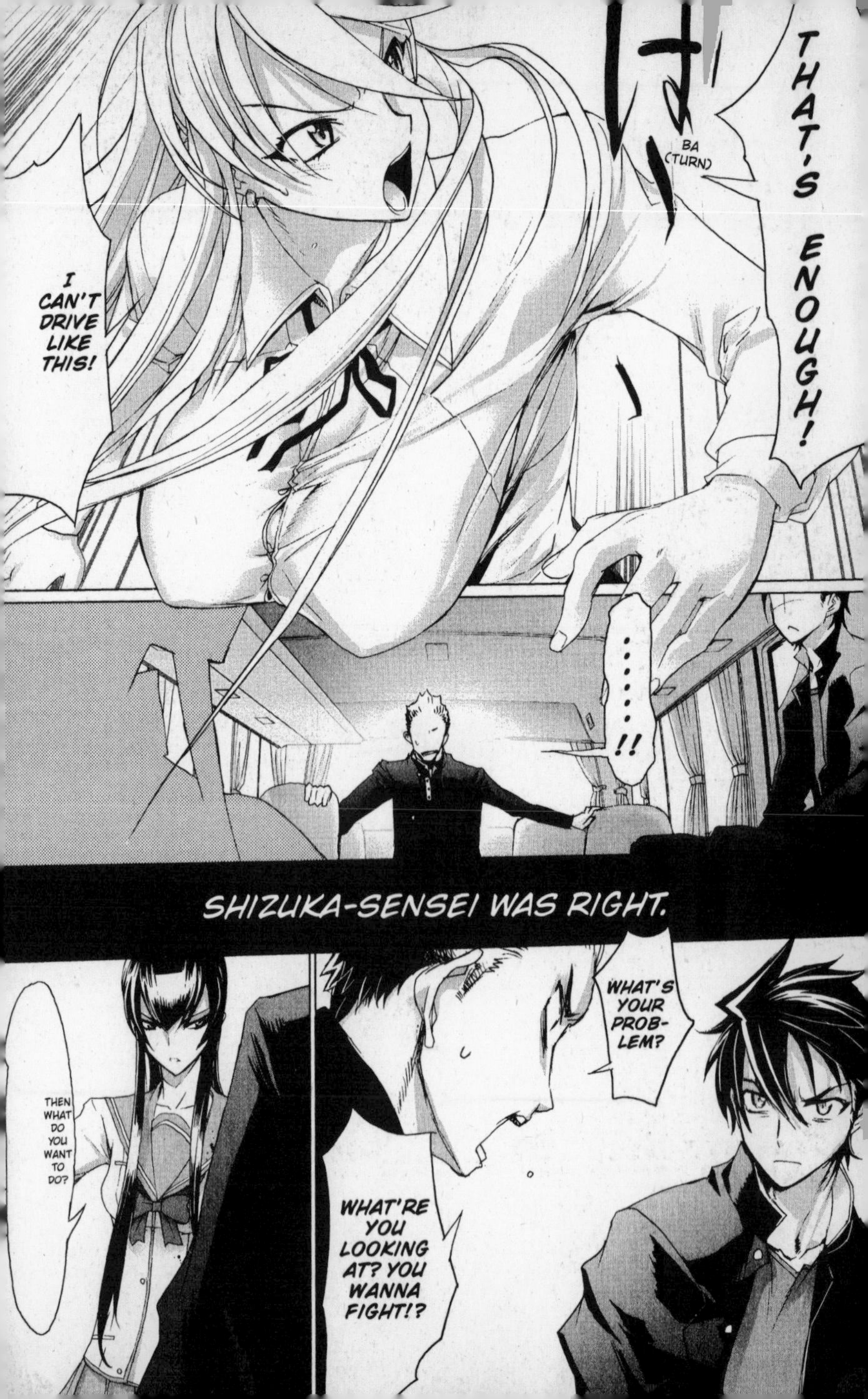
THAT'S ENOUGH!
BA (TURN)
I CAN'T DRIVE LIKE THIS!
......!!
SHIZUKA-SENSEI WAS RIGHT.
WHAT'S YOUR PROB-LEM?
WHAT'RE YOU LOOKING AT? YOU WANNA FIGHT!?
THEN WHAT DO YOU WANT TO DO?

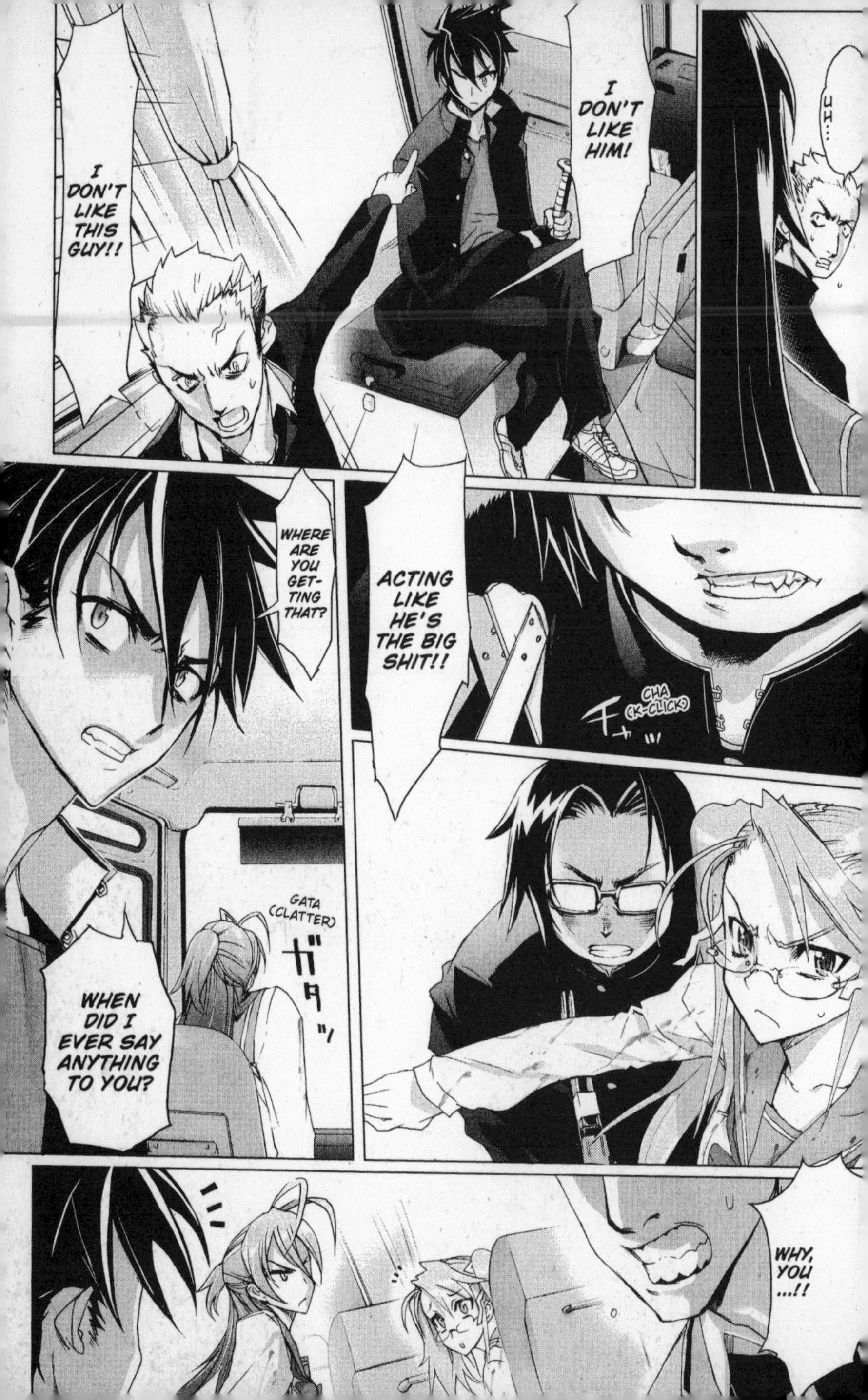

UH...
I DON'T LIKE HIM!
I DON'T LIKE THIS GUY!!
ACTING LIKE HE'S THE BIG SHIT!!
チャッ
CHA (K-CLICK)
WHERE ARE YOU GET-TING THAT?
ガタッ
GATA (CLATTER)
WHEN DID I EVER SAY ANYTHING TO YOU?
WHY, YOU ...!!

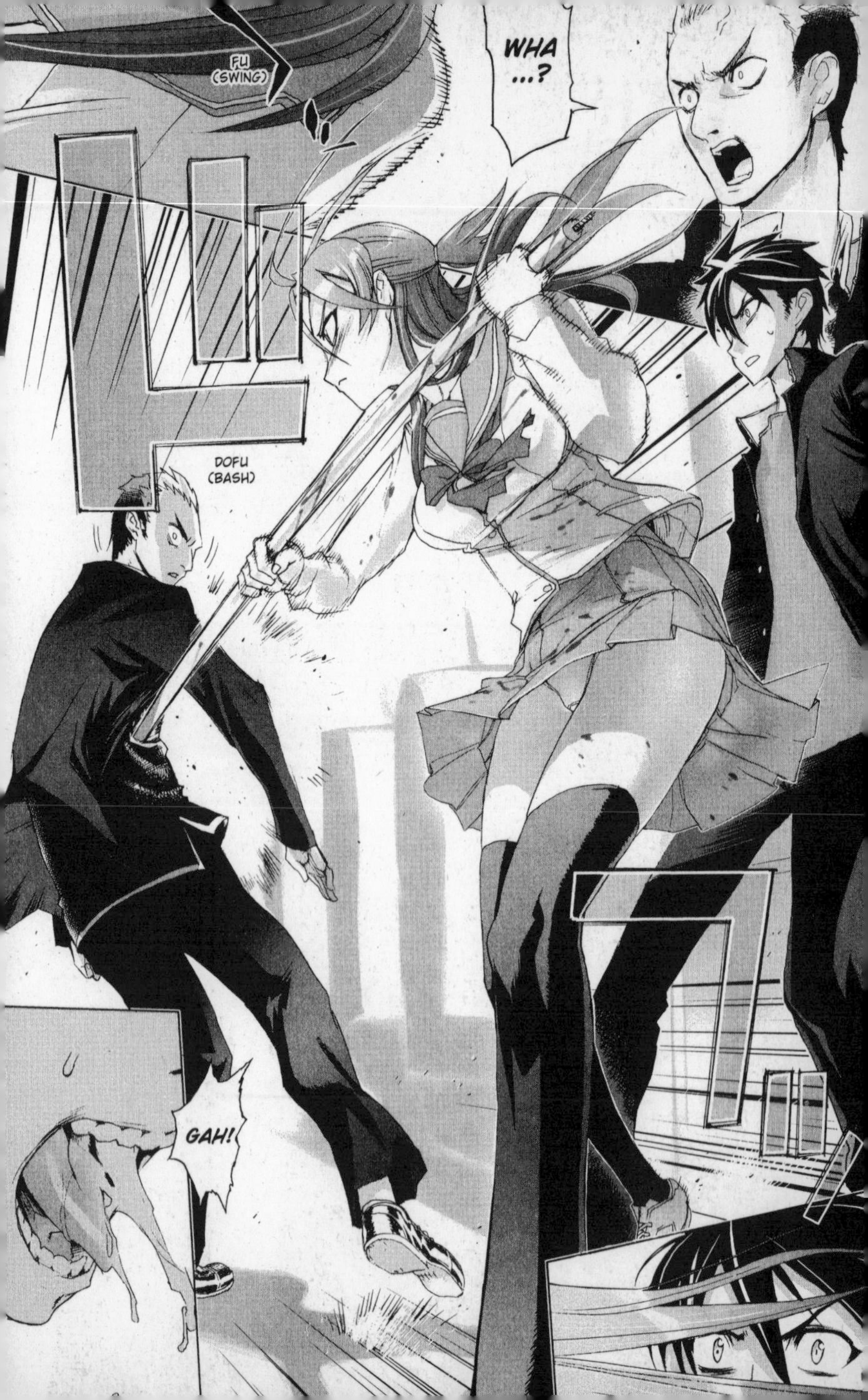
WHA ...?
FU (SWING)
DOFU (BASH)
GAH!

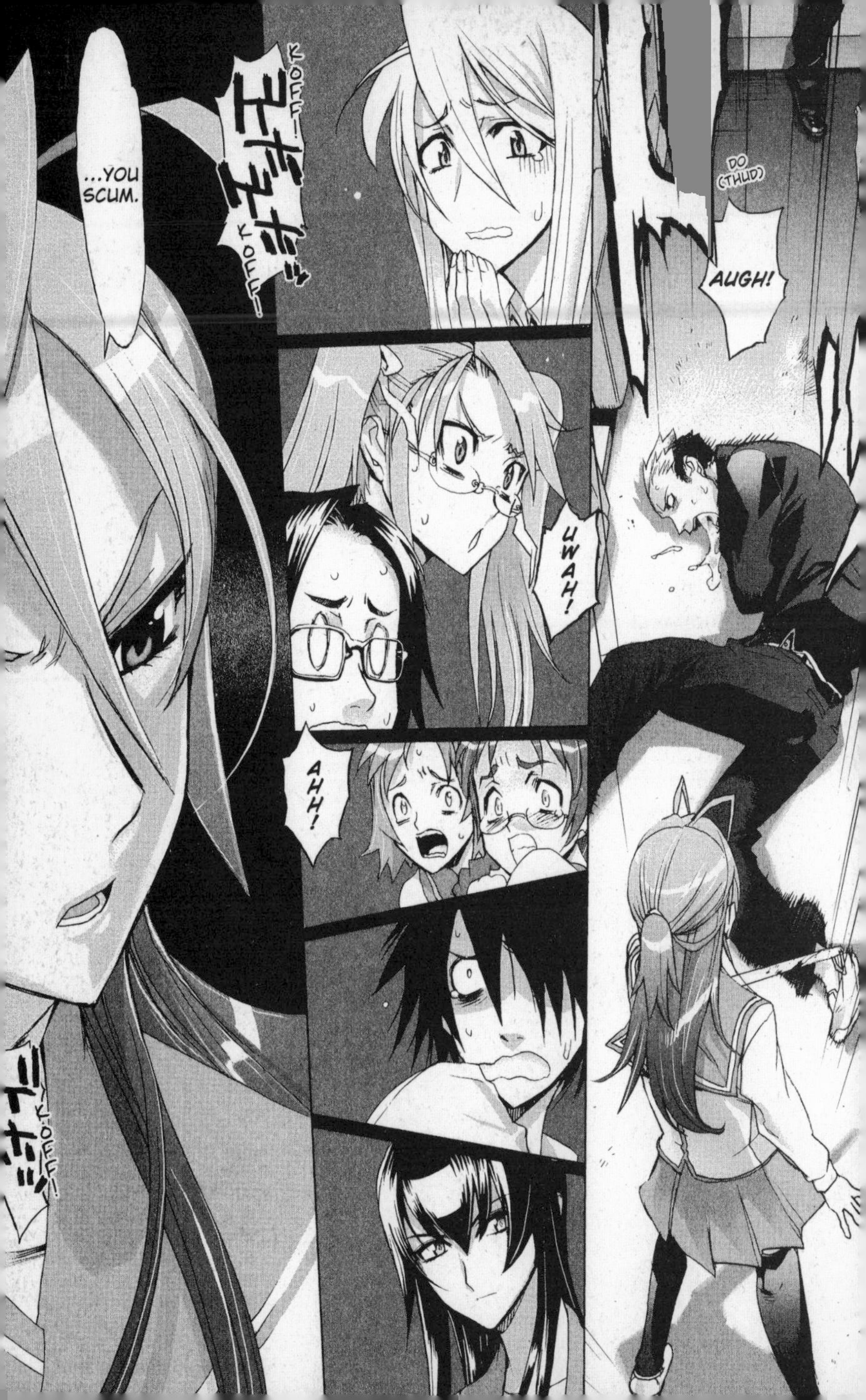
DO
(THUD)
AUGH!
UWAH!
AHH!
KOFF! KOFF!
...YOU SCUM.
KOFF!

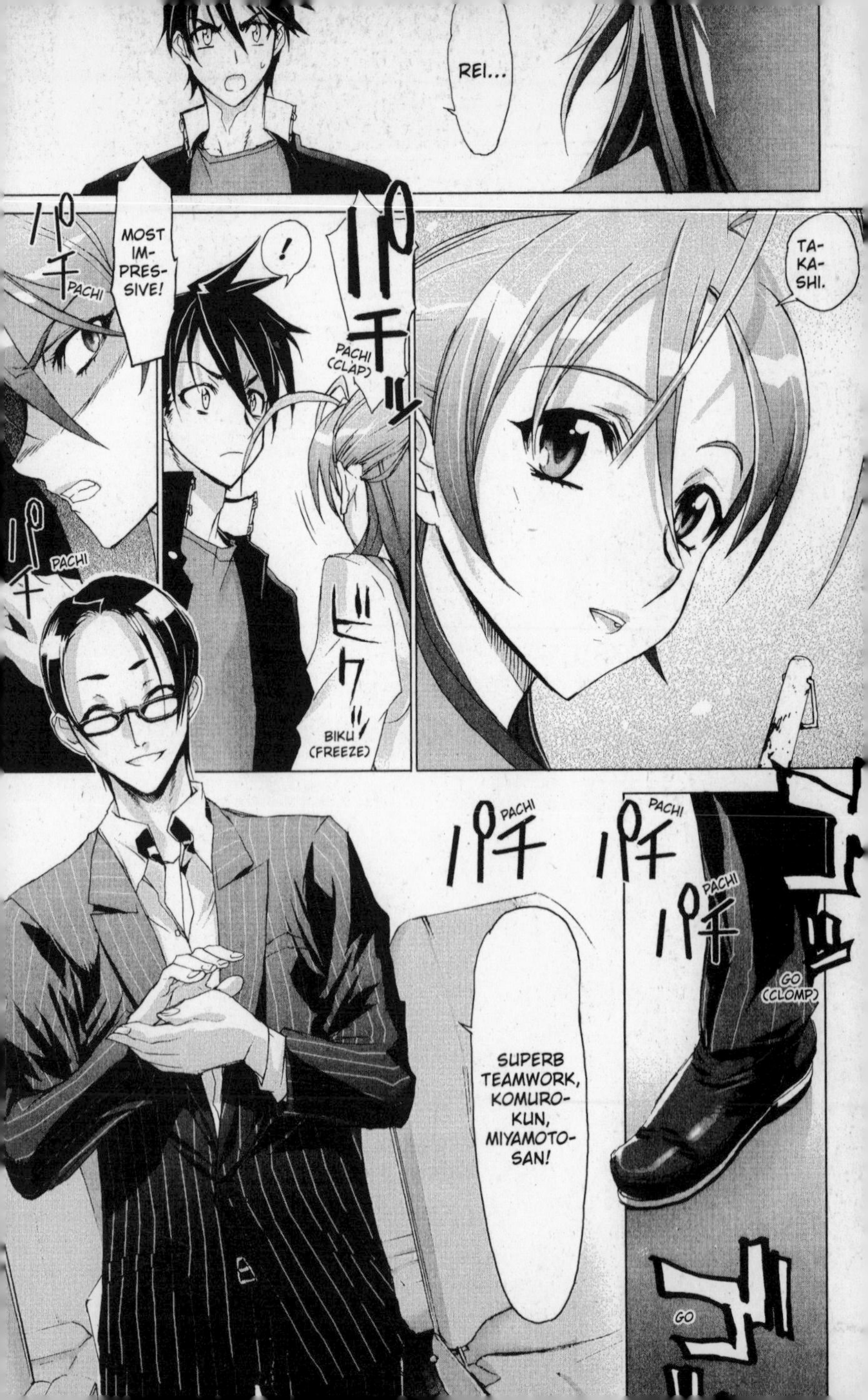
REI...
TA-KA-SHI.
PACHI (CLAP)
!
BIKU (FREEZE)
PACHI
MOST IM-PRES-SIVE!
PACHI
GO (CLOMP)
GO
PACHI
PACHI
PACHI
SUPERB TEAMWORK, KOMURO-KUN, MIYAMOTO-SAN!

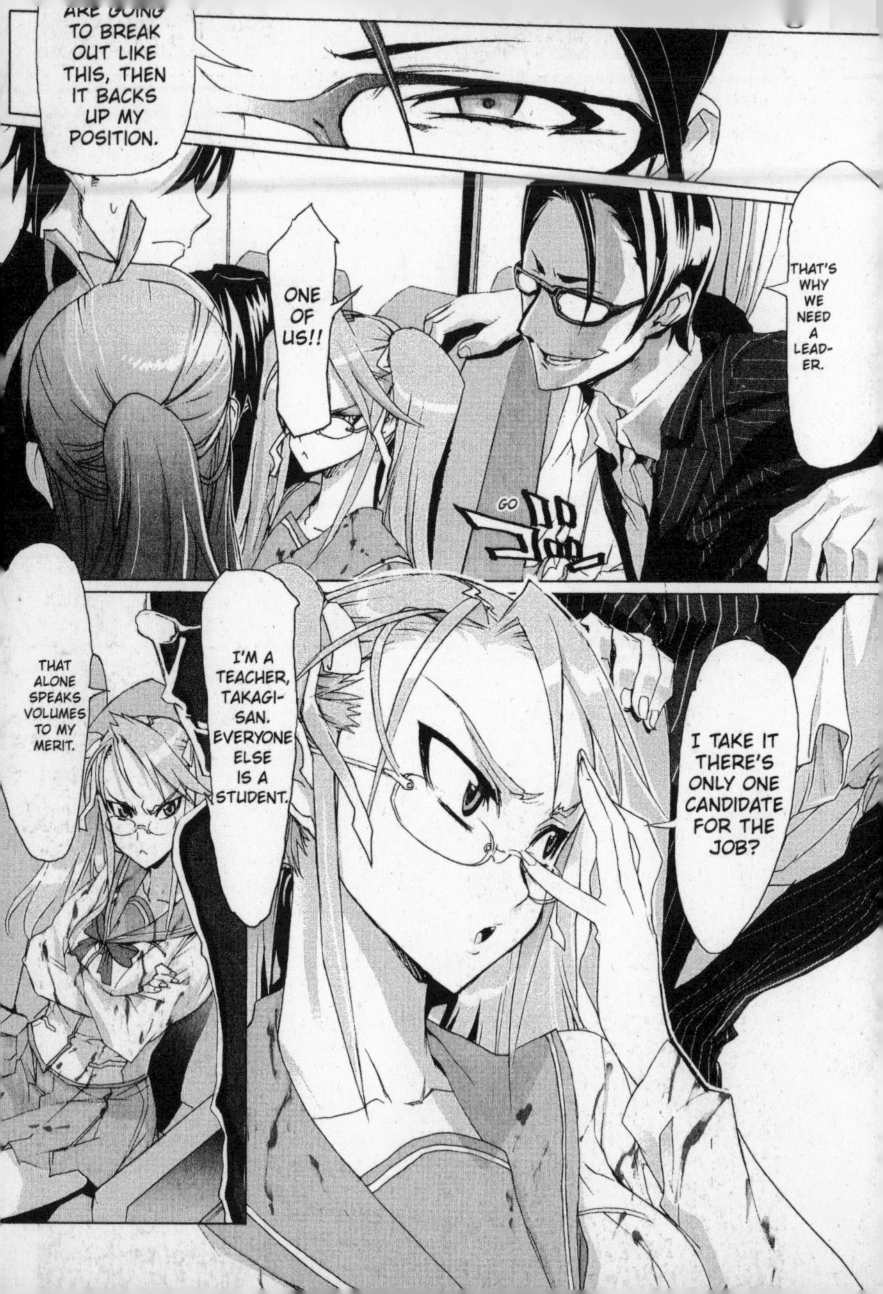
ARE GOING TO BREAK OUT LIKE THIS, THEN IT BACKS UP MY POSITION.
THAT'S WHY WE NEED A LEADER.
ONE OF US!!
GO
I TAKE IT THERE'S ONLY ONE CANDIDATE FOR THE JOB?
I'M A TEACHER, TAKAGI-SAN. EVERYONE ELSE IS A STUDENT.
THAT ALONE SPEAKS VOLUMES TO MY MERIT.

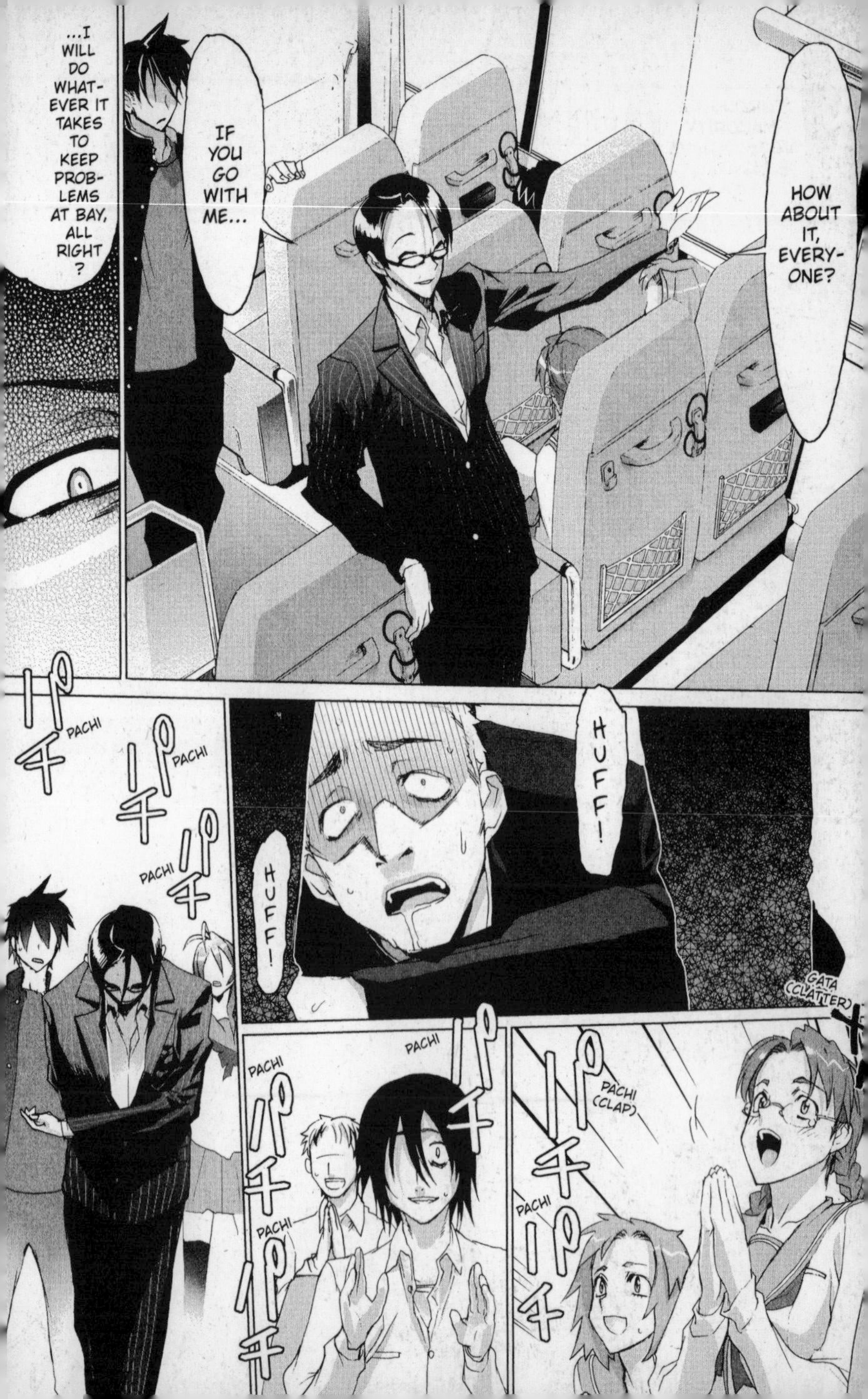
HOW ABOUT IT, EVERYONE?
IF YOU GO WITH ME...
...I WILL DO WHATEVER IT TAKES TO KEEP PROBLEMS AT BAY, ALL RIGHT?
HUFF!
HUFF!
GATA (CLATTER)
パチ
PACHI (CLAP)
パチ
PACHI
パチ
PACHI
パチ
PACHI
パチ
PACHI
パチ
PACHI
パチ
PACHI
パチ
PACHI

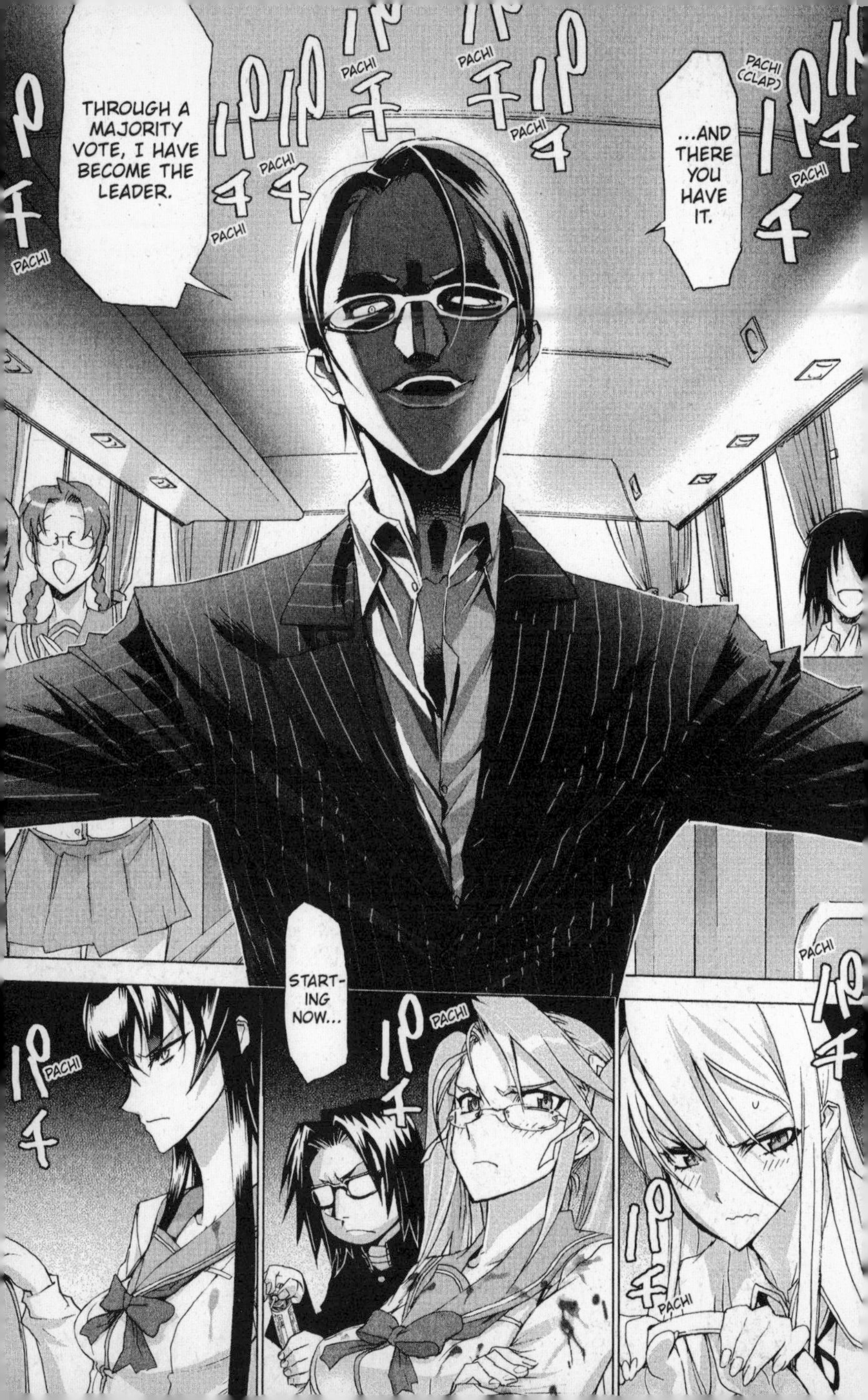
PACHI (CLAP)
PACHI
...AND THERE YOU HAVE IT.
PACHI
PACHI
PACHI
PACHI
PACHI
THROUGH A MAJORITY VOTE, I HAVE BECOME THE LEADER.
PACHI
PACHI
PACHI
STARTING-ING NOW...
PACHI
PACHI

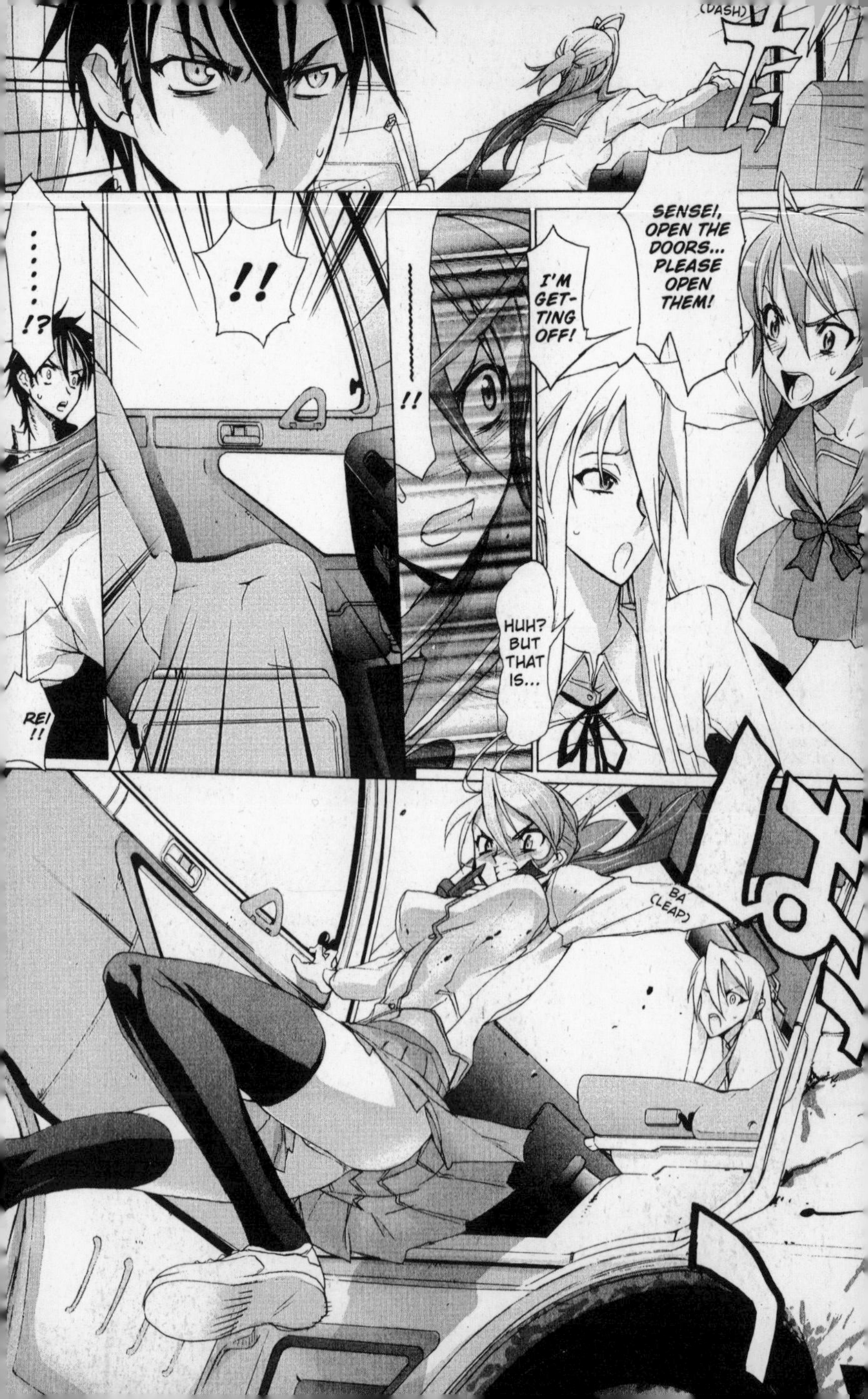
(DASH)
SENSEI, OPEN THE DOORS... PLEASE OPEN THEM!
I'M GETTING OFF!
HUH? BUT THAT IS...
————!!
!!
......!?
REI!!
BA (LEAP)

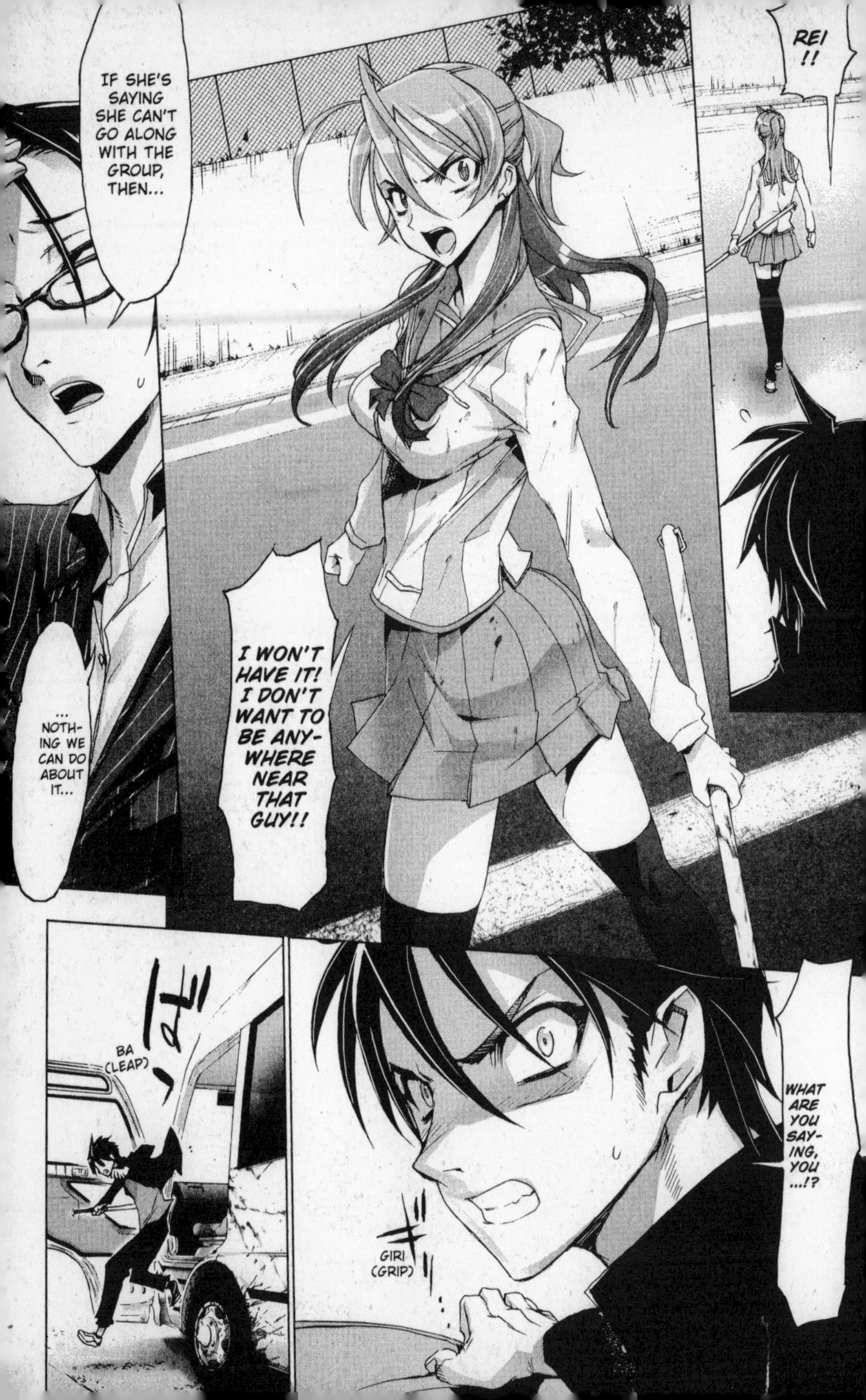
REI!!
I WON'T HAVE IT! I DON'T WANT TO BE ANY-WHERE NEAR THAT GUY!!
IF SHE'S SAYING SHE CAN'T GO ALONG WITH THE GROUP, THEN...
...NOTHING WE CAN DO ABOUT IT...
WHAT ARE YOU SAYING, YOU...!?
GIRI (GRIP)
BA (LEAP)

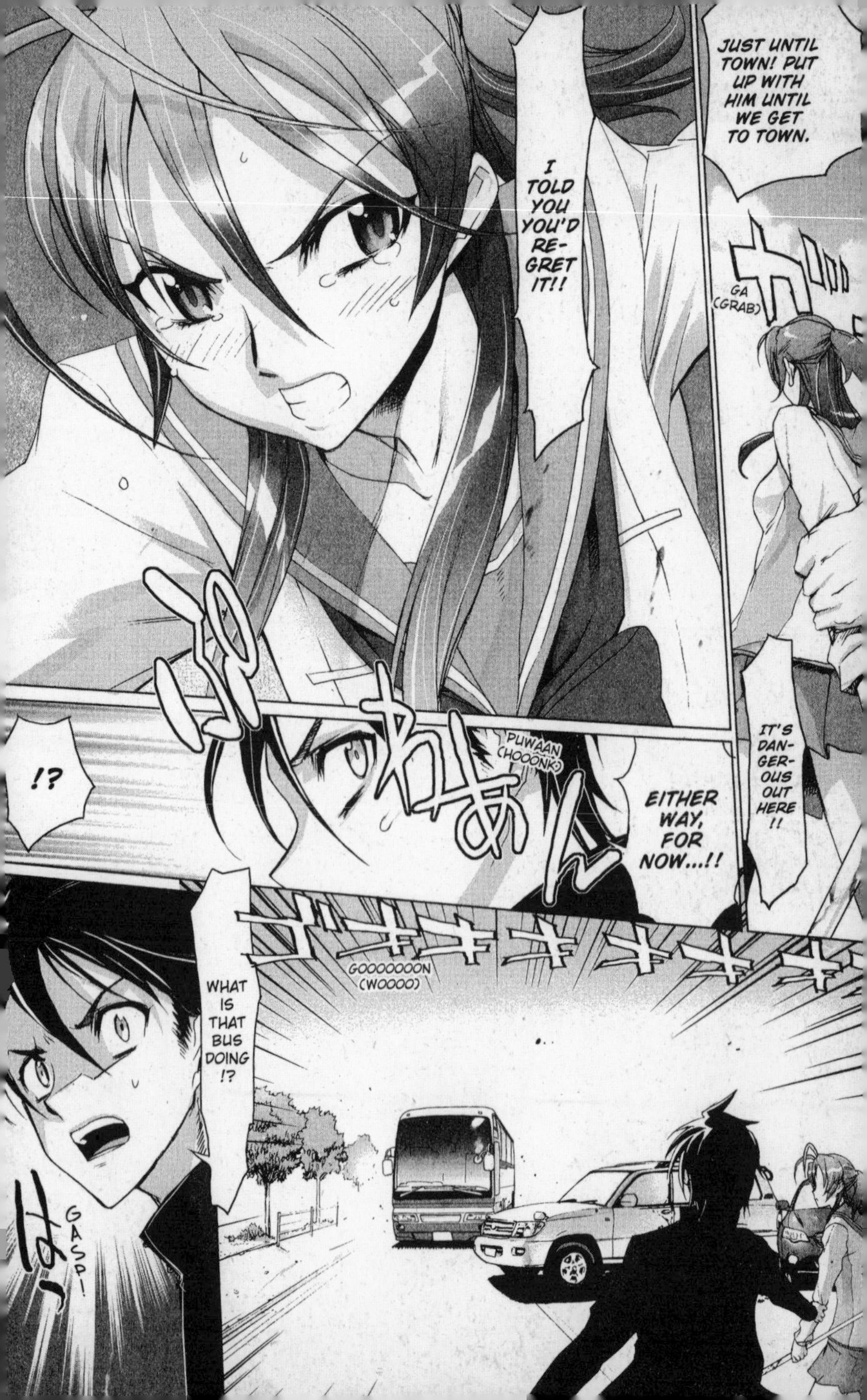
JUST UNTIL TOWN! PUT UP WITH HIM UNTIL WE GET TO TOWN.
GA (GRAB)
IT'S DAN-GER-OUS OUT HERE!!
I TOLD YOU YOU'D RE-GRET IT!!
EITHER WAY, FOR NOW...!!
PUWAAN (HOOONK)
!?
GOOOOOOON (WOOOO)
WHAT IS THAT BUS DOING!?
GASP!

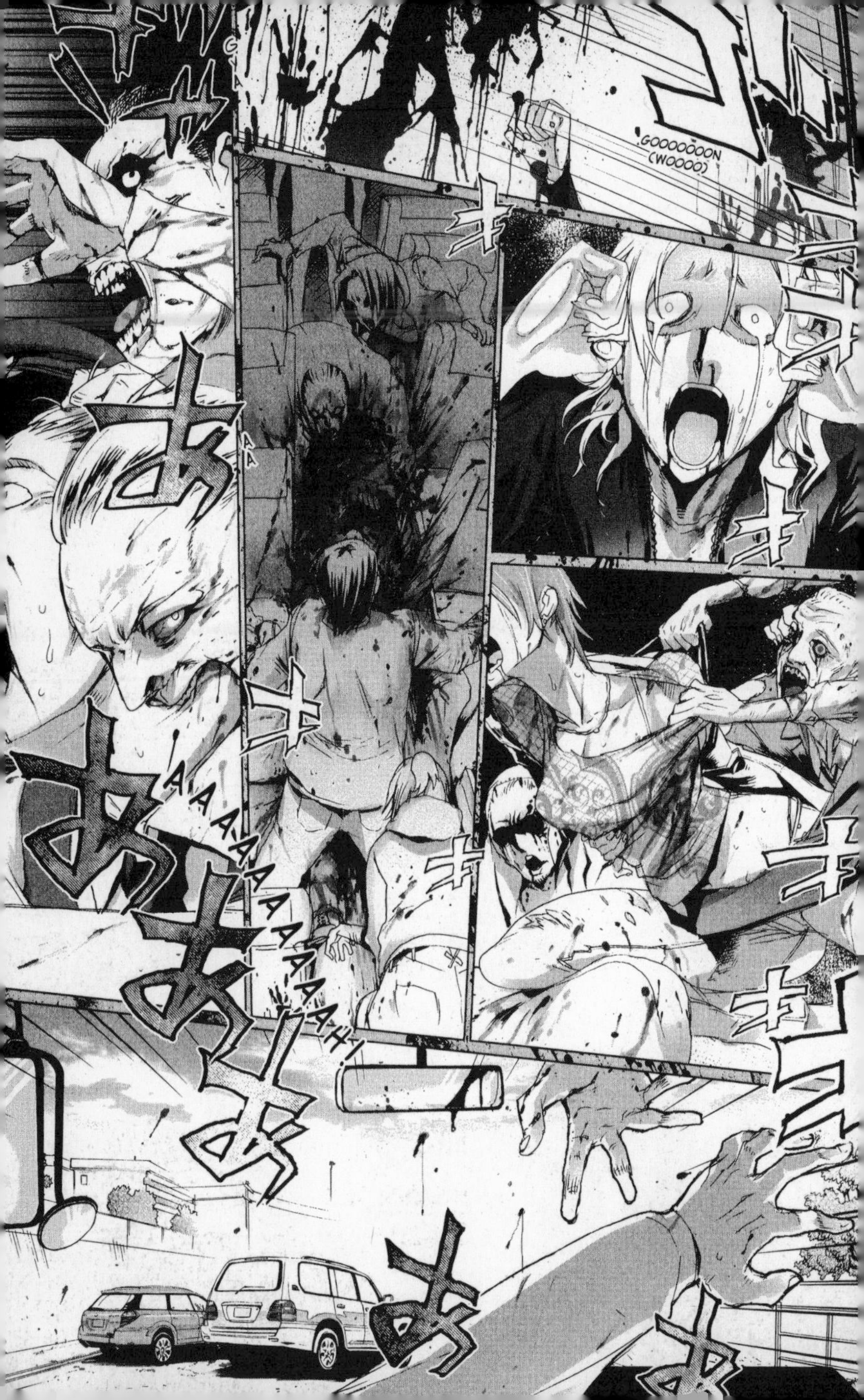
GOOOOOOON
(WOOOO)
GA
AA
AAAAAAAAAAH!

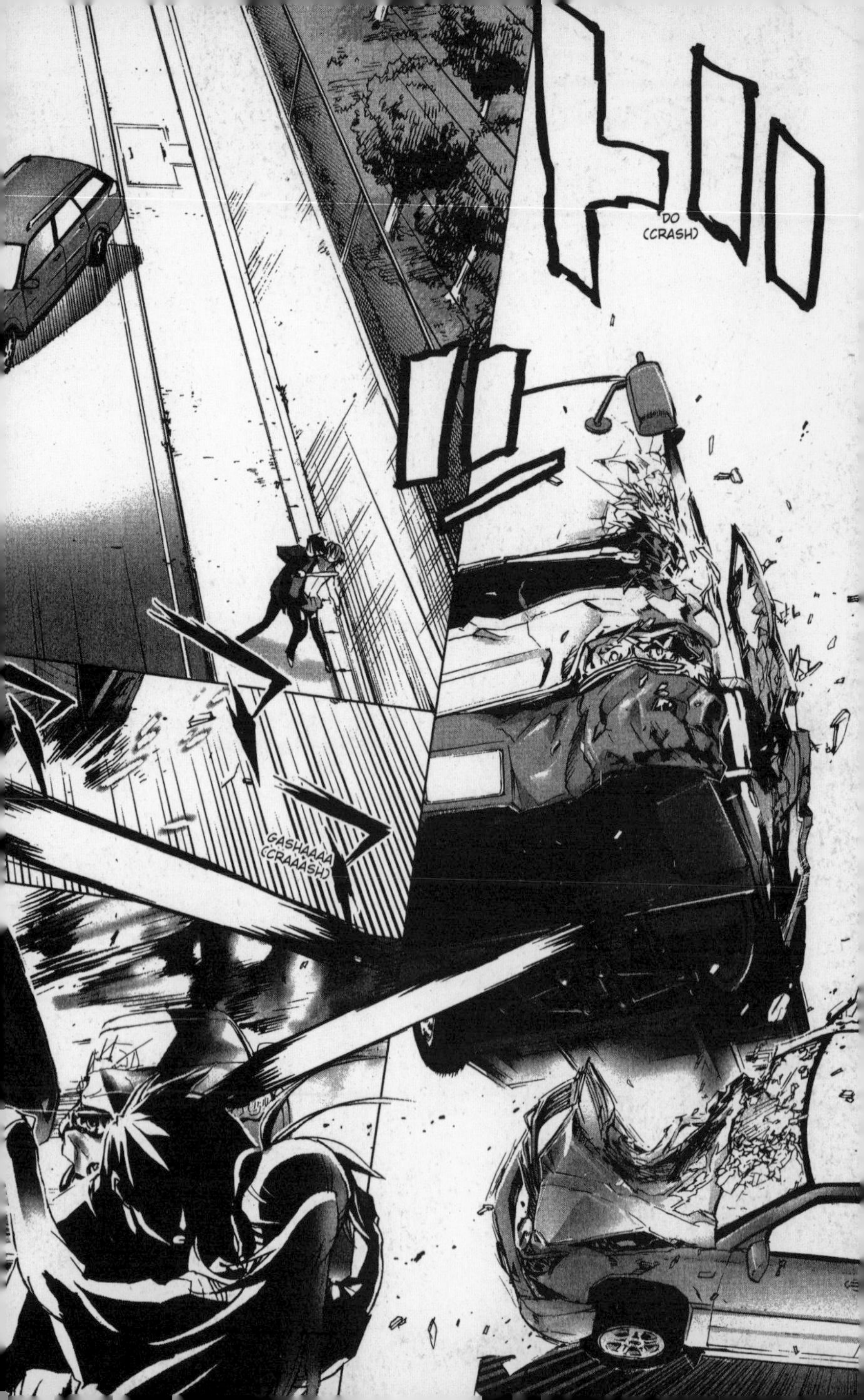
DO
(CRASH)
GASHAAAA
(CRAAASH)

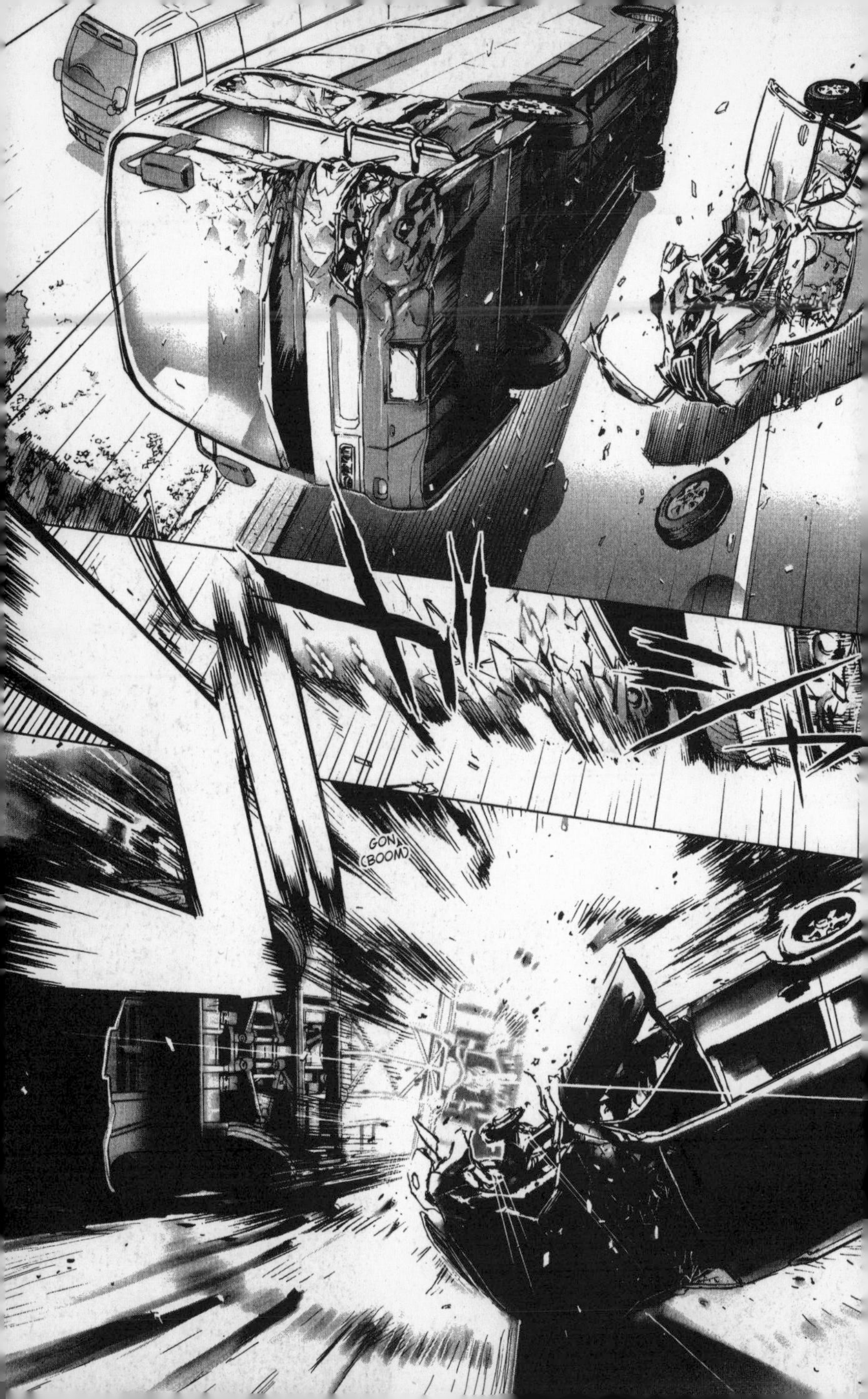
GON
(BOOM)

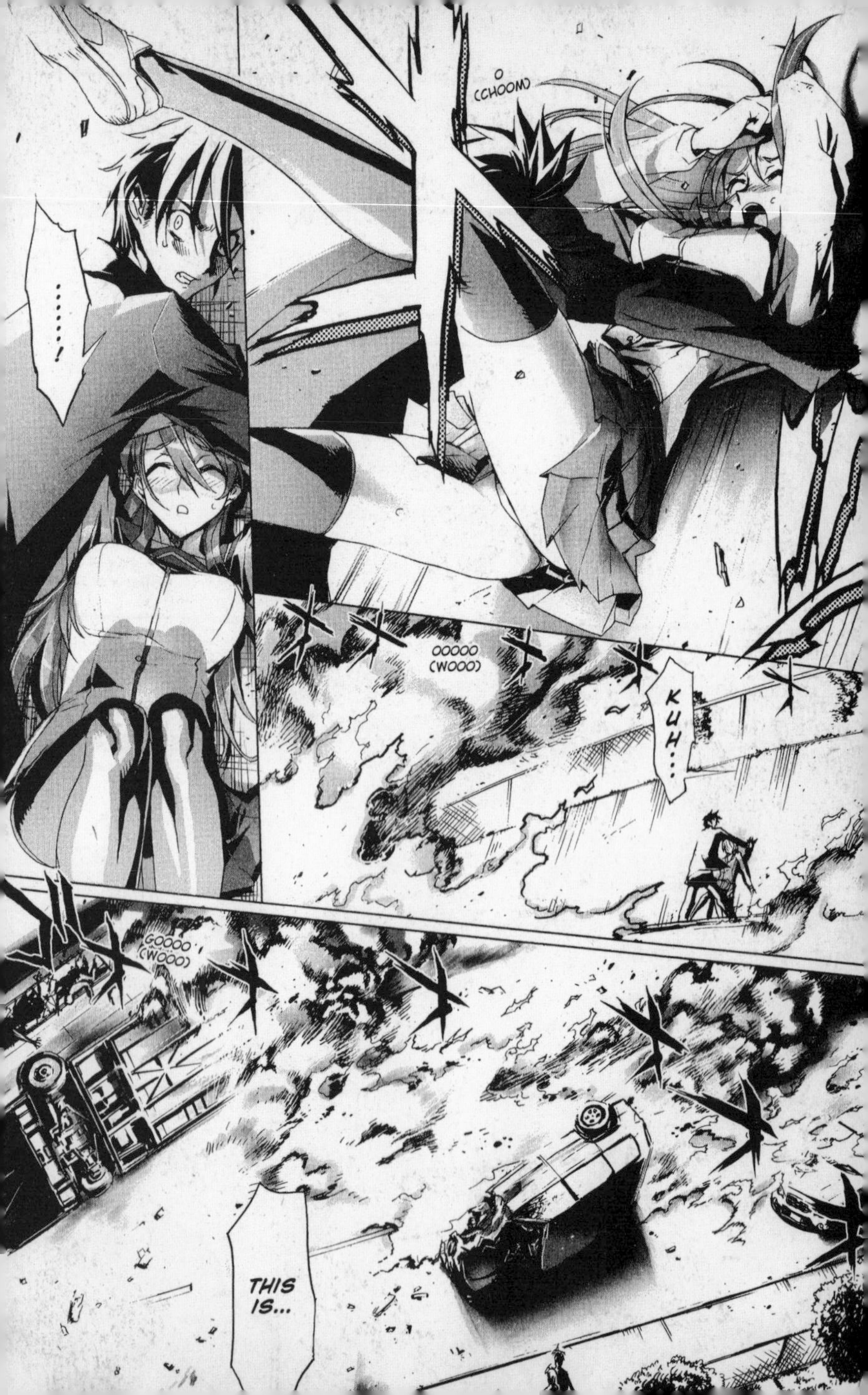
O
(CHOOM)
......!
OOOOO
(WOOO)
KUH...
GOOOO
(WOOO)
THIS IS...

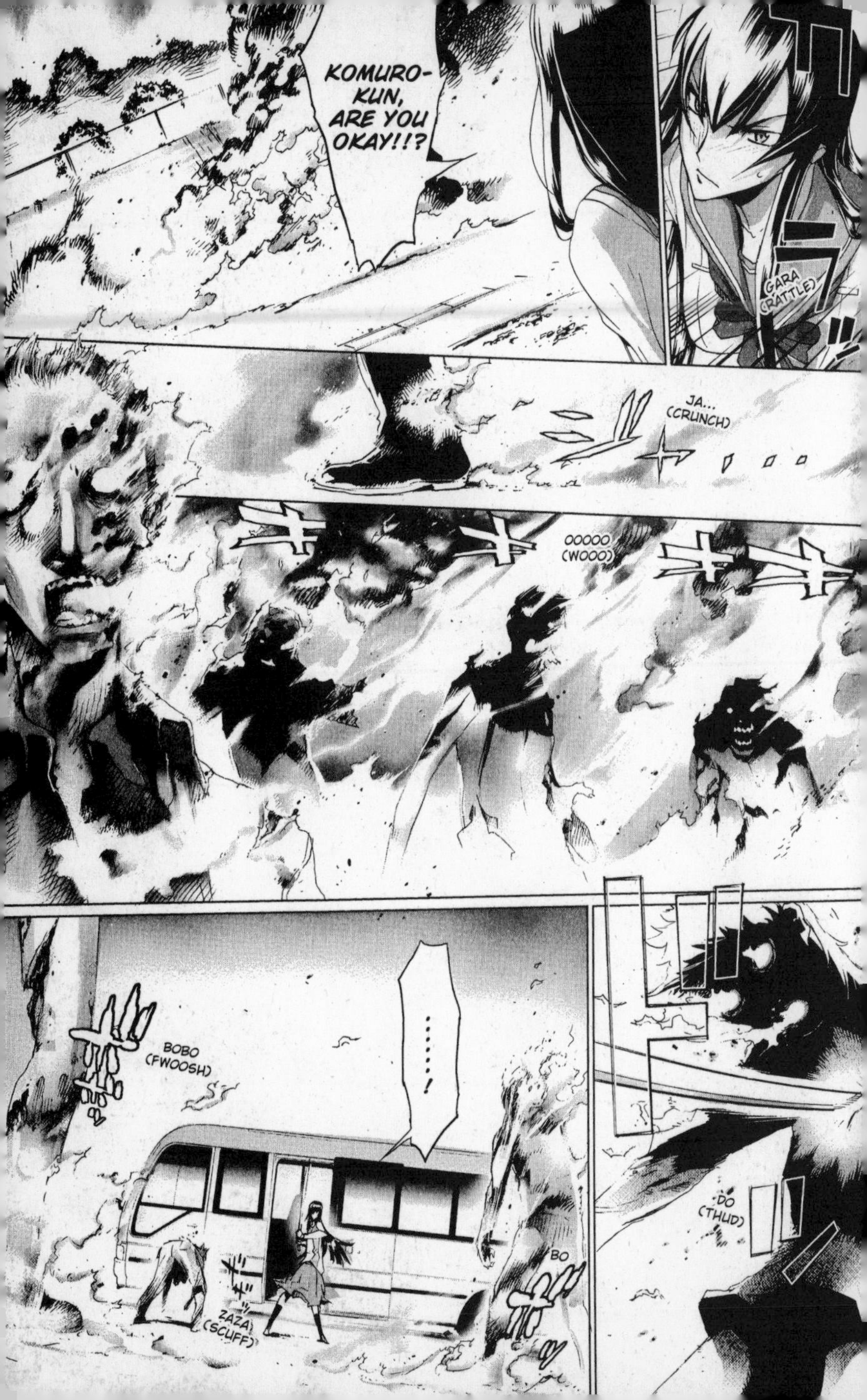
GARA (RATTLE)
KOMURO-KUN, ARE YOU OKAY!!?
JA... (CRUNCH)
OOOOO (WOOO)
DO (THUD)
......!
BO
ZAZA (SCUFF)
BOBO (FWOOSH)

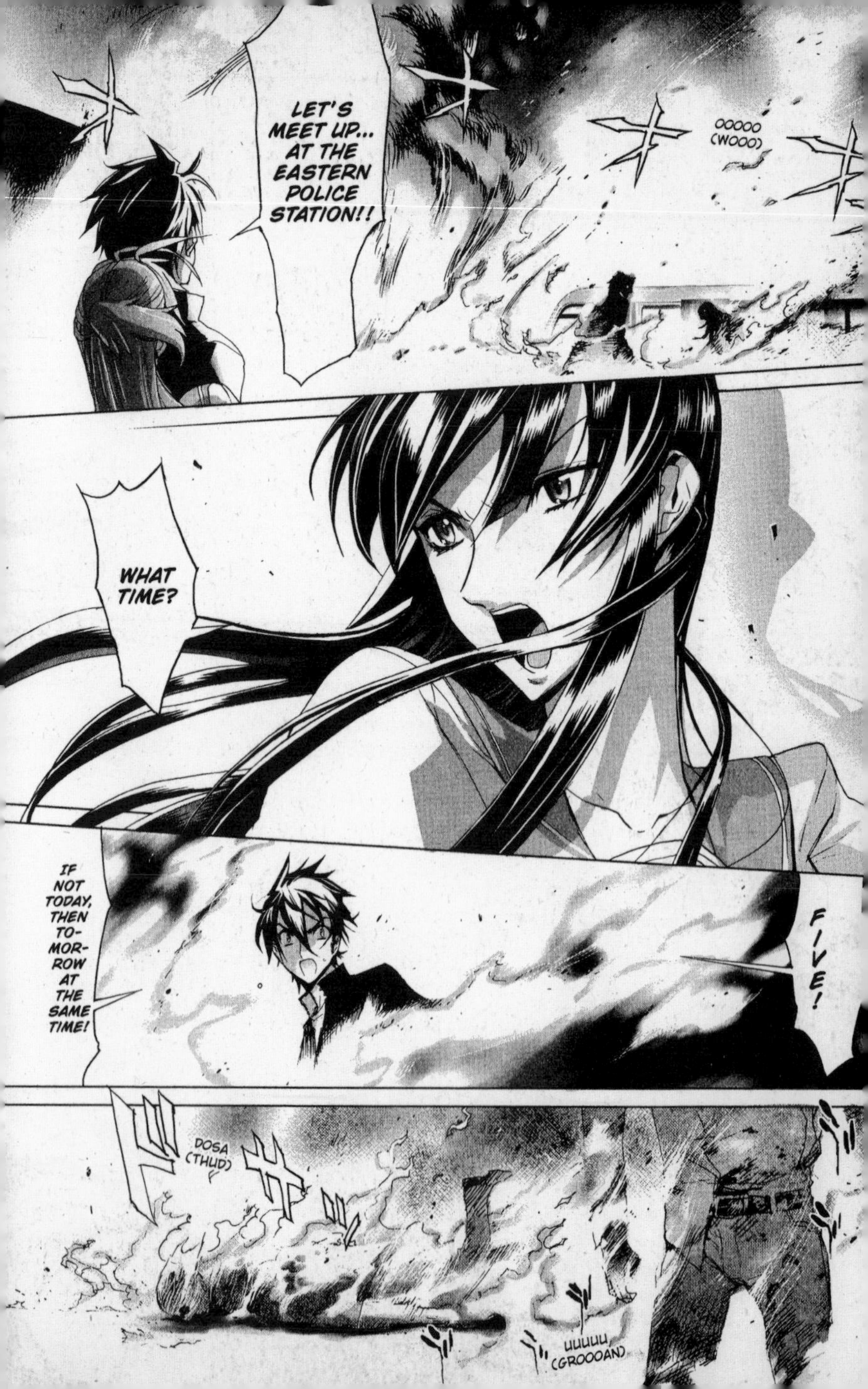
OOOOO
(WOOO)
LET'S MEET UP... AT THE EASTERN POLICE STATION!!
WHAT TIME?
FIVE!
IF NOT TODAY, THEN TO-MOR-ROW AT THE SAME TIME!
UUUUU
(GROOOAN)
DOSA
(THUD)

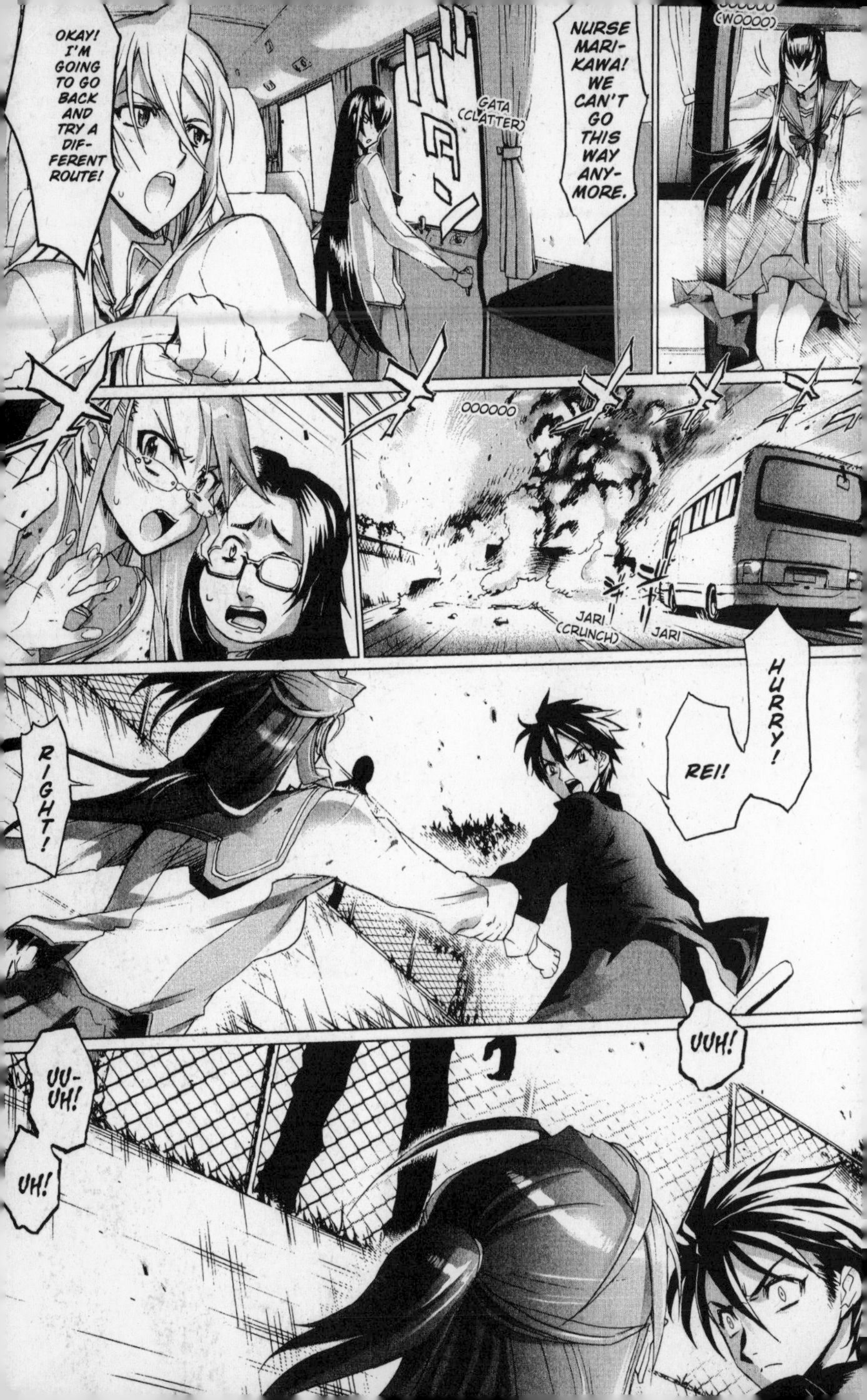
(WOOOO)
NURSE MARI-KAWA! WE CAN'T GO THIS WAY ANY-MORE.
GATA (CLATTER)
OKAY! I'M GOING TO GO BACK AND TRY A DIF-FERENT ROUTE!
OOOOOO
JARI
JARI (CRUNCH)
HURRY!
REI!
RIGHT!
UUH!
UU-UH!
UH!

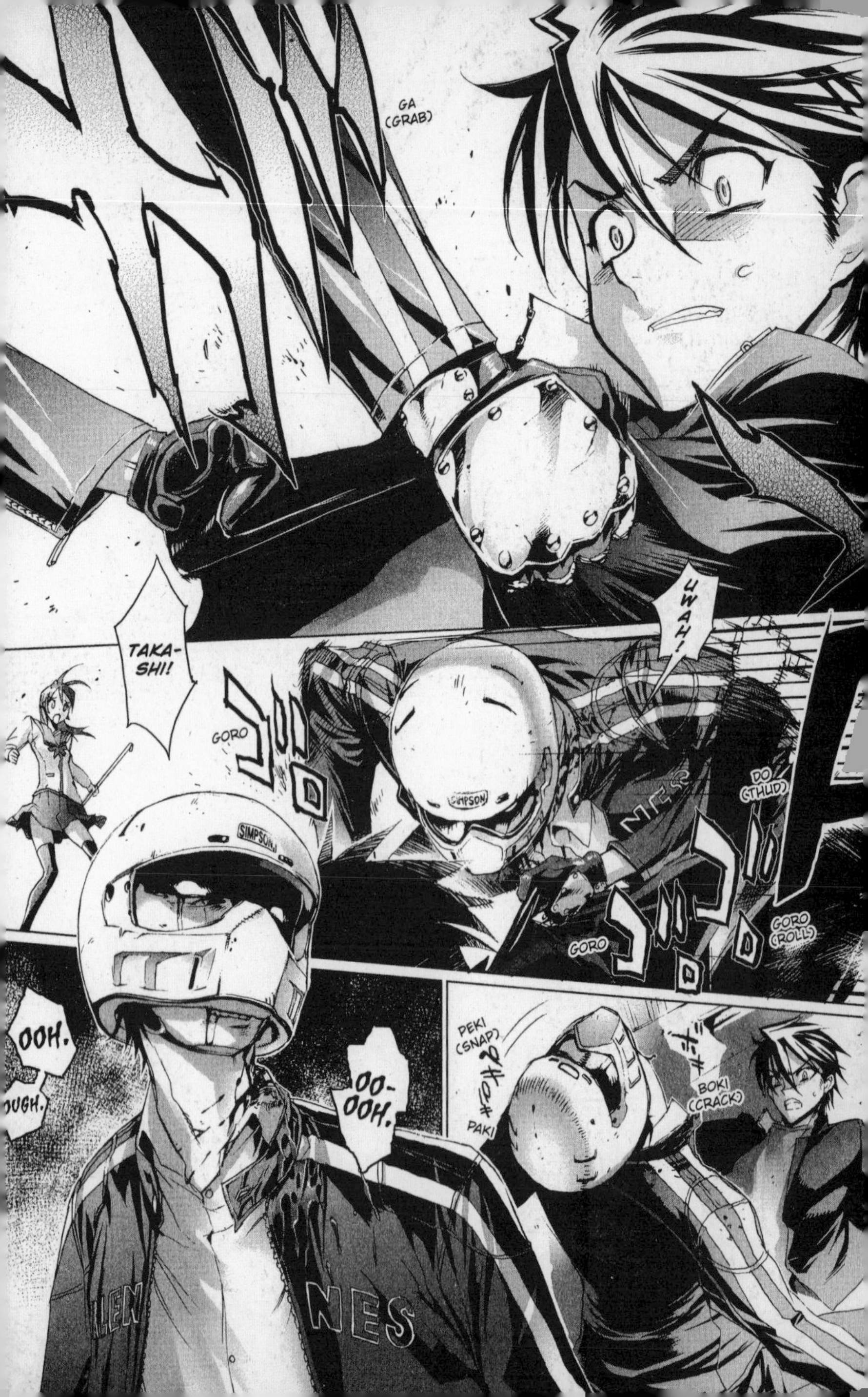
GA (GRAB)
UWAH!
DO (THUD)
GORO (ROLL)
GORO
TAKA-SHI!
GORO
BOKI (CRACK)
PEKI (SNAP)
PAKI
OO-OOH.
OOH.
OUGH.

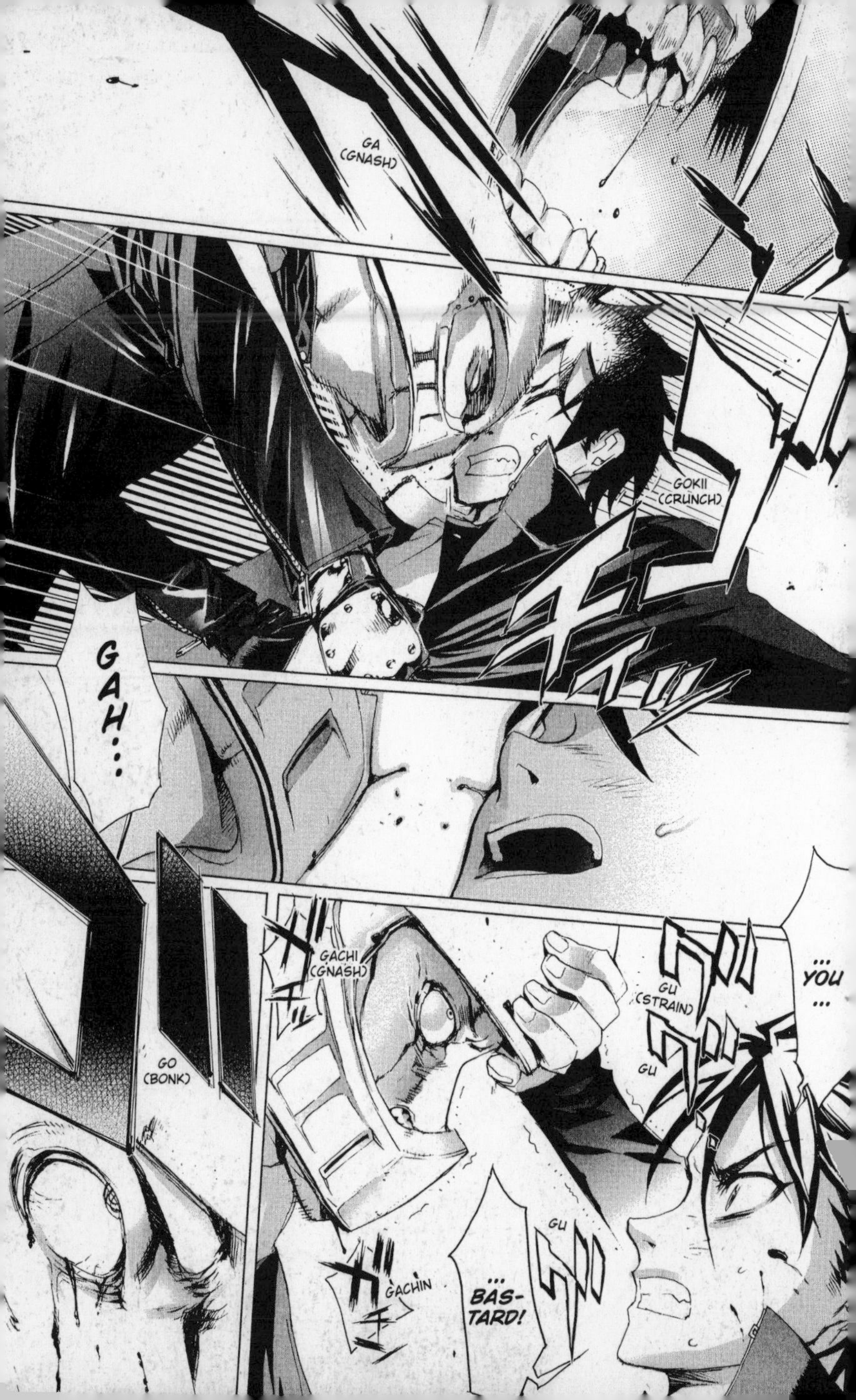
GA (GNASH)
GOKII (CRUNCH)
GAH...
...YOU...
GU (STRAIN)
GU
GACHI (GNASH)
GU
...BAS-TARD!
GACHIN
GO (BONK)

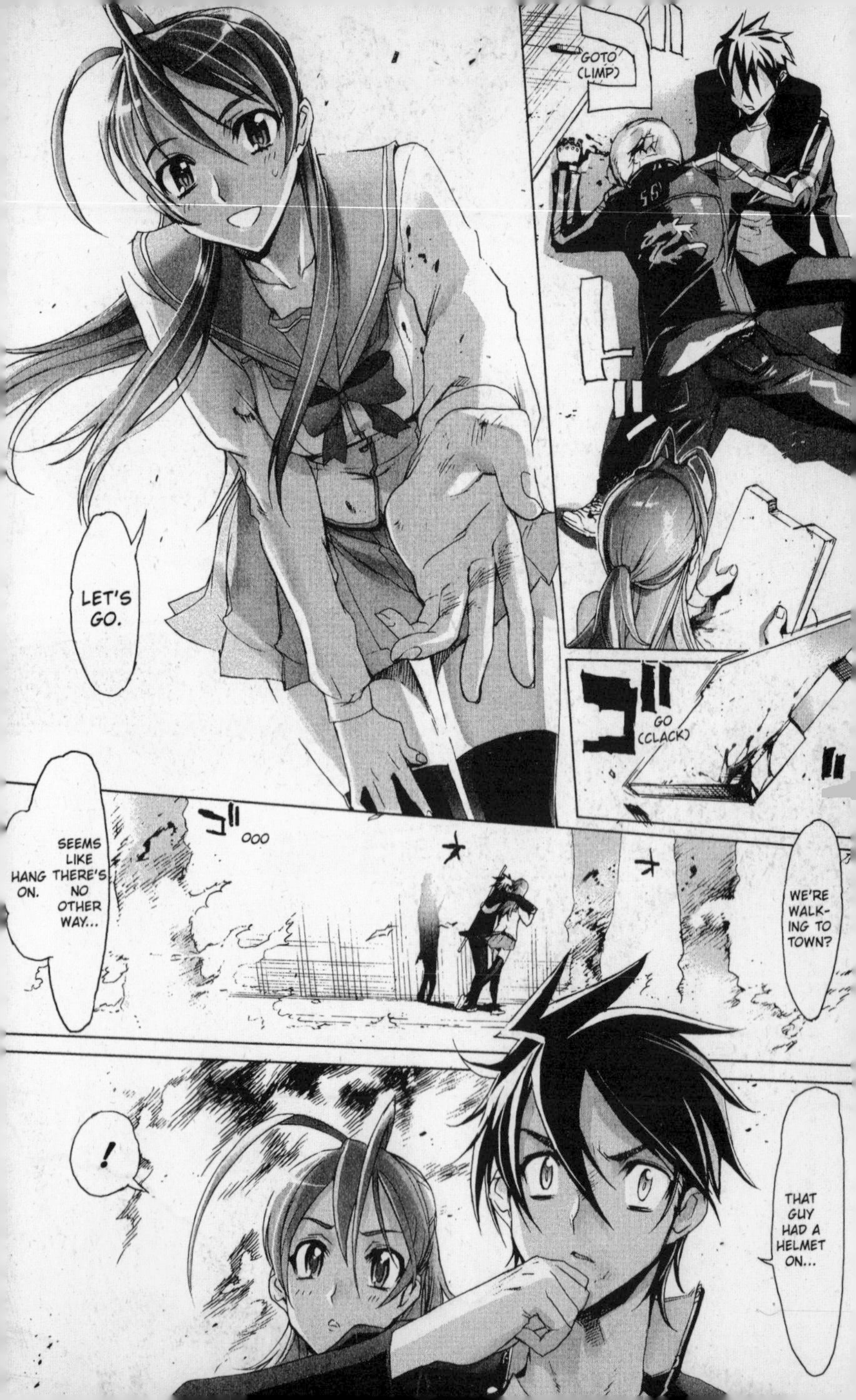
GOTO (LIMP)
GO (CLACK)
LET'S GO.
WE'RE WALKING TO TOWN?
GOOO
SEEMS LIKE THERE'S NO OTHER WAY...
HANG ON.
THAT GUY HAD A HELMET ON...
!

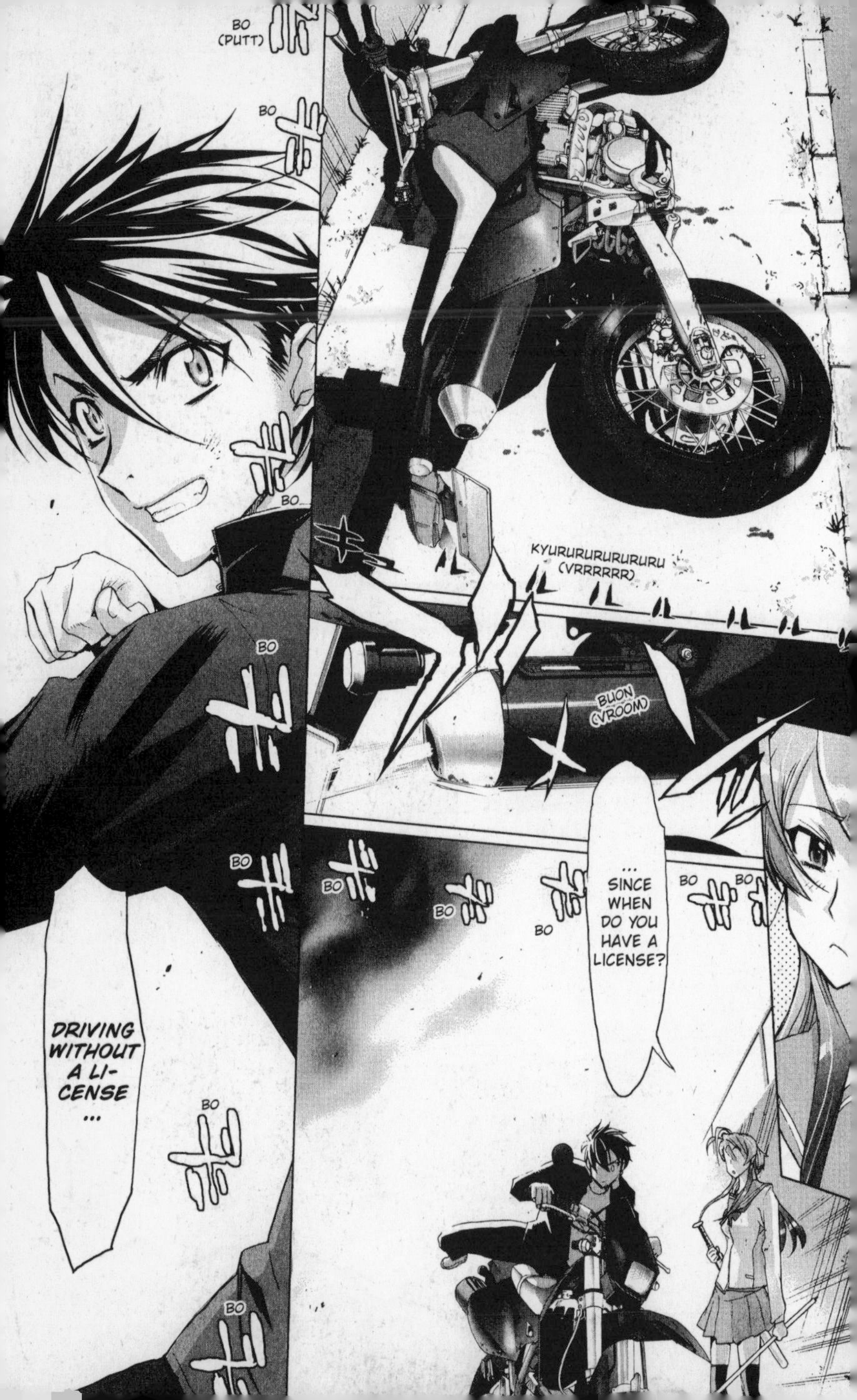
KYURURURURURURU (VRRRRRR)
BUON (VROOM)
BO BO
BO
BO
BO
... SINCE WHEN DO YOU HAVE A LICENSE?
BO (PUTT)
BO
BO
BO
BO
DRIVING WITHOUT A LICENSE ...
BO
BO

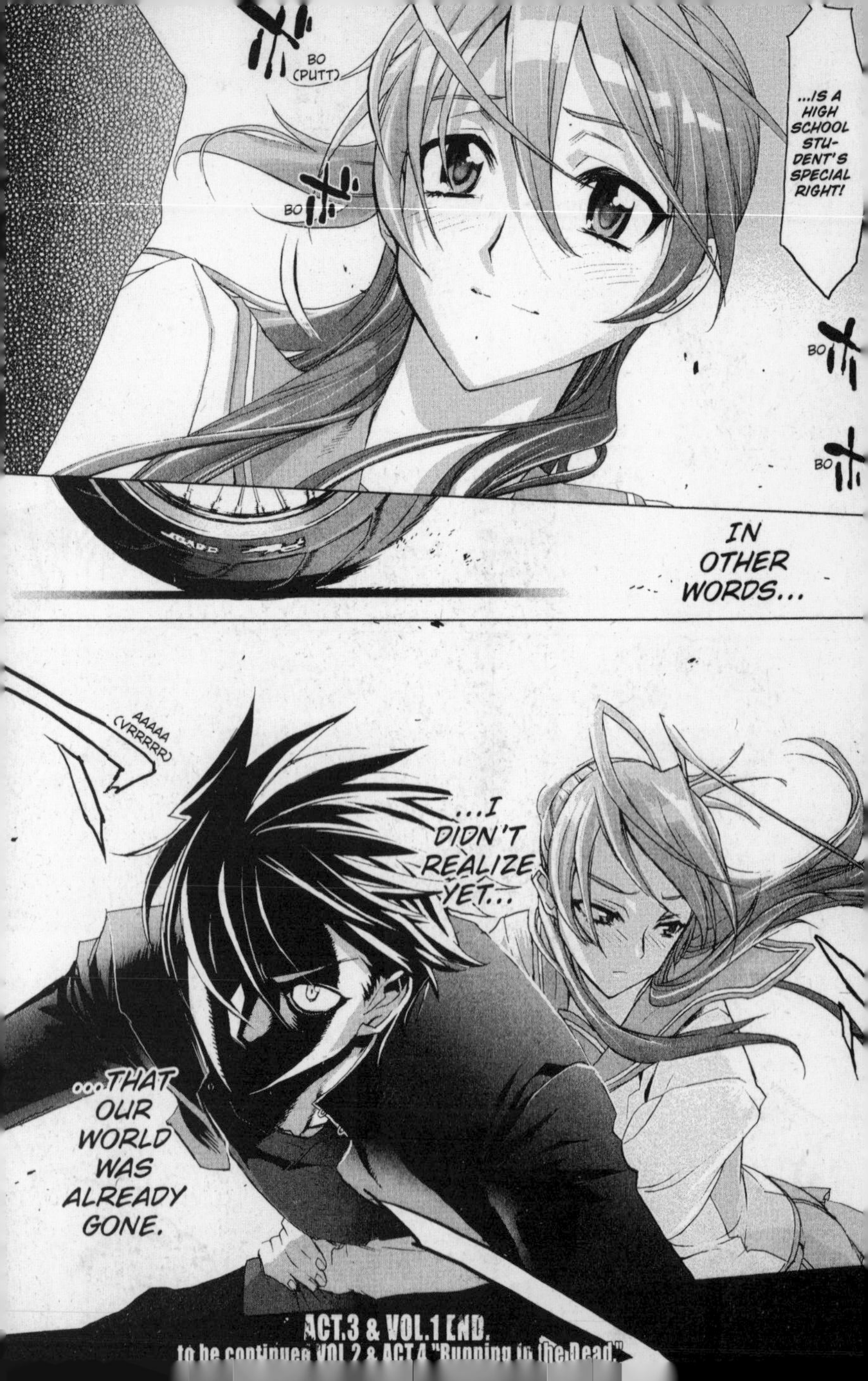
...IS A HIGH SCHOOL STU-DENT'S SPECIAL RIGHT!
BO (PUTT)
BO
BO
BO
IN OTHER WORDS...
...I DIDN'T REALIZE YET...
AAAAA (VRRRRR)
...THAT OUR WORLD WAS ALREADY GONE.
ACT.3 & VOL.1 END.
to be continued VOL.2 & ACT.4 "Running in the Dead."

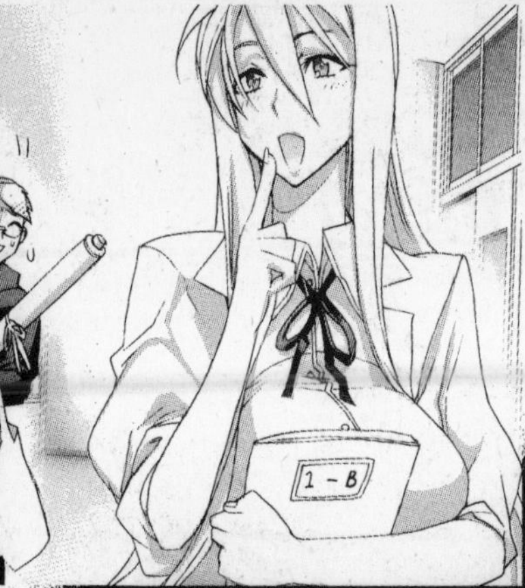
1－B

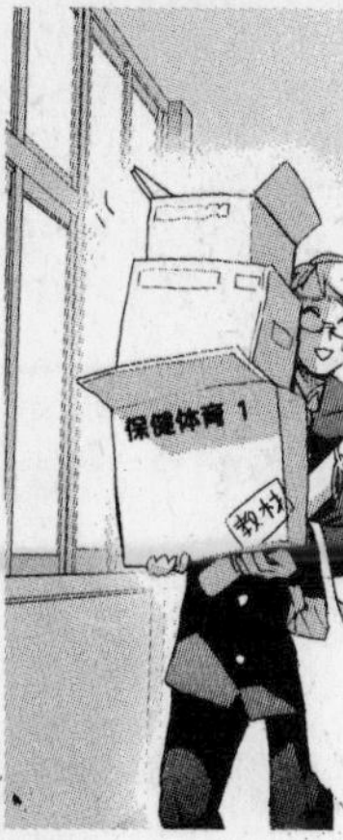
保健体育 1
教材

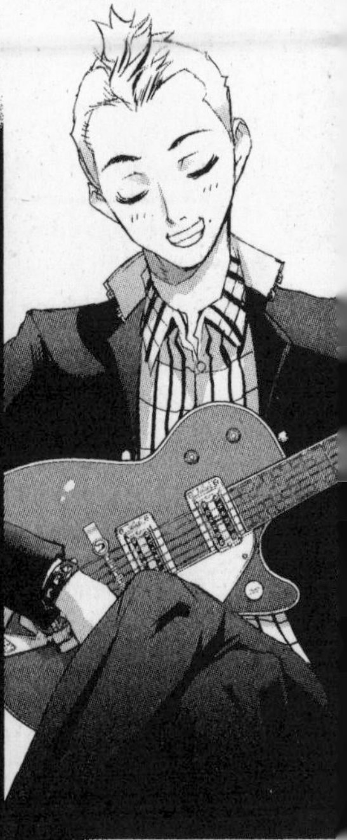

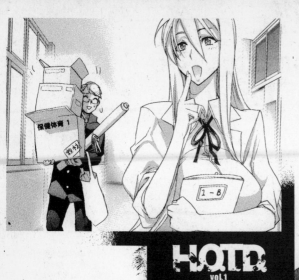

H.O.T.D.

vol.1
STAFF

Original Story
Daisuke Sato

Illustrations
Shouji Sato

Hisayoshi Misasagi

Taiheitengoku
Mirai Kobayashi
Yuuji Isono

Special Thanks
Koushi Rikudou
Kouta Hirano

Editor
Akira
Kawashima

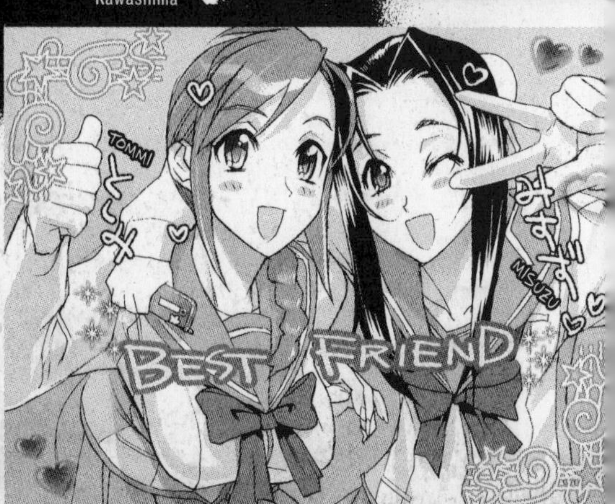
TOMMI
MISUZU
BEST FRIEND

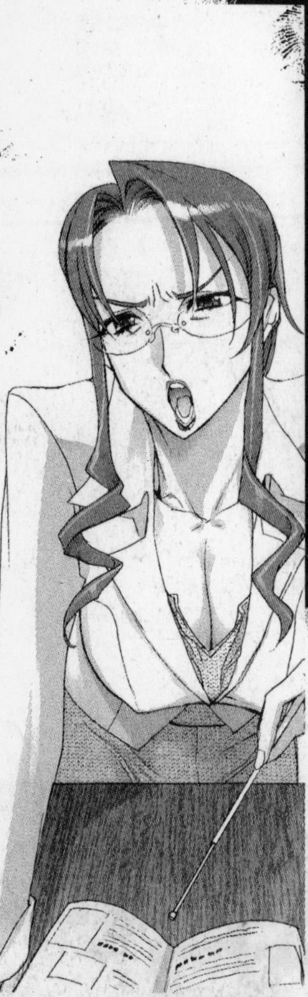

HIGHSCHOOL OF THE DEAD ❶

DAISUKE SATO
SHOUJI SATO

Translation: Christine Dashiell

Lettering: Chris Counasse

GAKUENMOKUSIROKU HIGHSCHOOL OF THE DEAD Volume 1 ©2007 DAISUKE SATO ©2007 SHOUJI SATO. First published in Japan in 2007 by FUJIMISHOBO CO., LTD., Tokyo. English translation rights arranged with KADOKAWA SHOTEN Publishing Co., Ltd., Tokyo through TUTTLE-MORI AGENCY, INC., Tokyo.

Translation © 2011 by Hachette Book Group, Inc.

Yen Press
Hachette Book Group
237 Park Avenue, New York, NY 10017

www.HachetteBookGroup.com
www.YenPress.com

Yen Press is an imprint of Hachette Book Group, Inc.
The Yen Press name and logo are trademarks of Hachette Book Group, Inc.

First Yen Press Edition: January 2011

ISBN: 978-0-316-13225-1

10 9 8 7 6 5 4 3 2

BVG

Printed in the United States of America